Adaptive Code via C#: Agile coding with design patterns and SOLID principles

Gary McLean Hall

PUBLISHED BY
Microsoft Press
A division of Microsoft Corporation
One Microsoft Way
Redmond, Washington 98052-6399

Library of Congress Control Number: 2014943458
ISBN: 978-0-7356-8320-4

Printed and bound in the United States of America.

First Printing

Microsoft Press books are available through booksellers and distributors worldwide. If you need support related to this book, email Microsoft Press Book Support at mspinput@microsoft.com. Please tell us what you think of this book at http://aka.ms/tellpress.

Acquisitions Editor: Devon Musgrave
Developmental Editor: Devon Musgrave
Project Editor: Devon Musgrave
Editorial Production: Online Training Solutions, Inc. (OTSI)
Technical Reviewer: Jeremy Johnson
Copyeditor: Kathy Krause (OTSI)
Indexer: Krista Wall (OTSI)
Cover: Twist Creative • Seattle and Joel Panchot

For Amelia Rose

—Gary McLean Hall

Contents at a glance

Contents

What do you think of this book? We want to hear from you!

Microsoft is interested in hearing your feedback so we can continually improve our books and learning resources for you. To participate in a brief online survey, please visit:

microsoft.com/learning/booksurvey

What do you think of this book? We want to hear from you!

Microsoft is interested in hearing your feedback so we can continually improve our
books and learning resources for you. To participate in a brief online survey, please visit:

microsoft.com/learning/booksurvey

Introduction

The first words of the title of this book, *Adaptive Code*, provide a good description of the outcome of applying the principles in the book: the ability of code to adapt to any new requirement or unforeseen scenario while avoiding significant rework. The aim of this book is to aggregate into one volume many of the current best practices in the world of C# programming with the Microsoft .NET Framework. Although some of the content is covered in other books, those books either focus heavily on theory or are not specific to .NET development.

Programming can be a slow process. If your code is adaptive, you will be able to make changes to it more quickly, more easily, and with fewer errors than you would if you were working with a codebase that impedes changes. Requirements, as every developer knows, are subject to change. How change is managed is a key differentiating factor between successful software projects and those that atrophy due to scope creep. Developers can react in many ways to requirement changes, with two opposing viewpoints highlighting the continuum that lies between.

First, developers can choose a rigid viewpoint. In this approach, from the development process down to class design, the project is as inflexible as if it were implemented 50 years ago by using punch cards. Waterfall methodologies are conspicuous culprits in ensuring that software cannot change freely. Their determination that the phases of analysis, design, implementation, and testing be distinct and one-way make it difficult—or at least expensive—for customers to change requirements after implementation has begun. The code, then, does not *need* to be built for change: the process all but forbids alterations.

The second approach, Agile methodology, is not just an alternative to such rigid methodologies, but a *reaction* to them. The aim of Agile processes is to embrace change as a necessary part of the contract between client and developer. If customers want to change something in the product that they are paying for, the temporal and financial cost should be correlated to the size of the change, not the phase of the process that is currently in progress. Unlike physical engineering, software engineering works with a malleable tool: source code. The bricks and mortar that form a house are literally fused together as construction progresses. The expense involved in changing the design of a house is necessarily linked to the completion of the building phase. If the project has not been started—if it is still just in blueprints—change is relatively cheap. If the windows are in, the electricity wired up, and the plumbing fitted, moving the upstairs bathroom down next to the kitchen could be prohibitively expensive. With code, moving features around and reworking the navigation of a user interface should not be as significant. Unfortunately, this is not always the case. The temporal cost alone often prohibits such changes. This, I find, is largely a result of a lack of adaptability in code.

This book demonstrates the second approach and explains, with real-world examples, the practicalities of implementing adaptive code.

Who should read this book

This book is intended to bridge a gap between theory and practice. The reader for whom this book is written is an experienced programmer who seeks more practical examples of design patterns, SOLID principles, unit testing and refactoring, and more.

Capable intermediate programmers who want to plug the gaps in their knowledge or have doubts and questions about how some of the industry's best practices fit together will benefit most from this book, especially because the day-to-day reality of programming rarely matches simple examples or theory. Much of SOLID is now understood, but the intricacies of the open/closed principle (covered in Chapter 6) and Liskov substitution (covered in Chapter 7) are not fully comprehended. Even experienced programmers sometimes do not fully realize the benefits provided by dependency injection (covered in Chapter 9). Similarly, the flexibility—adaptability— that interfaces (covered in Chapter 3) lend to code is often overlooked.

This book can also help the more junior developer learn, from the ground up, which aspects of common patterns and practices are benevolent and which are, in the long term, malevolent. The code samples that I see from prospective employees have a lot in common. The general theme is that the candidate is *almost there* with respect to many skills but just needs a slight push in the right direction to become a significantly better programmer. Specifically, the Entourage anti-pattern (covered in Chapter 2) and the Service Locator anti-pattern (covered in Chapter 9) are very prevalent in sample code. Practical alternatives, and their rationales, are provided in this book.

Assumptions

Ideally, you should have some practical experience of programming in a language that is syntactically similar to C#, such as Java or C++. You should also have a strong foundation in core procedural programming concepts such as conditional branching, loops, and expressions. You should also have some experience of object-oriented programming using classes, and at least a passing familiarity with interfaces.

This book might not be for you if...

This book might not be for you if you are just starting out on a journey to learn how to program. This book covers advanced topics that assume a thorough understanding of fundamental programming concepts.

Organization of this book

This book is made up of three parts, each of which builds on the last. That said, the book can also be read out of order. Each chapter covers a self-contained subject in detail, with cross references included where appropriate.

Part I: An Agile foundation

This part lays the foundation for building software in an adaptive way. It covers the high-level Agile process known as *Scrum*, which requires code to be adaptive to change. The chapters in this part focus on details around interfaces, design patterns, refactoring, and unit testing.

- **Chapter 1: Introduction to Scrum**   This chapter sets the scene for the book by introducing Scrum, which is an Agile project management methodology. The chapter gives an in-depth overview of the artifacts, roles, metrics, and phases of a Scrum project. Finally, it shows how developers should organize themselves and their code when operating in an Agile environment.

- **Chapter 2: Dependencies and layering**   This chapter explores dependencies and architectural layering. Code can only be adaptive if the solution's structure allows it to be. The different types of dependencies are described: first-party, third-party, and framework. The chapter describes how to manage and organize dependencies, from anti-patterns (which should be avoided) to patterns (which should be embraced). It also introduces advanced topics such as aspect-oriented programming and asymmetric layering, providing further depth.

- **Chapter 3: Interfaces and design patterns**   Interfaces are, by now, ubiquitous in modern .NET development. However, they are often misapplied, misunderstood, and misappropriated. This chapter shows some of the more common and practically useful design patterns, exploring how versatile an interface can be. Leading the reader beyond the simple extraction of an interface, the chapter shows how interfaces can be elaborated in many different ways to solve a problem. Mixins, duck-typing, and interface fluency further underscore the versatility of this key weapon in the programmer's arsenal.

- **Chapter 4: Unit testing and refactoring** Two practices that are becoming prerequisite skills are unit testing and refactoring. The two are closely related and work in unison to produce adaptive code. Without the safety net of unit tests, refactoring is prone to error; without refactoring, code becomes unwieldy, rigid, and hard to comprehend. This chapter takes an example of unit testing from humble beginnings and expands it to use more advanced—but practical—patterns and practices such as fluent assertions, test-driven development, and mocking. For refactoring, the chapter provides examples of real-world refactors that improve the readability and maintainability of the source code.

Part II: Writing SOLID code

This part builds on the foundation laid in Part I. Each chapter is devoted to examining one principle of SOLID. The emphasis in these chapters is on practical examples for implementing the principles, rather than solely on the theory of why. By placing each example in a real-world context, the chapters in this part of the book clearly demonstrate the utility of SOLID.

- **Chapter 5: The single responsibility principle** This chapter shows how to implement the single responsibility principle in practice by using the Decorator and Adapter patterns. The outcome of applying the principle is an increase in the number of classes and a decrease in the size of those classes. The chapter shows that, in contrast with monolithic classes that provide extensive features, these smaller classes are more directed and focused on solving only a small part of a larger problem. It is in their aggregation that these classes then become more than the sum of their parts.

- **Chapter 6: The open/closed principle** The open/closed principle (OCP) is simply stated, but it can have a significant impact on code. It is responsible for ensuring that code that follows SOLID principles is only appended to and never edited. This chapter also discusses the concept of predicted variation in relation to OCP and explores how it can help developers identify extension points for further adaptability.

- **Chapter 7: The Liskov substitution principle** This chapter shows the positive effects that result from applying the Liskov substitution principle on code, particularly the fact that the guidelines help enforce the open/closed principle and prevent the unintended consequences of change. Contracts—through preconditions, postconditions, and data invariants—are covered by using the Code Contracts tooling. The chapter also describes subtyping guidelines such as covariance, contravariance, and invariance, along with the negative impact of breaking these rules.

- **Chapter 8: Interface segregation**   Not only should classes be smaller than they commonly are, this chapter shows that interfaces are, similarly, often too big. Interface segregation is a simple practice that is often overlooked; this chapter shows the benefits of limiting interfaces to the smallest size possible, along with the benefits of working with smaller interfaces. It also explores the different reasons that might motivate the segregation of interfaces, such as client need and architectural need.

- **Chapter 9: Dependency injection**   This chapter contains the cohesive glue that holds together the rest of the features in the book. Without dependency injection (DI), there is a lot that would not be possible—it is really that important. This chapter contains an introduction to DI and a comparison of the different methods of implementing it. The chapter includes discussions on managing object lifetimes, working with Inversion of Control containers, avoiding common anti-patterns relating to service location, and identifying composition roots and resolution roots.

Part III: Adaptive sample

This part uses a sample application as a way of tying together the rest of the book. Although there is a lot of code in these chapters, there is ample accompanying explanation. Because this book is about working in an Agile environment, the chapters map to Scrum sprints, and all work is the result of backlog items and client change requests.

- **Chapter 10: Adaptive sample: Introduction**   This first chapter describes the application that is to be developed: an online chat application developed in ASP.NET MVC 5. A brief design is provided as a guideline for the planned architecture, in addition to an explanation of the features on the backlog.

- **Chapter 11: Adaptive sample: Sprint 1**   Using a test-driven development (TDD) approach, the first features of the application are developed, including viewing and creating chat rooms and messages.

- **Chapter 12: Adaptive sample: Sprint 2**   The client, inevitably, makes some changes to the requirements of the application, and the team accommodates those changes through adaptive code.

Appendices

Some reference material is available in the appendices, specifically for working with Git source control and to explain how the code for this book is organized on GitHub.

- **Appendix A: Adaptive tools**   This is a very brief introduction to Git source control that should, at the very least, allow you to download the code from GitHub and compile it in Microsoft Visual Studio 2013. It is not intended as a thorough guide to Git—there are some excellent sources already out there, such as the official Git tutorial:

    http://git-scm.com/docs/gittutorial

    A quick web search will find other sources.

    This appendix also looks at other developer tools, such as continuous integration and the development environment.

- **Appendix B (available online only): GitHub code samples**   By putting the code for this book on GitHub, I am able to make changes in a centralized location. The repository is read-only, but Appendices A and B together show you how to find the code for a listing, download it, compile it, run it, and make local changes. If you think you have found a defect or want to suggest a change, you can issue a pull request to the main AdaptiveCode repository and I will gladly take a look. You can find Appendix B via this book's page at *microsoftpressstore.com*.

Conventions and features in this book

Throughout this book, there are a number of repeated conventions. These are mainly standard to Microsoft Press publications, but it won't hurt to explain them up front.

Code listings

Code listings are included where appropriate, and a call-out is made to them where relevant, as shown in Listing I-1.

LISTING I-1 This is a code listing. There are plenty of these in the book.

```
public void MyService : IService
{

}
```

Whenever your attention should be drawn to a certain part of the code—for instance, when changes have been made to a previous example—the code will be highlighted in bold.

Readeraids and sidebars

Readeraids are used for small asides, such as notes or warnings, whereas sidebars are reserved for larger digressions. Here are some examples:

> **Note** This is a readeraid. It contains small information nuggets that relate to the main content but have some kind of added importance.

> **This is a sidebar**
>
> Although this one is necessarily short, sidebars are usually reserved for longer discussions on topics that are somewhat tangential to the main topic.

Images

Sometimes, an explanation—no matter how florid—is not enough. In these cases, an image is provided. All diagrams were created in Microsoft Visio 2013 with no theming, to create a high contrast and to focus solely on exposition. Screenshots were taken with a high-contrast theme applied.

System requirements

You will need the following hardware and software to use the code samples in this book:

- Either Windows XP Service Pack 3 (except Starter Edition), Windows Vista Service Pack 2 (except Starter Edition), Windows 7, Windows Server 2003 Service Pack 2, Windows Server 2003 R2, Windows Server 2008 Service Pack 2, or Windows Server 2008 R2

- Visual Studio 2013, any edition (multiple downloads might be required if you are using Express Edition products)

- Microsoft SQL Server 2008 Express Edition or higher (2008 or R2 release), with SQL Server Management Studio 2008 Express or higher (included with Visual Studio; Express Editions require a separate download)

- A computer that has a 1.6-gigahertz (GHz) or faster processor (2 GHz recommended)

- 1 gigabyte (GB) (32 bits) or 2 GB (64 bits) of RAM (add 512 megabytes [MB] if running in a virtual machine or using SQL Server Express Editions, more for advanced SQL Server editions)

- 3.5 GB of available hard disk space

- A 5,400-RPM hard disk drive

- A DirectX 9–capable video card running at 1024 x 768 or a higher-resolution display

- A DVD-ROM drive (if installing Visual Studio from DVD)

- An Internet connection for downloading software or code samples

Depending on your Windows configuration, you might require Local Administrator rights to install or configure Visual Studio 2013 and SQL Server 2008 products.

Downloads: Code samples

As far as possible, I ensured that the code listings were part of a larger example that could be run either as a stand-alone application or a unit test. I wrote many of the simpler unit tests by using MSTest, so that no external test runner was needed, but I wrote the more complex unit tests by using NUnit. I used Visual Studio 2013 Ultimate to write all of the code. Although I wrote some of it by using the preview version, it has all been compiled and tested on the full version. As far as possible, I didn't use features that were unavailable to the Express Editions of Visual Studio 2013, but for some topics, this was not possible. Readers wanting to run this code will need to install a paid-for version.

The code itself is available from GitHub, at the following address:

http://aka.ms/AdaptiveCode_CodeSamples

Appendix A contains explanations for using Git, and Appendix B (online only) details how the code in the AdaptiveCode repository is organized.

If you want to make a comment where I am likely to see it, my WordPress blog is here:

http://garymcleanhall.wordpress.com

Acknowledgments

The byline for this book is not really accurate. I couldn't have written any of this without the following people, all of whom have helped me in different ways.

Victoria, my wife, for making this book possible. That's not lip service—it's simply a fact.

Amelia, my daughter, for being perfect in every way.

Pam, my mother, for proofreading and for her wonderfully hyperbolic words of encouragement.

Les, my father, for all his hard work.

Darryn, my brother, for general, continual guidance.

Kathy Krause at Online Training Solutions, Inc., for her excellent work making this book readable.

Devon Musgrave, for his apparently limitless patience.

Errata, updates, & book support

We've made every effort to ensure the accuracy of this book and its companion content. You can access updates to this book—in the form of a list of submitted errata and their related corrections—at:

http://aka.ms/Adaptive/errata

If you discover an error that is not already listed, please submit it to us at the same page.

If you need additional support, email Microsoft Press Book Support at mspinput@microsoft.com.

Please note that product support for Microsoft software and hardware is not offered through the previous addresses. For help with Microsoft software or hardware, go to *http://support.microsoft.com*.

Free ebooks from Microsoft Press

From technical overviews to in-depth information on special topics, the free ebooks from Microsoft Press cover a wide range of topics. These ebooks are available in PDF, EPUB, and Mobi for Kindle formats, ready for you to download at:

http://aka.ms/mspressfree

Check back often to see what is new!

We want to hear from you

At Microsoft Press, your satisfaction is our top priority, and your feedback our most valuable asset. Please tell us what you think of this book at:

http://aka.ms/tellpress

We know you're busy, so we've kept it short with just a few questions. Your answers go directly to the editors at Microsoft Press. (No personal information will be requested.) Thanks in advance for your input!

Stay in touch

Let's keep the conversation going! We're on Twitter: *http://twitter.com/MicrosoftPress*.

An Agile foundation

This part of the book gives you a grounding in Agile principles and practices.

Writing code is the central pillar of software development. However, there are many different ways to achieve the goal of working code. Even if you don't count the selection of platform, language, and framework, there are a multitude of choices presented to a developer who is tasked with implementing even the simplest functionality.

The creation of successful software products has always been an obvious focus for the software development industry. But in recent years, developers have begun to emphasize the implementation of patterns and practices that are repeatable and have a positive effect on the quality of code. This is because the notion of code quality is no longer separate from the notion of quality in the software product. Over time, poor-quality code will degrade the quality of the product—at the very least, it will irretrievably delay the delivery of working software.

To produce high-quality software, developers must strive to ensure that their code is maintainable, readable, and tested. In addition to this, a new requirement has emerged that suggests that code should also be *adaptive to change*.

The chapters in this part of the book present modern software development processes and practices. These processes and practices are generally termed *Agile* processes and practices, which reflects their ability to change direction quickly. *Agile processes* suggest ways in which a software development team can elicit fast feedback and alter its focus in response, and *Agile practices* suggest ways in which a software development team can write code that is similarly able to change direction.

CHAPTER 1

Introduction to Scrum

After completing this chapter, you will be able to

- Assign roles to the major stakeholders in the project.

- Identify the different documents and other artifacts that Scrum requires and generates.

- Measure the progress of a Scrum project on its development journey.

- Diagnose problems with Scrum projects and propose remedies.

- Host Scrum meetings in an effective manner for maximum benefit.

- Justify the use of Scrum over other methodologies, both Agile and rigid.

Scrum is a project management methodology. To be more precise, it is an Agile methodology. Scrum is based on the idea of adding value to a software product in an iterative manner. The overall Scrum process is repeated—iterated—multiple times until the software product is considered complete or the process is otherwise stopped. These iterations are called *sprints,* and they culminate in software that is potentially releasable. All work is prioritized on the *product backlog* and, at the start of each sprint, the development team commits to the work that they will complete during the new iteration by placing it on the *sprint backlog*. The unit of work within Scrum is the *story*. The product backlog is a prioritized queue of pending stories, and each sprint is defined by the stories that will be developed during an iteration. Figure 1-1 shows an overview of the Scrum process.

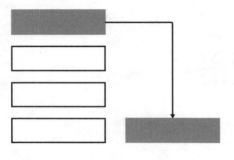 

Product backlog	Sprint backlog	Sprint	Release
The product backlog contains features and stories to be implemented.	Stories that have been committed to the sprint are moved to the sprint backlog. Each story is implemented in priority order.	Each sprint lasts between one and four weeks. With each day of the sprint, the team works toward completing the committed stories.	After each sprint, newly implemented features are released in a new version of the product.

FIGURE 1-1 Scrum works like a production line for small features of a software product.

Scrum involves a mixture of documentation artifacts, roles played by people inside and outside the development team, and ceremonies—meetings that are attended by appropriate parties. Although a single chapter is not enough to explore the entirety of what Scrum offers as a project management discipline, this chapter offers enough detail to provide both a springboard to further learning and an orientation for the day-to-day practices of Scrum.

> ### Scrum is Agile
>
> *Agile* is a family of lightweight software development methods that embrace the changing requirements of customers even as the project is in progress. Agile is a reaction to the failings of more rigidly structured practices. The Agile Manifesto exemplifies the contrast. It can be found on the web at *www.agilemanifesto.org*.
>
> The Agile Manifesto was signed by 17 software developers. The Agile method has grown in influence in the intervening years to the extent that experience in an Agile environment is now a common prerequisite for software development roles. Scrum is one of the most common implementations of an Agile process.

Scrum versus waterfall

In my experience, the Agile approach works better than the waterfall method of software development, and I evangelize only in favor of Agile processes. The problem with the waterfall method is its rigidity. Figure 1-2 provides a representation of the process involved in a waterfall project.

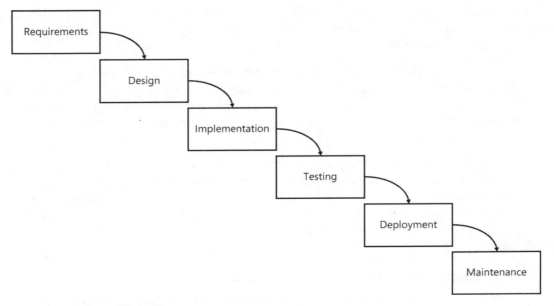

FIGURE 1-2 The waterfall development process.

Note that the output from one stage becomes the input to the next. Also note that each phase is completed before moving to the next phase. This assumes that no errors, issues, problems, or mis-understandings are discovered after a phase has completed. The arrows only point one way.

The waterfall process also assumes that there will be no changes made after a phase has completed, something that seems quite contrary to empirical and statistical evidence. Change is a natural part of life, not just of software engineering. The attitude toward change that waterfall approaches espouse is that it is expensive, undesirable, and—most damningly—*avoidable*. Waterfall methods assert that change can be circumnavigated by spending more time on requirements and design, so that changes simply *do not occur* during subsequent phases. This is preposterous, because change will *always* happen.

Agile responds to this fact by adopting a different approach, which welcomes change and allows everyone to adapt to any changes that occur. Although Agile—and therefore Scrum—allows for change at a process level, *coding for change* is one of the hardest, yet most important, tenets of modern software development. This book is dedicated to showing you how to produce code that is Agile and adaptive enough to survive change.

Waterfall methodologies are also document-centric, generating a lot of documentation that does not directly improve the software product. Agile, on the other hand, considers working software to be the most important document of a software product. The behavior of software is, after all, dictated by its source code—not by the documents that accompany that code. Furthermore, because documentation is a separate entity from the source code, it can easily fall out of sync with software.

Scrum prescribes some metrics that provide feedback on the progress of a project and its overall health, but this differs from explicative documentation about the product. Agile, in general, favors just enough documentation to avoid being irresponsible, but it does not mandate such documentation.

Some code can certainly benefit from supporting documentation, providing that it is not written once and never read again. For this reason, living documents that are easy to use, such as wikis, are common tools in Scrum teams.

The rest of this chapter covers the most important aspects of Scrum in more depth, although the focus is not purely Scrum, but a common variant thereof. The aim of Scrum as a process is not only to iteratively refine the software product, but also to iteratively refine the development process. This encourages teams to adopt subtle changes to ensure that the process is working for them, given their unique situations and context.

After discussing the constituent elements of Scrum, this chapter examines its flaws. This chapter sets the scene for the rest of the book, which details how to implement code in such a way that it remains adaptive to the change that is embraced by the Scrum process. There is little point in having a process in which you claim to be able to handle change gracefully when the reality is that change is incredibly difficult to *implement* down at a code level.

Different forms of Scrum

Whenever a development team claims that they follow the Scrum methodology, it is common for them to mean that they follow some *variant* of Scrum. Pure Scrum does not include a lot of common practices that have been taken from other Agile methods, such as Extreme Programming (XP). There are three different subcategories of Scrum that progressively veer further away from the purist implementation.

Scrum and...

Common practices like writing unit tests first and pair-programming are not part of Scrum. However, they are useful and worthy additions to the process for many teams, and so they are considered complementary practices. When certain practices are added from other Agile methods such as XP or Kanban, the process becomes "Scrum and..."—that is: Scrum plus extra best practices that enhance, rather than detract from, the default Scrum process.

Scrum but...

Some development teams claim to be practicing Scrum, but they omit key aspects. Their work is ordered on a backlog that is carried into iterative sprints, and they have retrospectives and daily stand-up meetings. However, they don't estimate in story points and instead favor real-time estimates. This sort of diluted version of Scrum is termed "Scrum but...". Although the team is aligned with Scrum in a lot of areas, they are misaligned in one or two key areas.

Scrum not...

If a development team moves far enough away from the Scrum method, they end up doing "Scrum not..." This causes problems, particularly when team members expect an Agile methodology and the actual process in place is so different that it barely resembles Scrum at all. I find that the daily stand-up meeting is the easiest part of Scrum to adopt, but relative estimation and the positive attitude to change are much more difficult. When enough parts of the Scrum process are neglected, the process is no longer Scrum.

Roles and responsibilities

Scrum is just a process, and—I cannot stress this enough—it is only as effective as the people who follow the process. These people have roles and responsibilities that guide their actions.

Product owner

The role of product owner (sometimes called the PO) is vital. The product owner provides the link between the client or customer and the rest of the development team. Product owners take ownership of the final product and, accordingly, their responsibilities include:

- Deciding which features are built.

- Setting the priority of the features in terms of business value.

- Accepting or rejecting "completed" work.

As a key stakeholder to the success of the project, the PO must be available to the team and be able to communicate the vision clearly. The long-term goal of the project should be clear to the development team, with changes in focus propagated throughout the team in a timely manner. In short-term sprint planning, the product owner sets out what will be developed and when. Product owners determine the features that will be needed along the road to making a release of the software, and they set the priorities for the product backlog.

Although the product owner's role is key, he or she does not have unlimited influence over the process. The product owner cannot influence how much the team commits to for a sprint, because this is determined by the team itself based on its velocity. Product owners also do not dictate *how* work is done—the development team has control over the details of how it implements a certain story at a technical level. When a sprint is underway, the product owner cannot change the sprint goals, alter acceptance criteria, or add or remove stories. After the goals are decided and the stories committed to the sprint during sprint planning, the sprint in progress becomes immutable. Any changes must wait until the next sprint—unless the change is to cancel the sprint or project in its entirety and start again. This allows the development team to retain total focus on achieving the sprint goal without moving the goalposts.

Throughout the sprint, as stories progress and are completed, the product owner will be asked to verify how a feature works or comment on a task that is in progress. It is important that product owners be able to devote some time during the sprint to liaise with the development team, in case the unexpected occurs and confusion arises. In this way, by the end of the sprint, the product owner is not presented with "completed" stories that deviate from their initial vision. Product owners do, however, get to decide whether a story meets the acceptance criteria supplied and whether it is considered complete and can be demonstrated at the end of the sprint.

Scrum master

The Scrum master (SM) shields the team from any external distractions during the sprint and tackles any of the impediments that the team flags during the daily Scrum meeting. This keeps the team fully functional and productive for the duration of the sprint, allowing it to focus wholly on the sprint goals.

Just as the product owner owns the product—what is to be done—the Scrum master owns the process—the framework surrounding how it is to be done. Thus it is the Scrum master's responsibility to ensure that the process is being followed by the team. Although the Scrum master can make some suggestions for improving the process (such as switching from a four-week sprint duration to a two-week duration), the Scrum master's authority is limited. Scrum masters cannot, for instance, specify how the team should implement a story, beyond ensuring that it follows the Scrum process.

As owners of the process, Scrum masters also own the daily Scrum meeting. The Scrum master ensures the team's attendance and takes notes throughout in case any actionable items are uncovered. The team is not, however, reporting to the Scrum master during the Scrum meeting; they are informing *everyone* present of their progress.

Development team

Ideally, an Agile team consists of *generalizing specialists*. That is, each member of the team should be multidisciplinary—capable of operating effectively on several different technologies, but with an aptitude, preference, or specialization in a certain area. For example, a team could consist of four developers, each of whom is capable of working very competently on ASP.NET MVC, Windows Workflow, and Windows Communication Foundation (WCF). However, two of the developers specialize in Windows Forms, and the remaining pair prefer to work with Windows Presentation Foundation (WPF) and Microsoft SQL Server.

Having a cross-functional team prevents siloes where one person—the "web person," the "database person," or the "WPF person"—has sole knowledge of how that part of the application works. Siloes are bad for everyone involved, and there should be heavy emphasis placed on breaking down siloes wherever possible. In Scrum, the code is owned by the team collectively. Siloes are bad for the business because it makes them depend too heavily on a single resource to provide value in a certain area. And the individuals themselves suffer because they become entrenched in roles that "only they can do."

Software testers are responsible for maintaining the quality of the software while it is being developed. Before a story is started, the testers might discuss automated test plans for verifying that the implementation of a story meets all of the acceptance criteria. They might work with the developers to implement those test plans, or they might write such tests themselves. After a story is implemented, the developer can submit it for testing, and the test analyst will verify that it is working as required.

Pigs and chickens

Each role of the Scrum process can be categorized as a pig or a chicken. These characterizations relate to the following story: A chicken approaches his friend, the pig, and says, "Hello pig, I've had an idea. I think we should open a restaurant!" At first, the pig is enthusiastic and enquires, "What should we call it?" The chicken replies, "We could call it Ham 'n' Eggs." The pig ponders this briefly before exclaiming in outrage, "No way! I'd be *committed*, but you'd only *contribute*!"

This fun allegory merely highlights the level of involvement that certain members need to have in a project. Pigs are entirely committed to a project and will be accountable for its outcome, whereas chickens merely contribute and are involved in a more peripheral manner. The product owner, the Scrum master and the development team are all pigs inasmuch as they are committed to the delivery of the product. Most often, customers are merely contributing chickens. Similarly, executive management will contribute to the project, so they are also considered chickens rather than pigs.

Artifacts

Throughout the lifetime of any software project, many documents, graphs, diagrams, charts, and metrics are created, reviewed, analyzed, and dissected. In this respect, a Scrum project is no different from any other. However, Scrum documents are distinct from documents of other types of project management in their type and purpose. A key difference between all Agile processes and more rigid processes is the relative importance of documentation. Structured Systems Analysis and Design Methodology (SSADM), for example, places a heavy emphasis on writing lots of documentation. This is referred to pejoratively as Big Design Up Front (BDUF): the errant belief that all fear, uncertainty, and doubt can be eliminated from a project if sufficient attention is paid to documentation. Agile processes aim to reduce the amount of documentation produced to only that which is absolutely necessary for the project to succeed. Instead, Agile favors the idea that the code—which is highly authoritative documentation—can be deployed, run, and used at any time. It also prefers that all stakeholders communicate with each other directly rather than write documents that might never be read by their most important audience. Documentation is still important to an Agile project, but its importance does not supersede that of working software or communication.

The Scrum board

Central to the daily workings of a Scrum project is the Scrum board. There should be a generous amount of wall space reserved for the Scrum board—if the board is too small, the temptation is to omit important details. Wall space might well be at a premium in your office, but there are tricks that you can use. Perhaps that large, neglected whiteboard could be repurposed as a Scrum board. With the aid of magnets, metal filing cabinets can double as the Scrum board. If your office is rented or you otherwise cannot deface the walls, "magic" whiteboards—which are simply wipe-clean sheets of static paper—are ideal. Try to identify a suitable place that could perform this function in your office.

Whatever you choose, however you designate it, if it doesn't feel right after a couple of iterations, feel free to change it. Physical Scrum boards are an absolute must. There is nothing that can replace the visceral experience of standing in front of a Scrum board. Though digital Scrum tools have their uses, I believe that they are complementary, rather than primary, to the Scrum process. Figure 1-3 shows an example of a typical Scrum board.

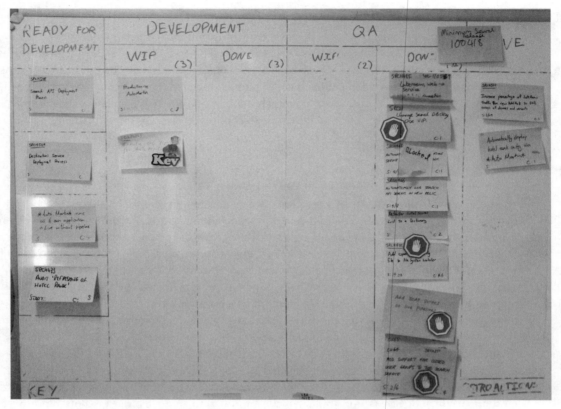

FIGURE 1-3 A Scrum board is a snapshot of the state of the work currently in development.

A Scrum board is a hive of information. It holds a lot of details, and discerning what is happening might be daunting. The rest of this section explains each aspect in detail.

Cards

The primary items on the Scrum board are the cards. The cards represent different elements of progress for a software product—from a physical release of the software down to the smallest distinct task. Each of these card types is typically represented by a different color, for clarity. Due to space constraints, the Scrum board usually shows only the stories, tasks, defects, and technical debt associated with the current sprint.

Tip Colors alone might not be sufficient for the requirements of everyone on the team. For example, consider coupling colors with distinct shapes for team members who can't distinguish colors.

Hierarchy of composition Figure 1-4 shows how the cards on a Scrum board are related. Note that it is implied that a product is composed of many tasks. Even the most complex software can be distilled into a finite list of discrete tasks that must be performed, each paving the way to completion.

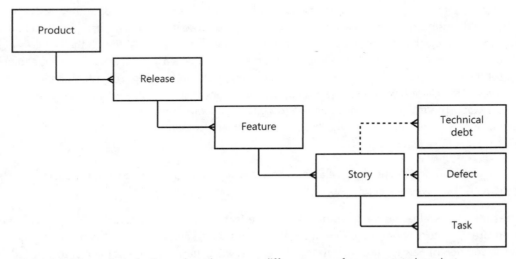

FIGURE 1-4 The cards on the Scrum board represent different parts of an aggregated product.

Product At the top of the Scrum food chain is the software product that is being built. Examples of products are bountiful: integrated development environments, web applications, accounting software, social media apps, and many more. This is the software that you are developing and the product you intend to deliver.

Teams usually work toward only one product at a time, but sometimes teams are responsible for delivering multiple products.

Release For every product that you develop, there will be multiple releases. A release is a version of the software that end users can purchase or use as a service. Sometimes a release is made only to address defects, but a release could also be intended to provide value-add features to key clients or to make a beta version of the software available as a sneak preview.

Web applications are often implicitly versioned with only a single deployment that supersedes all prior releases. In fact, the Google Chrome web browser is an interesting example. Although it is a desktop application, it is deployed as a stream of micro-releases that are seamlessly deployed to desktops without the usual fanfare that accompanies rival browsers. Internet Explorer 8, 9, and 10 each had their own advertisements on television, but Chrome does not follow this pattern—Google simply advertises the browser itself, irrespective of version. And iterative releases like this are becoming more common. Scrum can direct this release pattern by focusing on the potential to deliver working software after every sprint.

Minimum viable release

The first release can be aligned to a *minimum viable release (MVR)*—the basic set of features that are deemed sufficient to fulfill the fundamental requirements. For accounting software, for example, this feature set could be limited to the ability to create new clients, add transactions (both deposits and withdrawals) to their accounts, and present a total. The idea here is to bootstrap the project so that it becomes self-funding as soon as possible. Although this is unlikely to occur as a result of the MVR, the hope is that the MVR will at least bring in some revenue to offset the ongoing costs of development. Not only this, but that first deployment, even if it targets a restricted client base, is likely to provide vital feedback that can influence the direction of the software. This is the nature of Scrum—and Agile in general—constantly evolving the software product with the knowledge that all software is subject to change.

Regardless of the intent of the release or how it is deployed (or even how often), ideally a single product will survive several releases.

Feature   Each release is made up of one or more features that were previously not present in the software. The most significant difference between version 1.0 and version 2.0 of any piece of software is the addition of new features that the team believes will generate sufficient interest to persuade new users to make a purchase and existing users to upgrade.

The term *minimum marketable feature (MMF)* is useful to delineate features and compose a release. The following is a list of example features that are generic enough to be applied to many different projects, yet specific enough to be real-world features:

- Exporting application data to a portable XML-based format

- Servicing webpage requests within 0.5 seconds

- Archiving historical data for future reference

- Copying and pasting text

- Sharing files across a network with colleagues

Features are marketable if they have some value for the customer. When distilled down to the smallest amount of functionality possible while still retaining its value, the feature is also minimal.

> ## Epics/features vs. MMFs vs. themes
>
> You might be more used to the term *epic* rather than *feature* when talking about Scrum, but I have taken the liberty of switching this out for my preferred term. Epics and features are often considered "large stories": that is, stories that are much larger than MMFs and that cannot be delivered in a single sprint.
>
> Features are also similar to Scrum *themes* in that they serve to group stories that fulfill a common goal.

Features can be broadly grouped into three categories for each release: required, preferred, and desired. These are mutually exclusive options that reflect the overall priority assigned to each feature. Typically, the development team is instructed to work on all required features before tackling the preferred features, with the desired features being addressed only if time allows. As you might have guessed, these categories—and, indeed, the features themselves—are always changeable. They can be canceled, reprioritized, altered, and superseded at any time, with the team expected to switch focus gracefully (with the proviso, however, that deadlines and funding might also change in kind). Everything in Scrum is a moveable feast, and this book is aimed to help you deal with that reality.

User story   The user story is probably the Scrum artifact that most people are familiar with, but ironically, it is not prescribed by Scrum. User stories are an artifact of Extreme Programming, but they have been co-opted by Scrum because they are so commonly used. User stories are specified by using the following template:

"As a [user role], I want to [verb-centric behavior], so that [user value added]."

The square brackets denote parameterization that distinguishes one user story from another. A concrete example should illuminate further:

"As an unauthenticated but registered user, I want to reset my password, so that I can log on to the system if I forget my password."

There are many things to note about this user story. First of all, *there is not nearly enough detail to actually implement the behavior required.* Note that the user story is written from the perspective of a *user.* Although this would seem to be obvious, this point is missed by many and, too often, stories are wrongly written from the perspective of developers. This is why the first part of the template— *As a [user role]*—is so important. Similarly, the *[user value added]* portion is just as important because, without this, it is easy to lose sight of the underlying reason that the user story exists. This is usually what ties the user story is to its parent feature; the example just given could belong to a feature such as *"Forgotten user credentials are recoverable."* And the story would probably be grouped with the story in which the user has forgotten his or her logon name and the story in which the user has forgotten both logon name and password.

Given that this user story is not sufficient to begin development, what is its value? A user story represents a conversation that is yet to occur between the development team and the customer. When it comes time to implement the story, the developers assigned to it will start by taking the story to the customer and talking through the customer's requirements. This analysis phase will produce several acceptance criteria that must be adhered to throughout the lifetime of the user story, so that the user story can be deemed complete.

After the requirements have been gathered, the developers convene and lay out some design ideas to meet these requirements. This phase might include user interface mockups that use Balsamiq, Microsoft Visio, or some other tool. Some technical design concepts will detail how the existing code base must be altered to meet these new requirements, often using Unified Modeling Language (UML) diagrams.

After the design is ratified, the team can start to break the user story down into tasks and then work toward implementing the story by performing these tasks. When they reach a point when they are satisfied that the story is working as required, they can hand it over to be acceptance tested. This final phase of quality assurance (QA) double-checks the working software against the acceptance criteria and either approves or rejects it. When it is approved, the user story is complete.

Let's recap for a minute. With a user story for guidance, developers gathered requirements in an analysis phase, generated a design, implemented a working solution, and then tested this against the acceptance criteria. This sounds a lot like waterfall development methodologies! Indeed, that's the whole point of user stories—to perform the entire software development life cycle, in miniature, for each story. This helps to prevent any wasted effort because it is not until the user story is ready to be taken from the Scrum board and implemented that the developers can be sure it is still relevant to the software product.

User stories are the main focus of work in Scrum; they hold the incentive that Scrum provides for team members: story points. The team assigns each user story its own story point score during sprint planning and, after the user story is complete, the story points are considered to be earned and are deducted from the sprint total. Story points are explained in further detail later in this chapter.

Task There is a unit of work smaller than a user story—the task. Stories can be broken down into more manageable tasks, which can then be split between the developers assigned to the story. I prefer to wait until the story is taken off the board before I split it into tasks, but I have also seen this done as part of sprint planning.

Although user stories must incorporate a full vertical slice of functionality, tasks can be split at the layer level to take advantage of developer specializations within the team. For example, if a new field is required on an existing form, there will probably need to be changes to the user interface, business logic, and data access layers. You could divide this into three tasks that target these three layers and assign each to the relevant specialist: the WPF developer, the core C# expert, and the database guru, respectively. Of course, if you are lucky enough to have a team of generalizing specialists, anyone should really be able to *volunteer* for any task. This allows everyone to work on various parts of the code, which improves their understanding in addition to boosting their job satisfaction.

The vertical slice

When I was growing up, every Christmas my father would make trifle. This is a traditional English dessert that is made from various layers. At the bottom there is sliced fruit; then there are layers of sponge cake, jelly, and custard; and on top is whipped cream. My brother used to dig his spoon all the way through the layers, whereas I would eat each layer in turn.

Well-designed software is layered just like a trifle. The bottom layer is dedicated to data access, with layers in between for object-relational mappers, domain models, services, and controllers—with the user interface on top. Much like eating trifle, there are two ways to slice any part of a layered application: vertically and horizontally.

By slicing horizontally, you take each layer and implement what is required of those layers as a whole. But there is no guarantee that each slice will align at the same time. The user interface might allow the user to interact with certain features that layers below have not yet implemented. The net effect is that the client cannot use the application until a significant proportion of each layer has been completed. This delays the important feedback loop that Agile methods give you and increases the likelihood that you will build more than is needed—or simply the wrong thing.

Slicing vertically is what you should aim for. Each user story should incorporate functionality at each layer and should be tethered at the top to the user interface. This way, you can demonstrate the functionality to the user and receive feedback quickly. This also avoids writing user stories that are developer-centric, such as, *"I want to be able to query the database for customers who have not paid this month."* This sounds too much like a task; the story could be about generating a report on the outstanding unpaid accounts.

It is important to note that the user stories are the bearers of story points and that these do not transfer down to their constituent tasks. A five-point story that is broken into three distinct tasks is not composed of two one-point tasks and a three-point task. This is because there is neither incentive nor credit for partially completed work. Unless the story—as a whole—is proven complete by the QA process before the end of the sprint, the points that it contains are not claimed, even in part. The story remains in progress until the next sprint, when ideally it will be completed early in the iteration. If a story takes too long to complete and remains in progress for a long time—more than a full sprint's length—then it was probably too big in the first place and should have been sliced into smaller, more manageable stories.

Technical debt   Technical debt is a very interesting concept, but it is easily misunderstood. Technical debt is a metaphor for the design and architectural compromises that have been made during a story's journey across the Scrum board. Technical debt has its own section later in this chapter.

Defect   A defect card is created whenever acceptance criteria are not met on a previously complete user story. This highlights the need for automated acceptance testing: each batch of tests written for a story forms a suite of regression tests to ensure that no future work is able to introduce a breaking change.

Defect cards, like technical debt, do not have story points assigned to them, thus removing the incentive to create defects and technical debt—something that developers want to avoid even if full eradication of defects and technical debt is unattainable.

All software has defects. That is just a fact of software development, and no amount of planning or diligence will ever account for the fallibility of humans. Defects can be broadly categorized as A, B, or C: *apocalyptic* defects, *behavioral* errors, and *cosmetic* issues.

Apocalyptic defects result in an outright crash of the application or otherwise prevent the continuation of the user's work. An uncaught exception is the classic example because the program must terminate and be restarted or—in a web scenario—the webpage must be reloaded. These defects should be assigned the highest priority and should be fixed before a release of the software.

Behavioral errors are often not quite as serious but can infuriate users. These types of errors could be even more damaging than simply crashing the application. Imagine erroneous currency conversion logic that rounds data badly. Whether the algorithm favors the customer or the business, someone is going to lose money. Of course, not all logic errors are quite this serious, but it is easy to understand why they should be given medium-priority to high-priority.

Cosmetic issues are typically problems with the user interface—badly aligned images, a window that doesn't expand to full screen gracefully, or an image on the web that never loads. These issues do not affect the use of the software, just its appearance. Although these issues are often given a lower priority, it is still important to remember that appearances count toward the user's expectations of the software. If the user interface is badly designed with buttons that don't work and images that don't load, users are less inclined to trust the internal workings of that software. Conversely, a shiny user interface with plenty of bells and whistles might convince users that your software is just as well designed internally. A common trick for projects that have developed a poor reputation is to redesign the user interface—perhaps even rebranding the entire product—to improve perceptions and reset expectations.

Card sharp

A lot of options are available for customizing and personalizing the cards on the Scrum board.

Color scheme

Any color scheme will suffice for the cards, but there are a few that, in my experience, make the most sense. Index cards are ideal for features and user stories, whereas sticky notes make excellent task, defect, and technical debt cards because they can be stuck to a relevant story. Here are my recommendations:

- Features: green index cards
- User stories: white index cards
- Tasks: yellow sticky notes
- Defects: red/pink sticky notes
- Technical debt: purple/blue sticky notes

Note that user stories and tasks, being the most common kinds of cards you will create, use the most commonly available index cards and sticky notes. The last thing you need is to run out of index cards, so try to use the most commonly available colors.

Who creates cards?

The simple answer to the question, "Who can create the cards?" is: anyone. This does, of course, come with some conditions. Though anyone can create a card, its validity, priority, criticality, and other such states are not something that should be decided by one person alone. All feature and story cards should be verified by the product owner, but task, defect, and technical debt cards are entirely the domain of the development team.

Avatars

Much like the avatars found online in forums, on blogs, and on Twitter, these are miniature representations of the various members of the team. Feel free to allow your team members to express themselves through their avatars, because it certainly adds a sense of fun to the Scrum process. Of course, steer them away from anything likely to cause offense, but there should be a sense of distinct identity for each person's avatar.

Over the course of an iteration, these avatars will be moved around a lot and will be handled on a daily basis. Because you have index-card stories and sticky-note tasks already on the board, these avatars should be no bigger than 2-inch squares. Laminating them will also help to protect them from becoming dog-eared or torn, and reusable adhesive or a little piece of tape should hold them in place.

Swimlanes

Scrum boards have vertical lines drawn on them to demarcate the swimlanes. Each swimlane can contain multiple user story cards to denote the progress of that story throughout its development life cycle. From left to right, the basic swimlanes are Backlog, In Progress, QA, and Done.

A story in the backlog has been "committed to" for the sprint and should—unless canceled—be taken from the board and work on it should begin. This column can be ordered by priority so that the top item is always the next one that should be implemented.

After the story is taken from the backlog and a conversation has taken place with the product owner about the scope and requirements, the card is returned—with newly derived tasks—to the In Progress swimlane. At this point, the avatars of all team members involved in the story should also be attached. The story now counts toward any swimlane limits that might be associated with the in-progress phase. For example, you might require that only three user stories be in progress at a time, thus coercing the team to complete already-started stories in preference to those that have not yet been started. Remember: there is no incentive for partially completed work.

After analysis, design, and implementation have been carried out for a story, it is considered "developer complete" and can be moved to the Quality Assurance (QA) swimlane. Ideally, the QA environment should mirror the production environment as closely as possible, to avoid any environmental errors that can occur from even minor differences in deployment. The test analysts will assess the story in conjunction with the acceptance criteria. In essence, they try to break the story and prove that the code does not behave in the manner in which it ought. Typically, they attempt to provide unusual and erroneous input to certain operations, ensuring that validation works correctly. They might even look for security loopholes to ensure that malicious end users cannot gain access above their specified privilege level. When it is fully complete, the user story is moved across to the Done swimlane. Any story points associated with the story are then claimed, and the sprint burndown chart (which shows the progress of the sprint) can be amended. These artifacts are covered in more detail later.

Horizontal swimlanes   The Scrum board can be further split by using horizontal swimlanes. These swimlanes can be used to group the stories by feature, so that everyone can see at a glance where effort is being concentrated, and thus where bottlenecks need to be alleviated.

One special swimlane at the top of the board is the Fast-Track lane, into which any very high priority tasks can be placed. Team members can be instructed to "swarm" on a fast-track item so that it is completed as quickly as possible, often to the detriment of any other outstanding work. Swarming ensures that the team stops what they are doing to collaborate on a problem or task that has overriding priority. It is a useful tool and should be used sparingly, when such a priority occurs. Apocalyptic defects found in production are the most common fast-track items.

Technical debt

The term *technical debt* deserves further explanation. Throughout the course of implementing a user story, it is likely that certain compromises will need to be made between the "ideal code" and code that is good enough to meet the deadline. This is not to say that poor design should be willingly tolerated (nor actively encouraged) in order to hit a deadline, but that there is value in doing something simpler now, with a view to improving it later.

Good and bad technical debt   Debt is likely to accrue gradually over the lifetime of a project. It is termed *debt* because that is a great metaphor for how it should be viewed. There is nothing wrong with certain types of financial debt. If, for example, you have the option of spreading the payments for a car over 12 months and these payments are interest-free, you are in debt, but this could be a good decision if you need the car for commuting and cannot afford the payment in full. The car will allow you to generate the revenue necessary to pay for it, because you can now get to work on time.

Of course, some debt is bad. If you take out a credit card and pay for something extravagant without first calculating how you will repay the debt, you can end up in a cycle of balance transfers, trying to keep interest payments at a minimum. This will, in hindsight, look like a bad financial decision based around bad debt. The key is to look carefully at the options and decide whether the debt is worth taking on or whether you should just pay up front.

The tradeoff is the same in software. You could implement a suboptimal solution now and meet a deadline or spend the extra time now to improve the design, perhaps missing the deadline. There is no right answer that fits all situations, just guidelines for detecting good and bad technical debt.

The technical debt quadrant   Martin Fowler, a prominent Agile evangelist, defined a technical debt quadrant for categorizing the concessions and compromises that might be needed to mark a story as done. The two axes that divide a plane into quadrants, x and y, correspond to the questions, "Are we accruing this technical debt for the correct reasons?" and "Are we aware of alternatives to avoid this technical debt?", respectively.

If you answer "Yes" to the former question, you are adding prudent technical debt: you can point to valid reasons for adding it, and your conscience is clear. If you answer "No," then this debt is reckless and you would be better advised to deal with this debt now, rather than allow it to accumulate.

For the latter question, an affirmative answer means that you have considered the alternatives and decided to take the debt. A negative answer indicates that you cannot think of other alternatives.

The results of these questions generate four possible scenarios, as shown in Figure 1-5:

- **Reckless, deliberate**   This type of debt is the most poisonous. It is equivalent to saying something like, "We don't have time for design," which indicates a very unhealthy working environment. A decision such as this should alert everyone that the team is not adaptive, and is marching steadily toward inevitable failure.

- **Reckless, inadvertent**   This type of debt is most likely created by a lack of experience. It is the result of not knowing best practices in modern software engineering. It is likely that the code is a mess, much like in the previous case, but the developer did not know any better and therefore could not find any other options. Education is the answer here: as long as developers are willing to learn, they can stop introducing this kind of technical debt.

- **Prudent, inadvertent**   This occurs when you follow best practices but it turns out that there was a better way of doing something, and "now you know how you should have done it." This is similar to the previous case, but all of the developers were in agreement at the time that there was no better way of solving the problem.

- **Prudent, deliberate**   This is the most acceptable type of debt. All of the choices have been considered, and you know exactly what you are doing—and why—by allowing this debt to remain. It is most commonly associated with a late decision to "ship now and deal with the consequences."

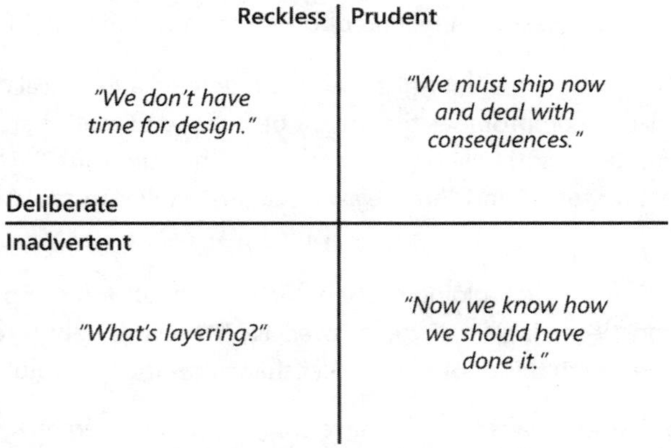

	Reckless	Prudent
Deliberate	"We don't have time for design."	"We must ship now and deal with consequences."
Inadvertent	"What's layering?"	"Now we know how we should have done it."

FIGURE 1-5 The technical debt quadrant, as explained by Martin Fowler, helps developers visualize the four different categories of debt.

Repaying debt   Technical debt is not directly associated with any story points, yet the debt must be repaid despite the lack of direct incentive. It is best to try to attach a technical debt card to a story and refactor the code so that the new design is implemented along with associated new behavior. The next time that a story is taken from the board, check whether any of the code that will be edited has a technical debt attached, and try to tackle the two together.

Digital Scrum boards

A digital Scrum board, unless constantly projected on a wall, hides some of the most important information about a project. By being open with this information and displaying it for the whole company to see, you invite questions about process that otherwise would not be asked. Being transparent with process is a huge benefit, especially when you are implementing Scrum for the first time in a company. It encourages buy-in from important stakeholders that you would do well to involve in the process.

It is a cliché, but people really do fear change. Fear is just a natural reaction to the unknown. By educating people on what you are doing and what certain charts mean (and why their wall is now covered in dozens of index cards), you foster a spirit of collaboration and communication that really is priceless. Being required to explain these things to a layman can also be helpful to you, because in doing so you might come to understand the process better yourself.

As with all tools, the best ones are high-touch and low-resistance. They will be used very often, and there will be no barriers to their use. When a tool becomes even mildly inconvenient to use, it will gradually be more and more neglected. What was initially used often and diligently kept up to date will no longer be tended, and it will rapidly fall behind reality.

The definition of done

Every project needs a *definition of done (DoD)*. This is the standard that every user story must adhere to in order to be considered done. How many times have you heard these lines from a developer?

> *"It's done, I just have to test it...."*

> *"It's done, but I found a defect that I need to fix...."*

> *"It's done, but I'm not 100-percent happy with the design, so I'm going to change the interface...."*

I have used these myself in the past. If the story truly was done, there would be no caveats, conditions, or clauses required. These examples are what developers say when they need to buy themselves a little more time due to a bad estimate or an unforeseen problem. Everyone must agree on a definition of "done" and stick to it. If a user story doesn't meet the criteria, it can't possibly be done. Story points are never claimed until the story meets the definition of done.

What goes into a definition of done? That is entirely up to you, your team, and how stringent you want your quality assurance process to be. However, the following demonstrates a stock DoD as a starting point.

In order to claim that a user story is done, you must:

- Unit-test all code to cover its success and failure paths, with all tests passing.

- Ensure that all code is submitted to the Continuous Integration builds and compiles—without errors—with all tests passing.

- Verify behavior against the acceptance criteria with the product owner.

- Peer-review code by a developer who did not work on the story.

- Document just enough to communicate intent.

- Reject reckless technical debt.

Feel free to remove, amend, or append any rules, but be strict with this definition. If one story cannot meet all criteria, you either ensure that this story can meet all criteria or drop prohibitive criteria from the definition of done altogether. For example, if you feel that code reviews are arcane or pedantic, feel free to omit that criterion from your DoD.

Charts and metrics

There are several charts that can be used to monitor the progress of a Scrum project. Scrum charts can indicate the health and historical progress of a Scrum project, in addition to predicting probable future achievement. All of these charts should be displayed prominently by the Scrum board in a size sufficient to be read from a few feet away. This shows the team that these metrics are not being used behind their back, that they are not a way of measuring their progress for the consumption of management. Instead, be very up front about how progress is measured, and make it clear that these charts are not being made for performance reasons, but to diagnose problems with the project as a whole.

On a related note, try to avoid measuring anything on a personal level—such as story points achieved per developer. This conveys a poor message to the team: that they can sacrifice team progress for personal progress. Developers will readily attach themselves to such measurements and try to save face by monopolizing larger stories, trying to achieve points all by themselves. Be careful what you incentivize.

Caution Be wary of what you measure—there is an "observer effect." For instance, for some metrics, the act of measuring is not possible without first altering that which is measured. Take, for example, measuring tire pressure on a car. It is very difficult to measure the pressure without first letting a little air out of the tire, thus altering the pressure. This same principle applies quite aptly to human nature, too. When the team knows that they are going to be measured by some criteria, they will do whatever they can to improve their statistics to look good. This is not to say that you are managing a group of Machiavellian troublemakers, but when the team realizes that story points will be used to measure their progress, they might be inclined to assign higher points for the same effort. Use triangulation (which is covered in the "Sprint retrospective" section later in this chapter) to reconcile estimated effort with actual effort.

Story points

Story points are intended to incentivize the team to add business value with every sprint. Story points are assigned to user stories by the whole development team during the sprint planning meeting (see the "Sprint planning" section later in this chapter). A story point is a measure of relative effort required to implement the behavior that the user story represents. This is the inclusive effort required to fulfill the entire software life cycle—requirements analysis, technical design, and code implementation with unit testing, plus quality assurance against acceptance criteria and deployment to a staging environment. Although every story should already be small enough to fit comfortably inside a sprint, stories might still vary significantly in size.

At one end of the scale is a "one-point story" which requires minimal effort to implement. An interesting and important fact about story points is that they are absolutely meaningless outside of the team that assigned them. A one-point story for one team might be a three-point story for another team. What occurs over multiple sprints is a consensus on the approximate effort required for a story.

One thing that a story point definitely does not represent is effort measured in absolute terms—days, hours, or any other temporal measurement. Story points do, very roughly, correspond to a historical range of times, as shown in Figure 1-6. In this chart, the vertical bars represent estimated times, and the horizontal dashes attached to the bars represent actual effort spent on a story of the corresponding number of points.

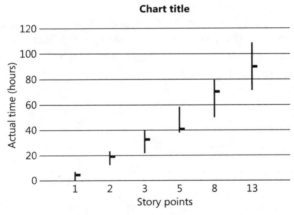

FIGURE 1-6 Min/max/average chart showing correlation between estimated effort and actual effort.

The main takeaway from this chart is that larger stories have correspondingly larger ranges—the larger a story is assumed to be, the harder it is to accurately predict how long it will take to complete.

Velocity

Over multiple sprints, it is possible to calculate a running average of the achieved story points. Let's say that a team has completed three sprints, meeting the definition of done on stories totaling 8, 12, and 11 story points. This is a running total of 31 and a running average of 10 points. This can be said to be the team's velocity, and it can be used in two ways.

First, a team's velocity can form a ceiling for how many points a team should commit to for the next sprint. If the team is averaging 10 points per sprint, committing to more than that amount for a single iteration would be more than just optimistic—it would be setting them up for a morale-sapping failure. It is better to set an achievable goal and meet or exceed it than to set an unrealistic goal and fall short. If the team took these 10 points and actually implemented 11, it would feed into a new velocity of 11: (12 + 11 + 11) / 3. This is the Scrum feedback loop in action.

A second use for the velocity is to analyze problems with delivery. If the velocity of a team drops by a significant percentage for one sprint, this probably indicates that something bad happened during that sprint that needs to be rectified. Perhaps the stories were too large and their true scale was underestimated, thus keeping them in progress for a long time and requiring them to survive for more than one sprint. Alternatively, a simpler explanation could be possible—that too many key staff members were on vacation (or ill) all at once and progress naturally slowed. On the other hand, perhaps too much time was spent refactoring existing, working code, with not enough emphasis on introducing new behavior to the system. Whatever the reason, a 25-percent drop in velocity is not *always* disastrous, but it *could* be indicative of further problems to come that you should address as soon as possible. Week-after-week reductions in velocity—protracted deceleration—is a definite problem and probably points to code that is not adaptive to change; something that this book will help you address.

Sprint burndown chart

At the start of each sprint, a two-dimensional Cartesian graph is created and placed by the Scrum board. The total number of story points is charted along the y-axis, and the number of working days is plotted along the x-axis. A straight diagonal line (also known as the *line of best fit*) is then drawn to show the ideal progression of the sprint, as shown in Figure 1-7.

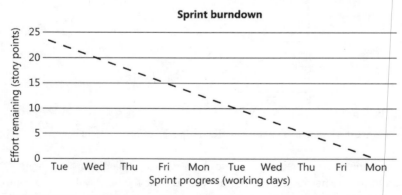

FIGURE 1-7 A sprint burndown chart at the beginning of a sprint. The straight line shows the "line of best fit" to the sprint goal (23 story points, in this example).

At each morning's stand-up Scrum meeting, the points associated with any completed user stories are claimed and deducted from the current remaining total. As illustrated in Figure 1-8, this shows the actual progress of the sprint against the necessary progress in order to achieve the sprint goal.

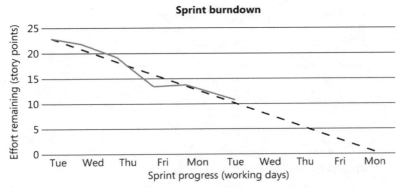

FIGURE 1-8 A sprint burndown chart partway through a sprint. In this instance, the team is sticking closely to the "path of perfection," although no progress was made between Friday and Monday of the first week.

Drawing the actual-progress line and required line in different colors helps differentiate the two. If at any time during the sprint the actual line is above the required line, the chart is indicating that there is a problem and that the amount of work that will be delivered is less than planned. Conversely, if the actual line is below the required line, the project is ahead of schedule. It is likely that during the course of a sprint, the actual line will oscillate above and below the line somewhat, without indicating any real problems. It is the larger divergences that need to be explained.

Burndown charts are useful when there is a fixed amount of work required in a fixed amount of time. Under these conditions, it is not possible to dip below the x-axis. (When y=0, you have completed all work assigned.)

Feature burnup chart

Just as the sprint burndown chart tracks progress at story level throughout a sprint, the feature burnup chart shows the progress of completed features as they are implemented. At the end of each sprint, it is possible that a new feature might have been implemented in its entirety. The best thing about this graph is that it is impossible to fake the delivery of completed features without having symptoms manifest quite quickly. The idea is to watch this graph increase linearly over time, ideally without significant plateaus. Figure 1-9 shows an example of a good feature burnup chart.

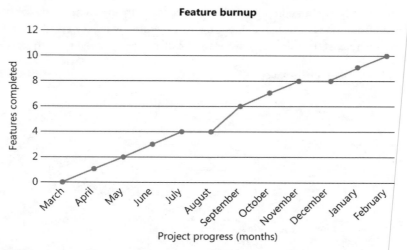

FIGURE 1-9 The feature burnup chart covering an adjusted calendar year for a healthy project making consistent progress.

Although the gradient might be shallow, this graph implies that the team has found a good rhythm to their development and is consistently delivering features at a fairly predictable rate. Though there are slight deviations from a perfectly straight line, these are nothing to worry about.

On the other hand, the burnup chart shown in Figure 1-10 shows that a definite issue has occurred during development. The team started very strongly, delivering lots of features extremely quickly, but they have since stalled and only delivered two completed features over the past eight months.

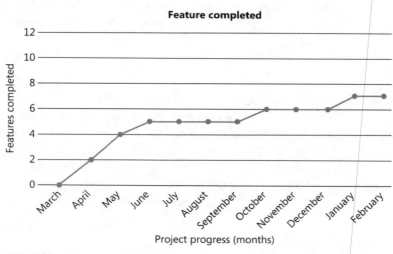

FIGURE 1-10 The feature burnup chart covering an adjusted calendar year for a project that has stalled.

The problem here is quite clear: the code was not adaptive to change. The initial dash from the starting line could indicate a lack of unit testing and neglect for layering or other best practices. By omitting these details, the team managed to complete features early. However, as the code base became bloated and disorganized, progress began to slow down significantly and the amount of features delivered ground to a halt. A progression like this is likely to be accompanied by an increase in the amount of defects and bad—reckless—technical debt. Eventually, if the project continues to follow this path, it would probably be better to start over—the refactoring effort required to get it back on track would outweigh the benefits. If the problem was caught early enough, of course, the team and project could recover. However, it is probably best to start with Agile development practices in place from the outset, rather than trying to crowbar them in to a brownfield project.

 Note *Brownfield* here means a project that is already in progress. It is the opposite of a *greenfield* project, which is a new project. The terms are taken from the construction industry.

Backlogs

A backlog is a list of pending items that are yet to be addressed. These items are waiting for their time to be taken from the backlog and acted on until they are complete. Each item in the list has an assigned priority and an estimated required effort, and the list is ordered first by priority and then by effort.

Two backlogs are maintained in Scrum, each with its own distinct purpose: the product backlog and the sprint backlog.

Product backlog

At any point during a product's life, the product backlog contains features that are waiting to be implemented. These features have not been committed to a sprint, so the development team is not actively working on the items on this backlog. However, the development team—or its key representatives—will have spent time estimating the effort required on these features. This helps to prioritize the items on the product backlog so that it remains in priority order.

The priority of each item is primarily dictated by the value that implementing the feature would represent to the business. This business value must be determined by the owner of the product backlog: the product owner. This person represents the business to the development team and can speak authoritatively for it. The product owner's knowledge of the business and its working practices is vital for correctly assigning the business value intrinsic to any particular feature. If two items on the product backlog have the same relative business value, their priority is decided based on the relative effort required. Given two features of high business value, if one is estimated to be small and another estimated to be large, it makes business sense to implement the small feature first. This is because smaller features pose less of a risk; the probable range of time required to implement a small feature will not vary as much as that of a larger feature. Also, the return on investment (ROI) is larger for a feature that requires less effort than for one of equal value that requires more.

When the business wants to release a new version of the product, the product backlog can be consulted to determine which features are most valuable to the release. This can occur in one of two ways: either the business sets an absolute deadline for the release and commits to the amount of work likely to be accomplished in that timeframe, given the effort estimates attached; or the business selects the features that are required for the release and the likely release date is determined from the estimates.

Aside from features, the product backlog can also contain defects that must be fixed but that have not yet found their way into a sprint. Just like features, defects will have some assigned business value. The estimate of effort required for a defect is difficult to ascertain, because there is less known about the cause of defects and some time might be required to find an estimate.

The product backlog should reflect the open nature of Agile reporting. It should be visible to everyone so that anyone can contribute ideas, offer suggestions, or indicate possible surprises along the way. It is also important that this list remain authoritative, containing the true state of the product backlog at any time. Poor decisions are often made due to poor information, and an out-of-date product backlog could be disastrous if key release-planning decisions are ill-informed.

Sprint backlog

The sprint backlog contains all of the user stories that are to be completed in the coming sprint. At the start of the sprint, the team selects enough work to fill a sprint based on their current velocity and the relative size of the user stories that are yet to be developed. After the stories are committed to the sprint, the team can start to break down each story into tasks that have real-world time estimates in hours. Each individual then elects to implement enough tasks to fill his or her time during the sprint.

The sprint backlog and all of the time estimates are owned by the team. No one outside of the development team can add items to the sprint backlog, nor can they reliably estimate the relative effort or absolute hours required to complete work. The team alone is responsible for the sprint backlog, but they must take work from the product backlog in priority order.

The sprint

The iterations of a Scrum project are called *sprints*. Sprints should last between one and four weeks, with two-week sprints commonly favored. A shorter sprint might leave too little time to accomplish the sprint goals, and a longer sprint might cause the team to lose focus.

Sprints are generally referred to by their index number, starting with sprint zero. Sprint zero is intended to prepare the development environment for the whole team, and to carry out some preliminary planning meetings before the first actual sprint begins. There will probably not be any points associated with sprint zero, but a lot can be achieved in those first weeks to make the transition to Scrum easier during subsequent sprints.

The temptation is to align sprints to the working week by starting them on a Monday and ending them on a Friday. The trouble with this is that the sprint retrospective (which will be covered shortly) involves quite a lot of time in meetings, and there is nothing more energy-sapping than sitting in meetings on a Friday afternoon. Some people also tend to leave early on Fridays, and concentration levels are likely to dip before the weekend. Similarly, no one looks forward to starting their week with meetings, so it is perhaps best to avoid this and start your sprints around midweek: Tuesday, Wednesday, or Thursday.

The following is an explanation of all of the meetings that form part of each sprint, in order, unless otherwise stated.

Release planning

At some point before the sprint begins, the release of the software must be planned. This involves the customer and the product owner deciding on a release date and prioritizing and sizing the features that are to be included.

Feature estimation

Features can involve a lot of effort, even on the smaller end of the scale. Thus, any attempts to accurately predict the amount of effort required will likely be off by a wide margin. For this reason, feature effort can be stated in common T-shirt sizes:

- Extra-large (XL)
- Large (L)
- Medium (M)
- Small (S)
- Extra-small (XS)

Feature priority

It might be difficult to predict how many features can fit into a release, which is why feature priority is so important. For a specific release, all features can be given one of three priorities:

- Required (R)
- Preferred (P)
- Desired (D)

Required features form part of the Minimum Viable Release. Preferred features are the features that should be tackled if any time is available before the deadline looms. Desired features are the lowest priority, those features that are not essential—but that the customer would certainly like to have implemented—for this release, anyway.

In addition, business stakeholders should number the features so that the development team can be sure to implement each feature in priority order.

Sprint planning

The expected outcome of sprint planning is to estimate user stories. As with all parts of the Scrum process, there are variations of the story estimation process. This section discusses planning poker, which is one of the more common ways to generate discussion, and affinity estimation, a quicker way to estimate the relative size of stories. Affinity estimation is better when there are a large number of stories to estimate. For an individual sprint, it is possible to use planning poker if there are only a few stories to estimate or to use affinity estimation if there are a larger number of stories or if time is short.

Planning poker

The planning poker session involves the whole development team—business analysts, developers, and test analysts—including the Scrum master and the product owner. For every user story that is currently on the product backlog, a small scope explanation is given, and then everyone is asked to vote on its size in story points.

In order to avoid a lot of small-scale differences, it is best to limit the voting options. For example, a common choice is a modified Fibonacci scale: 1, 2, 3, 5, 8, 13, 20, 40, and 100. Regardless of the scale chosen, the choices should be limited overall and the gaps between the options should increase in size as the number of points goes up. At the lower end of the scale, zero can be added to represent "no work required," for a story that requires a negligible amount of work. At the upper end of the scale, team members can vote that a story is too big to implement within a sprint and must be vertically split further before being taken off the board to develop.

A few decks of playing cards double well as voting cards, but you can also fashion voting cards from spare index cards or even just scribble numbers on pieces of scrap paper. When it comes time to vote, everyone should show their cards at the same time, to avoid being influenced by the choices of others. It is unlikely that consensus will be achieved all the time, and there could be some large divergences between individual estimates. This is perfectly normal—there is sure to be a couple of outliers who deviate from the average vote. These voters should be asked to justify their choice in light of the general consensus. For example, if someone votes a 1 when the average vote was 8, that person would be asked—politely, of course—to explain why they think the story requires that much less effort. Similarly, voters who vote above the average should be asked to explain their reasons, too. All that is occurring here is that a discussion is generated about how much effort the team believes is required to carry a story to its conclusion.

After the justifications have been aired, a revote might be necessary because other people could have been persuaded that their vote was actually too big or too small and that the outlier was in fact correct. Eventually, consensus should be achieved, with all parties agreeing on a suitable number of story points. Each story should be estimated until the number of points assigned reaches the team's current velocity, which is the maximum amount of work that the team should commit to in each sprint.

> ## Avoiding Parkinson's Law
>
> Parkinson's Law states:
>
> *"Work expands so as to fill the time available for its completion."*
>
> —Cyril Northcote Parkinson
>
> When you untether the estimates of stories from real-world time, there is less likelihood of succumbing to Parkinson's Law. The focus should remain on completing the story—that is, on meeting the definition of done—as quickly as possible.

Affinity estimation

Affinity estimation is provided as a counterpoint to planning poker, which can take a significant amount of time to generate estimates if there are a lot of stories. Rather than entering into a discussion for each story, the team picks two stories from the top of the product backlog and then decides which is the smaller of the two. The smaller is placed on the left side of a table and the larger on the right.

The team then proceeds to take a single story from the product backlog and places it where they believe it should go on the spectrum between the existing smaller and larger stories. It could feasibly be placed to the left of the smaller story, indicating that it is smaller still; to the right of the larger, indicating that it is larger still; on top of the small or large story, indicating that it is roughly the same; or anywhere in between the two stories. This process then continues for each story on the product backlog, until there is no more room in the sprint for extra work.

With the stories grouped together by relative size, the team can start at the leftmost group and proceed toward the rightmost group, allocating points to the stories according to the modified Fibonacci sequence. If there are many stories to estimate, or if time is scarce, this is a good way of achieving a ballpark estimate of relative size.

Daily Scrum

Although there are several meetings that will last a couple of hours, the Scrum process itself is only really visible day to day at the daily Scrum, or "stand-up meeting."

The team should gather around the Scrum board in a horseshoe shape and each person, in turn, should address the whole team. The daily Scrum should not last longer than 15 minutes. To focus the meeting, everyone should answer these three questions:

- What did you do yesterday?

- What will you do today?

- What impediments do you face?

The key issues that the daily stand-up meeting addresses are yesterday's actual progress and to-day's estimated progress. In discussing what you did yesterday, refer to the Scrum board and feel free to move cards across from one swimlane to another or move your avatar from one card to another, thus keeping the Scrum board current. Outline what you worked on and how the day went. If you do not have anything to do at this point, notify the Scrum master and request a new work item. Impediments include anything that might prevent you from completing your goal for the day. Because you will refer back to what you claim you will be doing today in tomorrow's daily Scrum, it is important to enumerate anything that might prevent you from achieving what you plan to do. The impediment could be directly work related, as in, "I will not be able to continue if the network keeps going down like it did yesterday," or it might be a personal matter, as in "I have an appointment with the dentist at 14:00, so I'm unlikely to complete everything." Regardless, the Scrum master should be taking notes so that she knows how everyone is progressing with their stories.

Niko-niko calendar

A "niko-niko calendar"—also sometimes referred to as a "mood board" (in Japanese, "niko-niko" has a meaning close to "smiley")— provides a good barometer of how the team feels about their progress during the sprint. A table is drawn by the Scrum board, with the days of the sprint across the top and the names of the team members down the side, as shown in Figure 1-11.

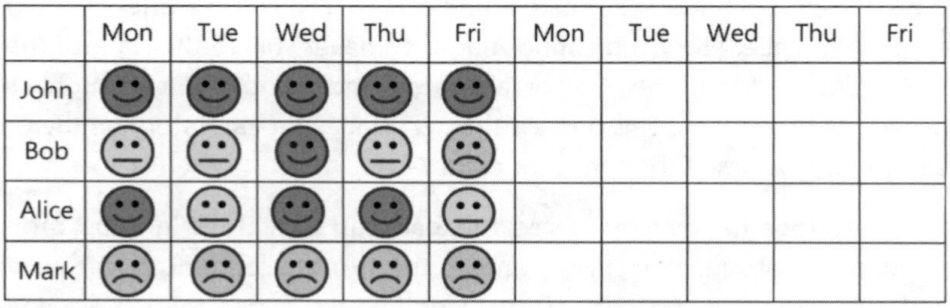

	Mon	Tue	Wed	Thu	Fri	Mon	Tue	Wed	Thu	Fri
John	🙂	🙂	🙂	🙂	🙂					
Bob	🙂	😐	🙂	😐	🙁					
Alice	🙂	😐	🙂	🙂	😐					
Mark	🙁	🙁	🙁	🙁	🙁					

FIGURE 1-11 A niko-niko calendar quickly shows who is having a good sprint and who is not.

At the Scrum meeting, each person is asked to place one of three stickers on the board—green, yellow, or red—in their square for the previous day. Each sticker corresponds to an over-all summary of how the previous day went: good, okay, or bad, respectively. This will quickly show when team members are having consecutive frustrating days and require help, which they might not otherwise seek.

This is just another metric to improve the feedback loop. If all of your team members are consistently feeling bad about their work, perhaps morale needs to be boosted. Or if one of the team is consistently unhappy but the rest of the team is happy, this could indicate that someone is being left behind or doesn't feel like he/she fits in. Worst of all, if the whole team feels happy when sprints are running late, the code is in a mess, and clients are knocking down the door for their money back—the team has stopped caring!

After everyone has spoken, the meeting is over. One thing to be vigilant against is tangential conversations. It is extremely tempting to try to talk through problems during the Scrum. If someone mentions an impediment of some weird and wonderful behavior in the code base, all of the developers will likely want to hypothesize about the possible causes. Be aware of who needs to be present for such conversations—do the test analysts really need to listen to a discussion on why Microsoft Visual Studio is using the coders' entire available RAM? No, most likely not. Make a note of the problem and ask the appropriate people to take the discussion offline (after the meeting).

Sprint demo

A sprint demo is a key event to put in the sprint calendar. It is a showcase of all of the completed stories—those that have met the definition of done during the sprint—in action in a real environment. The entire development team should be present, and you could also invite other stakeholders to the meeting, such as management or sales team representatives. Anyone who might have an interest in the project's progress should be free to attend. This further fosters an openness that all projects should have.

Collect all of the completed user stories from the Scrum board and, for each one, explain its scope and what it was intended to achieve as part of the project as a whole. Refer to the feature to which the story belongs, and the change in application behavior that has occurred as a result of its implementation. Proceed to demonstrate this behavior by using a real deployment of the system. Invite questions from the audience, but do be careful about off-topic issues or getting sidetracked by irrelevance. Keep the conversation focused, and offer to talk to people individually after the demo has completed. Any suggestions for improvements should feed back into the product backlog so that they are correctly prioritized and scheduled. It sometimes feels that improvements suggested in the demo are suddenly the most important things to be done, but this is rarely a reflection of reality.

The demo should not be feared, but it certainly incentivizes progress. No one wants to cancel a demo because nothing has been completed, but resist the temptation to circumvent the definition of done just to demonstrate something. By being honest about progress, you will not have to hide any problems. Instead, point to the charts and metrics to explain probable causes for the reduced output.

Specifying a time before the demo when code will be locked is also a good idea, to prevent those tempting last-minute changes to try to claim more points. Dedicate a realistic amount of time before the demo to set up the environment and ensure that everyone is ready, and guard against throwing reckless technical debt into the code for a short-term boost.

> *Discipline is the ability to consistently choose perpetual benefit over fleeting temptation.*
>
> *Mike Alexander, Fitness Expert*

Sprint retrospective

When the sprint demo is complete, it is time to take stock of the iteration and gauge opinions about its overall success. For some team members, the sprint might have been a resounding success, whereas for others, it might have been an absolute disaster. The sprint retrospective can help you distill the elements that went well into actions that bear repeating and isolate problems so that they can be dealt with. The output from the sprint retrospective should not be written once and forever forgotten. It should be referred to at the end of the next sprint to ensure that requisite changes were made and that mistakes were not repeated.

The following questions should be asked of the team during the retrospective:

- What went well?

- What went badly?

- What do we need to start doing?

- What do we need to stop doing?

- What do we need to continue doing?

- Did we experience any surprises during the sprint?

Starting with the positive, ask each team member to elaborate on what they felt went well about the sprint. Perhaps they were very happy with the progress that was made, or with the quality of the work that was produced.

Next, ask them to explain what went badly in the sprint. Perhaps some tasks were more difficult and involved than first anticipated, thus causing an otherwise simple story to be delayed. Whatever the problem, it is certain that some kind of resolution can be found. There is nothing wrong with candidness, as long as it is accompanied by objectivity. No one should be accusatory against other team members, and all criticism should be given constructively and received gracefully. The goal is an improvement of the process and the product.

It could be that there are certain things that the team does not currently do that should be introduced to the process. Perhaps there are not yet any formal unit tests to accompany the code, and the team believes that this should be introduced at this stage. As with all suggestions, the Scrum master should be actively taking notes to take action later.

Equally, there could be things that the team is doing that they feel should be stopped. Prime examples are to stop unplanned digressions in meetings and to stop moving stories into the In Progress lane when there is plenty of work already there. This latter problem is quite common and can be solved by putting capacity limits on certain swimlanes. By enforcing that no more than three stories can be in progress at a time, team members are encouraged to help finish work that has already begun rather than start something afresh.

Some things that went well will yield actions that bear repeating. If the sprint demo went well and it was decided that this was due to good preparation beforehand, make a note to continue to do this. It is quite surprising how quickly good habits can be forgotten and bad habits take their place.

Finally, the team should recall any surprises—good or bad—that were revealed during the sprint. Any bad surprise should result in an action item to avoid such an occurrence in the future, whereas a good surprise could result in behavior that bears repeating.

At least one action item from the retrospective should be prioritized for the next sprint. The outcomes of this meeting should not be forgotten; they should be acted on.

Story point triangulation

Some of the stories during the sprint might have required more or less effort than was estimated by the team during the sprint planning meeting. Taking 5 or 10 minutes at the end of the sprint retrospective to triangulate the estimated stories with the actual effort expended can be rewarding.

After a couple of sprints, there will be statistics available for how long each story actually took in comparison to its story point estimate. For example, you might have a table something like Table 1-1.

TABLE 1-1 Statistics for the average, minimum, and maximum actual effort compared to user story estimates on a hypothetical project

Story points	Average actual effort (hours)	Minimum actual effort (hours)	Maximum actual effort (hours)
1	5.5	1	19
2	9.5	2	23
3	17	7.5	40
5	36	20	76
8	56	40	86
13	88	68	154

If a one-point story for a sprint actually took 60 hours to complete, it was probably closer to an eight-point story. As long as there were no mitigating circumstances—such as a lack of developer resources because of absence—the estimate can be safely deemed to have been erroneous. If you claim the eight story points instead, your velocity will not suffer as a result, and the amount of stories that the team can commit to does not decrease.

Focus on the stories that are significantly out of range. If a one-point story fits into the range for a two-point or three-point story, it is unlikely to make a significant difference to take more points.

Scrum calendar

For clarity, a calendar showing the typical Scrum meetings over the course of a sprint is shown in Table 1-2.

TABLE 1-2 A possible calendar for organizing the Scrum meetings of a sprint for a hypothetical project

Date (April 2013)	Time	Type of meeting	Attendees
Tuesday 2nd	13:00-15:30	Sprint planning	Development team; product owner
Wednesday 3rd	09:30-09:45	Daily Scrum	Development team
Thursday 4th	09:30-09:45	Daily Scrum	Development team
Friday 5th	09:30-09:45	Daily Scrum	Development team
Monday 8th	09:30-09:45	Daily Scrum	Development team
Tuesday 9th	09:30-09:45	Daily Scrum	Development team
Wednesday 10th	09:30-09:45	Daily Scrum	Development team
Thursday 11th	09:30-09:45	Daily Scrum	Development team
Friday 12th	09:30-09:45	Daily Scrum	Development team
Monday 15th	09:30-09:45	Daily Scrum	Development team
Tuesday 16th	10:00-11:20	Sprint demonstration	Anyone
	11:30-12:00	Sprint retrospective	Development team
	13:00-15:30	Sprint planning	Development team; product owner

Observe that almost a whole day is dedicated to the end of a sprint and the beginning of a new sprint. This is called Sprint Handover Day and, to maintain concentration levels, it is sometimes split between two consecutive days: an afternoon and the following morning. The sprint demo and retrospective would then be held Tuesday afternoon, and the sprint planning meeting would be moved to Wednesday morning.

Another interesting point is the timing of the daily Scrum. If it is too early in the day, attendance can be a problem because people could be delayed by traffic or otherwise waylaid. Similarly, if it is too late, dragging people from their desks when they are already involved in a task is also difficult.

These meetings can be added to Microsoft Outlook or some other calendar program, with the relevant people attached as attendees.

Problems with Scrum and Agile

Agile processes are not a miracle solution, destined to turn every failing project to profitability and success. The aim of any software development process is to create repeatable success when delivering software, but that software still needs to be written. No amount of documentation can remove the fact that a software product is the result of working source code.

This book teaches developers how to create software solutions that are *adaptive*. This means that they are resilient to the sort of change to which all software is subjected. It is irrational to assume that the first attempt at a solution will meet all of the needs of the customer, so change is inevitable. Agile processes—and Scrum is no exception—aim to embrace this change and seek to ensure that customers are allowed to make alterations to the behavior of the software as it is developed. Otherwise, they would be forced to accept a substandard solution that misses the mark.

Maladaptive code

Code that is not adaptive is *maladaptive*. If code is maladaptive, it does not readily lend itself to change. The estimates that the team assigned to various tasks could be significantly different from reality because the code takes much longer to change than it really should. Changing the code might also result in the introduction of defects that will eventually take further time, effort, and resources to be fixed.

Rigidity

Code can display a few different signs of rigidity, each of which needs to be addressed so that changes don't become increasingly difficult, limiting the number of features that can be delivered.

Lack of abstractions   An abstraction hides the details of something, showing instead a much simpler representation. Abstractions are all around us. The steering wheel in your car abstracts the mechanical implementation that eventually turns the wheels in either direction. In fact, there are two common types of steering: rack-and-pinion steering and recirculating-ball steering. In either implementation, the end result is that both of the wheels turn to match how much you have turned the steering wheel, in relative terms. Also, the left and right wheels do not turn the same amount. Because the inside wheel traces a circle of smaller radius than the outside wheel, it must turn more tightly than the outside wheel.

Of course, you do not need to know any of this to drive a car. Sure, it might help you diagnose problems or explain how it works, but as an everyday driver, all this is extraneous information that is not vital to you. The abstraction hides as many details as it can and gives you just enough to get by.

In software, abstractions are key. The user interface does not need to know what storage medium is being used to house the user's input. In fact, if it does know this, there is a lack of abstraction, and the user interface becomes hopelessly obsessed with details that it need not and should not be concerned with.

Code with sufficient abstractions will be better organized, easier to understand and communicate to others, and easier to maintain, and it will contain fewer errors.

Mixed responsibilities   Often, code gradually grows organically from something small, perhaps even trivial, to something much bigger and more important. Incremental changes are made, one on top of the other, until some critical point is reached when a single change can have many related and unpredictable consequences.

This sort of code contains methods, classes, and possibly even whole modules that have no single discernable purpose. Instead, each fulfills several different responsibilities that cannot be easily separated. In this code, a change that should only take a few hours to complete can easily end up taking a day or more of wrestling with the side-effects that one change has on another, ostensibly unrelated, area of the code.

To avoid this, ensure that code at every level—methods, classes, and modules—focuses on one well-defined responsibility.

Untestability

Unit testing has been an established practice for many years now. It is a reliable method of ensuring code correctness that should feel entirely natural to many developers. However, it takes constant discipline and diligence to ensure that code remains testable over the long term.

If code is untestable, it is untested. If code is untested, it *will* contain defects. There is no quantum state indeterminacy at play here: you must simply assume that untested code contains defects. That is the level of suspicion with which you should treat such code.

The following concepts, and testability in general, are discussed in further detail in Chapter 4, "Unit testing and refactoring."

Skyhooks vs. cranes   Daniel C. Dennett wrote in his 1995 book, "Darwin's Dangerous Idea" [emphasis mine]:

> "A **skyhook** is ... an exception to the principle that all design, and apparent design, is ultimately the result of mindless, motiveless mechanicity. A **crane**, in contrast, is a subprocess or special feature of a design process that can be demonstrated to permit the local speeding up of the basic, slow process of natural selection, and that can be demonstrated to be itself the predictable (or retrospectively explicable) product of the basic process."
>
> *Daniel C. Dennett,*
> *Darwin's Dangerous Idea: Evolution and the Meaning of Life, 1995 [Simon & Schuster]*

Sidestepping the religiosity of the content, put simply, a skyhook is a way to explain something without reference to a prior antecedent. Conversely, cranes have explicable antecedents—perhaps until arriving at some primary axiom.

This is a useful analogy in programming, too. Skyhooks are indicative of a deeper problem. All skyhooks should be replaced with appropriate cranes.

The presence of a skyhook in code is difficult to replace with a fake implementation, thereby reducing testability. Examples of skyhooks are:

- Static methods

- Static classes (including singletons)

- Object construction that uses new

- Extension methods

Each of these make testing more difficult[1] by hindering your ability to inject mocks into your code; they are skyhooks and thus they are undesirable. Each is used *ex nihilo*—from nothing.

Luckily, each of these can be replaced with a suitable crane, such as the following, that will facilitate some kind of external injection (that is, it can be used *ex materia*—from something).

- Interfaces

- Dependency injections

- Inversion of control

- Factories

In subsequent chapters of this book, each of these "cranes" of programming are explained in more detail.

Metrics

Source code has been subject to many different metrics through the years, each attempting to reduce the complexity of code down to numbers that indicate the health—or otherwise—of the project as a whole.

This might seem rather reductive, but metrics have evolved somewhat since middle-management obsessed over source lines of code (SLOC). Although SLOC correlates well to the effort required—it takes longer to write more lines of code than it does to write fewer—it does not necessarily correlate to the level of functionality of a system. Nor, indeed, is it a reliable measure of a developer's productivity.

---

1 Difficult, though not impossible. Some mocking frameworks, such as TypeMock (*www.typemock.com*), are able to mock skyhooks. However, this should only be considered if the skyhooks are in third-party, unchangeable code.

Unit test coverage   *Unit test coverage* is a measurement of the percentage of the code that is covered by unit tests. This ranges from 0 percent, indicating that none of the code is covered by any tests, to 100 percent, where every line of code is covered by at least one unit test. Typically, coverage of 80 percent is considered a minimum acceptable level.

In addition to the unit tests, unit test coverage tools should be run by the continuous integration server, which will compile the code every time it is committed to source control. This will allow you to gain fast feedback on any movements in code coverage.

Test coverage is somewhat misleading, because it is a quantitative measure of the unit tests, as opposed to a qualitative measure. It is easy to increase code coverage with *any* tests, as opposed to the *right* tests.

If test coverage is below 80 percent—or whatever your chosen benchmark is—then it can be incrementally increased over time toward your overall coverage goal. With each increase, the continuous integration build should be configured to fail if the coverage percentage slips backward. This means that no new production code can be added without accompanying unit tests, otherwise the coverage percentage would be diluted and would decline.

Cyclomatic complexity   *Cyclomatic complexity* is a measure of the number of paths that exist in the code. With each additional branch in the code—*if* statements, loops, or *switch* statements—the cyclomatic complexity increases. As Figure 1-12 shows, a simple *if* statement and inner loop can be modeled as a graph As the figure shows, the total number of paths through the statement and loop is equal to the cyclomatic complexity of the code.

The edge labeled 1 is the case when the *if* statement has a *false* condition, thus its body is not executed. Edge 2 is when the *if* statement's body is executed, but the contained loop is not. Edge 3 is the case when both the *if* statement and loop are executed.

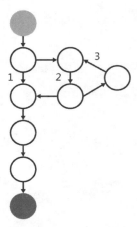

FIGURE 1-12 Each extra path through the code adds further complexity.

As cyclomatic complexity increases, the testing effort required in order to gain unit test code coverage on each branch also increases. Therefore, it is best to keep branching, thus cyclomatic complexity, low to avoid extra test code.

There is also a statistical correlation between high complexity and defect count. That is, code with more branching tends to have more defects.

Conclusion

This chapter has served as an introduction to the Scrum process. If you have never worked on a Scrum project, I hope that your interest has now been piqued sufficiently to do so. On the other hand, if you do work on a Scrum project, perhaps there were some new ideas in this chapter that you want to use.

Though there is admittedly a lot of ground still not covered in this chapter with respect to Scrum, the rest of the book is dedicated more to the developer's point of view of an Agile project. However, there are plenty of resources available for learning more about Scrum and discovering whether it is a good fit for your company and your projects.

Scrum projects, like any software projects, are vulnerable to failure. Spotting when something is going wrong is a significant part of the battle, but spotting why it is happening can be even harder. The internal machinations of the code might be designed in a way that makes change very difficult—no matter what process is in place for managing this change. The rest of this book will provide advice and guidelines for ensuring that code is adaptive from the bottom up, making change easier and allowing you to focus solely on adding business value with every sprint.

CHAPTER 2

Dependencies and layering

After completing this chapter, you will be able to

- Manage complex dependencies from method level to assembly level.

- Identify areas where dependency complexity is greatest and use tools to reduce complexity.

- Decompose your code into smaller, more adaptive pieces of functionality that promote reuse.

- Apply layering patterns where they are most useful.

- Understand how dependencies are resolved and debug dependency problems.

- Hide implementations behind simple interfaces.

All software has dependencies. Each dependency is either a first-party dependency within the same code base, a third-party dependency on an external assembly, or the ubiquitous dependency on the Microsoft .NET Framework. Most nontrivial projects make use of all three types of dependency.

A dependency abstracts functionality away from calling code. You don't need to worry too much about what a dependency is doing, much less *how* it is doing it, but you should ensure that all dependencies are correctly managed. When a dependency chain is poorly managed, developers force dependencies that need not exist and tangle the code into knots with spurious assembly references. You might have heard the adage that "the most correct code is that which is not written." Similarly, the best-managed dependency is that which does not exist.

To keep your code adaptive to change, you must manage dependencies effectively. This applies at all levels of the software—from architectural dependencies between subsystems to implementation dependencies between individual methods. A poorly architected application can slow down the delivery of working software, even halt it entirely in the worst case.

I cannot emphasize enough how important it is to take a purist approach to dependency management. If you compromise on such an important issue, you might notice a temporary increase in velocity, but the long-term effects are potentially fatal to the project. It is an all-too-familiar story: the short-lived productivity boost quickly dissipates as the amount of code and number of modules increases. The code becomes rigid and fragile, and progress slows to a crawl. In terms of Scrum artifacts and metrics, the sprint burndown chart flatlines because no story points are claimed and, as long as the problem is unaddressed, the feature burnup chart follows suit because no features are completed. Even the bug count increases. When the dependency structure is incomprehensible, a change in one module can cause a direct side effect in another, seemingly unrelated module.

With discipline and awareness, you can easily manage dependencies. There are established patterns that help you arrange your application in the short term so that it can adapt to changes in the long term. Layering is one of the most common architectural patterns, and this chapter elaborates on the different layering options available, in addition to other methods of dependency management.

The definition of dependency

What is a dependency? Generically, a *dependency* is a relationship between two distinct entities whereby one cannot perform some function—or exist—without the other. A good analogy of this is that one person can be said to be *financially dependent* on another. Often, in legal documents, you are required to state whether you have any dependents—that is, whether anyone depends on you for their living expenses and other basic necessities. This typically refers to a spouse or children. When I lived in Bermuda, for example, I had a work permit that stated that my wife and my daughter could stay there only as long as my work permit was valid. In this way, they were dependent on me and they were my dependents.

Transferring this definition to code, the entities are often assemblies: assembly A uses another assembly, B, and thus you can say that A *depends on* B. A common way of stating this relationship is that A is the *client* of B, and B is the *service* of A. Without B, A cannot function. However, it is very important to note that B is *not* dependent on A and, as you will learn, *must not* and *cannot* depend on A. This client/service relationship is shown in Figure 2-1.

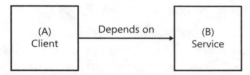

FIGURE 2-1 In any dependency relationship, the dependent is referred to as the *client*, and the entity that is being depended on is the *service*.

Throughout this book, code is discussed from the point of view of the *client* and the *service*. Although some services are hosted remotely, such as services that were created by using Windows Communication Foundation (WCF), this is not a prerequisite to code being termed a service. All code is service code and all code is client code depending on the perspective from which you are approaching the code. Any class, method, or assembly can call other methods, classes, and assemblies; thus the code is a client. The same class, method, or assembly can also be called by other methods, classes, and assemblies; thus the code is also a service.

A simple example

Let's look at how a dependency behaves in a practical situation. This example is a very simple console application that prints a message to the screen. It's the universal "Hello World!" example. This example is necessarily trivial, because I want to distill the problems with dependencies down to their essence.

You can follow the steps here manually or retrieve the solution from GitHub. See Appendix A, "Adaptive tools," for basic instructions on using Git, and Appendix B, "Git branches," (online only) for a reference of each code listing to a Git branch name.

1. Open Microsoft Visual Studio and create a new console application, as shown in Figure 2-2. I have called mine SimpleDependency, but the name is not important.

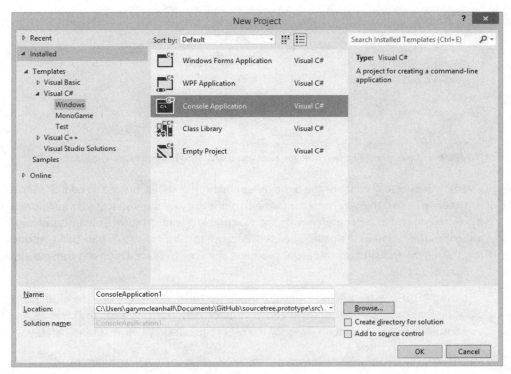

FIGURE 2-2 The New Project dialog box in Visual Studio allows you to select from many different project templates.

2. Add a second project to the solution, this time a class library. I have called mine Message-Printer.

3. Right-click the console application's *References* node and select Add Reference.

4. In the Add Reference dialog box, navigate to Projects and select the class library project.

You have now created a dependency from one assembly to another, as shown in Figure 2-3. Your console application depends on your class library, but the class library does not depend on your console application The console application is the client, and the class library is the service. Although this application does not do much at the moment, build the solution and navigate to the project's bin directory—this is where the executable file is.

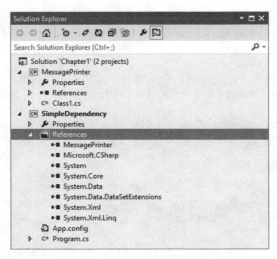

FIGURE 2-3 The referenced assemblies for any project are listed under its *References* node.

The `bin` directory contains the `SimpleDependency.exe` file, but it also contains the `Message-Printer.dll` file. This was copied into the `bin` directory by the Visual Studio build process because it was referenced as a dependency by the executable. I want to show you an experiment, but first a slight modification to the code is needed. Because this is a console application that does nothing, it will initialize and shut down before you have any time to react. Open the console application's `Program.cs` file.

Listing 2-1 shows the addition (in bold) inside the `Main` method. This is the entry point to the application that currently does nothing and exits quickly. By inserting a call to `Console.ReadKey()`, you ensure that the application waits for the user to press a key before it terminates.

LISTING 2-1 The call to ReadKey prevents the console application from exiting immediately.

```
namespace SimpleDependency
{
  class Program
  {
    static void Main()
    {
      Console.ReadKey();
    }
  }
}
```

Rebuild the solution and run the application. As expected, it shows the console window, waits for you to press a key on the keyboard, and then terminates after you do so. Place a breakpoint on the `Console.ReadKey()` line, and debug the solution from Visual Studio.

When the application pauses at the breakpoint, you can view the assemblies that have been loaded into memory for this application. To do this, you can either use the menu bar to select Debug > Windows > Modules, or you can use the keyboard shortcut Ctrl+D, M. Figure 2-4 shows the list of modules that have been loaded for the application.

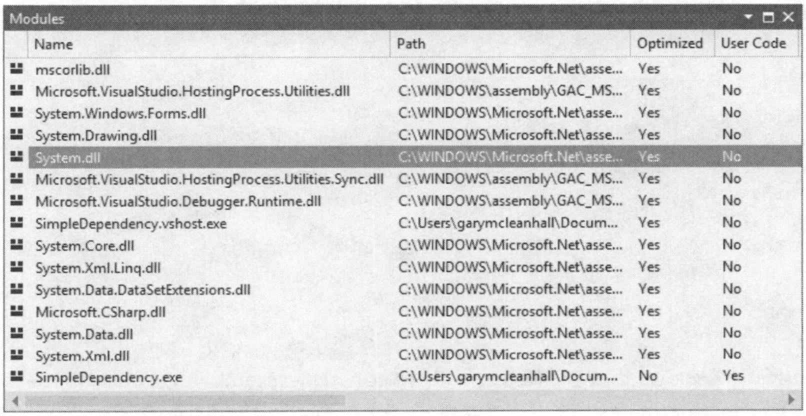

Name	Path	Optimized	User Code
mscorlib.dll	C:\WINDOWS\Microsoft.Net\asse...	Yes	No
Microsoft.VisualStudio.HostingProcess.Utilities.dll	C:\WINDOWS\assembly\GAC_MS...	Yes	No
System.Windows.Forms.dll	C:\WINDOWS\Microsoft.Net\asse...	Yes	No
System.Drawing.dll	C:\WINDOWS\Microsoft.Net\asse...	Yes	No
System.dll	C:\WINDOWS\Microsoft.Net\asse...	Yes	No
Microsoft.VisualStudio.HostingProcess.Utilities.Sync.dll	C:\WINDOWS\assembly\GAC_MS...	Yes	No
Microsoft.VisualStudio.Debugger.Runtime.dll	C:\WINDOWS\assembly\GAC_MS...	Yes	No
SimpleDependency.vshost.exe	C:\Users\garymcleanhall\Docum...	Yes	No
System.Core.dll	C:\WINDOWS\Microsoft.Net\asse...	Yes	No
System.Xml.Linq.dll	C:\WINDOWS\Microsoft.Net\asse...	Yes	No
System.Data.DataSetExtensions.dll	C:\WINDOWS\Microsoft.Net\asse...	Yes	No
Microsoft.CSharp.dll	C:\WINDOWS\Microsoft.Net\asse...	Yes	No
System.Data.dll	C:\WINDOWS\Microsoft.Net\asse...	Yes	No
System.Xml.dll	C:\WINDOWS\Microsoft.Net\asse...	Yes	No
SimpleDependency.exe	C:\Users\garymcleanhall\Docum...	No	Yes

FIGURE 2-4 When you are debugging, the Modules window shows all of the currently loaded assemblies.

Did you notice something strange? There is no mention of the class library that was created. For this example, shouldn't `MessagePrinter.dll` be loaded? Actually, no—this is exactly the expected behavior. Here's why: the application isn't using anything from inside the `MessagePrinter` assembly, so the .NET runtime does not load it.

Just to prove conclusively that the dependent assembly is not really a prerequisite, navigate again to the console application's `bin` directory and delete `MessagePrinter.dll`. Run the application again, and it will continue happily without raising an exception.

Let's repeat this experiment a couple more times to truly find out what is happening. First, add a `using MessagePrinter` directive to the top of the `Program.cs` file. This imports the `Message-Printer` namespace. Do you think this is enough to cause the Common Language Runtime (CLR) to load the module? It is not. The dependency is once again ignored, and the assembly is not loaded. This is because the `using` statement for importing a namespace is just syntactic sugar that only serves to reduce the amount of code you need to write. Rather than writing out the entire namespace whenever you want to use a type from inside it, you can import the namespace and reference the types directly. The `using` statement generates no instructions for the CLR to execute.

This next test builds on the first test, so you can leave the `using` statement in place. In `Program.cs`, above the call to `Console.ReadLine()`, add a call to the constructor for `MessagePrinting.Service`, as shown in Listing 2-2.

LISTING 2-2 Introducing a dependency by calling an instance method.

```
using System;
using MessagePrinter;

namespace SimpleDependency
{
  class Program
  {
    static void Main()
    {
      var service = new MessagePrintingService();
      service.PrintMessage();
      Console.ReadKey();
    }
  }
}
```

The Modules window now shows that the `MessagePrinter.dll` assembly has been loaded, because there is no way to construct an instance of the `MessagePrintingService` without pulling the contents of the assembly into memory.

You can prove this if you delete the `MessagePrinter.dll` from the `bin` directory and run the application again. An exception is thrown this time.

```
Unhandled Exception: System.IO.FileNotFoundException: Could not load file or assembly
'MessagePrinter, Version=1.0.0.0, Culture=neutral, PublicKeyToken=null' or one of its
dependencies. The system cannot find the file specified.
```

Framework dependencies

The dependency shown in the previous section is called a *first-party* dependency. Both the console application and the class library on which it depends belong to the same Visual Studio solution. This means that the dependency should always be accessible, because the dependency project can always be rebuilt from the source code if necessary. It also means that you can modify the source code of first-party dependencies.

Both projects have other dependencies in the form of .NET Framework assemblies. These are not part of the project but are expected to be available. Each .NET Framework assembly is versioned to the .NET Framework version for which it was built: 1, 1.1, 2, 3.5, 4, 4.5, and so on. Some .NET Framework assemblies are new to a particular version and cannot be referenced by projects that are using an earlier version of the .NET Framework. Other assemblies change from version to version of the .NET Framework, and a specific version must be used.

The `SimpleDependency` project has several references to the .NET Framework, as shown earlier in Figure 2-3. Many of these dependencies are defaults that are added to all console application projects. The example application doesn't use them, so they can be safely removed. In fact, for both projects, everything except `System` and `System.Core` are superfluous, so they can be removed from the references list. The application will still run correctly.

By removing unnecessary framework dependencies, you make it easier to visualize the dependencies required by each project.

> ## Framework assemblies always load
>
> It is worth noting that, unlike other dependencies, references to .NET Framework assemblies will always cause those assemblies to load. Even if you are not really using an assembly, it will still load at application startup. Fortunately, if multiple projects in the solution all reference the same assembly, only one instance of this assembly is loaded into memory and is shared among all dependents.

The default reference list The default references for a project vary depending on the project type. Each project type has a project template that lists the references required. This is how a Windows Forms application can reference the `System.Windows.Forms` assembly, whereas a Windows Presentation Foundation application can reference `WindowsBase`, `PresentationCore`, and `Presentation-Framework`.

Listing 2-3 shows the references for a console application. All Visual Studio project templates are located under the Visual Studio installation directory root `/Common7/IDE/ProjectTemplates/` and are grouped by language.

LISTING 2-3 Part of a Visual Studio project template for conditionally referencing different assemblies.

```
<ItemGroup>
  <Reference Include="System"/>
  $if$ ($targetframeworkversion$ >= 3.5)
  <Reference Include="System.Core"/>
  <Reference Include="System.Xml.Linq"/>
  <Reference Include="System.Data.DataSetExtensions"/>
  $endif$
  $if$ ($targetframeworkversion$ >= 4.0)
  <Reference Include="Microsoft.CSharp"/>
  $endif$
  <Reference Include="System.Data"/>
  <Reference Include="System.Xml"/>
</ItemGroup>
```

There is some logic in these files that can alter how the template generates a real project instance. Specifically, the references differ depending on the version of the .NET Framework that is being used for the resulting project. Here, the `Microsoft.CSharp` assembly is only referenced if the project is targeting .NET Framework 4, 4.5, or 4.5.1. This makes sense, because it is normally only required if you use the `dynamic` keyword that was introduced in the .NET Framework 4.

Third-party dependencies

The final type of dependency is that of assemblies developed by third-party developers. Typically, if something is not provided by the .NET Framework, you can implement a solution yourself by creating first-party dependencies. This could be a laborious task depending on the size of the solution required. Instead, you can elect to make use of prefabricated solutions. As an example, you are unlikely to want to implement your own Object/Relational Mapper (ORM), because such a large piece of infrastructural code could take months to be functional and years to be complete. Instead, you could look first to Entity Framework, which is part of the .NET Framework. If that did not meet your needs, you could look instead at NHibernate, which is a mature ORM library that has been extensively tested.

The main reason to use a third-party dependency is to exchange the effort required for implementing some features or infrastructure for the effort of integrating something that is already written and suitable for the job. Do not forget that this integration effort could still be significant, depending on the structure of both your first-party code and the interface of the third-party code. When your aim is to deliver increments of business value on an iterative basis—as in Scrum—using third-party libraries allows you to maintain this focus.

Organizing third-party dependencies   The simplest way to organize dependencies that are external to your project and the .NET Framework is to create a solution folder called Dependencies under the Visual Studio solution of a project and to add the .dll files to that folder. When you want to add references to these assemblies to the projects of the solution, you can do so by browsing to the files in the Reference Manager dialog box (shown in Figure 2-5).

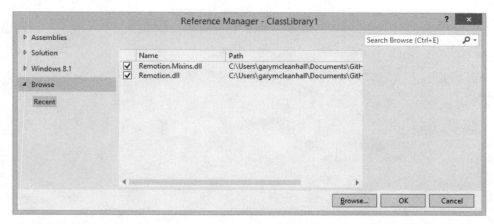

FIGURE 2-5 Third-party references can be stored in a Dependencies folder in the Visual Studio solution.

The other advantage of this approach is that all of the external dependencies are stored in source control. This allows other developers to receive the dependencies just by retrieving the latest version of the source from a central repository. This is a much simpler approach than requiring all of the developers to install or download the files themselves.

A better way to organize third-party dependencies is demonstrated later in this chapter, in the "Dependency management with NuGet" section. In brief, the NuGet dependency management tool manages a project's third-party dependencies for you, including downloading a package containing all relevant artifacts, referencing assemblies, and upgrading library versions.

Modeling dependencies in a directed graph

A *graph* is a mathematical construct that consists of two distinct elements: nodes and edges. An edge can only exist between two nodes and serves to connect them in some way. Any node can be connected to any number of the other nodes in a graph. A graph can be one of several types, depending on variations in the graph's properties. For example, the graph in Figure 2-6 shows edges that are directionless: the edge between nodes A and C is neither from A to C nor from C to A—the presence of the edge is all that matters. This is called an *undirected graph*.

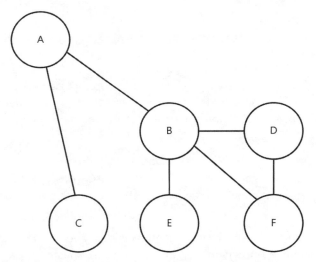

FIGURE 2-6 A graph consists of nodes that are connected by edges.

If, as in Figure 2-7, the edges have arrowheads at one end, you can determine the direction of the edges. There is an edge from A to C, but not an edge from C to A. This is called a directed graph, or a *digraph*.

There are many areas of software engineering in which graphs are excellent models, but graphs are extremely applicable to modeling code dependencies. As you have already learned, dependencies consist of two entities with a direction applied from the dependent code to the dependency. You can think of the entities as nodes and draw a directed edge from dependent to dependency. When you extend this to the rest of the entities, you form a *dependency digraph*.

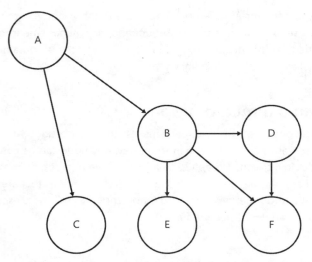

FIGURE 2-7 The edges of this graph are specifically directed, so there is no edge (B,A), yet the edge (A,B) exists.

This structure can be applied at several different granularities, as Figure 2-8 shows. The nodes in the graph could represent the classes in a project, different assemblies, or groups of assemblies that form a subsystem. In all cases, the arrows between the nodes represent the dependencies between components. The source of the arrow is the dependent component and the target of the arrow is the dependency.

For each node at a coarse-grained granularity, there is a set of nodes at a more fine-grained granularity. Inside subsystems are assemblies; inside assemblies are classes; inside classes are methods. This exemplifies how a dependency on a single method can pull in a whole subsystem of chained dependencies.

However, with all of these examples, you do not know what *sort* of dependency you are dealing with (inheritance, aggregation, composition, or association), just that there is a dependency. This is still useful, because managing dependencies only requires knowledge of the binary relationship between two entities: *is there a dependency or not?*

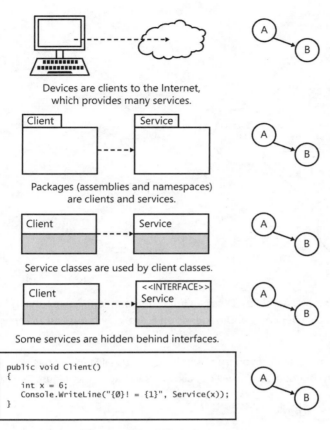

Devices are clients to the Internet,
which provides many services.

Packages (assemblies and namespaces)
are clients and services.

Service classes are used by client classes.

Some services are hidden behind interfaces.

```
public void Client()
{
    int x = 6;
    Console.WriteLine("{0}! = {1}", Service(x));
}
```

Even down at the method level, a method that
calls another method is the client of a service.

FIGURE 2-8 Dependencies at all levels can be modeled as graphs.

Cyclic dependencies

Another part of graph theory is that directed graphs can form cycles: the ability to traverse from one node back to itself by following the edges. The graphs shown so far are said to be *acyclic digraphs*—containing no cycles. Figure 2-9 shows an example of a *cyclic digraph*. If you start at node D, you can follow the edge to E, then B, and finally, end up back at D again.

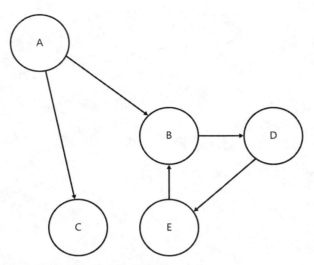

FIGURE 2-9 This digraph contains cycles.

Imagine that these nodes represent assemblies. D has an implicit dependency on anything that its explicit and implicit dependencies also depend on. D depends on E explicitly but B and D implicitly. Therefore, D depends on *itself*.

For assemblies, this is actually not possible. If you try to set this up in Visual Studio, when you come to assigning the reference from E to B, Visual Studio will not allow this to happen, as Figure 2-10 shows.

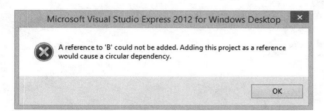

FIGURE 2-10 It is not possible to create a cyclic dependency in Visual Studio.

So, although modeling dependencies as graphs might seem academic, it has clear benefits when you are organizing your dependencies. Cyclic dependencies between assemblies are not a diversion from a purist ideal but are completely disallowed, and their avoidance is mandatory.

Loops are specializations of the cycles in digraphs. If a node is connected with an edge to *itself*, that edge becomes a loop. Figure 2-11 shows an example of a graph with a loop.

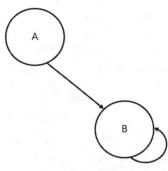

FIGURE 2-11 In this digraph, node B links to itself with a loop.

In practice, assemblies always explicitly self-depend, and such an observation is not particularly noteworthy. However, at the method level, a loop is evidence of *recursion*, as shown in Listing 2-4.

LISTING 2-4 A self-loop in a digraph that represents methods results in recursion.

```
namespace Graphs
{
  public class RecursionLoop
  {
    public void A()
    {
      int x = 6;
      Console.WriteLine("{0}! = {1}", x, B(x));
    }

    public int B(int number)
    {
      if(number == 0)
      {
        return 1;
      }
      else
      {
        return number * B(number - 1);
      }
    }
  }
}
```

The class in Listing 2-4 shows the functional equivalent of the dependency graph in Figure 2-11. Method A calls method B; therefore, you say that method A is dependent on method B. However, more interesting is method B's dependency on itself—B is an example of a recursive function; that is, a function that calls itself.

Managing dependencies

You have learned so far that dependencies are necessary but also must be carefully managed lest they present you with problems later in development. These problems can be quite difficult to back out of after they have manifested themselves. Therefore, it is best to manage your dependencies correctly from the outset and to stay vigilant so that no problems creep in. Poorly managed dependencies can quickly escalate from a small compromise to become an overall architectural problem.

The rest of this chapter is focused on the more practical aspects of continually managing dependencies. This includes avoiding anti-patterns and, more importantly, understanding why these common patterns are *anti*-patterns. Conversely, some patterns are benevolent and should be embraced; these are offered as direct alternatives to the noted anti-patterns.

Patterns and anti-patterns

As an engineering discipline, object-oriented software development is a relatively new endeavor. Over the last few decades, some repeatable collaborations between classes and interfaces have been identified and codified as *patterns*.

There are many software development patterns, each providing a generic solution that can be repurposed to a specific problem domain. Some patterns can be used in conjunction with each other to produce elegant solutions to complex problems. Of course, not all patterns are applicable all the time, and it takes experience and practice to recognize when and where certain patterns might apply.

Some patterns are not so benevolent. In fact, they are quite the opposite. They are considered *anti-patterns*. These patterns harm the adaptability of your code and should be avoided. Some anti-patterns began as patterns before slowly falling out of favor due to perceived negative side effects.

Implementations versus interfaces

Developers who are new to the concept of programming to interfaces often have difficulty letting go of what is behind the interface.

At compile time, any client of an interface should have no idea which implementation of the interface it is using. Such knowledge can lead to incorrect assumptions that couple the client to a specific implementation of the interface.

Imagine the common example in which a class needs to save a record in persistent storage. To do so, it rightly delegates to an interface, which hides the details of the persistent storage mechanism used. However, it would not be right to make any assumptions about which implementation of the interface is being used at run time. For example, casting the interface reference to any implementation is *always* a bad idea.

The *new* code smell

Interfaces describe *what* can be done, whereas classes describe *how* it is done. Only classes involve the implementation details—interfaces are completely unaware of how something is accomplished. Because only classes have constructors, it follows that constructors are an implementation detail. An interesting corollary to this is that, aside from a few exceptions, you can consider an appearance of the new keyword to be a *code smell*.

Code smells

Saying that code *smells* is a way of saying that some code is *potentially* problematic. The word "potentially" is chosen deliberately because two occurrences of a code smell might not be equally problematic. Unlike anti-patterns, which are more universally considered bad practice, code smells are not necessarily bad practice. Code smells are warnings that something could be wrong and that the root cause might need to be corrected.

Code smells might be indicative of technical debt that will need to be repaid—and the longer the debt remains unpaid, the harder it might be to fix.

There are many different categories of code smell. The use of the new keyword—direct object instantiation—is an example of "inappropriate intimacy." Because constructors are implementation details, their use can cause unintended (and undesirable) dependencies to be required by client code.

Code smells, like anti-patterns, are fixed by refactoring the code so that it has a better, more adaptive design. Although the code might fulfill its requirements, its current design is suboptimal and might cause issues in the future. This is undoubtedly a development task that yields no immediate tangible benefit to the business. As with all refactor work, there appears to be no business value associated with fixing the problem. However, just as financial debt can lead to crippling interest repayments, technical debt can spiral out of control and ruin good dependency management practices, jeopardizing future enhancements and code fixes.

Listing 2-5 shows a couple of examples where directly instantiating an object instance by using the new keyword is a code smell.

LISTING 2-5 An example of how instantiating objects prevents code from being adaptive.

```
public class AccountController
{
    private readonly SecurityService securityService;

    public AccountController()
    {
        this.securityService = new SecurityService();
    }
```

```
[HttpPost]
public void ChangePassword(Guid userID, string newPassword)
{
    var userRepository = new UserRepository();
    var user = userRepository.GetByID(userID);
    this.securityService.ChangeUsersPassword(user, newPassword);
}
}
```

The AccountController class is part of a hypothetical ASP.NET MVC application. Do not worry too much about the specifics; concentrate on the inappropriate object construction, highlighted in bold. The controller's responsibility is to allow the user to perform account queries and commands. There is only one command shown: ChangePassword.

There are several problems with this code, and they are caused directly by the two occurrences of new:

- The AccountController is forever dependent on the SecurityService and User-Repository implementations.

- Whatever dependencies the SecurityService and UserRepository have are now implicit dependencies of the AccountController.

- The AccountController is now extremely difficult to unit test—the two classes are impossible to mock with conventional methods.

- The SecurityService.ChangeUsersPassword method requires clients to load User objects.

These problems are addressed in greater detail in the following sections.

Inability to enhance the implementations

If you want to change your implementation of the SecurityService, your two options are to change the AccountController directly to refer to this new implementation or add the new functionality to the existing SecurityService. Throughout this book, you will learn why neither option is preferred. For now, consider that the aim is to never edit either the AccountController or the SecurityService class after they have been created.

Chain of dependency

The SecurityService is also likely to have some dependencies of its own. By having a default constructor, it is making the bold claim that it does not have any dependencies. However, what if the code shown in Listing 2-6 is the implementation of the SecurityService constructor?

```
public SecurityService()
{
    this.Session = SessionFactory.GetSession();
}
```

This service actually depends on NHibernate, the Object/Relational Mapper, which is being used to retrieve a *session*. The session is NHibernate's analogy for a connection to persistent, relational storage, such as Microsoft SQL Server, Oracle, or MySQL. As you saw previously, this means that the AccountController also depends—implicitly—on NHibernate.

Furthermore, what if the signature of the SecurityService constructor changes? That is, what if it suddenly requires clients to provide the connection string to the database that the Session needs? Any client using the SecurityService, including the AccountController, would have to be updated to provide the connection string. Again, this is a change that you should not have to make.

Lack of testability

Testability is a very important concern, and it requires code to be designed in a certain fashion. If it is not, testing is extremely difficult. Unfortunately, neither the AccountController nor the Security-Service is easily tested. This is because you cannot replace their dependencies with fake versions that do not perform any action. For example, when testing the SecurityService, you do not want it to make any connections to the database. That would be needless and slow, and would introduce another large failure point in the test: what if the database is unavailable? There are ways to test these classes by replacing their dependencies at run time with fakes. Tools such as Microsoft Moles and Typemock can hook into constructors and ensure that the objects that they return are fakes. But that is an example of treating the symptoms and not the cause.

More   inappropriate intimacy

The AccountController.ChangePassword method creates a UserRepository class to retrieve a User instance. It only needs to do this because that is what the SecurityService.ChangeUsers-Password method demands of it. Without a User instance, the method cannot be called. This is indicative of a badly designed method interface. Instead of requiring all clients to retrieve a User, the SecurityService should, in this case, retrieve the User itself. The two methods would then look like Listing 2-7.

LISTING 2-7 An improvement is made to all clients of SecurityService.

```
[HttpPost]
public void ChangePassword(Guid userID, string newPassword)
{
    this.securityService.ChangeUsersPassword(userID, newPassword);
}
//...
public void ChangeUsersPassword(Guid userID, string newPassword)
{
    var userRepository = new UserRepository();
    var user = userRepository.GetByID(userID);
    user.ChangePassword(newPassword);
}
```

This is definitely an improvement for the AccountController, but the ChangeUsersPassword method is still directly instantiating the UserRepository.

Alternatives to object construction

What would improve the AccountController and SecurityService—or any other example of inappropriate object construction? How can they be made demonstrably correct so that none of the aforementioned problems apply? There are a few options, all complementary, that you can choose from.

Coding to an interface

The first and most important change that you should make is to hide the implementation of Security-Service behind an interface. This allows the AccountController to depend only on the interface, and not on the implementation, of SecurityService. The first refactor is to extract an interface out of SecurityService, as shown in Listing 2-8.

LISTING 2-8 Extracting an interface from SecurityService.

```
public interface ISecurityService
{
    void ChangeUsersPassword(Guid userID, string newPassword);
}
//...
public class SecurityService : ISecurityService
{
    public ChangeUsersPassword(Guid userID, string newPassword)
    {
        //...
    }
}
```

The next step is to update the client so that it no longer depends on the `SecurityService` class, but rather on the `ISecurityService` interface. Listing 2-9 shows this refactor applied to the `AccountController`.

LISTING 2-9 The `AccountController` now uses the `ISecurityService` interface.

```
public class AccountController
{
    private readonly ISecurityService securityService;

    public AccountController()
    {
        this.securityService = new SecurityService();
    }

    [HttpPost]
    public void ChangePassword(Guid userID, string newPassword)
    {
        securityService.ChangeUsersPassword(user, newPassword);
    }
}
```

This example is not yet complete—you are still dependent on the `SecurityService` implementation because of its constructor. The concrete class is still being instantiated in the constructor of `AccountController`. To separate the two classes completely, you need to make a further refactor: introduce *dependency injection* (DI).

Using dependency injection

This is a large topic that cannot be covered in a small amount of space. In fact, Chapter 9, "Dependency injection," is devoted to the subject, and there are entire books dedicated to it. Luckily, DI is not particularly complex or difficult, so the basics can be covered here from the point of view of classes that make use of DI. Listing 2-10 shows another refactor that has been applied to the constructor of the `AccountController` class. The constructor is the only change here, highlighted in bold. It is a very minor change as far as this class is concerned, but it makes a huge difference to your ability to manage dependencies. Rather than constructing the `SecurityService` class itself, the `AccountController` now requires some other class to provide it with an `ISecurityService` implementation. Not only that, a precondition has been introduced to the constructor that prevents its clients from passing in a `null` value for the `securityService` parameter. This ensures that, when you use the `securityService` field in the `ChangePassword` method, you are guaranteed to have a valid instance and do not have to check for `null` anywhere else.

LISTING 2-10 Using dependency injection allows you to remove the dependency on the `SecurityService` class.

```
public class AccountController
{
    private readonly ISecurityService securityService;

    public AccountController(ISecurityService securityService)
    {
        if(securityService == null) throw new ArgumentNullException("securityService");

        this.securityService = securityService;
    }

    [HttpPost]
    public void ChangePassword(Guid userID, string newPassword)
    {
        this.securityService.ChangeUsersPassword(user, newPassword);
    }
}
```

The `SecurityService` also needs to follow suit and apply dependency injection. Listing 2-11 shows how it looks after refactoring.

LISTING 2-11 Dependency injection is a ubiquitous pattern that can be applied liberally almost everywhere.

```
public class SecurityService : ISecurityService
{
    private readonly IUserRepository userRepository;

    public SecurityService(IUserRepository userRepository)
    {
        if(userRepository == null) throw new ArgumentNullException("userRepository");
        this.userRepository = userRepository;
    }

    public ChangeUsersPassword()
    {
        var user = userRepository.GetByID(userID);
        user.ChangePassword(newPassword);
    }
}
```

Just as the `AccountController` enforces its dependency on a valid `ISecurityService` instance, so too does the `SecurityService` enforce its dependency on a valid `IUserRepository`—by throwing an exception if it is given a `null` reference on construction. Similarly, the `UserRepository` class dependency has been entirely removed, in favor of an `IUserRepository` interface.

The Entourage anti-pattern

The *Entourage anti-pattern* gets its name from the fact that even though you think you are asking for just one simple thing, it brings along all of its friends. This is much like music or film stars who are followed by hangers-on and moochers: their entourage. It is a name that I have created to best describe undesirable dependency management.

The Entourage anti-pattern is a common mistake that is made when developers explain programming to an interface. Rather than providing a full solution, the demonstration commonly stops short of saying, unequivocally, that interfaces and their dependencies *should not be in the same assembly*.

The Unified Modeling Language (UML) diagram in Figure 2-12 shows how the `AccountController` example is organized at the package level. The `AccountController` depends on the `ISecurity-Service` interface, which is implemented by the `SecurityService` class. The diagram also shows the packages—in the .NET Framework these are assemblies or Visual Studio projects—where each entity is. This is an example of the Entourage anti-pattern: the implementation of an interface in the same assembly as the interface itself.

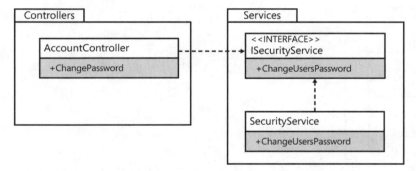

FIGURE 2-12 The `AccountController` assembly depends on the `Services` assembly.

You have already learned that the `SecurityService` class has some dependencies of its own, and how the chain of dependencies results in implicit dependencies from client to client to client. Expanding on the package diagram, Figure 2-13 displays the full extent of the Entourage problem.

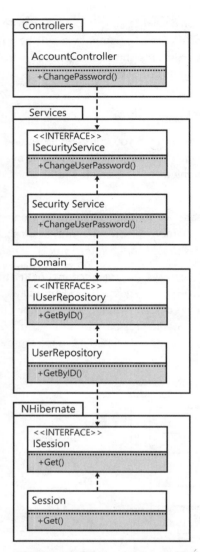

FIGURE 2-13 The AccountController is still at the mercy of too many implementations.

If you build the Controllers project in isolation, you will still find NHibernate in the bin/ directory, indicating that it is still an implicit dependency. Although you have made excellent steps to separate the AccountController *class* from any unnecessary dependencies, it is still not loosely coupled from the implementations in each dependent *assembly*.

There are two problems caused by this anti-pattern. The first issue is that of programmer discipline. You need the interfaces in each of the packages—`Services`, `Domain`, and `NHibernate`—to be marked as `public`. However, you also need the concrete classes—the implementations—to be marked as `public` to make them available for construction at some point (just not inside the client classes). This means that there is nothing to stop an undisciplined developer from making a direct reference to the implementation. There is a temptation to cut corners and just call new on the class to get an instance of it.

Second, what happens if you create a new implementation of the `SecurityService` that, instead of depending on a domain model that is persisted by using NHibernate, instead uses a third-party service bus, such as NServiceBus, to send a command message to a handler? Adding it into the `Services` assembly creates yet another dependency, leading to a bloated, fragile codebase that will be very difficult to adapt to new requirements.

It is a general rule that implementations should be split from their interfaces by placing them in separate assemblies. For this, you can use the Stairway pattern.

The Stairway pattern

The Stairway pattern is the correct way to organize your classes and interfaces. By putting interfaces and their implementations in different assemblies, you can vary the two independently, and clients only need to make a single reference—to the interface assembly.

You might be thinking, "But how many assemblies am I going to need to keep track of? If I split every interface and class into its own assembly, I would have a solution with 200 projects!" Fear not, because applying the Stairway pattern should only increase the number of projects by a few while giving you the benefit of a well-organized and easy-to-understand solution. It is possible that the number of overall projects will *decrease* when you apply the Stairway pattern, if the projects were particularly badly arranged before.

The running example of the `AccountController`, refactored to use the Stairway pattern, is shown in Figure 2-14. Each implementation—that is, each class—only references the assembly that contains the interface on which it is dependent. It does not reference the implementation assembly, not even implicitly. Each implementation class *also* references its interface's assembly. This really is the best of all worlds: interfaces without any dependencies, client code without any implicit dependencies, and implementations that continue the pattern by depending only on other interface assemblies.

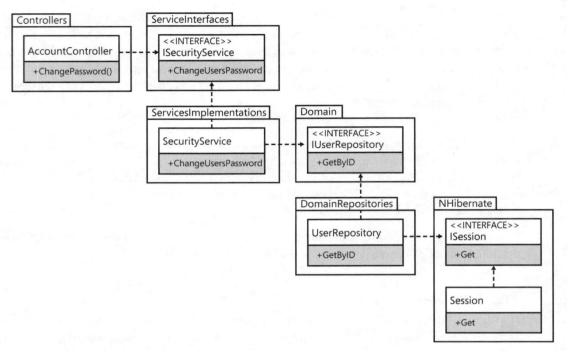

FIGURE 2-14 The Stairway pattern is aptly named.

I now want to focus on one of those benefits in greater detail: interfaces should not have any external dependencies. As far as possible, this should always be adhered to. Interfaces should not have methods or properties that expose any data objects or classes defined in third-party references. Although they can, and certainly will, need to depend on classes and data types from other projects in the solution and common .NET Framework libraries, a reference to infrastructural entities should be avoided. Third-party libraries are commonly used for infrastructure purposes. Even the interfaces from libraries such as Log4Net, NHibernate, and MongoDB are infrastructural dependencies that will tie your interfaces to a specific implementation. This is because those libraries are packaged by using the Entourage anti-pattern, rather than the Stairway pattern. They each provide a single assembly that contains both the interface you *want* to depend on and the implementation that you *do not* want to depend on.

To get around this problem, you can refer instead to your own interfaces for logging, domain persistence, and document storage. You can write a simple interface that hides the third-party dependency behind a first-party dependency. Then, if you ever need to replace the third-party dependency, you can do so by writing a new adapter to your interface for the new library.

On a pragmatic level, this might not be entirely feasible. In instances where converting a third-party dependency to a first-party dependency presents an inordinate amount of work, the team must acknowledge that they will have to retain the dependency and it will become omnipresent. If the library is outgrown, it will be incredibly difficult and time-consuming to replace. This sort of concession is commonly made for *frameworks*, which are much larger than simple libraries.

Resolving dependencies

Knowing how to arrange your projects and the dependencies that they have will not help when it comes to debugging a dependency between assemblies. Sometimes assemblies are not available at run time and it becomes necessary to find out why.

Assemblies

The Common Language Runtime (CLR), which is the virtual machine that the .NET Framework uses to execute code instructions, is a software product like any other and has been programmed to behave in a predictable and logical way when hosting applications. A good grounding in the theory and practice of how assemblies are resolved and how errors in resolution can be fixed is very useful. A little knowledge can go a long way when you need to track down a problem with finding assemblies.

Resolution process   The assembly resolution process is an important facet of the CLR. This covers the gap between adding a reference to an assembly or project and having the application running with this assembly loaded. There are several steps involved, and little more is needed than an overview so that, when something goes wrong during the process, you can reason about the probable causes of the problem.

Figure 2-15 shows the assembly resolution process as a flow chart. This flow chart is at a high level and does not include every detail, but there is enough to show the headline items in the process. The process is as follows:

- The CLR uses a just-in-time (JIT) model to resolve assemblies. As was already proven earlier in the chapter, the references contained in an application are not resolved as you start up the application, but rather when you first make use of a feature of that assembly—literally just in time.

- Each assembly has an identity that is a composite of its name, version, culture, and public key token. Features such as binding redirects can change this identity, so determining it is not quite as simple as it might seem.

- When the assembly's identity has been established, the CLR is able to determine whether it has already attempted to resolve this dependency previously during the current execution of the application, as shown in the following snippet taken from a Visual Studio project file.

```
<reference include="MyAssembly, Version=2.1.0.0, Culture=neutral,
    PublicKeyToken=17fac983cbea459c" />
```

- Asking this question causes the CLR to branch depending on the answer. If you have attempted to resolve this assembly, that process has either already succeeded or failed. If it succeeded, the CLR can use the assembly that has already been loaded, and it exits early. If not, the CLR knows that it need not continue attempting to resolve this assembly because it will fail.

- Alternatively, if this is the first attempt to resolve the assembly, the CLR first checks the global assembly cache (GAC). The GAC is a machine-wide assembly repository that allows multiple versions of the same assembly to be executed in the same application. If the assembly is found in the GAC, the resolution process is successful and the discovered assembly is loaded. So you now know that, because the GAC is searched first, the presence of an applicable assembly in the GAC will take precedence over an assembly on the file system.

- If the assembly could not be found in the GAC, the CLR starts probing a variety of directories in search of it. The directories searched depend on the `app.config` settings. If there is a `codeBase` element in the `app.config`, that location is checked and—if the assembly is not found—no other locations are subsequently checked. However, the default is for the application's root directory to be searched, which is typically the `/bin` folder that relates to the entry point or web application. If the assembly cannot be found there, the resolution process fails and an exception is thrown by the CLR. Typically, this results in the termination of the application.

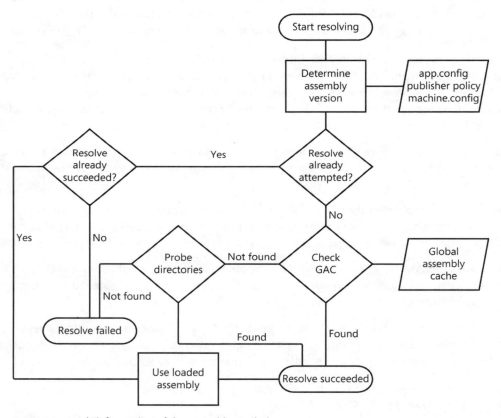

FIGURE 2-15 A brief overview of the assembly resolution process.

The Fusion log   This is a very useful tool for debugging failed attempts by the CLR to bind to an assembly at run time. Rather than trying to step through the application in the Visual Studio debugger, it is better to turn Fusion on and read the log file that results.

To enable Fusion you must edit the Windows registry, as shown in the following code.

```
HKLM\Software\Microsoft\Fusion\ForceLog 1
HKLM\Software\Microsoft\Fusion\LogPath C:\FusionLogs
```

The ForceLog value is a DWORD, whereas the LogPath is a string. You can set the LogPath to whatever path you choose. An example of a failed binding is shown in Listing 2-12.

LISTING 2-12 Sample output from Fusion for a failed attempt to bind an assembly.

```
*** Assembly Binder Log Entry  (6/21/2013 @ 1:50:14 PM) ***

The operation failed.
Bind result: hr = 0x80070002. The system cannot find the file specified.

Assembly manager loaded from:  C:\Windows\Microsoft.NET\Framework64\v4.0.30319\clr.dll
Running under executable  C:\Program Files\1UPIndustries\Bins\v1.1.0.242\Bins.exe
--- A detailed error log follows.

=== Pre-bind state information ===
LOG: User = DEV\gmclean
LOG: DisplayName = TaskbarDockUI.Xtensions.Bins.resources, Version=1.0.0.0, Culture=en-US,
    PublicKeyToken=null (Fully-specified)
LOG: Appbase = file:///C:/Program Files/1UPIndustries/Bins/v1.1.0.242/
LOG: Initial PrivatePath = NULL
LOG: Dynamic Base = NULL
LOG: Cache Base = NULL
LOG: AppName = Bins.exe
Calling assembly : TaskbarDockUI.Xtensions.Bins, Version=1.0.0.0, Culture=neutral,
    PublicKeyToken=null.
===
LOG: This bind starts in default load context.
LOG: No application configuration file found.
LOG: Using host configuration file:
LOG: Using machine configuration file from C:\Windows\Microsoft.NET\Framework64
    \v4.0.30319\config\machine.config.
LOG: Policy not being applied to reference at this time (private, custom, partial, or
    location-based assembly bind).
LOG: Attempting download of new URL file:///C:/Program Files/1UPIndustries/
    Bins/v1.1.0.242/en-US/TaskbarDockUI.Xtensions.Bins.resources.DLL.
LOG: Attempting download of new URL file:///C:/Program Files/1UPIndustries/
    Bins/v1.1.0.242/en-US/TaskbarDockUI.Xtensions.Bins.resources/
    TaskbarDockUI.Xtensions.Bins.resources.DLL.
LOG: Attempting download of new URL file:///C:/Program Files/1UPIndustries/Bins/
    v1.1.0.242/en-US/TaskbarDockUI.Xtensions.Bins.resources.EXE.
LOG: Attempting download of new URL file:///C:/Program Files/1UPIndustries/
    Bins/v1.1.0.242/en-US/TaskbarDockUI.Xtensions.Bins.resources/
    TaskbarDockUI.Xtensions.Bins.resources.EXE.
LOG: All probing URLs attempted and failed.
```

After the registry is edited, all attempts, successful or otherwise, to resolve an assembly by any managed application will be written to the logs. This is obviously a lot of log files, which can be good, but it can start to become a needle-in-a-haystack sort of problem.

Luckily, Fusion has a UI application, shown in Figure 2-16, which makes it slightly easier to find the right file for your application, rather than scouring the file system.

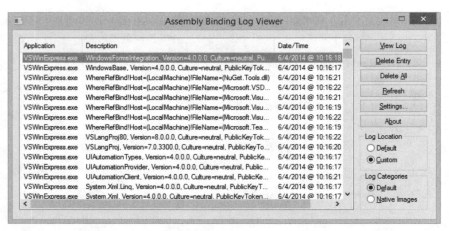

FIGURE 2-16 Fusion has a user interface for finding the log file for your application.

Not all dependencies require assembly references. One alternative is to deploy the service code as a hosted service. This requires inter-process or inter-network communication, but it minimizes the assembly references required between client and server, as the next section examines.

Services

In comparison to assemblies, the coupling of a client to a hosted service can be much looser, which is beneficial but also comes at a cost. Depending on your application's requirements, you could have the client know a lot or a little about the location of the service. Also, you can vary how the service is implemented so that it has very few requirements. With each of these options, there are different tradeoffs to be considered.

Known endpoint   When the location of the service is known to clients at compile time, you can create a service proxy on the client side. This proxy can be created in at least two ways: by using Visual Studio to add a service reference to a project, and by creating the service proxy yourself via the ChannelFactory class in the .NET Framework.

Adding a service reference in Visual Studio is very easy: just select Add Service Reference on the shortcut menu for the project. All the Add Service Reference dialog box needs is the location of the Web Services Definition Language (WSDL) file, which provides a metadata description of the service, its data types, and available behavior. Visual Studio then generates a set of proxy classes for this service, saving a lot of time. It can even generate asynchronous versions of the service methods to mitigate against blocking. However, the tradeoff of using this method is the loss of control over the code that is generated. The code that Visual Studio generates is unlikely to match up to your in-house coding standards, which might be a problem depending on how strict those standards are. Another issue is that the generated service proxy does not lend itself to unit testing: it does not generate any interfaces, just implementing classes.

An alternative to adding a service reference is to create a service proxy yourself in code. This method is best used when the client has access to the interface of the service and can reuse it directly by reference. Listing 2-13 shows an example of creating a service proxy by using the ChannelFactory class.

LISTING 2-13 The ChannelFactory class allows you to create a service proxy.

```
var binding = new BasicHttpBinding();
var address = new EndpointAddress("http://localhost/MyService");
var channelFactory = new ChannelFactory<IService>(binding, address);
var service = channelFactory.CreateChannel();
service.MyOperation();
service.Close();
channelFactory.Close();
```

The ChannelFactory class is generic, and its constructor requires the interface for the service proxy that you want it to create. Because this code also requires a Binding and an Endpoint-Address, you must furnish the ChannelFactory with the full address/binding/contract (ABC). In this example, the IService interface is the same interface that the service implements. What you receive from ChannelFactory.CreateChannel is a proxy that, for each call made, will call the equivalent method on the server-side implementation. Because the same interface is used, client-side classes can require this interface as a constructor parameter to be resolved by dependency injection, and the client classes instantly become testable. In addition, they don't have to know that they are calling a remote service.

Service Discovery   Sometimes you might know the binding type of a service or its contract, but not the address where it is hosted. In this case, you can use Service Discovery, which was introduced to Windows Communication Foundation (WCF) in the .NET Framework 4.

Service Discovery comes in two flavors: managed and ad hoc. In managed mode, a centralized service called a discovery proxy is well known to clients, which directly send it queries for finding other services. This is the less interesting mode, because it introduces a single point of failure (SPOF): if the discovery proxy is not available, clients cannot access *any* other services because they are not discoverable.

Ad hoc mode obviates the need for a discovery proxy by using multicast network messages. The default implementation of this uses the User Datagram Protocol (UDP), with each discoverable service listening on a specified IP address[1] for queries. Clients effectively ask the network whether there is a service that matches its query criteria—a contract or binding type, for example. In this scenario, if one of the services is unavailable, only that service cannot be discovered, whereas the rest will respond to requests. Listing 2-14 shows how to host a discoverable service programmatically, and Listing 2-15 shows how to add discoverability to a service via configuration.

---

[1] The IP address used is 239.255.255.250 (IPv4) or [FF02::C] (IPv6). The port used is 3702. This is set by the WS-Discovery standard, so is not configurable.

LISTING 2-14 Programmatically hosting a discoverable service.

```
class Program
{
    static void Main(string[] args)
    {
        using (ServiceHost serviceHost = new ServiceHost(typeof(CalculatorService)))
        {
            serviceHost.Description.Behaviors.Add(new ServiceDiscoveryBehavior());

            serviceHost.AddServiceEndpoint(typeof(ICalculator), new BasicHttpBinding(),
    new Uri("http://localhost:8090/CalculatorService"));
            serviceHost.AddServiceEndpoint(new UdpDiscoveryEndpoint());

            serviceHost.Open();
            Console.WriteLine("Discoverable Calculator Service is running...");
            Console.ReadKey();
        }
    }
}
```

LISTING 2-15 Hosting a discoverable service via configuration.

```
<system.serviceModel>
    <behaviors>
      <serviceBehaviors>
        <behavior>
          <serviceMetadata httpGetEnabled="true" httpsGetEnabled="true"/>
          <serviceDebug includeExceptionDetailInFaults="false"/>
        </behavior>
        <behavior name="calculatorServiceDiscovery">
          <serviceDiscovery />
        </behavior>
      </serviceBehaviors>
      <endpointBehaviors>
        <behavior name="calculatorHttpEndpointDiscovery">
          <endpointDiscovery enabled="true" />
        </behavior>
      </endpointBehaviors>
    </behaviors>
    <protocolMapping>
        <add binding="basicHttpsBinding" scheme="https" />
    </protocolMapping>
    <serviceHostingEnvironment aspNetCompatibilityEnabled="true"
    multipleSiteBindingsEnabled="true" />
    <services>
      <service name="ConfigDiscoverableService.CalculatorService"
    behaviorConfiguration="calculatorServiceDiscovery">
        <endpoint address="CalculatorService.svc"
    behaviorConfiguration="calculatorHttpEndpointDiscovery"
```

```
        contract="ServiceContract.ICalculator" binding="basicHttpBinding" />
            <endpoint kind="udpDiscoveryEndpoint" />
        </service>
      </services>
    </system.serviceModel>
```

To become discoverable, all a service needs to do is add the ServiceDiscoveryBehavior and host a DiscoveryEndpoint. In this example, the UdpDiscoveryEndpoint is used for receiving multicast network messages from clients.

> **Note** Service Discovery in WCF complies with the WS-Discovery standard. This makes it interoperable with different platforms and languages, not just the .NET Framework.

Clients make use of the DiscoveryClient class to find a discoverable service, which also needs a DiscoveryEndpoint. The Find method is then called with a configured FindCriteria instance, which describes the attributes of the service to be found. Find returns a FindResponse instance that contains an Endpoints property—a collection of EndpointDiscoveryMetadata instances, one per matching service. Listing 2-16 shows these steps to find a discoverable service.

LISTING 2-16 Service Discovery is a good way to decouple code.

```
class Program
{
    private const int a = 11894;
    private const int b = 27834;

    static void Main(string[] args)
    {
        var foundEndpoints = FindEndpointsByContract<ICalculator>();

        if (!foundEndpoints.Any())
        {
            Console.WriteLine("No endpoints were found.");
        }
        else
        {
            var binding = new BasicHttpBinding();
            var channelFactory = new ChannelFactory<ICalculator>(binding);
            foreach (var endpointAddress in foundEndpoints)
            {
                var service = channelFactory.CreateChannel(endpointAddress);
                var additionResult = service.Add(a, b);
                Console.WriteLine("Service Found: {0}", endpointAddress.Uri);
                Console.WriteLine("{0} + {1} = {2}", a, b, additionResult);
```

```
        }
    }

    Console.ReadKey();
}

private static IEnumerable<EndpointAddress> FindEndpointsByContract
<TServiceContract>()
{
    var discoveryClient = new DiscoveryClient(new UdpDiscoveryEndpoint());
    var findResponse = discoveryClient.Find(new
FindCriteria(typeof(TServiceContract)));
    return findResponse.Endpoints.Select(metadata => metadata.Address);
}
}
```

Bear in mind that with UDP, as opposed to TCP, there is no guarantee of message delivery. It is possible for datagrams to be lost in transmission, so either the request might not reach a viable service or the response might not make it back to the client. In either scenario, it would appear to the client that there wasn't a service available to handle the request.

Tip When hosting a discoverable service in Internet Information Services (IIS) or Windows Process Activation Service (WAS), ensure that you use the Microsoft AppFabric AutoStart functionality. Discoverability depends on the availability of the service, meaning that it must be running in order to receive queries from clients. AppFabric AutoStart allows the service to run when the application is started in IIS. Without AutoStart, the service is not started until the first request is made.

RESTful services   The most compelling reason to create RESTful services (REST: REpresentational State Transfer) is the very low dependency burden expected of clients. All that is needed is an HTTP client, which is commonly provided by the frameworks and libraries of languages. This makes RESTful services ideal for developing services that need to have wide-ranging, cross-platform support. For example, both Facebook and Twitter have REST APIs for various queries and commands. This ensures that clients can be developed for a large number of platforms: Windows Phone 8, iPhone, Android, iPad, Windows 8, Linux, and much more. Having a single implementation that can service all of these clients would be more difficult without the very low dependency requirements that REST allows.

The ASP.NET Web API is used for creating REST services that use the .NET Framework. Similar to the ASP.NET MVC framework, it allows developers to create methods that map directly to web requests. The Web API provides a base controller class called `ApiController`. You inherit from this controller and add methods named like the HTTP verbs: GET, POST, PUT, DELETE. HEAD, OPTIONS, and PATCH. Whenever an HTTP request arrives using one of these verbs, the corresponding method is called. Listing 2-17 shows an example of a service that implements all of these verbs.

LISTING 2-17 Almost all of the HTTP verbs are supported by the ASP.NET Web API.

```
public class ValuesController : ApiController
{
    public IEnumerable<string> Get()
    {
        return new string[] { "value1", "value2" };
    }

    public string Get(int id)
    {
        return "value";
    }

    public void Post([FromBody]string value)
    {
    }

    public void Put(int id, [FromBody]string value)
    {
    }

    public void Head()
    {
    }

    public void Options()
    {
    }

    public void Patch()
    {
    }

    public void Delete(int id)
    {
    }
}
```

Listing 2-18 shows the client code for accessing the GET and POST methods of this service, using the HttpClient class. Although this is by no means the only way to access REST services in the .NET Framework, it relies on only the framework itself.

LISTING 2-18 Clients can use the `HttpClient` class to access RESTful services.

```
class Program
{
    static void Main(string[] args)
    {
        string uri = "http://localhost:7617/api/values";

        MakeGetRequest(uri);
        MakePostRequest(uri);

        Console.ReadKey();
    }

    private static async void MakeGetRequest(string uri)
    {
        var restClient = new HttpClient();
        var getRequest = await restClient.GetStringAsync(uri);

        Console.WriteLine(getRequest);
    }

    private static async void MakePostRequest(string uri)
    {
        var restClient = new HttpClient();
        var postRequest = await restClient.PostAsync(uri,
                new StringContent("Data to send to the server"));

            var responseContent = await postRequest.Content.ReadAsStringAsync();
            Console.WriteLine(responseContent);
        }
    }
}
```

Just to emphasize the point that multiple clients can be written with equally low dependency requirements, Listing 2-19 shows a Windows PowerShell 3 script for accessing the GET and POST methods of the service.

LISTING 2-19 Accessing the REST service from Windows PowerShell 3 is extremely trivial.

```
$request = [System.Net.WebRequest]::Create("http://localhost:7617/api/values")
$request.Method ="GET"
$request.ContentLength = 0

$response = $request.GetResponse()
$reader = new-object System.IO.StreamReader($response.GetResponseStream())
$responseContent = $reader.ReadToEnd()
Write-Host $responseContent
```

This code uses the WebRequest object from the .NET Framework to call the RESTful service. This class is the superclass of the HttpRequest class. The Create method is a factory method that returns an HttpRequest instance because an http:// URI was provided.

Dependency management with NuGet

Dependency management can be greatly simplified with the use of dependency management tools. Such tools are responsible for following dependency chains to ensure that all dependent artifacts are available. They also manage the versioning of dependencies: you can specify that you want to depend only on specific versions of dependencies, and the dependency management tools do the rest.

NuGet is a package management utility for the .NET Framework. NuGet refers to a dependency as a *package*, but the tool is not limited to assemblies. NuGet packages can also include configuration, scripts, and images—almost anything you need. One of the most compelling reasons to use a package manager such as NuGet is that it has knowledge of a package's dependencies and will bring the entire dependency chain with it when a project references a package.

As of Visual Studio 2013, NuGet is fully integrated as the default package management utility.

Consuming packages

NuGet adds some new commands to the shortcut menu in the Solution Explorer window of Visual Studio. From there, you can open the NuGet package management window and add a reference to a dependency.

For this example, I'm going to add a dependency to CorrugatedIron, the .NET Framework client driver for the Riak NoSql key/value store. Figure 2-17 shows the NuGet package management window.

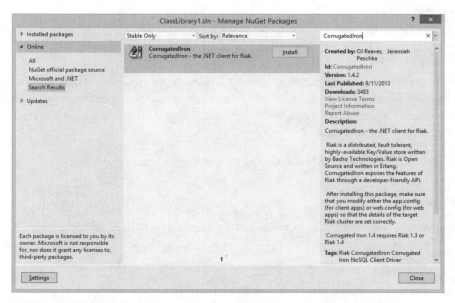

FIGURE 2-17 NuGet packages have a lot of useful metadata associated with them.

Whenever a package is selected in the list, the information pane on the right shows some metadata about the package. This includes its unique name in the gallery, the author or authors of the package, the version of the package, the date it was last published, a description of the package, and any dependencies that it has. The dependencies are very interesting, because they show what else is going to be installed as a result of referencing this package, in addition to the required or supported versions of the dependencies. CorrugatedIron, for example, requires at least version 4.5.10 of Newtonsoft.Json, a .NET Framework JSON/class serializer, and at least version 2.0.0.602 of protobuf-net. Both of these packages could have dependencies of their own.

When you choose to install this package, NuGet will first try to download all the files and place them in a `packages/` folder under the solution's root folder. This allows you to put this entire directory into source control, exactly as you did earlier with a `dependencies/` folder. NuGet then references the downloaded assemblies in the project where you want to use this library. Figure 2-18 shows the references for the project after Riak is added.

In addition to making the references, NuGet also creates a `packages.config` file that contains information about which packages—and which versions—are referenced by the project. This is useful when it comes to upgrading or uninstalling packages, which is also something that NuGet is able to do.

FIGURE 2-18 The target package and all of its dependencies are referenced by the project.

Riak also needs some default configuration before it is ready to be used. So not only has NuGet downloaded and referenced a lot of assemblies, it has also edited your `app.config` to include some sensible default values for required settings that Riak needs. Listing 2-20 shows the current state of the `app.config` after Riak is installed.

LISTING 2-20 NuGet has added a new `configSection` to the `app.config` specifically for Riak.

```
<configuration>
  <configSections>
    <section name="riakConfig" type="CorrugatedIron.Config.RiakClusterConfiguration,
    CorrugatedIron" />
  </configSections>
  <riakConfig nodePollTime="5000" defaultRetryWaitTime="200" defaultRetryCount="3">
    <nodes>
      <node name="dev1" hostAddress="riak-test" pbcPort="10017" restScheme="http"
```

```
restPort="10018" poolSize="20" />
    <node name="dev2" hostAddress="riak-test" pbcPort="10027" restScheme="http"
restPort="10028" poolSize="20" />
    <node name="dev3" hostAddress="riak-test" pbcPort="10037" restScheme="http"
restPort="10038" poolSize="20" />
    <node name="dev4" hostAddress="riak-test" pbcPort="10047" restScheme="http"
restPort="10048" poolSize="20" />
  </nodes>
 </riakConfig>
</configuration>
```

Clearly, this is a great timesaver because you haven't had to search the Riak site for a download of CorrugatedIron or any of its dependencies. Everything has been put into a state where you can concentrate on developing. And when it comes time to upgrade CorrugatedIron to the next version, you can also use NuGet to automatically update all of the packages that depend on it in the entire solution.

Producing packages

NuGet also allows you to create packages. You might want to create packages for publication on the official NuGet package gallery so that other developers can use them, or you might want to host your own package feed for first-party dependencies. Figure 2-19 shows the NuGet Package Explorer, which can be used to create your own packages. In this package, I have configured CorrugatedIron to be a dependency, so it will also depend on Newtonsoft.Json and protobuf-net, implicitly. I have added a library artifact that is targeted specifically to the .NET Framework 4.5.1 and a text file that will be created in the referenced assembly under My folder/NewFile.txt. There is even a Windows PowerShell script that is instructed to run during installation. This could feasibly be used to do almost anything—thanks to the flexibility of Windows PowerShell.

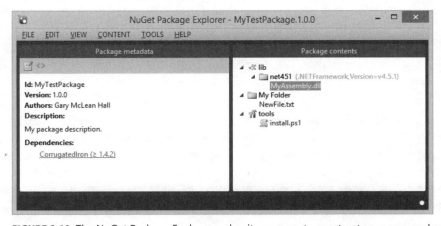

FIGURE 2-19 The NuGet Package Explorer makes it very easy to construct your own packages.

Each package has an XML file that details the metadata that is shown in the installation window. Listing 2-21 shows some of the syntax of this file.

LISTING 2-21 The package XML definition, including metadata.

```xml
<package xmlns="http://schemas.microsoft.com/packaging/2010/07/nuspec.xsd">
    <metadata>
        <id>MyTestPackage</id>
        <version>1.0.0</version>
        <authors>Gary McLean Hall</authors>
        <requireLicenseAcceptance>false</requireLicenseAcceptance>
        <description>My package description.</description>
        <dependencies>
            <dependency id="CorrugatedIron" version="1.0.1" />
        </dependencies>
    </metadata>
</package>
```

NuGet is such a productivity and organizational bonus that it is painful to return to manually managing third-party dependencies, if a package does not exist for a particular library. In fact, NuGet is not only for third-party dependencies. When a solution becomes large enough it is advisable to split the solution into multiple parts, sliced by layer. The assemblies for each layer can then be packaged by using NuGet and consumed by layers above. This keeps solutions small and easy to work with.

Chocolatey

The best way to describe Chocolatey is that it is a package management tool, just like NuGet, but its packages are applications and tools, not assemblies. Developers with some Linux knowledge will find that Chocolatey is like `apt-get`, which is Debian and Ubuntu's package manager. Again, many of the benefits of package management apply: simplified installation, dependency management, and ease of use.

The following Windows PowerShell script can be used to download and install Chocolatey.

```
@powershell -NoProfile -ExecutionPolicy unrestricted -Command "iex ((new-object
    net.webclient).DownloadString('https://chocolatey.org/install.ps1'))" && SET
    PATH=%PATH%;%systemdrive%\chocolatey\bin
```

After Chocolatey is installed, you can use the command line to search for and install various applications and tools. The installation procedure will have already updated the command-line path to include the `chocolatey.exe` application. Much like Git, Chocolatey has subcommands such as `list` and `install`, but these also have synonyms that can be used as shortcuts: `clist` and `cinst`, respectively. Listing 2-22 shows a sample Chocolatey session that finds the package name for Filezilla, the FTP client, and then installs it.

LISTING 2-22 First you search the packages for the application that you want, and then you install it.

```
C:\dev> clist filezilla
ferventcoder.chocolatey.utilities 1.0.20130622
filezilla 3.7.1
filezilla.commandline 3.7.1
filezilla.server 0.9.41.20120523
jivkok.tools 1.1.0.2
kareemsultan.developer.toolkit 1.4
UAdevelopers.utils 1.9
C:\dev> cinst filezilla
Chocolatey (v0.9.8.20) is installing filezilla and dependencies. By installing you accept
the license for filezilla and each dependency you are installing.
. . .
  This Finished installing 'filezilla' and dependencies - if errors not shown in console,
none detected. Check log for errors if unsure.
```

As long as no errors were reported by Chocolatey, the requested package is now installed. Be aware that Chocolatey *should* have altered your system PATH so that any new binaries can be executed from the command line, but it does not always do so. There are a lot of packages available via Chocolatey, and the convenience that it provides is a compelling reason to use it.

Layering

To this point, this chapter has looked primarily at managing dependencies at the assembly level. This is a natural first step to organizing your application, because all classes and interfaces are contained in assemblies, and how they reference each other is a common concern. When correctly organized, your assemblies will contain classes and interfaces that only pertain to a single group of related functionality. Taken in aggregate, however, how can you ensure that groups of assemblies are also correctly organized?

Groups of two or more interrelated assemblies form *components* of the software system that is being developed. It is equally important—if not more so—that these components interact in a similarly well-defined and structured fashion. As Figure 2-20 shows, components are not physical artifacts of deployment, like assembly dynamic-link libraries (DLLs), but are logical groupings of assemblies that share a similar theme.

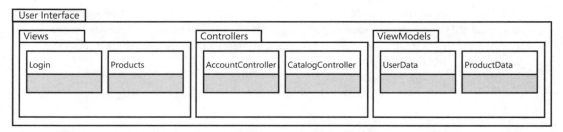

FIGURE 2-20 By grouping related assemblies together, you can define logical components.

There are three assemblies included in the diagram: Views, Controllers, and ViewModels. Each assembly contains two classes that serve different purposes and might require different dependencies. Although the classes and assemblies are constructs provided by the .NET Framework, the User Interface package that groups everything is logical. The three assemblies might be located in the solution in a folder called UserInteraces, but there is nothing preventing you from polluting this layer with another project that does not belong. Nothing, that is, except your own diligence.

In dependency management, components are no different from other programming constructs at lower levels. As with methods, classes, and assemblies, you can consider layers to be another node in the dependency graph shown earlier in this chapter. Thus, the same rules apply: keeping the digraph acyclic and ensuring a single responsibility.

Layering is an architectural pattern that encourages you to think of software components as horizontal layers of functionality that build on each other to form a whole application. Components are layered, one on top of another, and the dependency direction must always point downward. That is, the bottom layer of the application has no dependencies[2], and each layer upward depends on the layer immediately below it. At the top of the stack is the user interface. If the application is a service layer, the top layer will be the API that clients will use to interact with the system.

Common patterns

There are several common layering patterns from which to choose for any project. Each one presented here should be used as a guide to be tailored to the specific requirements and restrictions of your situation. The differentiating factor between the layering patterns is simply the *number* of layers used. This section starts with a simple architecture made up of only two layers, then inserts a third layer in between, and finally, extrapolates to an arbitrary number of layers.

The number of layers required correlates to the complexity of the solution; the complexity of the solution correlates to the complexity of the problem. Therefore, the more complex the problem, the more inclined you might be to invest in a multilayered architecture. Complexity, in this instance, is measured by many factors: the time constraints placed on the project, its required longevity, how frequent requirements might change, and the importance that the development team places on patterns and practices, to name only a few.

Because this book is about adapting to changes in requirements, I advocate doing the *simplest thing possible first*, and refactoring toward something more complex *only when required*. This has positive effects on projects. First, it allows you to deliver something as soon as possible. Feedback should be sought early and frequently in software development. Trying to deliver the perfect solution is pointless if the customer's idea of perfection differs from the development team's idea of perfection. Developing a multilayer solution takes longer than a simple two-layer solution, delaying that all-important feedback loop.

---

[2] This isn't strictly true: there are likely to be some dependencies, but because it is the bottom layer with no other first-party code to depend on, they are likely to be third-party, infrastructural dependencies.

Layers vs. tiers

The difference between layers and tiers is the difference between the logical organization and physical deployment of code. Logically, you could separate an application in three or four *layers*, but physically deploy it into one *tier*. The number of tiers is somewhat related to the number of machines that the application is deployed to. If you deploy to a single machine, you are deploying an application in one tier. If you deploy the application to two machines, split by at least two layers, you are deploying to two tiers.

With every tier that you deploy to, you accept that you are crossing a network boundary, and with that comes a temporal cost: it is expensive to cross a processing boundary within the same machine, but it is much more expensive to cross a network boundary. However, deploying in tiers has a distinct advantage because it allows you to scale your applications. If you deploy a web application that consists of a user interface layer, a logic layer, and a data access layer onto a single machine—thus a single tier—that machine now has a lot of work to do, and the number of users you can support will necessarily be lower. Were you to split the application's deployment into two tiers—putting the database on one tier and the user interface and logic layers on another—you could actually scale the user interface layer both *horizontally* and *vertically*.

To scale vertically, you just increase the power of the computer by adding memory or processing units. This allows the single machine to achieve more by itself. However, you can also scale horizontally by adding completely new machines that perform exactly the same task. There would be multiple machines to host the web user interface code and a load balancer that would direct clients to the least busy machine at any point in time. Of course, this is not a panacea to supporting more concurrent users on a web application. This requires more care with data caching and user authentication, because each request made by a user could be handled by a different machine.

Two layers

A two-layered solution is the simplest step forward from having no discernable layering. It is only useful in a narrow set of circumstances, but it is extremely quick to implement. The only two layers included are the user interface layer and the data access layer. Remember that this does not limit you to just two *assemblies*, but two logical *groups* of assemblies: one focusing directly on the user interface, the other on data access.

Figure 2-21 shows the two layers as packages in a UML diagram, each layer containing assemblies relating to those layers. The only dependency shown is directed from the user interface layer down to the data access layer. This is the only way that the dependencies can ever be directed in any layered architecture.

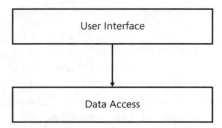

FIGURE 2-21 A two-layered application consists of the UI components and the data access components.

User interface The user interface layer is responsible for:

- Providing a way for the user to interact with the application (for example, desktop windows and controls, a webpage, or a console application's command line or menu).

- Presenting data and information to the user.

- Receiving requests from the user in the form of queries or commands.

- Validating input that the user has entered.

The user interface layer can vary in its implementation. It could be a Windows Presentation Foundation (WPF) client packed with fancy graphics and animation, a set of webpages that the user navigates through, or a simple console application that uses command-line switches or a simple menu for the user to select a command or query to execute.

> **Note** In some cases, the user interface could be replaced with a set of services that surface functionality to clients elsewhere. There isn't really a user interface, but the two-layer architecture is still apparent, with the UI layer being replaced by an API layer.

The user interface layer sits on top of the data access layer and can make use of it. However, as discussed previously in relation to assembly references, the user interface layer should not make direct reference to any of the data access layer's implementation assemblies. There should be a strict separation between the interface and implementation assemblies of the two layers. This makes the layering diagram look a little more like Figure 2-22.

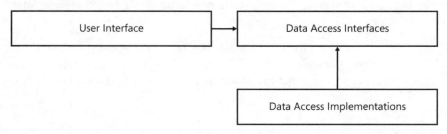

FIGURE 2-22 The two layers are separated into implementation assemblies and interface assemblies.

This is solving the Entourage anti-pattern with the Stairway pattern, but this time it is doing so at the architectural level. Each layer is the combination of an abstraction of the functionality that a higher layer depends on, along with an implementation of this abstraction. If a layer above starts referencing part of the implementation of a layer, that layer is called a *leaky abstraction*. The dependencies of that layer's implementation will begin to leak into layers further up the stack, resulting in avoidable dependencies.

Data access The responsibilities of the data access layer are:

- Servicing queries for data.

- Serializing and deserializing object models to and from a relational model.

The implementation of the data access layer can be just as varied as that of the user interface layer. This layer typically includes some kind of persistent data store that could include a relational database such as SQL Server, Oracle, MySQL, or PostgreSQL or a document database such as MongoDB, RavenDB, or Riak. In addition to the data storage mechanism, there is likely to be one or more supporting assemblies for executing queries or insert/update/delete commands by calling stored procedures, or for mapping data to a relational database via Entity Framework or NHibernate.

Data access layers should be hidden behind interfaces that do not depend on any of these technology choices. As with all interfaces, there should be no reference to a third-party dependency, thus keeping clients separated from the choice of implementation.

A well-designed data access layer is reusable across multiple applications. If two different user interfaces require the same data but present it in different forms, the same data access layer can be shared between them. Imagine an application that runs across multiple platforms: Windows 8 and Windows Phone 8. Both have different user interface requirements, but each could use the same data access layer.

As with any architecture, using only two layers has some tradeoffs that must be considered carefully before adoption. The two-layer architecture is a good choice when:

- There is little or no logic to the application beyond some trivial validation. This can easily be encapsulated in either the data access layer or the user interface layer.

- The application performs mainly CRUD operations on data. Creating, reading, updating, and deleting data becomes more difficult with every additional layer placed between the user interface and the data itself.

- Time is short. If only a prototype or a bootstrap needs to be developed, limiting the number of layers can save a lot of time and the feasibility of a proof of concept can be ascertained. When you stick to good practices such as the Stairway pattern, it is easier to insert additional layers as necessary later.

However, the two-layer architecture has some obvious drawbacks and is a bad choice when:

- There is significant logic in the application, or logic is subject to change. Any logic placed in the user interface layer or data access layer is technically a pollution of that layer and decreases its flexibility and maintainability.

- The application is certain to outgrow two layers within one or two sprints. Any concessions made to obtain quick feedback are not worth the investment if that architecture will only last a matter of weeks.

The two-layer architecture is still very much a viable alternative. Too many developers are enchanted by the latest architectural trend and overlook simpler designs. This causes an otherwise trivial application to receive feedback too late and makes it fragile and hard to maintain. Often, the simplest thing possible is the right thing to do.

Three layers

The three-layer architecture adds an extra layer between the user interface and the data access layer. This is the logic layer. The addition of the logic layer allows the application to encapsulate more complex processing. The logic layer, like the data access layer, can be reused across multiple applications, so it need not be implemented multiple times. Figure 2-23 shows the typical three-layer architecture.

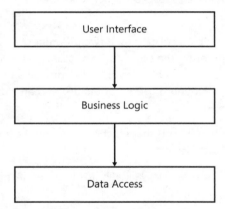

FIGURE 2-23 The third layer contains processing or business logic for the application.

Again, like the data access layer, the logic layer provides interface and implementation assemblies to clients, to avoid a leaky abstraction.

> **Note** Although the three-layer architecture is very common for web applications, it is typically deployed in only two *tiers*. One node handles the database, and another node handles almost everything else: the user interface, the logic, and even part of the data access.

Business logic   The business logic layer's responsibilities are to:

- Handle commands from the user interface layer.

- Model the business domain to capture business processes, rules, and workflow.

The logic layer might be a command processor that receives commands from the user via the user interface layer and, by collaborating with the data access layer, solves a specific problem or executes a particular task. It could also be a fully developed domain model that aims to map a business's processes into software. For the latter, it is common for the data access layer to include an Object/Relational Mapping component so that the logic layer can be implemented directly into classes, possibly by using domain-driven design (DDD). In a domain model, there should be no dependencies, either further down the stack or via some implementation-specific technology. For example, the domain model's assemblies should have no dependencies on an Object/Relational Mapping library. Instead, a separate mapping assembly should be created that is implementation specific and instructs the ORM how to map to the domain model. This allows the domain model's core classes to be reused without depending on the ORM, and the ORM could be replaced without affecting the domain model or its clients. Figure 2-24 shows a possible implementation of a logic layer that uses a domain model.

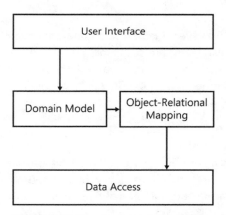

FIGURE 2-24 How the assemblies of a domain model collaborate to form a logic layer.

The addition of a logic layer is necessary when there is complex logic in the application, such as business rules that aim to reflect the real-world workflows of people's jobs. Even if the logic is not particularly complex but changes often, this is a good argument for introducing a separate layer for encapsulating this behavior. It simplifies the user interface and data access layers, allowing them to concentrate fully on their only purpose.

Cross-cutting concerns

Sometimes a component's responsibilities are not easily limited to a single layer. Functions such as auditing, security, and caching can permeate through the entire application, because they are applicable at *every* layer. Tracing the code's actions at each method call and return, for example, is a useful debugging tool when the application has been deployed and if the Visual Studio debugger cannot be attached to step through the code. You can manually produce an output of the values of parameters as they are passed around, and the return values of various methods, as shown in Listing 2-23.

LISTING 2-23 Manually applying cross-cutting concerns quickly swamps the real intent of the code.

```
public void OpenNewAccount(Guid ownerID, string accountName, decimal openingBalance)
{
    log.WriteInfo("Creating new account for owner {0} with name '{1}' and an opening
    balance of {2}", ownerID, accountName, openingBalance");

    using(var transaction = session.BeginTransaction())
    {
        var user = userRepository.GetByID(ownerID);
        user.CreateAccount(accountName);
        var account = user.FindAccount(accountName);
        account.SetBalance(openingBalance);

        transaction.Commit();
    }
}
```

This is laborious and error-prone, and it instantly pollutes every method with irrelevant boilerplate code, increasing the noise-to-signal ratio. Instead, you can factor out such cross-cutting concerns into encapsulated functionality and apply them to the code in a much less invasive fashion. The most common way of adding functionality non-invasively is through aspect-oriented programming.

Aspects

Aspect-oriented programming (AOP) is the application of cross-cutting concerns—or aspects—to multiple layers in the code. The .NET Framework has several AOP libraries to choose from (search NuGet for *AOP*), but the examples given here are for PostSharp, which has a free Express version, though with reduced functionality. Listing 2-24 shows tracing code factored out into a PostSharp aspect and applied as an attribute to some methods.

LISTING 2-24 Aspects are a great way to implement cross-cutting concerns.

```
[Logged]
[Transactional]
public void OpenNewAccount(Guid ownerID, string accountName, decimal openingBalance)
{
    var user = userRepository.GetByID(ownerID);
    user.CreateAccount(accountName);
    var account = user.FindAccount(accountName);
    account.SetBalance(openingBalance);
}
```

The two attributes decorating the `OpenNewAccount` method provide the same functionality as shown in Listing 2-23, but the intent of the method is clearer. The `Logged` attribute writes information about the method call to a log, including parameter values. The `Transactional` attribute wraps the method in a database transaction and commits the transaction on success or rolls back the transaction on failure. The key here is that both of these attributes are generic enough to be applied to *any* method, not specifically this one, so they can be reused many times.

Asymmetric layering

All of the users' requests to an application occur through the provided user interface. However, the path that the requests follow after that is not necessarily always the same. The layering could be asymmetrical, depending on the type of request being made. This is motivated by the need to be pragmatic and to consider whether the layering in place is overkill for some requests or even insufficient for some requests.

A pattern of asymmetric layering that has rapidly gained popularity in the last few years is Command/Query Responsibility Segregation (CQRS). Before discussing CQRS, which is an architectural pattern, a grounding in its method-level influencer, command/query separation, is required.

Command/query separation

Bertrand Meyer, in his book *Object-Oriented Software Construction* (Prentice Hall, 1997), used the phrase *command/query separation (CQS)* to explain that all object methods should be one of only two things: a *command* or a *query*.

Commands are imperative calls to action, requiring the code to *do* something. These methods are allowed to change the state of a system but should not also return a value. Listing 2-25 shows an example of a CQS-compliant command method, followed by one that is noncompliant.

LISTING 2-25 CQS-compliant and non–CQS-compliant command methods.

```
// Compliant command
Public void SaveUser(string name)
{
    session.Save(new User(name));
}
// Non-compliant command
public User SaveUser(string name)
{
    var user = new User(name);
    session.Save(user);
    return user;
}
```

Queries are requests for data, requiring the code to *get* something. These methods return data to calling clients but should not also change the state of a system. Listing 2-26 shows an example of a CQS-compliant query method, followed by one that is noncompliant.

LISTING 2-26 CQS-compliant and non–CQS-compliant query methods.

```
// Compliant query
Public IEnumerable<User> FindUserByID(Guid userID)
{
    return session.Get<User>(userID);
}
// Non-compliant query
public IEnumerable<User> FindUserByID(Guid userID)
{
    var user = session.Get<User>(userID);
    user.LastAccessed = DateTime.Now;
    return user;
}
```

Commands and queries are thus differentiated by the presence of a return value. If a method returns a value (and is CQS-compliant) you can safely assume that it does not change any state of the object. The advantage here is that you can reorder query calls knowing that they have no other effect on the object. A method having no return value (and that is CQS-compliant) indicates that you can assume that it does change the state of the object. For these calls, you would have to be more careful in your call order.

Command/Query Responsibility Segregation

The Command/Query Responsibility Segregation pattern is attributed to Greg Young. The pattern is the application of CQS at an architectural level and is an example of asymmetric layering. Commands and queries follow much the same rules as with CQS, but CQRS goes one step further: it acknowledges that commands and queries might need to follow different paths through the layering in order to be best handled.

An example of where minimal CQRS can be applied is when you are developing a three-layer architecture with a domain model. In this instance, the domain model is only ever used by the commanding side of the application, with a much simpler two-layer architecture used for the querying side. Figure 2-25 exemplifies this design.

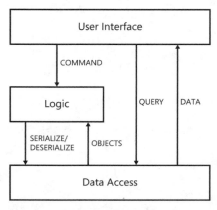

FIGURE 2-25 Domain models should only be used for handling commands.

Querying data often needs to be fast and is allowed to provide few guarantees of transactional consistency: phantom reads or nonrepeatable reads can be an acceptable tradeoff for increased responsiveness. Command processing, though, is often required to have transactional consistency, hence the differing layers in place to handle commands and queries. Sometimes, the data access layers can also differ between commands and queries. A fully ACID-compliant (*ACID* stands for atomic, consistent, isolated, durable) database might be needed for commands, whereas simple document storage might suffice for queries. The document storage would be updated asynchronously by events published from the command layer, giving eventual consistency to the query reads.

Conclusion

This chapter has shown how the organization of dependencies presents a significant problem when creating software applications. The long-term health, adaptability, and possibly the viability of a project relies on sound management of dependencies. A mess of spaghetti-like interdependencies will occur if developers create classes that reference each other without careful consideration, which can seriously affect a team's ability to deliver business value in a consistent, predictable fashion.

Dependencies must be managed at all levels, from individual classes and methods interacting with each other, through assembly references, to the high-level architecture of components. Developers must be constantly vigilant that spurious dependencies do not leak outside of their method, class, assembly, or layer.

In some ways, this chapter underpins a lot of the content of the rest of this book. The content provides a solid foundation for maintainable, adaptive code that is reinforced with each chapter. If your assemblies are a spaghetti of references, and your layers do not hide their infrastructural dependencies, your code will become harder to test, amend, and understand, no matter what other patterns or practices you attempt to follow.

CHAPTER 3

Interfaces and design patterns

After completing this chapter, you will be able to

- Define interfaces and identify the primary ways in which they differ from classes.

- Apply design patterns, such as the Adapter and Strategy patterns, to interfaces.

- Understand an interface's versatility through duck-typing, mixins, and fluent interfaces.

- Identify the limitations of interfaces and implement workarounds.

- Spot common anti-patterns and abuses of interfaces.

The interface is a powerful construct in Microsoft .NET Framework development. Although the `interface` keyword is very simple, what it represents is a very powerful paradigm. When used correctly, interfaces provide your code with the extension points that make it extremely adaptive. However, some uses of interfaces are not so good; yet they remain in common use.

This chapter provides a reminder of the differences between classes and interfaces and describes how best to use the two together both to protect client code from implementation changes and to facilitate polymorphism.

It also covers the versatility of interfaces and how they are a ubiquitous tool in modern software solutions. This encompasses some powerful design patterns that, when applied correctly (in conjunction with other patterns in this book) yield code that is incredibly flexible and able to adapt to the changing requirements that Agile projects embrace.

Interfaces alone are, however, no panacea. A judicious sprinkling of interfaces can certainly help a project, but the interfaces must be applied in the correct manner. This chapter explores some of the common abuses of interfaces.

What is an interface?

An interface defines the behavior that a class has, but not *how* this behavior is implemented. Interfaces stand as separate constructs from classes, but they require a class to provide the working code to fulfill the interface.

Interfaces are defined by their syntax—that is, the language-construct side of the interface: the `interface` keyword and everything that this implies and entails. But they are also defined by their features: the concepts that they represent and enable.

Syntax

Interfaces are defined by using the `interface` keyword. They can contain properties, methods, and events, just as classes can. However, no element of an interface can be given an access modifier: the implementing class must implement an interface as `public`. Listing 3-1 shows the declaration of an interface, along with a possible implementation.

LISTING 3-1 Declaring and implementing an interface.

```
public interface ISimpleInterface
{
    void ThisMethodRequiresImplementation();

    string ThisStringPropertyNeedsImplementingToo
    {
        get;
        set;
    }

    int ThisIntegerPropertyOnlyNeedsAGetter
    {
        get;
    }

    public event EventHandler<EventArgs> InterfacesCanContainEventsToo;
}
// . . .
public class SimpleInterfaceImplementation : ISimpleInterface
{

    public void ThisMethodRequiresImplementation()
    {

    }

    public string ThisStringPropertyNeedsImplementingToo
    {
        get;
        set;
    }
```

```
public int ThisIntegerPropertyOnlyNeedsAGetter
{
    get
    {
        return this.encapsulatedInteger;
    }
    set
    {
        this.encapsulatedInteger = value;
    }
}

event EventHandler<EventArgs> InterfacesCanContainEventsToo = delegate { };

private int encapsulatedInteger;
}
```

The .NET Framework does not support the concept of multiple inheritance of classes, but it does support multiple interface implementation for a single class.

There is no limit imposed on the number of interfaces that a class can implement; the number of interfaces that really make sense on one class is more of a practical concern. Listing 3-2 extends the prior example to implement a second interface on the implementing class.

LISTING 3-2 Multiple interfaces can be implemented by a single class.

```
public interface IInterfaceOne
{
    void MethodOne();
}
// . . .
public interface IInterfaceTwo
{
    void MethodTwo();
}
// . . .
public class ImplementingMultipleInterfaces : IInterfaceOne, IInterfaceTwo
{
    public void MethodOne()
    {
    }

    public void MethodTwo()
    {
    }
}
```

Though there can be multiple interfaces implemented on a single class, a single interface can similarly be implemented multiple times by different classes.

Multiple inheritance

Some languages support the concept of inheriting from multiple base classes. C++, in particular, allows this construct. However, .NET Framework languages do not permit it, and the compiler will generate a warning if a class attempts to inherit from two or more classes, as Figure 3-1 shows.

> ⊗ 2 Class 'TheInterface.AttemptedMultipleInheritance' cannot
> have multiple base classes: 'TheInterface.BaseClassOne'
> and 'BaseClassTwo'

FIGURE 3-1 Multiple inheritance is prevented by the compiler.

Diamond inheritance problem

One reason that multiple inheritance is disallowed is because of the diamond inheritance problem. This problem occurs when two or more classes are inherited by the same class. If each of those base classes contains identical methods, which one should be used? Figure 3-2 shows a Unified Modeling Language (UML) diagram of the problem.

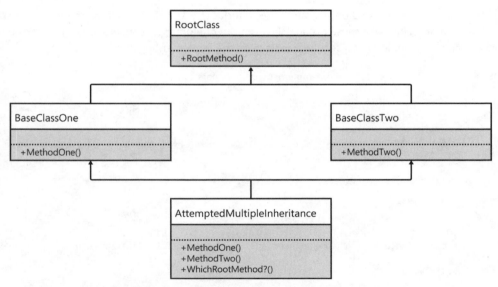

FIGURE 3-2 A UML diagram showing the diamond inheritance problem.

In this case, which version of `RootMethod()` should class `AttemptedMultipleInheritance` inherit—the one that `BaseClassOne` inherited from `RootClass`, or the one that `BaseClass-Two` inherited from `RootClass`? Because of this ambiguity, the .NET Framework does not allow multiple inheritance of classes.

Explicit implementation

Interfaces can also be implemented *explicitly*. Explicit interface implementation differs from implicit interface implementation, which is what was shown in the previous examples. Listing 3-3 shows the same example class from before, but this time it implements its interface explicitly.

LISTING 3-3 Implementing an interface explicitly.

```
public class ExplicitInterfaceImplementation : ISimpleInterface
{
    public ExplicitInterfaceImplementation()
    {
        this.encapsulatedInteger = 4;
    }

    void ISimpleInterface.ThisMethodRequiresImplementation()
    {
        encapsulatedEvent(this, EventArgs.Empty);
    }

    string ISimpleInterface.ThisStringPropertyNeedsImplementingToo
    {
        get;
        set;
    }

    int ISimpleInterface.ThisIntegerPropertyOnlyNeedsAGetter
    {
        get
        {
            return encapsulatedInteger;
        }
    }

    event EventHandler<EventArgs> ISimpleInterface.InterfacesCanContainEventsToo
    {
        add { encapsulatedEvent += value; }
        remove { encapsulatedEvent -= value; }
    }

    private int encapsulatedInteger;
    private event EventHandler<EventArgs> encapsulatedEvent;
}
```

To use an explicitly implemented interface, clients must have a reference to an instance of the interface—a reference to an implementation of the interface will not suffice. Listing 3-4 explores this in further detail.

LISTING 3-4 When implemented explicitly, the interface methods are not visible on class instances.

```
public class ExplicitInterfaceClient
{
    public ExplicitInterfaceClient(ExplicitInterfaceImplementation
        implementationReference, ISimpleInterface interfaceReference)
    {
        // Uncommenting this will cause compilation errors.
        //var instancePropertyValue =
        //implementationReference.ThisIntegerPropertyOnlyNeedsAGetter;
        //implementationReference.ThisMethodRequiresImplementation();
        //implementationReference.ThisStringPropertyNeedsImplementingToo = "Hello";
        //implementationReference.InterfacesCanContainEventsToo += EventHandler;

        var interfacePropertyValue =
            interfaceReference.ThisIntegerPropertyOnlyNeedsAGetter;
        interfaceReference.ThisMethodRequiresImplementation();
        interfaceReference.ThisStringPropertyNeedsImplementingToo = "Hello";
        interfaceReference.InterfacesCanContainEventsToo += EventHandler;
    }

    void EventHandler(object sender, EventArgs e)
    {

    }
}
```

Explicit implementation is only really useful when you want to avoid a signature clash, when the class already possesses a method signature that must be implemented by an interface.

Every method that can be defined in the .NET Framework has a specific method signature. This signature helps to distinguish methods as unique and to differentiate methods that have been overridden. A method's signature consists of its name and its parameter list. Note that a method's access level, return value, abstract, or sealed status all affect the method signature. Listing 3-5 shows a variety of method signatures, some of which clash. Method signatures clash if they are equal in all aforementioned criteria. No `class`, `interface`, or `struct` can contain methods with clashing signatures.

LISTING 3-5 Some of these methods have the same signature.

```
public class ClashingMethodSignatures
{
    public void MethodA()
    {

    }

    // This would cause a clash with the method above:
    //public void MethodA()
    //{
```

```
//}

// As would this: return values are not considered
//public int MethodA()
//{
//    return 0;
//}

public int MethodB(int x)
{
    return x;
}

// There is no clash here: the parameters differ.
// This is an overload of the previous MethodB.
public int MethodB(int x, int y)
{
    return x + y;
}
}
```

Properties, because they don't have parameter lists, are differentiated solely on their name. Thus, two properties' signatures clash if they possess the same name.

Imagine the class shown in Listing 3-6, which is needed to implement the aforementioned interface, `InterfaceOne`.

LISTING 3-6 The interface that this class needs to implement will cause method signature collisions.

```
public class ClassWithMethodSignatureClash
{
    public void MethodOne()
    {
    }
}
```

First, because the method signatures are the same, you only need to add the interface implementation notation to the class declaration, as shown in Listing 3-7.

LISTING 3-7 Implicitly implementing the interface will allow reuse of the existing methods.

```
public class ClassWithMethodSignatureClash : IInterfaceOne
{
    public void MethodOne()
    {
    }
}
```

Whenever a client calls the interface methods on this class, the same methods that are already in place will be used. An example of where this can be useful is when you are implementing the Model-View-Presenter (MVP) pattern in Windows Forms and adding an IView interface that requires a Close method to be implemented on a Form. Listing 3-8 shows this in practice.

LISTING 3-8 Sometimes the presence of a clashing method can be neatly capitalized on.

```
public interface IView
{
    void Close();
}
// . . .
public partial class Form1 : Form, IView
{
    public Form1()
    {
        InitializeComponent();
    }
}
```

However, if the class needs to provide different method bodies for the interface implementation, the class should implement the interface explicitly, avoiding the method signature clash. Listing 3-9 shows a class with clashing methods that provides different implementations of those methods.

LISTING 3-9 Explicitly implementing an interface to avoid clashing method signatures.

```
public class ClassAvoidingMethodSignatureClash : IInterfaceOne
{
    public void MethodOne()
    {
        // original implementation
    }

    void IInterfaceOne.MethodOne()
    {
        // new implementation
    }
}
```

In a similar regard, if a class needs to implement two different interfaces that are unrelated but that both contain a method with the same signature, you can implement them both implicitly and share the same method implementation. Or, as shown in Listing 3-10, you can implement them both explicitly—for clarity—to demarcate which implementation belongs to which interface.

LISTING 3-10 When implementing two interfaces with a common method signature, only explicit implementation is sufficient.

```
public class ClassImplementingClashingInterfaces : IInterfaceOne, IAnotherInterfaceOne
{
    void IInterfaceOne.MethodOne()
    {

    }

    void IAnotherInterfaceOne.MethodOne()
    {

    }
}
```

Polymorphism

The ability to use an object of one type and have it implicitly act as if it were of a different type is called *polymorphism*. Client code can interact with an object as if it is one type when it is actually another. This programmatic sleight of hand is one of the most important tenets of object-oriented programming and underpins some of the most elegant, adaptive solutions to programming problems.

Figure 3-3 shows an interface representing the behavior of vehicles, and some possible implementing classes for cars, motorcycles, and speedboats. Note that each of these three vehicle types is quite distinct, but they all exhibit the same behavior due to their unifying interface.

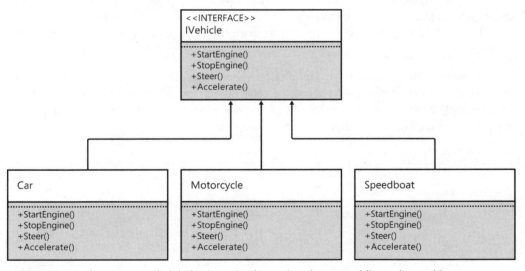

FIGURE 3-3 Interfaces pass on their behavior to implementing classes, enabling polymorphism.

In this example, vehicles are assumed to have an engine that can be started and stopped, some provision for steering, and the ability to accelerate. Polymorphism allows client code to hold a reference to an IVehicle interface and treat all concrete types as if they were the same. The details of how a car steers or accelerates compared to a motorcycle, or how a speedboat engine is started and stopped compared to a train, is irrelevant to the client. And this is a very good thing. In reality, we are all clients to this interface whenever we use a vehicle. Sure, a real interface for a vehicle is more nuanced than that which is shown here, but the principle is the same. Do you need to know how the engine of your car works in order to start and stop the engine? No, not at all. Those are all implementation details that can have no bearing on your knowledge of driving. That is good interface design.

The design patterns and interface features that make up the rest of this chapter all facilitate the creation of adaptive code. Polymorphism enables each one to be useful for any class that fulfils an expected interface, whether it has already been written or is yet to be conceived.

Adaptive design patterns

Design patterns were popularized by the Gang of Four[1] book, *Design Patterns* (Addison-Wesley Professional, 1994). Despite the fact that this book is almost 20 years old (which is at least four ice ages in software development terms), it is still extremely relevant today. Some of the patterns have crossed over to be reclassified as anti-patterns, but others are used constantly and enhance the adaptability of code.

Good design patterns are reusable collaborations between interfaces and classes that can be applied repeatedly in many different scenarios, across projects, platforms, languages, and frameworks. As with most notable best practices, design patterns are another theoretical tool that it is better to know than not know. They can be overused, and they are not always applicable, sometimes over-complicating an otherwise simple solution with an explosion of classes, interfaces, indirection, and abstraction.

In my experience, design patterns tend to be either underused or overused. In some projects, there are not enough design patterns and the code suffers from a lack of discernable structure. Other projects apply design patterns too liberally, adding indirection and abstraction where the benefit is negligible. The balance is in finding the right places to apply the right patterns.

---

[1] So called because of its four authors: Erich Gamma, Richard Helm, Ralph Johnson, and John Vlissides.

The Null Object pattern

The Null Object pattern is one of the most common design patterns—and it is one of the easiest to comprehend and implement. Its purpose is to allow you to avoid accidentally throwing a Null-ReferenceException and a plethora of null object checking code. The UML class diagram in Figure 3-4 shows how the Null Object pattern is applied.

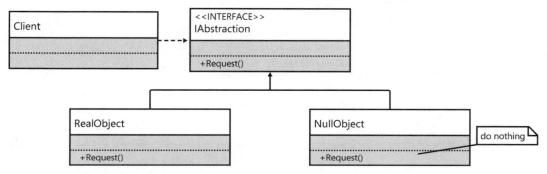

FIGURE 3-4 The Null Object pattern demonstrated as a UML class diagram.

Listing 3-11 shows some typical code that can throw a NullReferenceException.

LISTING 3-11 If you don't check return values for null, there is a chance of throwing a NullReference-Exception.

```
class Program
{
    static IUserRepository userRepository = new UserRepository();

    static void Main(string[] args)
    {
        var user = userRepository.GetByID(Guid.NewGuid());
        // Without the Null Object pattern, this line could throw an exception
        user.IncrementSessionTicket();
    }
}
```

Every client that calls IUserRepository.Get(Guid uniqueID) is in danger of throwing a null reference. In practice, this means that every client must check that the return value is not null, to avoid attempting to dereference null, causing a NullReferenceException to be thrown. This would make the client shown previously look more like the code in Listing 3-12.

```
class Program
{
    static IUserRepository userRepository = new UserRepository();

    static void Main(string[] args)
    {
        var user = userRepository.GetByID(Guid.NewGuid());
        if(user != null)
        {
            user.IncrementSessionTicket();
        }
    }
}
```

The Null Object pattern indicates that you are placing too much unnecessary burden on all of the clients of IRepository. The more clients that use this method, the greater the probability of forgetting a null reference check. Instead, you should change the source of the problem to perform the check for you, as shown in Listing 3-13.

LISTING 3-13 The service code should implement the Null Object pattern.

```
public class UserRepository : IUserRepository
{
    public UserRepository()
    {
        users = new List<User>
        {
            new User(Guid.NewGuid()),
            new User(Guid.NewGuid()),
            new User(Guid.NewGuid()),
            new User(Guid.NewGuid())
        };
    }

    public IUser GetByID(Guid userID)
    {
        IUser userFound = users.SingleOrDefault(user => user.ID == userID);
        if(userFound == null)
        {
            userFound = new NullUser();
        }
        return userFound;
    }

    private ICollection<User> users;
}
```

First, this code attempts to retrieve the `User` from the in-memory collection, which is no change from the previous implementation. Now, though, you check whether the `User` instance returned is actually a `null` reference. If it is, you return a special subclass of the `IUser` type: the `NullUser`. This subclass overrides the `IncrementSessionTicket` method to do precisely nothing, as shown in Listing 3-14. In fact, a proper `NullUser` implementation overrides *all* methods to do as close to nothing as possible.

LISTING 3-14 The `NullUser` method implementations all do nothing.

```
public class NullUser : IUser
{
    public void IncrementSessionTicket()
    {
        // do nothing
    }
}
```

Additionally, whenever a method or property of the `NullUser` object is expected to return a reference to another object, it should return a special Null Object implementation of *those* types, too. In other words, all Null Object implementations should return recursive Null Object implementations. This obviates the need for any `null` reference checking in clients.

This also has the added benefit of reducing the number of unit tests that you need to write. Previously, when each client had to implement the check, there would also be concomitant unit tests to confirm that the check was in place. Instead, the repository implementation is unit tested to ensure that it returns the `NullUser` implementation.

The IsNull property anti-pattern

Sometimes the Null Object pattern involves adding a Boolean `IsNull` property to the interface. All real implementations of this interface return the value `false` for this property. The Null Object implementation of the interface returns `true`. Listing 3-15 shows how this might work, given the previous example.

LISTING 3-15 The `IsNull` property is only true for Null Object implementations.

```
public interface IUser
{
    void IncrementSessionTicket();

    bool IsNull
    {
        get;
    }
}
```

```
// . . .
public class User : IUser
{
    // . . .
    public bool IsNull
    {
        get
        {
            return false;
        }
    }

    private DateTime sessionExpiry;
}
// . . .
public class NullUser : IUser
{
    public void IncrementSessionTicket()
    {
        // do nothing
    }

    public bool IsNull
    {
        get
        {
            return true;
        }
    }
}
```

The problem with this property is that it causes logic to spill out of the objects whose purpose is to encapsulate behavior. For example, if statements will start to creep into client code to differentiate between real implementations and the Null Object implementation. This obviates the whole purpose of the pattern, which is to avoid proliferating this logic to its various clients. Listing 3-16 is a typical example of this problem.

LISTING 3-16 Logic based on the IsNull property makes this an anti-pattern.

```
static void Main(string[] args)
{
    var user = userRepository.GetByID(Guid.NewGuid());
    // Without the Null Object pattern, this line would throw an exception
    user.IncrementSessionTicket();

    string userName;
    if(!user.IsNull)
```

```
    {
        userName = user.Name;
    }
    else
    {
        userName = "unknown";
    }

    Console.WriteLine("The user's name is {0}", userName);

    Console.ReadKey();
}
```

This can easily be fixed by encapsulating the name of a null user inside the NullUser class, as in Listing 3-17.

LISTING 3-17 With proper encapsulation, the IsNull property is obsolete.

```
public class NullUser : IUser
{
    public void IncrementSessionTicket()
    {
        // do nothing
    }

    public string Name
    {
        get
        {
            return "unknown";
        }
    }
}
// . . .
static void Main(string[] args)
{
    var user = userRepository.GetByID(Guid.NewGuid());
    // Without the Null Object pattern, this line would throw an exception
    user.IncrementSessionTicket();

    Console.WriteLine("The user's name is {0}", user.Name);

    Console.ReadKey();
}
```

Cascading Nulls

A requested feature of the C# language is that it mimic Groovy[2] and include a "Cascading Nulls" operator. Consider the following code snippet.

```
if(person != null && person.Address != null && person.Address.Country == "England")
{
    // . . .
}
```

The theory is that it could be replaced with the following.

```
if(person?.Address?.Country == "England")
{
    // . . .
}
```

The `?.` operator thus becomes a way of safely dereferencing any object and, at worst, being handed a `default(T)` of the property type. I am not against any progression in the syntax of the language that others might find useful, but I would be reluctant to use this as an alternative to a proper Null Object implementation, for three reasons.

First, there are too many instances in which a default value of a type is simply not going to suffice. The previous example of using a sensible user name to avoid throwing a `Null-ReferenceException` illustrates that the alternative is not a default value but something more meaningful to the application.

Second, this would require all clients of this code to be programmed with the possibility of `null` in mind. Part of the reason to use the Null Object pattern is to obviate `null` checking and give you the freedom to dereference with impunity. If you reject the Null Object pattern in favor of the Cascading Nulls syntax, you open yourself up to forgetting to dereference again.

A third, more subjective reason is that such syntax would likely become ubiquitous. The occasional `int?` to represent an `int` with optional/reference semantics is fair enough, but littering the code with `?.` for every dereference? No, thanks.

Given a proper Null Object implementation, this example could be written succinctly as shown here.

```
if(person.Address.Country == "England")
{
    // . . .
}
```

This, surely, offers the most benefit: client code that is less obfuscated but that is safe from the perils of a `NullReferenceException`.

---

[2] Groovy is a dynamically typed Java variant (*http://groovy.codehaus.org*).

The Adapter pattern

The Adapter pattern allows you to provide an object instance to a client that has a dependency on an interface that your instance does not implement. An `Adapter` class is created that fulfills the expected interface of the client but that implements the methods of the interface by delegating to different methods of another object. It is typically used when the target class cannot be altered to fit the desired interface. This could be because it is `sealed` or because it belongs to an assembly for which you do not have the source. You can implement the Adapter pattern in two ways: by using the Class Adapter pattern or by using the Object Adapter pattern.

The Class Adapter pattern

Figure 3-5 shows the collaborating classes and interfaces used in the Class Adapter pattern.

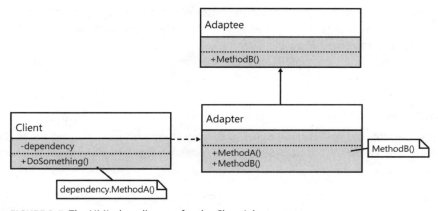

FIGURE 3-5 The UML class diagram for the Class Adapter pattern.

The Class Adapter pattern makes use of inheritance for the adapter—a subclass of the target class is what needs to be adapted to fit the expected interface of clients. Listing 3-18 shows how this works in practice.

LISTING 3-18 The Class Adapter pattern uses implementation inheritance.

```
public class Adaptee
{
    public void MethodB()
    {

    }
}
// . . .
public class Adapter : Adaptee
{
    public void MethodA()
```

```
    {
        MethodB();
    }
}
// . . .
class Program
{
    static Adapter dependency = new Adapter();
    static void Main(string[] args)
    {
        dependency.MethodA();
    }
}
```

This is the less common of the two types of Adapter pattern, mostly because developers are told to favor composition over inheritance. This is because inheritance, which is *whitebox* reuse, makes the subclass dependent on the implementation of a class, rather than merely on its interface. Composition, which is *blackbox* reuse, limits the dependency to the interface, so that the implementation can vary without adversely affecting clients.

The Object Adapter pattern

The Object Adapter pattern uses composition to delegate from the methods of the interface to that of a contained, encapsulated object. Figure 3-6 shows the collaborating classes and interfaces used in the Object Adapter pattern.

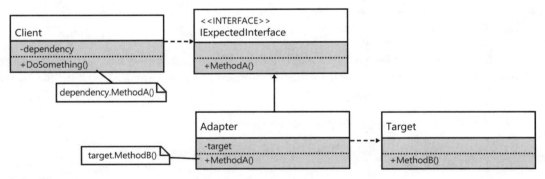

FIGURE 3-6 The UML class diagram for the Object Adapter pattern.

Listing 3-19 shows how this works in practice.

LISTING 3-19 The adaptor accepts the target class as a constructor parameter and delegates to it.

```
public interface IExpectedInterface
{
    void MethodA();
}
// . . .
public class Adapter : IExpectedInterface
{
    public Adapter(TargetClass target)
    {
        this.target = target;
    }

    public void MethodA()
    {
        target.MethodB();
    }

    private TargetClass target;
}
//
public class TargetClass
{
    public void MethodB()
    {

    }
}
// . . .
class Program
{
    static IExpectedInterface dependency = new Adapter(new TargetClass());
    static void Main(string[] args)
    {
        dependency.MethodA();
    }
}
```

The Strategy pattern

The Strategy pattern allows you to change the desired behavior of a class without requiring recompilation, potentially even during run-time execution. Figure 3-7 shows the UML class diagram for the Strategy pattern.

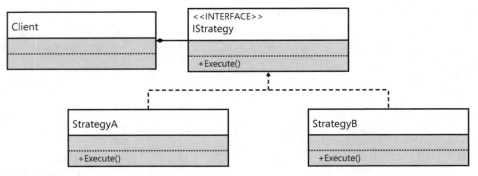

FIGURE 3-7 The UML class diagram of the Strategy pattern.

The Strategy pattern is used whenever a class needs to exhibit variant behavior depending on the state of an object. If this behavior can change at run time depending on the current state of the class, the Strategy pattern is a perfect fit for encapsulating this variant behavior. Listing 3-20 shows how to create the Strategy pattern and use it in a class.

LISTING 3-20 The Strategy pattern in action.

```
public interface IStrategy
{
    void Execute();
}
// . . .
public class ConcreteStrategyA : IStrategy
{
    public void Execute()
    {
        Console.WriteLine("ConcreteStrategyA.Execute()");
    }
}
// . . .
public class ConcreteStrategyB : IStrategy
{
    public void Execute()
    {
        Console.WriteLine("ConcreteStrategyB.Execute()");
    }
}
// . . .
public class Context
{
    public Context()
    {
        currentStrategy = strategyA;
    }
```

```
    public void DoSomething()
    {
        currentStrategy.Execute();

        // swap strategy with each call
        currentStrategy = (currentStrategy == strategyA) ? strategyB : strategyA;
    }

    private readonly IStrategy strategyA = new ConcreteStrategyA();
    private readonly IStrategy strategyB = new ConcreteStrategyB();

    private IStrategy currentStrategy;
}
```

With every call that is made to `Context.DoSomething()`, the method first delegates to the current strategy and then swaps between strategy A and strategy B. The next call delegates to the newly selected strategy before again swapping back to the original strategy.

The way the strategies are selected is an implementation detail—it does not alter the net effect of the pattern: that the behavior of the class is hidden behind an interface whose implementations are used to perform the real work.

Further versatility

The utility of interfaces is not limited to design patterns. There are some other, more specialized uses of interfaces that are worth investigation. Though these features are not generally applicable, there are situations in which they are the right tool for the job.

Just as with design patterns, their *overuse* can be detrimental to the readability and maintainability of code. It is a difficult balancing act to find the correct number of collaborating patterns and techniques to solve a problem elegantly, so exercise some caution when using interfaces in the following ways.

Duck-typing

C# is a statically typed language, whereas duck-typing is more commonly found in dynamically typed languages. Duck-typing uses the duck test:

> *When I see a bird that walks like a duck and swims like a duck and quacks like a duck, I call that bird a duck.*
>
> —*James Whitcomb Riley*

Applied to types in a programming language, the duck test suggests that, as long as an object exhibits the *behavior* of a certain interface, it should be treated as that interface. Unfortunately, this is not true by default in C#. Observe the example in Listing 3-21.

LISTING 3-21 Although the object Swan fulfills all of the methods of an IDuck, it is, in fact, *not* an IDuck.

```
public interface IDuck
{
    void Walk();

    void Swim();

    void Quack();
}
// . . .
public class Swan
{
    public void Walk()
    {
        Console.WriteLine("The swan is walking.");
    }

    public void Swim()
    {
        Console.WriteLine("The swan can swim like a duck.");
    }

    public void Quack()
    {
        Console.WriteLine("The swan is quacking.");
    }
}
// . . .
class Program
{
    static void Main(string[] args)
    {
        var swan = new Swan();

        var swanAsDuck = swan as IDuck;

        if(swan is IDuck || swanAsDuck != null)
        {
            swanAsDuck.Walk();
            swanAsDuck.Swim();
            swanAsDuck.Quack();
        }
    }
}
```

The is predicate and the as cast return false and null, respectively. The Common Language Runtime (CLR) does not consider a Swan as being an IDuck, even though it actually fulfils that interface. A type must *implement* the interface via interface inheritance.

There are a couple of tricks that you can employ to enable the Swan class to be usable as an instance of the IDuck interface *without* having to implement it. Either you can take advantage of the dynamic typing extensions in newer versions of the CLR, or you can make use of a third-party library called Impromptu Interface.

Using the Dynamic Language Runtime

As of version 4, the .NET Framework was no longer strictly statically typed. With the introduction of the dynamic keyword, and some supporting types, you can avoid the CLR's static typing and switch to the dynamic typing of the Dynamic Language Runtime (DLR). An example of dynamic typing in C# is shown in Listing 3-22.

LISTING 3-22 The DLR can be used for duck typing.

```
class Program
{
    static void Main(string[] args)
    {
        var swan = new Swan();

        DoDuckLikeThings(swan);

        Console.ReadKey();
    }

    static void DoDuckLikeThings(dynamic duckish)
    {
        if (duckish != null)
        {
            duckish.Walk();
            duckish.Swim();
            duckish.Quack();
        }
    }
}
```

Notice, however, that the method parameter is of type dynamic. Not only do you need to target the .NET Framework 4, dynamic typing needs to be designed into clients specifically. On both counts, this is sometimes infeasible. You can't, for example, simply start creating all methods to take dynamic parameters everywhere, or else you would be better off using a dynamically typed .NET Framework language, such as IronPython[3].

---

[3] *http://ironpython.net/*

Using Impromptu Interface

Impromptu Interface is a .NET Framework library that can be installed via NuGet. After it is installed, you can use the `ActLike<T>()` method to pass in your Swan and receive an `IDuck` instance that delegates to your instance. Listing 3-23 shows how this works.

LISTING 3-23 Impromptu Interface allows duck-typing in C#.

```
class Program
{
    static void Main(string[] args)
    {
        var swan = new Swan();

        var swanAsDuck = Impromptu.ActLike<IDuck>(swan);

        if(swanAsDuck != null)
        {
            swanAsDuck.Walk();
            swanAsDuck.Swim();
            swanAsDuck.Quack();
        }

        Console.ReadKey();
    }
}
```

What the `ActLike` method is doing is creating a new type at run time by using Reflection Emit. This is a powerful part of the .NET Framework Reflection API that allows the creation of new types at run time. This new type fulfills the `IDuck` interface, but it also contains the Swan instance as an encapsulated field. Whenever one of the `IDuck` interface methods is called, the new type trivially delegates to the Swan instance. It is, in effect, a run-time version of the Adapter pattern. Impromptu Interface is an automatic way of applying the Object Adapter pattern.

CLR duck-typing support

Interestingly, the CLR already supports duck-typing. Unfortunately, this is only for one uncommon case: implementing something that is enumerable. A type that is the target of the `foreach` loop must conform to a certain interface, but that interface is not formalized and can be implemented *ad hoc* on the target class. In the example in Listing 3-24, the Duck class is the target of a `foreach` loop.

LISTING 3-24 The CLR implicitly supports duck-typing for enumerable types.

```
class Program
{
    static void Main(string[] args)
    {
        var duck = new Duck();
```

```
        foreach (var duckling in duck)
        {
            Console.WriteLine("Quack {0}", duckling);
        }

        Console.ReadKey();
    }
}
```

The Duck does not implement any interface, but the GetEnumerator() method is required by the foreach loop, as the compiler instructs, as shown in Figure 3-8.

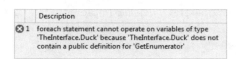

FIGURE 3-8 Without requiring a specific interface, the compiler complains that a public method is missing from the class.

When you implement this method with a void return type, you receive a new error stating that this type does not support some other required methods and properties, as shown in Figure 3-9.

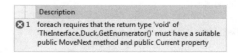

FIGURE 3-9 The return type of the GetEnumerator method must also match an implicit contract.

These properties can then be implemented as shown in Listing 3-25.

LISTING 3-25 Completing the implied interface of the DuckEnumerator class.

```
public class DuckEnumerator
{
    int i = 0;

    public bool MoveNext()
    {
        return i++ < 10;
    }

    public int Current
    {
        get
        {
            return i;
        }
    }
}
```

At this point, you have successfully implemented the implicit interface that the `foreach` requires—duck-typing in action!

Mixins

An extension of duck-typing is the concept of the mixin. A *mixin* is a class that contains the implementations from multiple other classes, without using implementation inheritance. As you have already learned, multiple implementation inheritance is not supported by C#, so you must look at other solutions for implementing mixins.

One trivial but limited way of implementing mixins is to use extension methods. This allows you to add methods to a type that has already been defined, which can be very useful. An alternative is to use a third-party library such as Re-motion Re-mix, which operates much like Impromptu Interface in that it generates a new type at run time that contains all of the interfaces you specify and acts as a multifaceted adapter.

Using extension methods

Since the .NET Framework 3.5, extension methods have allowed the addition of new functionality to already existing types. Without needing to access the source of a type, nor requiring the type to be a `partial` definition, you can extend a type. Listing 3-26 shows the interface that will be enhanced in this section, along with a pair of trivial extension methods.

LISTING 3-26 Extension methods can enhance an existing interface.

```
public interface ITargetInterface
{
    void DoSomething();
}
// . . .
public static class MixinExtensions
{
    public static void FirstExtensionMethod(this ITargetInterface target)
    {
        Console.WriteLine("The first extension method was called.");
    }

    public static void SecondExtensionMethod(this ITargetInterface target)
    {
        Console.WriteLine("The second extension method was called.");
    }
}
```

Now, whenever a client has access to an `ITargetInterface` instance, and it also references the `MixinExtensions` class, these two extension methods will be available. Any number of extension methods can be created, spread across multiple static classes. Listing 3-27 shows another pair of extension methods; this time they take extra parameters.

LISTING 3-27 Extension methods can take parameters.

```
public static class MoreMixinExtensions
{
    public static void FurtherExtensionMethodA(this ITargetInterface target, int
        extraParameter)
    {
        Console.WriteLine("Further extension method A was called with argument {0}",
            extraParameter);
    }

    public static void FurtherExtensionMethodB(this ITargetInterface target, string
        stringParameter)
    {
        Console.WriteLine("Further extension method B was called with argument {0}",
            stringParameter);
    }
}
```

These extension methods can be called just like any other by any client, as in Listing 3-28.

LISTING 3-28 Clients have access to extension methods as if they were declared directly on the target interface.

```
public class MixinClient
{
    public MixinClient(ITargetInterface target)
    {
        this.target = target;
    }

    public void Run()
    {
        target.DoSomething();
        target.FirstExtensionMethod();
        target.SecondExtensionMethod();
        target.FurtherExtensionMethodA(30);
        target.FurtherExtensionMethodB("Hello!");
    }

    private readonly ITargetInterface target;
}
```

There are a few notable limitations to this approach to mixins. The first is the testability of the client. As Chapter 4, "Unit testing and refactoring," will show, static classes do not lend themselves to be easily mocked. This makes all clients of these extension methods more difficult to properly unit test.

Worse still, also due to extension methods being static classes, they cannot hold any extra per-instance state related to the object. Sure, there are workarounds, such as storing a static dictionary that maps instances to some extra values, but this is not ideal.

Notice also that the extension methods are all targeting the same interface, and that all instances to be enhanced must implement this interface. True mixins, on the other hand, implement multiple different interfaces and act as aggregate adapters.

Using Re-motion Re-mix

An alternative way of implementing mixins is by using a third-party library such as Re-motion Re-mix. Re-mix allows you to specify, via run-time configuration, which classes to combine when creating a new instance of a certain target class. As with Impromptu Interface, it generates a new type on the fly that fulfills all of the interfaces present on the mixins requested, with each instance of this type delegating to an instance of the mixin whenever an interface method is called. The interfaces, and some sample implementations, are shown in Listing 3-29.

LISTING 3-29 The disparate interfaces to be combined as a mixin.

```csharp
public interface ITargetInterface
{
    void DoSomething();
}
// . . .
public class TargetImplementation : ITargetInterface
{
    public void DoSomething()
    {
        Console.WriteLine("ITargetInterface.DoSomething()");
    }
}
// . . .
public interface IMixinInterfaceA
{
    void MethodA();
}
// . . .
public class MixinImplementationA : IMixinInterfaceA
{
    public void MethodA()
    {
        Console.WriteLine("IMixinInterfaceA.MethodA()");
    }
}
// . . .
public interface IMixinInterfaceB
{
    void MethodB(int parameter);
}
```

```
// . . .
public class MixinImplementationB : IMixinInterfaceB
{
    public void MethodB(int parameter)
    {
        Console.WriteLine("IMixinInterfaceB.MethodB({0})", parameter);
    }
}
// . . .
public interface IMixinInterfaceC
{
    void MethodC(string parameter);
}
// . . .
public class MixinImplementationC : IMixinInterfaceC
{
    public void MethodC(string parameter)
    {
        Console.WriteLine("IMixinInterfaceC.MethodC(\"{0}\")", parameter);
    }
}
```

Note that there is no single class that implements all of these interfaces. Instead, the next step is to configure Re-mix so that, when it is asked for an instance of `TargetImplementation`, it will return a mixin containing all of the interfaces and classes combined. Listing 3-30 shows such a configuration.

LISTING 3-30 Instructing Re-mix how to construct `TargetImplementation` instances.

```
var config = MixinConfiguration.BuildFromActive()
    .ForClass<TargetImplementation>()
    .AddMixin<MixinImplementationA>()
    .AddMixin<MixinImplementationB>()
    .AddMixin<MixinImplementationC>()
    .BuildConfiguration();

MixinConfiguration.SetActiveConfiguration(config);
```

Unfortunately, you cannot simply call new on the `TargetImplementation` and expect a mixin. Instead, you have to ask Re-mix to create a `TargetImplementation` instance so that it can build a new type to your specification and instantiate it. Listing 3-31 shows how it can do that—and luckily, it is trivial.

LISTING 3-31 Re-mix is in charge of creating mixins.

```
ITargetInterface target = ObjectFactory.Create<TargetImplementation>(ParamList.Empty)
```

One of the limitations of Re-mix is that you do not—and cannot—know the exact type of the instance returned by `ObjectFactory.Create`. All you know is that it is an instance of a *subclass* `TargetImplementation`. This is sort of bad news for clients, because the only interface you can guarantee that `TargetImplementation` fulfills at compile time is `ITargetInterface`. Clients of the mixin, therefore, must type-sniff by using `is` and `as` to cast the mixin to the desired interface. Listing 3-32 highlights this problem.

LISTING 3-32 Type-sniffing is bad practice but necessary for using mixins.

```
public class MixinClient
{
    public MixinClient(ITargetInterface target)
    {
        this.target = target;
    }

    public void Run()
    {
        target.DoSomething();

        var targetAsMixinA = target as IMixinInterfaceA;
        if(targetAsMixinA != null)
        {
            targetAsMixinA.MethodA();
        }

        var targetAsMixinB = target as IMixinInterfaceB;
        if(targetAsMixinB != null)
        {
            targetAsMixinB.MethodB(30);
        }

        var targetAsMixinC = target as IMixinInterfaceC;
        if(targetAsMixinC != null)
        {
            targetAsMixinC.MethodC("Hello!");
        }
    }

    private readonly ITargetInterface target;
}
```

Applying mixins to a solution works best when type-sniffing is already present or necessary. This is true with some libraries and frameworks. For example, Prism (the Windows Presentation Foundation/Model-View-Viewmodel library) makes use of type-sniffing, and the functionality required of client classes can be segregated into different implementations and recombined via mixins.

Fluent interfaces

An interface is said to be *fluent* if it returns itself from one or more of its methods. This allows clients to chain calls together, as shown in Listing 3-33.

LISTING 3-33 Fluent interfaces allow method chaining.

```
public class FluentClient
{
    public FluentClient(IFluentInterface fluent)
    {
        this.fluent = fluent;
    }

    public void Run()
    {
        // without using fluency
        fluent.DoSomething();
        fluent.DoSomethingElse();
        fluent.DoSomethingElse();
        fluent.DoSomething();
        fluent.ThisMethodIsNotFluent();

        // using fluency
        fluent.DoSomething()
            .DoSomethingElse()
            .DoSomethingElse()
            .DoSomething()
            .ThisMethodIsNotFluent();
    }

    private readonly IFluentInterface fluent;
}
```

This improves readability because it avoids repeated references to the instance of the interface. It is an increasingly popular way to implement configuration or finite state machines, as described in Chapter 8, "Interface segregation."

Fluent interfaces are easy to implement, too. All the class has to do is return `this` from the method. Because the class is already an implementation of the interface, by returning `this`, the class returns only the interface portion of itself, thus hiding the rest of the implementation. Listing 3-34 shows the definition of the `IFluentInterface` and the implementation used in this example.

LISTING 3-34 Implementing a simple fluent interface is easy.

```
public interface IFluentInterface
{
    IFluentInterface DoSomething();

    IFluentInterface DoSomethingElse();
```

```
    void ThisMethodIsNotFluent();
}
// . . .
public class FluentImplementation : IFluentInterface
{
    public IFluentInterface DoSomething()
    {
        return this;
    }

    public IFluentInterface DoSomethingElse()
    {
        return this;
    }

    public void ThisMethodIsNotFluent()
    {

    }
}
```

Note that one of the methods of the interface is not fluent—it returns void. If a method returns anything but an interface, it is not fluent. Any chaining of methods that a client does will be halted by a call to a method that is not fluent.

Conclusion

In this chapter, you have learned what interfaces are and why they are such a key facet of writing adaptive code. They are catalysts for polymorphism, which allows you to encapsulate variation in families of classes. They are the root around which design patterns grow. And yet they actually *do* nothing.

Remember, interfaces are useless without accompanying implementations. But without interfaces, implementations—and their associated dependencies—would infiltrate and pollute your code, making it hard to maintain and extend. A well-placed interface acts as a firewall between the dirty implementation details of service code and a clean, well-organized client.

Interfaces also have other, more specialized features, such as duck-typing and mixins. These are seldom used, but when applied in the right context, they can simplify otherwise convoluted code and add an extra dimension of adaptability.

The groundwork laid in this chapter will be of great importance as you experience the ubiquity of the interface throughout the rest of the book.

CHAPTER 4

Unit testing and refactoring

After completing this chapter, you will be able to

- Define unit testing and refactoring and explain why both are very useful techniques.

- Understand how unit testing and refactoring are intrinsically linked.

- Write code in a test-first fashion, focusing on implementing only that which the tests require.

- Refactor production code to improve its overall design.

- Recognize overspecified unit tests and refactor them.

This chapter focuses on two different techniques that are current programming best practices: unit testing and refactoring.

Unit testing is the discipline of writing code that tests other code. Unit tests themselves, being source code, can be compiled and executed. As each unit test runs, it reports the test's success or failure with a simple true or false, often a green or a red visual indicator. If all of the unit tests pass, the production code that they test is considered to possibly be working. If even a single unit test fails—out of possibly thousands—the production code overall is deemed to certainly be broken.

Refactoring is the process of incrementally improving the design of existing code. It is analogous to writing various drafts of code, much like I have written various drafts of this book. By acknowledging that we developers rarely get things right the first time, refactoring frees us to do the simplest thing first and gradually, through incremental improvements, arrive at a better solution later.

The freedom to refactor with impunity is made possible by unit testing. When you unit test as early as possible in the process—that is, before you write any production code—you create a safety net to catch any subsequent errors when you refactor code. If a unit test transitions from a passing state to a failing state, you know that the last change you made is responsible for breaking the code. The process of writing unit tests and then refactoring toward better design is an upward spiral whereby the code quality increases while you simultaneously make progress with implementing new features.

Unit testing

To some degree, unit testing should be considered a mandatory part of every programmer's daily discipline. For some developers, the ideal situation is when production code—the code that forms the basis of the software product—is *entirely* the result of the tests that were written to verify the application's behavior. Later in this chapter, you will learn how this can be achieved through test-driven development, but bear in mind that the aim is to be pragmatic rather than purist: it is surely better to ship something and accept some prudent technical debt than it is to be late for the sake of writing more unit tests. That said, every project is unique in its tolerance for timeliness versus completeness.

There are some recognized unit testing patterns and guidelines that will result in repeatable success. These patterns and guidelines are no longer new but expected, tried, and tested. The arrangement and naming of unit tests and, most of all, how to ensure the testability of the code are all primary concerns. If these concerns are neglected, unit tests will no longer be synchronized with the code that they test, test failures will be tolerated, and the safety net will wither and break.

Arrange, Act, Assert

Every unit test is composed of three distinct parts:

- The **arrange**ment of the preconditions of the test

- The performance of the **act** that is being tested

- The **assert**ion that the expected behavior occurred

These three parts form the *Arrange, Act, Assert* (AAA) pattern. Every test that you write should follow this pattern so that other people can read your unit tests.

> **Note** Some readers might be more familiar with this pattern expressed as *Given, When, Then*. This is directly analogous to Arrange, Act, Assert, but it goes like this: *given* some preconditions, *when* the target of the test is executed, *then* some expected behavior should have occurred.

Arranging the preconditions

Before you can execute the action that you need to test, you must set up the scenario that you are testing. For some tests, this will be as simple as constructing the system under test (SUT). The SUT is the class that you are testing. Without a valid instance of the class, you will not be able to test any of its methods.

Listing 4-1 shows a minimal Arrange section of a test for an `Account` class that represents a customer's balance and transactions. For this example, I am using MSTest. This chapter will continue to build on this example for the Act and Assert parts of the test, too. The test method's name, `Adding-TransactionChangesBalance()`, succinctly describes the intent of the test—to ensure that whenever a transaction is added to the account, the balance of the account is changed to include this new transaction.

LISTING 4-1 Constructing the SUT is a common first step in arranging a unit test.

```csharp
[TestClass]
public class AccountTest
{
    [TestMethod]
    public void AddingTransactionChangesBalance()
    {
        // Arrange
        var account = new Account();
    }
}
```

The Arrange step taken here is simple enough. The only precondition to this test is a new instance of the Account class. You create this directly in your test by calling the new operator. From here, you can move on to the next step in the AAA pattern.

Performing the testable act

Now that you have the system under test in a fit state to be acted on, you can execute the method that you are testing. Each test's Act phase should consist of just one interaction with the system under test—one method call or property get or set, for instance. This ensures that the tests are simple to both read and write and have clearly delineated execution paths.

Listing 4-2 shows the addition of the Act part of the test. In keeping with the test method's name, the test calls the account.AddTransaction() method.

LISTING 4-2 Every Act phase should consist of only one interaction with the SUT.

```csharp
[TestClass]
public class AccountTest
{
    [TestMethod]
    public void AddingTransactionChangesBalance()
    {
        // Arrange
        var account = new Account();

        // Act
        account.AddTransaction(200m);
    }
}
```

The test has passed a value into the AddTransaction method. This represents the monetary amount of the transaction that you are adding to the account. It is a decimal value, meaning that it has very high precision, but there is no currency value associated with this amount. For simplicity, the assumption is that all accounts and transactions are in US dollars.

With the Arrange and Act phases complete, you can move on to the final part of the test.

Asserting the expectations

Both of the phases up to this point have really been a preamble to the crux of this and every unit test: the assertion. This is the part that will give you the green indicator of success or the red indicator of failure of the test as a whole. The test method name is again the reference point for the assertion that you are making—that the account balance has changed. In this case, the assertion is going to be a comparison of an *actual* value and an *expected* value. This is a common kind of assertion in state-based tests, which are tests whose assertions depend on the state of the SUT. This particular assertion is going to require the actual and expected values to be equal.

The Account class's Balance property will be queried for the actual value, and you will provide the expected value as a constant. This means that you must have prior knowledge of the expected value, which is a key factor to consider when writing tests. Rather than deriving the expected value in code, you should know what the expected value is ahead of time. In this scenario, it is easy. Given a new account, whose opening balance is unspecified and thus zero, if you add $200.00 to that account, what should the expected balance be?

$$\$0.00 + \$200.00 = \$200.00$$

Thus, you can write your Assert phase and complete your AAA test, as shown in Listing 4-3.

LISTING 4-3 An assertion of expected behavior has been added to the unit test.

```
[TestClass]
public class AccountTest
{
    [TestMethod]
    public void AddingTransactionChangesBalance()
    {
        // Arrange
        var account = new Account();

        // Act
        account.AddTransaction(200m);

        // Assert
        Assert.AreEqual(200m, account.Balance);
    }
}
```

This test is now ready to run. By running the test, you can verify whether or not the system under test behaves as expected.

Running the tests

When the test is complete, you need to run it by using a unit test runner. Unit tests are contained in test projects whose output is assemblies, not executables. This means that the test projects cannot be run by themselves but must instead be provided as input to a unit test runner. Microsoft Visual Studio supports MSTest unit tests with its integrated test runner, whereas some other kinds of unit tests require plugins to provide integrated support in Visual Studio.

In Visual Studio, you can run MSTest unit tests by selecting one of the options from the Test > Run menu. For now, you can select the All Tests option, which is aliased to the keyboard shortcut Ctrl+R, A. The output of running the AAA unit test is shown in Figure 4-1.

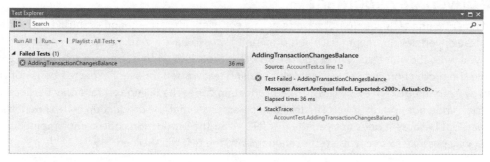

FIGURE 4-1 Running the unit test in the Visual Studio integrated MSTest unit test runner.

The test runner shows a master details view of the unit tests that you have chosen to run. The list of tests is enumerated in the left pane, with more details about the selected test shown in the right pane. You can tell that the test took 14 milliseconds to execute, which is not much at all. This is precisely one of the advantages of writing unit tests—it does not take long to run thousands of unit tests, compared to the effort required to test manually.

However, notice that the test assertion has *failed* because the expected value of 200 did not match the actual value provided. The `account.Balance` property was used for the actual value of the assertion, and it returned 0.

This is because you have not yet implemented the `Account` class. Listing 4-4 shows the minimal `Account` class implementation that was required up to this point.

LISTING 4-4 The system under test does not need to be implemented before the unit test.

```
public class Account
{
    public void AddTransaction(decimal amount)
    {

    }

    public decimal Balance
    {
        get;
        private set;
    }
}
```

As you can tell, this class does nothing with the provided transaction amount in the Add-Transaction method, and the `Balance` is just a default auto-property, though with a private setter. To make this test pass, you have to implement the `Account` class so that it meets your current expectations.

Test-driven development

To implement a unit test, you do not have to have a complete implementation of the system under test. In test-driven development (TDD), it is preferential *not* to have a working system under test before you write the unit tests. When you use a TDD approach to writing software, you write the unit tests and the production code in tandem, with a failing test written for every expected behavior exhibited by every method of every class in the production code. The failing test fails only because the production code does not exist yet. The test states—asserts—that the production code should act in some way, but because it does not yet, the test fails. After the production code is implemented in the simplest way possible to satisfy the test's requirements, the test will succeed.

Red, green, refactor!

What has been produced so far with the AAA `AddingTransactionChangesBalance()` test is the first part of a three-phase process called *red, green, refactor*.

1. Write a failing test that targets the expected behavior of the SUT.

2. Implement just enough of the SUT so that the new test passes without breaking existing successful tests.

3. If any refactoring can be done on the SUT to improve its design or overall quality, now is the time to do so.

The first phase generates a failing test, which test runners indicate with a red icon. The second phase makes that failing test succeed, turning the icon green. The third phase allows you to incrementally improve the production code piece by piece without fear of breaking its functionality.

To turn the failing test from red to green (from failure to success), you need to look at the second phase of the process: *implement just enough of the SUT so that the test passes*. Because this is currently the only test, you need not concern yourself with breaking any existing successful tests.

The behavior asserted with the test was that the balance was 200 after a transaction for that amount was added to a new account. Listing 4-5 shows the bare minimum needed to make the unit test pass.

LISTING 4-5 Always do the bare minimum when transitioning a test from red to green.

```
public class Account
{
    public Account()
    {
        Balance = 200m;
    }

    public void AddTransaction(decimal amount)
    {

    }

    public decimal Balance
    {
        get;
        private set;
    }
}
```

The changed code is highlighted in bold. To transition the test from red to green, the code has introduced a default constructor to the Account class that initializes the Balance property to 200m. To prove that this works—that the test now passes—Figure 4-2 shows a screenshot of the Visual Studio test runner after the failing test was rerun.

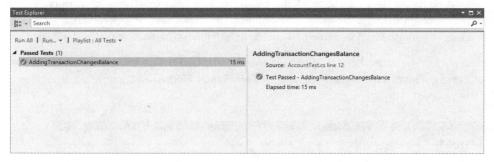

FIGURE 4-2 The test does, indeed, now pass—but is it correct?

Before you pat yourself on the back and move on to the final refactoring phase, you should assess whether this is the correct way to implement the expected behavior that the test specified. You can prove that it is *not* the correct implementation by adding another expectation in the form of another unit test.

The test to be added defines the expected value for the `Balance` field given a newly created `Account` object. Recall how the expected value of the `Balance` field was calculated after a transaction of $200 was added to the account; it included the *assumption* that an unspecified opening balance was *zero*. This is an expected behavior, just like any other, and so you should write a test that asserts that your expectations of the code are correctly implemented. Listing 4-6 shows the AAA pattern applied to such a unit test.

LISTING 4-6 The Arrange part of this test is omitted.

```
[TestMethod]
public void AccountsHaveAnOpeningBalanceOfZero()
{
    // Arrange

    // Act
    var account = new Account();

    // Assert
    Assert.AreEqual(0m, account.Balance);
}
```

First, notice that the name of the test method is again descriptive of the expected behavior that it asserts. In this case, though, the Arrange part of the unit test is blank, meaning that this part of the AAA syntax is optional. The part of the SUT that is being tested is the behavior of its default constructor, which is the only interaction with the SUT as part of the Act phase. The assertion, finally, codifies the previously stated assumption that a new `Account` will have a balance of 0m.

The fact that this unit test fails, even though the first unit test passes, indicates that the implementation of the expectations of the first unit test was erroneous. Figure 4-3 shows the output from the MSTest runner.

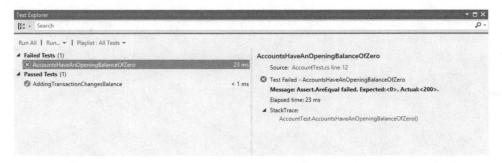

FIGURE 4-3 The second unit test fails because of the implementation of the first unit test's expectations.

From this position, if you revert your previous changes to the Account class, you will transition your failing *opening balance* test from red to green, while correctly causing your *adding transaction* test to fail again. By doing this, you have proven that you have the correct implementation of the Account class for the *opening balance* test, but the wrong implementation for the *adding transaction* test.

The effect of adding each new test is that further constraints are created on viable implementations of the SUT. Each test carries with it an expectation of behavior, and each expectation requires balancing in the SUT. The alternative simplest possible implementation to ensure that both tests pass is shown in Listing 4-7.

LISTING 4-7 Both tests now pass with this implementation, but is it correct?

```
public class Account
{
    public void AddTransaction(decimal amount)
    {
        Balance = 200m;
    }

    public decimal Balance
    {
        get;
        private set;
    }
}
```

The balance of a new account will now be zero on creation but will change to 200m when a call is made to AddTransaction. Of course, despite the fact that both tests now pass, intuition should tell you that this is absolutely wrong. The point of writing the simplest thing first—rather than jumping directly to the obvious correct solution—is to derive coded assertions from your intuition. Can you write another unit test that fails and proves that this implementation is not right? Listing 4-8 shows an example.

LISTING 4-8 This test is identical to the prior version but has a different amount value.

```
[TestMethod]
public void Adding100TransactionChangesBalance()
{
    // Arrange
    var account = new Account();

    // Act
    account.AddTransaction(100m);

    // Assert
    Assert.AreEqual(100m, account.Balance);
}
```

This test method does the same job as the first, which tested adding a transaction, but it adds a transaction of $100 rather than $200. Although the differentiating factor is small, it is sufficient to prove that the `Account.AddTransaction` method is wrong.

As expected, this new test fails. If you alter the `Account` class so that the value 100m is hardcoded into the `AddTransaction` method, you will fail the original test and transition this test from red to green. Instead, you can now implement the correct solution, as Listing 4-9 shows.

LISTING 4-9 All three tests pass with this implementation, but it is *still* wrong!

```
public class Account
{
    public void AddTransaction(decimal amount)
    {
        Balance = amount;
    }

    public decimal Balance
    {
        get;
        private set;
    }
}
```

With this implementation in place and all three of your unit tests passing—all having previously failed—the sun is shining and everything is right in the world. Except that it isn't! Again, the expectations of the `AddTransaction` method do not match up to the reality of the implementation. A fourth unit test highlights the problem, as Listing 4-10 shows.

LISTING 4-10 This unit test should finally help crack the `AddTransaction` method.

```
[TestMethod]
public void AddingTwoTransactionsCreatesSummationBalance()
{
    // Arrange
    var account = new Account();
    account.AddTransaction(50m);

    // Act
    account.AddTransaction(75m);

    // Assert
    Assert.AreEqual(125m, account.Balance);
}
```

This test finally allows you to discover the absolutely right functionality of the `AddTransaction` method—at least for the moment. The point is that, with requirements changing and new features being added, you need to codify your expectations of your classes so that you can fall back on existing unit tests, which form a safety net. Without this, you could easily make a change to your code that appears to work in the narrow circumstances under which you are manually testing it, but that breaks under unusual input or breaks something ostensibly unrelated elsewhere.

The test you have added asserts that an account's balance is the summation of all of its transactions. Previously, your most correct implementation would set the balance to the value of the last transaction that occurred, meaning that this test will fail and your implementation is not yet right. Listing 4-11 shows the implementation of the AddTransaction method that allows all four unit tests to pass.

LISTING 4-11 This implementation is so far the best for AddTransaction.

```
public class Account
{
    public void AddTransaction(decimal amount)
    {
        Balance += amount;
    }

    public decimal Balance
    {
        get;
        private set;
    }
}
```

After the transition from red to green for each unit test, you had the opportunity to refactor the implementation of the SUT, but this example was very simple. This phase of the process becomes more important with each new method added to the SUT. Refactoring in this manner is covered in more detail later in this chapter.

More complex tests

The previous example involved unit testing a class that forms part of the domain model of an application in a test-first manner. As described in Chapter 2, "Dependencies and layering," the domain model is an implementation of a business logic layer that sits between the user interface and the data access layers.

Specification

For the next set of tests, which build on this Account class, you will test a different part of the business logic layer: a service. The user interface for this hypothetical application could be tethered to any framework—ASP.NET MVC, Windows Presentation Foundation (WPF), or Windows Forms—and your service should be reusable regardless of the framework. This means that the service will contain no dependency specific to any of these frameworks, but it will depend on the Account class, though indirectly. Figure 4-4 shows the dependencies between the layers and classes that will form this example.

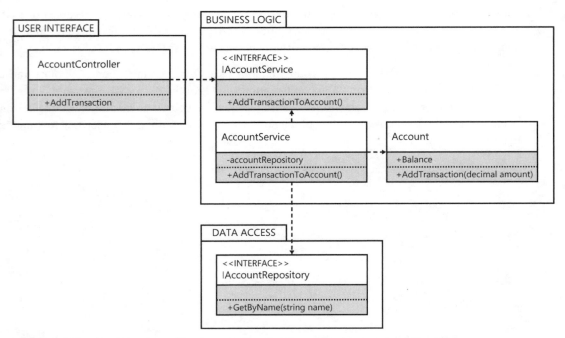

FIGURE 4-4 The dependencies and implementations that form the subsystem you will now test.

The Unified Modeling Language (UML) diagram shows the three packages that make up the three-layered architecture that you will create. The user interface will contain Model-View-Controller (MVC) controllers, although these could be view models or presenters for Model-View-ViewModel (MVVM) or Model-View-Presenter (MVP), respectively. Specifically, the `AccountController` will have a handler for the user interface action of adding a transaction to an account. This controller has a dependency on the interface of the `AccountService` that you are preparing to implement.

The `AccountService` lives in the business logic layer, along with its interface and the domain model, represented by the `Account` class that was previously implemented. Note that the packages represent the logical layers of the application, as opposed to mapping directly to Visual Studio projects and, therefore, to assemblies. This means that you are still preferring the Stairway pattern over the Entourage anti-pattern. The `AccountService` will require some way to retrieve `Account` instances from whichever persistent storage you are using. Because you are using a domain model in the business logic layer, the data access layer is implemented by using an Object/Relational Mapper (ORM).

A repository interface is used to hide the specific persistence logic from client code. The `IAccountRepository` is responsible for returning `Account` instances. The service depends on this interface because it will need to retrieve an account as part of its implementation.

Designing the test

The tests for the `AccountService.AddTransactionToAccount` method are written by using TDD and AAA, exactly as before. First, you need to think of what to expect of the method: that it delegates to the correct `Account` instance's `AddTransaction` method, passing in the correct value for the transaction amount. Let's specify the Arrange, Act, and Assert phases:

- **Arrange** Ensure that there is an available instance of the SUT—the `AccountService` class.

- **Act** Call the `AddTransactionToAccount` method.

- **Assert** The SUT calls the `AddTransaction` method on an `Account` instance, passing in the correct `amount` value.

Listing 4-12 shows a first attempt at writing this test.

LISTING 4-12 The first attempt at this new test is incomplete.

```
[TestClass]
public class AccountServiceTests
{
    [TestMethod]
    public void AddingTransactionToAccountDelegatesToAccountInstance()
    {
        // Arrange
        var sut = new AccountService();

        // Act
        sut.AddTransactionToAccount("Trading Account", 200m);

        // Assert
        Assert.Fail();
    }
}
```

Everything looks fine until you get to the assertion. The assertion is that a certain method is called on an object and a particular value is passed in, but how do you assert that? This is where *mocks* come in.

Testing with fakes

The first requirement before you can write your assertion is an `Account` instance to assert against. The `IAccountRepository` interface will be used by the `AccountService` to retrieve the `Account` that it will interact with, so you cannot just give the `AccountService` such an instance. Instead, you need to give the `AccountService` an `IAccountRepository`—but you do not have any implementations available. Because you depend on interfaces, instead of classes, you can write a fake implementation of an interface that will be sufficient only for the test. Listing 4-13 shows such a class, which lives in the unit testing assembly.

LISTING 4-13 A very simple implementation of a repository that is only for testing purposes.

```
public class FakeAccountRepository : IAccountRepository
{
    public FakeAccountRepository(Account account)
    {
        this.account = account;
    }

    public Account GetByName(string accountName)
    {
        return account;
    }

    private Account account;
}
```

You can now edit your account service implementation so that you can provide this fake repository. Listing 4-14 shows the new implementation of the `AccountService` class.

LISTING 4-14 The present state of the account service class.

```
public class AccountService : IAccountService
{
    public AccountService(IAccountRepository repository)
    {
        this.repository = repository;
    }

    public void AddTransactionToAccount(string uniqueAccountName, decimal
transactionAmount)
    {

    }

    private readonly IAccountRepository repository;
}
```

The unit test can now be completed, with new Arrange criteria:

- Ensure that there is an `Account` instance available to assert against.

- Ensure that there is a fake `IAccountRepository` instance available to pass to the service on construction.

These criteria, and the correct assertion, form the failing test in Listing 4-15.

LISTING 4-15 This test fails for the right reasons: the service method is not yet implemented.

```
[TestClass]
public class AccountServiceTests
{
    [TestMethod]
    public void AddingTransactionToAccountDelegatesToAccountInstance()
    {
        // Arrange
        var account = new Account();
        var fakeRepository = new FakeAccountRepository(account);
        var sut = new AccountService(fakeRepository);

        // Act
        sut.AddTransactionToAccount("Trading Account", 200m);

        // Assert
        Assert.AreEqual(200m, account.Balance);
    }
}
```

First you create an account that has an opening balance of zero. You then create an instance of your fake account repository, passing into it your account. Because the fake implements the interface of an account repository, the fake can easily be passed to the AccountService class, your SUT.

After calling the method that is the target of the test, you then assert that the account has the expected balance of 200m. As demonstrated by Figure 4-5, this assertion fails because the target method has not yet been implemented.

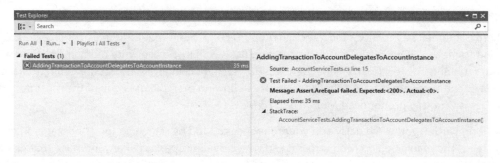

FIGURE 4-5 Continuing the red-to-green transition, you have your failing test.

Now that you have a unit test that specifies some behavior that is missing from your production code, you can do the simplest thing possible to make the unit test pass, as shown in Listing 4-16.

LISTING 4-16 This implementation of the `AccountService` makes the test pass.

```
public class AccountService : IAccountService
{
    public AccountService(IAccountRepository repository)
    {
        this.repository = repository;
    }

    public void AddTransactionToAccount(string uniqueAccountName, decimal
transactionAmount)
    {
        var account = repository.GetByName(uniqueAccountName);
        account.AddTransaction(transactionAmount);
    }

    private readonly IAccountRepository repository;
}
```

The unit test has guided you into doing the right thing in this implementation. You had to use the repository to retrieve the account, and you had to call the `AddTransaction` method on that account to mutate the read-only `Balance` property. If anyone subsequently breaks this method so that it no longer matches the expectations set out in the unit test, you will know about it very quickly.

Testing with mocks

It requires little power of the imagination to realize that mocking by writing fakes can quickly become laborious. Imagine all of the permutations of unit tests that you might write, and all of the different interfaces that your SUTs might need. This is a lot of extra code just to support your unit test.

There is another way to mock the `IAccountRepository`, but it requires the use of an external mocking framework. One positive aspect of writing fakes is that you can write them in isolation without requiring any third-party dependencies. However, mocking frameworks are commonplace nowadays, and there are many to choose from. The following example uses one of the most popular: Moq. This is variously pronounced *Moh-kyoo* and *Mok*.

By using NuGet, you can quickly add your reference to Moq by searching for its package on the online feed. The magic behind Moq is that it can create dynamic proxies of any interface that you ask it to mock. You will edit your existing test to use a Moq mock instead of your manual fake, as shown in Listing 4-17.

LISTING 4-17 Mocking frameworks such as Moq allow you to create mocks very easily.

```
[TestMethod]
public void AddingTransactionToAccountDelegatesToAccountInstance()
{
    // Arrange
    var account = new Account();
    var mockRepository = new Mock<IAccountRepository>();
    mockRepository.Setup(r => r.GetByName("Trading Account")).Returns(account);
    var sut = new AccountService(mockRepository.Object);

    // Act
    sut.AddTransactionToAccount("Trading Account", 200m);

    // Assert
    Assert.AreEqual(200m, account.Balance);
}
```

The changes to the test are highlighted in bold. Rather than instantiating your own fake repository, you now create a new Mock<IAccountRepository>() object. This object is very powerful and allows you to set all sorts of expectations and behavior on your mocked interfaces. This class does not implement your interface, so, unlike your fake, it is not directly a viable instance of the IAccount-Repository. This is because the Common Language Runtime (CLR) does not allow classes to inherit from generic parameters. Instead, there is a composition relationship between the mock and the proxy instance that it creates. The Object property allows you to access the underlying mocked interface, which is passed in to the AccountService in this example.

Before you provide your mock to the SUT, you need to specify how it should behave. By default, Moq defines *loose* mocks, which means that all of their return values are default. The default for any reference type is null and this applies to the Account class. The alternative to the loose mock is the *strict* mock, which will throw an exception whenever it is faced with a method call or property access that you have not already specified. Neither of these options is what you need, so you have to set up some expected behavior manually.

The Setup method of a Mock instance is very clever. It accepts a lambda expression that provides an instance of the underlying mocked type as a context parameter. By calling a method on the type, you are effectively specifying that you want something to happen when the method is called, with the exact arguments provided. What you choose to specify depends on your test situation. Moq lets you set the following expectations on a method call:

- Call some other lambda expression.

- Return a specific value.

- Throw a specified type of exception.

- Verify that this method was called.

For this test, you want the second option: return a specified value. The fluent interface of the `Mock.Setup` method call allows you to chain the call to the `Returns` method. This improves readability and reduces what is already becoming a rather large Arrange phase of the test. The `Returns` method is given the `Account` instance that you have already created, and with this you have completed setting your expectations of this mock. In brief, you have given the mock the following instruction:

> When the `GetByName` method is called for this `IAccountRepository` instance, and the account name provided is "`Trading Account`", return this instance of the `Account` class.

When you run your test again it will pass, just as before, as proven by Figure 4-6.

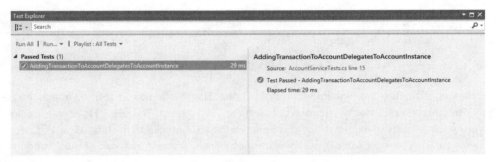

FIGURE 4-6 After being mocked with stubs, the test passes again.

Before you rejoice, you need to acknowledge that you have cheated. You have edited a unit test and not transitioned it from red to green. The test was already successful and, perhaps despite the change, it is still successful. In order to fail this test and then verify that it only passes as a result of a correctly implemented SUT, you should remove the code inside the `AddTransactionToAccount` method. When you do so, the test will pass, and reinstating the code causes the test to succeed. This is an important part of the unit test editing process that avoids false positives—that is, it prevents you from writing a test that succeeds despite not being implemented correctly.

Mocks and test over-specification

Testing with mocks is a common but potentially onerous practice. Tests that rely on mocks can easily become *over-specified*. An over-specified test is fragile, but you can avoid this fragility by changing what you assert. The problem arises when the test includes intimate knowledge of how the system under test (SUT) works. In other words, a test is over-specified when it has knowledge of the SUT's *implementation* rather than its expected *behavior*.

A unit test that uses mocks might need to know how the SUT is implemented. However, you should always remember that a unit test is a specification of expected behavior, so you should avoid introducing tests against implementation details. Such details include calls to other interfaces on which the SUT might depend. If you assert that a method on an interface must be called, the test has become wedded not to a certain behavior but to a specific implementation.

Over-specified tests are undesirable because they prevent refactoring of the production code that they test. A suite of passing unit tests accompanying a method or class is a signal that the implementation of the method or class can be altered with impunity: the only way that the tests will fail is if the expected behavior of the code is broken. Over-specified tests do not provide such a guarantee, because they will fail if the implementation of the method or class has changed—even if the expected behavior remains intact.

There are two options for avoiding test over-specification when testing with mocks. The first is to test behavior only. State-based tests are the best example of testing expected behavior. If a method accepts data as input and returns altered data as output, the method can be treated as a black box for testing purposes. If the method accepts inputs A, B, and C and returns outputs X, Y, and Z, it is irrelevant to the test how it arrived at such answers. The method can then be refactored without breaking the unit tests.

The second option is less attractive but is sometimes the only option. You can treat the unit test and the implementation that it tests as one atomic unit: if one changes, so must the other. This is akin to accepting that the unit test is over-specified and planning to throw away the unit test along with the production implementation if a refactor is ever required. This isn't quite as wasteful as it might seem. As you'll see in Part II, "Writing SOLID code," SOLID code yields smaller, more directed classes that are never altered anyway.

Further tests

Your first attempt at completing a working `AccountService` by using a TDD approach has been successful. There are potential problems that will require further tests to ensure that this method is much more robust. So far, you have tested only the *Happy Path*: the execution path through the code that yields no errors and causes no problems. There are a few gaps that need to be addressed:

- What if the account repository is a `null` reference?

- What if the repository cannot find the account?

- What if the account method throws an exception?

With each extra test that you write, you either uncover a defect that exists in your implementation (if the test fails) or you add extra confidence that your implementation is correct not only for the Happy Path, but also for error paths (if the test succeeds).

Under what circumstances might the account repository be a `null` reference? This will occur only if the `AccountService` is constructed with a `null` passed in as its constructor parameter. Because a valid account repository is a required dependency for the account service, you could say that this is a *precondition* of the constructor. Thus, you can write the test in Listing 4-18.

LISTING 4-18 No Arrange and no Assert, yet this is a valid test pattern for exceptions.

```
[TestMethod]
[ExpectedException(typeof(ArgumentNullException))]
public void CannotCreateAccountServiceWithNullAccountRepository()
{
    // Arrange

    // Act
    new AccountService(null);

    // Assert
}
```

This test is slightly different from the previous ones; the assertion is not in the usual place. MSTest requires you to apply the ExpectedExceptionAttribute to the test method with a parameter describing the type of exception that you require. What this test is specifying is that you expect an ArgumentNullException to be thrown if you construct an AccountService with a null reference for the IAccountRepository instance. This is precisely the precondition that you need, to ensure that in any method of the account service, you always have a valid instance of the repository and do not need to handle the case where it is null. This test fails for the right reasons, as shown here.

```
Test method ServiceTests.AccountServiceTests.CannotCreateAccountServiceWithNullAccountRepository
    did not throw an exception. An exception was expected by attribute
    Microsoft.VisualStudio.TestTools.UnitTesting.ExpectedExceptionAttribute defined on the test
    method.
```

To make this test pass, you need to implement the precondition. The manual approach is shown in Listing 4-19.

LISTING 4-19 Passing a null account repository into the constructor will cause an exception.

```
public AccountService(IAccountRepository repository)
{
    if (repository == null) throw new ArgumentNullException("repository", "A valid account
    repository must be supplied.");

    this.repository = repository;
}
```

The added line is in bold. This is an example of ensuring that you fail fast. Without this precondition, an exception would eventually have been thrown, but it would have been a NullReference-Exception and it would have occurred whenever you first tried to access the null repository.

With your constructor test passing, you can move on to the next test case: when the repository cannot find the account. Assume that your repository does not implement the Null Object pattern, which, as described in Chapter 3, "Interfaces and design patterns," would mean that it never returned a null object or threw an exception if the repository could not find the account requested. Instead, your repository should return a null reference for the account. Listing 4-20 shows the unit test that enforces the expected behavior for this case.

LISTING 4-20 No expected exception attribute and no assertion!

```
[TestMethod]
public void DoNotThrowWhenAccountIsNotFound()
{
    // Arrange
    var mockRepository = new Mock<IAccountRepository>();
    var sut = new AccountService(mockRepository.Object);

    // Act
    sut.AddTransactionToAccount("Trading Account", 100m);

    // Assert
}
```

The Assert phase of this test is blank, and there is no ExpectedException attribute, either. This is because your expectations are that there should *not* be an exception thrown during the Act phase of the test. If an exception is thrown at that point, the test fails. If an exception is not thrown—and there are no other assertions that could potentially fail—the test will *pass*, by default.

In the Arrange phase of the test, you mock the repository and pass it to the SUT (avoiding the precondition by providing a valid instance of the repository) but set up no expectations. This means that the call to IAccountRepository.GetByName() will return null. The next thing that you do with this return value is attempt to call Account.AddTransaction(). Because the instance is null, this causes a NullReferenceException and this test fails. To transition this test to green, you need to prevent this exception from being thrown in your method, as Listing 4-21 shows.

LISTING 4-21 The if statement protects this method from a NullReferenceException.

```
public void AddTransactionToAccount(string uniqueAccountName, decimal transactionAmount)
{
    var account = repository.GetByName(uniqueAccountName);
    if (account != null)
    {
        account.AddTransaction(transactionAmount);
    }
}
```

By adding a simple `if` statement that ensures that the account is not `null` before attempting to use it, you prevent the exception from being thrown, and the test passes.

The final extra test case required involves the behavior expected of the account service when the call to the account's `AddTransaction` method throws an exception. To avoid leaking dependencies between layers, it is good practice to wrap an exception thrown at a lower layer in a new exception for this layer. Figure 4-7 exemplifies this principle.

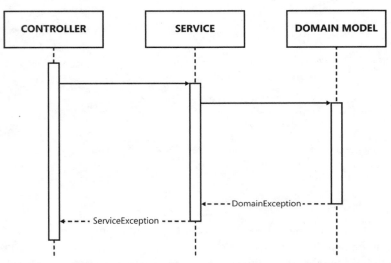

FIGURE 4-7 Each layer defines an exception type for wrapping exceptions at lower levels.

The exceptions that the domain model throws will be specific to that layer. If the service layer allows this to propagate up to the controller, the controller will have to have knowledge of the `Domain-Exception` type to effectively catch and handle these exceptions. This introduces a dependency between the controller and the domain model layer, which you want to avoid. Instead, the service will catch the domain model exceptions and *wrap* them in `ServiceException` instances before throwing them up to the controller. Due to the controller's dependency on the service layer, it is able to catch the exceptions that it defines. It is important to acknowledge that the `ServiceException` contains the `DomainException` as an inner exception—without this, you lose valuable context about why the original exception was thrown. Listing 4-22 shows the unit test required to enforce this behavior between your collaborating classes.

LISTING 4-22 The mock account is told to throw an exception when called.

```
[TestMethod]
[ExpectedException(typeof(ServiceException))]
public void AccountExceptionsAreWrappedInThrowServiceException()
{
    // Arrange
    var account = new Mock<Account>();
    account.Setup(a => a.AddTransaction(100m)).Throws<DomainException>();
    var mockRepository = new Mock<IAccountRepository>();
    mockRepository.Setup(r => r.GetByName("Trading Account")).Returns(account.Object);
    var sut = new AccountService(mockRepository.Object);

    // Act
    sut.AddTransactionToAccount("Trading Account", 100m);

    // Assert
}
```

The expected exception attribute is used to assert that the SUT throws a `ServiceException`, whereas the account mock is told to throw a `DomainException`. Therefore, it is up to the SUT to convert one to the other. Your method is not currently doing this, so this test correctly fails, as shown here.

```
Test method ServiceTests.AccountServiceTests.AccountExceptionsAreWrappedInThrowServiceException
  threw exception Domain.DomainException, but exception Services.ServiceException was expected.
  Exception message: Domain.DomainException: Exception of type 'Domain.DomainException' was
  thrown.
```

The expected exception attribute has determined that the exception thrown is not of the correct type compared to that which was specified. The code in Listing 4-23 shows the changes required to the AddTransactionToAccount method.

LISTING 4-23 The try/catch block is introduced to map one exception with another.

```
public void AddTransactionToAccount(string uniqueAccountName, decimal transactionAmount)
{
    var account = repository.GetByName(uniqueAccountName);
    if (account != null)
    {
        try
        {
            account.AddTransaction(transactionAmount);
        }
        catch(DomainException)
        {
            throw new ServiceException();
        }
    }
}
```

Although the introduction of the try/catch block transitions your test from red to green, there is an expectation missing, which means that this is still incomplete.

Writing tests for defect fixes

Imagine that you receive a defect report relating to the current example code. The report states:

> *I received a* `ServiceException` *when adding a transaction to my account.*

You proceed to reproduce the problem and discover the exception that is thrown—this is the proximate cause. But, because the DomainException has been replaced with the ServiceException, it is very difficult to understand the ultimate cause of the error. Your original expectation that the new exception should wrap the existing one has not been fulfilled because you missed an assertion in your unit tests.

When a defect arises in this manner, the first thing you should do is to write a failing unit test that captures two things: the exact reproduction steps required to force the defect to occur, and the expected behavior that is not currently enforced. Listing 4-24 shows both of these elements in a unit test that fails.

LISTING 4-24 You are now manually asserting against the thrown exception.

```
[TestMethod]
public void AccountExceptionsAreWrappedInThrowServiceException()
{
    // Arrange
    var account = new Mock<Account>();
    account.Setup(a => a.AddTransaction(100m)).Throws<DomainException>();
    var mockRepository = new Mock<IAccountRepository>();
    mockRepository.Setup(r => r.GetByName("Trading Account")).Returns(account.Object);
    var sut = new AccountService(mockRepository.Object);

    // Act
    try
    {
        sut.AddTransactionToAccount("Trading Account", 100m);
    }
    catch(ServiceException serviceException)
    {
        // Assert
        Assert.IsInstanceOfType(serviceException.InnerException, typeof(DomainException));
    }
}
```

For this test, the `ExpectedException` attribute alone is insufficient. You need to examine the `InnerException` property of the thrown exception and assert that it is a `DomainException`. This proves that you have wrapped the domain exception, preserving the original error that occurred. All software defects can be viewed as the result of a missing unit test: an incomplete specification of expected behavior. Listing 4-25 shows how to make the test pass by editing the production code.

LISTING 4-25 The original exception is now wrapped properly by the new exception.

```
public void AddTransactionToAccount(string uniqueAccountName, decimal transactionAmount)
{
    var account = repository.GetByName(uniqueAccountName);
    if (account != null)
    {
        try
        {
            account.AddTransaction(transactionAmount);
        }
        catch(DomainException domainException)
        {
            throw new ServiceException("An exception was thrown by a domain object",
    domainException);
        }
    }
}
```

By making this test pass, you can then go back and reproduce the original exception from the defect report and, this time, determine the ultimate cause of the problem.

Test setup

Let's take stock of the tests you have written so far. Each has progressively become more complex, with more code required to set up your expectations. It would be nice if you could factor this out somewhere in order to clean up the tests and shorten them a little. MSTest, like other unit testing frameworks, allows you to write a special initialization method that will be called at the start of every test in your test class. This setup method can be called anything you want, but it must be tagged with the `TestInitialize` attribute.

The code to put into this method is the code common to nearly all of the unit tests: instantiating the mock objects. You can store mock objects as private fields in the class so that they are still available to each test. You can also do the same with the SUT, because that only requires the mock repository as a constructor parameter and its construction doesn't depend on anything specific to each unit test. Listing 4-26 shows the changes required to the test class to support the setup method.

LISTING 4-26 The mock objects and the SUT can be constructed in a setup method.

```
[TestClass]
public class AccountServiceTests
{

    [TestInitialize]
    public void Setup()
    {
        mockAccount = new Mock<Account>();
        mockRepository = new Mock<IAccountRepository>();
        sut = new AccountService(mockRepository.Object);
    }

    private Mock<Account> mockAccount;
    private Mock<IAccountRepository> mockRepository;
    private AccountService sut;
}
```

With these objects constructed as part of a test initialization method, which is called individually for each test method, you can simplify some of the unit test code by removing this object construction. Listing 4-27 shows the changes made to the most recent unit test, `AccountExceptionsAre-WrappedInThrowServiceException`.

LISTING 4-27 This test is a little shorter and a little easier to read.

```
[TestMethod]
public void AccountExceptionsAreWrappedInThrowServiceException()
{
    // Arrange
    mockAccount.Setup(a => a.AddTransaction(100m)).Throws<DomainException>();
    mockRepository.Setup(r => r.GetByName("Trading Account")).Returns(mockAccount.Object);

    // Act
    try
    {
        sut.AddTransactionToAccount("Trading Account", 100m);
    }
    catch(ServiceException serviceException)
    {
        // Assert
        Assert.IsInstanceOfType(serviceException.InnerException, typeof(DomainException));
    }
}
```

Three lines might not be a huge amount of code to remove, but the cumulative effect on all of the unit tests is more readable code. You know that, by convention, any variable with the prefix mock will be a mocked object, whereas the variable sut is your system under test.

Refactoring

Your code will be more robust if you follow a TDD process that writes a failing unit test before moving on to implement the expected behavior. However, this code might not be as organized or understandable as it could be. There are many times during the course of writing code when you should stop writing unit tests and code, and instead focus on *refactoring*.

Refactoring is the process of improving the design of existing code—after it has already been written. Each refactor differs in size and scope. A refactor could be a small tweak to a variable name to aid clarity, or it could be a more sweeping architectural change such as splitting user interface logic from domain logic when the two have become inappropriately intimate.

Changing existing code

In the rest of this chapter, you are going to make incremental changes to a class that will, at every step, improve the code in some meaningful way. The Account class is the target for refactoring, but it has gained a new method since its previous use: CalculateRewardPoints. As with many companies, your clients want to reward customer loyalty through the accumulation of reward points. These points are earned by the customer depending on a variety of criteria. Listing 4-28 shows the new Account class.

LISTING 4-28 The new class tracks reward points in addition to the account's balance.

```
public class Account
{
    public Account(AccountType type)
    {
        this.type = type;
    }

    public decimal Balance
    {
        get;
        private set;
    }

    public int RewardPoints
    {
        get;
        private set;
    }

    public void AddTransaction(decimal amount)
    {
        RewardPoints += CalculateRewardPoints(amount);
        Balance += amount;
    }
}
```

```
public int CalculateRewardPoints(decimal amount)
{
    int points;
    switch(type)
    {
        case AccountType.Silver:
            points = (int)decimal.Floor(amount / 10);
            break;
        case AccountType.Gold:
            points = (int)decimal.Floor((Balance / 10000 * 5) + (amount / 5));
            break;
        case AccountType.Platinum:
            points = (int)decimal.Ceiling((Balance / 10000 * 10) + (amount / 2));
            break;
        default:
            points = 0;
            break;
    }
    return Math.Max(points, 0);
}

private readonly AccountType type;
}
```

The most important changes to the class are summarized thus:

■ A new property tracks the number of reward points that the customer has linked to this account.

■ Each account has a type code that indicates the tier of the account: Silver, Gold, or Platinum.

■ Whenever a transaction is added to the account, the customer earns reward points.

■ The number of reward points earned is dependent on multiple factors, which complicate the calculation method:

  • The account type—more points are earned at higher tiers.

  • The amount of the transaction—the more customers spend, the more points they earn.

  • The current balance of the account—the Gold and Platinum tiers give customers more points for keeping their balance high.

Assuming that this code has been written alongside its unit tests, those tests will help greatly by ensuring that changes do not affect the specified behavior. This is an important point—refactoring changes the *arrangement* of the code, not the *outcome*. If you tried to refactor without unit tests, how would you know if you inadvertently broke the expected behavior? You would not fail fast but much later at run time during testing or, worse, after deployment.

Replacing "magic numbers" with constants

The first refactor is a simple but nonetheless important improvement to the readability of the code. There are a lot of "magic numbers" littering the `CalculateRewardPoints` method. Six distinct numbers are used without any context as to what they mean or why they are required. To the person who wrote the code, their significance might be obvious because that person has prior knowledge of what it all means. In reality, that will probably only be true for a week, perhaps two, before the person's memory starts to fade and he loses track of what that 5, or that 2, means. Listing 4-29 shows the changes made to the class as a result of this refactor.

LISTING 4-29 This code is more readable to people unfamiliar with it.

```
public class Account
{
    public int CalculateRewardPoints(decimal amount)
    {
        int points;
        switch(type)
        {
            case AccountType.Silver:
                points = (int)decimal.Floor(amount / SilverTransactionCostPerPoint);
                break;
            case AccountType.Gold:
                points = (int)decimal.Floor((Balance / GoldBalanceCostPerPoint) + (amount
/ GoldTransactionCostPerPoint));
                break;
            case AccountType.Platinum:
                points = (int)decimal.Ceiling((Balance / PlatinumBalanceCostPerPoint) +
(amount / PlatinumTransactionCostPerPoint));
                break;
            default:
                points = 0;
                break;
        }
        return Math.Max(points, 0);
    }

    private const int SilverTransactionCostPerPoint = 10;
    private const int GoldTransactionCostPerPoint = 5;
    private const int PlatinumTransactionCostPerPoint = 2;

    private const int GoldBalanceCostPerPoint = 2000;
    private const int PlatinumBalanceCostPerPoint = 1000;
}
```

Each of the "magic numbers" has been replaced with an equivalent variable. There is a set of three variables for the cost-per-point denominator of the transaction amount, one per account type. Then there are two variables for the cost-per-point denominator of the balance amount, for the Gold and Platinum account types, which are the only two account types that offer this incentive.

The benefit of this refactor is that the code is now understandable to people who are unfamiliar with it, because you have explained what the values mean through the variable names. It would not be an improvement if you merely replaced the "magic numbers" with variables named A, B, or X. Try to choose variable names that explain concisely their purpose. Never be afraid of verbosity, and take every opportunity to self-document code through variable, class, and method names.

Replacing a conditional expression with polymorphism

The next refactor is more involved. The `switch` statement, which alters the `CalculateRewards` algorithm depending on the account type, is problematic for two reasons. First, it adversely affects readability but, more pressingly, it introduces a maintenance burden. Imagine that you are given a new requirement at some time in the future: a new account type. It has been decided that not enough people are meeting the criteria for the Silver account, so you need to create a new Bronze account. To add the Bronze account, you would need to edit the `Account` class and add tests to it. Editing existing code in this way, after it has been verified and deployed, should be avoided. Instead, you should look to other ways that you can extend code so that it is adaptable without being editable.

What you are aiming to achieve is to make it easier to add a new account type while improving the readability of the code. For this, you will take advantage of polymorphism. You will model the account types as different subclasses of the `Account` class. The Gold account type will be represented by the `GoldAccount` class, and the same is true of the `SilverAccount` and `PlatinumAccount`.

The first step is to define these classes, as shown in Listing 4-30.

LISTING 4-30 Each account type is now a distinct class.

```
public class SilverAccount
{
    public int CalculateRewardPoints(decimal amount)
    {
        return Math.Max((int)decimal.Floor(amount / SilverTransactionCostPerPoint), 0);
    }

    private const int SilverTransactionCostPerPoint = 10;
}
// ...
public class GoldAccount
{

    public decimal Balance
    {
        get;
        set;
    }

    public int CalculateRewardPoints(decimal amount)
    {
        return Math.Max((int)decimal.Floor((Balance / GoldBalanceCostPerPoint) + (amount /
    GoldTransactionCostPerPoint)), 0);
    }
```

```
        private const int GoldTransactionCostPerPoint = 5;
        private const int GoldBalanceCostPerPoint = 2000;
}
// …
public class PlatinumAccount
{

    public decimal Balance
    {
        get;
        set;
    }

    public int CalculateRewardPoints(decimal amount)
    {
        return Math.Max((int)decimal.Ceiling((Balance / PlatinumBalanceCostPerPoint) +
(amount / PlatinumTransactionCostPerPoint)), 0);
    }

    private const int PlatinumTransactionCostPerPoint = 2;
    private const int PlatinumBalanceCostPerPoint = 1000;
}
```

Note that, at this stage, the original Account class has not been changed. These classes have been created as stand-alone classes. The unit tests for these classes would mirror the expectations of the CalculateRewardPoints class, but with a different SUT for each account type. The algorithms for determining the reward points due on the Platinum and Gold classes have a dependency on the current balance; that has been included so that these classes compile in isolation. The Balance property is also publically settable, which enables unit testing with different values. The UML class diagram in Figure 4-8 explains how these classes are related.

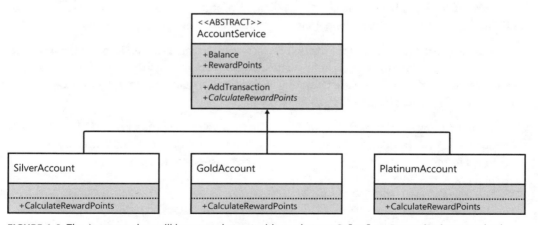

FIGURE 4-8 The Account class will become abstract with an abstract CalculateRewardPoints method.

This is merely an objective on the way to completing the goal of replacing the `switch` statement, of course. It is important not to do too much all at once, so that you can verify that you are on the right track with a succession of smaller changes. The next change, in Listing 4-31, is to link all four classes into an inheritance hierarchy.

LISTING 4-31 The complexity has been removed from the Account class.

```
public abstract class AccountBase
{
    public decimal Balance
    {
        get;
        private set;
    }

    public int RewardPoints
    {
        get;
        private set;
    }

    public void AddTransaction(decimal amount)
    {
        RewardPoints += CalculateRewardPoints(amount);
        Balance += amount;
    }

    public abstract int CalculateRewardPoints(decimal amount);
}
```

Without the `switch` statement, there is no reason for this class to be aware of its "type" anymore, so the constructor has been removed, too. The class is abstract due to the abstract calculation method, but this means that you can no longer instantiate it and, consequently, you can no longer test it.

An object instance is needed for the unit tests to work, so the next step is to link the three account types as subclasses of this base. A useful naming convention—along with prefixing interface names with a capital *I*—is to suffix abstract classes with *Base*. This a quick clue that the class cannot be instantiated and has associated subclasses.

When the three subclasses are created, you can remove the `Balance` property from the `Gold-Account` and `PlatinumAccount` because they will inherit the `Balance` and `AddTransaction` members from this base. Listing 4-32 shows all three classes after this step.

LISTING 4-32 Completing the refactor by inheriting from the base class.

```
public class SilverAccount : AccountBase
{
    public override int CalculateRewardPoints(decimal amount)
    {
        return Math.Max((int)decimal.Floor(amount / SilverTransactionCostPerPoint), 0);
    }

    private const int SilverTransactionCostPerPoint = 10;
}
// . . .
public class GoldAccount : AccountBase
{
    public override int CalculateRewardPoints(decimal amount)
    {
        return Math.Max((int)decimal.Floor((Balance / GoldBalanceCostPerPoint) + (amount /
    GoldTransactionCostPerPoint)), 0);
    }

    private const int GoldTransactionCostPerPoint = 5;
    private const int GoldBalanceCostPerPoint = 2000;
}
// . . .
public class PlatinumAccount : AccountBase
{
    public override int CalculateRewardPoints(decimal amount)
    {
        return Math.Max((int)decimal.Ceiling((Balance / PlatinumBalanceCostPerPoint) +
(amount / PlatinumTransactionCostPerPoint)), 0);
    }

    private const int PlatinumTransactionCostPerPoint = 2;
    private const int PlatinumBalanceCostPerPoint = 1000;
}
```

The refactor is now complete. From this point, it is easy to add a new account type by creating a subclass of the AccountBase and providing an implementation of the required CalculateReward-Points method. No existing code would have to be changed; you would just have to write a few unit tests to exercise the new algorithm for calculating reward points.

Replacing a constructor with a factory method

During the course of improving the Account class, there has probably been an adverse effect elsewhere in the code. Clients of the class were expecting to construct the account objects by using the Account constructor, and to pass in the type of account required. What will you now provide them by way of creating the correct account subclass for their situation?

The AccountType enumeration can be reused as a parameter to a new factory method on the AccountBase. Whereas a constructor, in conjunction with the new operator, returns an instance of the type in which it resides, a factory method is able to return many different types of object, all of which belong to the same inheritance hierarchy. Listing 4-33 shows such a factory method implemented on the base class.

LISTING 4-33 The switch statement returns, but in simplified form.

```
public abstract class AccountBase
{
    public static AccountBase CreateAccount(AccountType type)
    {
        AccountBase account = null;
        switch(type)
        {
            case AccountType.Silver:
                account = new SilverAccount();
                break;
            case AccountType.Gold:
                account = new GoldAccount();
                break;
            case AccountType.Platinum:
                account = new PlatinumAccount();
                break;
        }
        return account;
    }
}
```

There are two key features of the factory method that alleviate the burden on clients. First, it is static, meaning that clients call it on the type, rather than on an instance of that type. Second, the return type is the base class, allowing you to hide the subclass accounts from clients. In fact, you can hide them to the degree that they are internal and therefore invisible outside of this assembly. This disallows clients from directly constructing the subclasses, eliminating the new operator as a potential code smell. Listing 4-34 compares how a client would interact with the account before and after the refactor.

Although a switch statement still remains, it is far simpler in this instance and facilitates the prior refactor where it was replaced with polymorphism.

LISTING 4-34 How the AccountService creates a new account before and after the refactor.

```
public void CreateAccount(AccountType accountType)
{
    var newAccount = new Account(accountType);
    accountRepository.NewAccount(newAccount);
}
// . . .
public void CreateAccount(AccountType accountType)
{
    var newAccount = AccountBase.CreateAccount(accountType);
    accountRepository.NewAccount(newAccount);
}
```

This code is an example of how a client—in this case, the `AccountService`—would construct a new account before and after the refactor. The difference is negligible, but note that the new operator has been removed and replaced with the static call to the factory method. This is a common way to replace something very rigid with something much more adaptive. Factory methods open up many more possibilities because of what they can return, compared to methods that always return the same type.

Observant readers will note that the choice of a static factory method is suboptimal—it is a skyhook rather than a crane and thus affects the testability and adaptability of the code. A better implementation would place the `CreateAccount` method on a suitable interface, as explored in the next section.

Replacing a constructor with a factory class

There is an alternative to the factory method: the factory class. In fact, you do not need to couple clients to the implementation of a stand-alone factory, you can just give them the interface, as in Listing 4-35.

LISTING 4-35 The account factory hides the implementation details of creating an account instance.

```
public interface IAccountFactory
{
    AccountBase CreateAccount(AccountType accountType);
}
```

The interface of the method is actually identical to that of the factory method, except for the fact that it is an instance method. The implementation *could* be identical to the previous method body, meaning that it has perfect knowledge of all of the different types of account. The `AccountService`, and other clients, would then require this interface as a constructor parameter, as shown in Listing 4-36.

LISTING 4-36 The service now receives a factory as a constructor parameter and uses it to create the account.

```
public class AccountService
{
    public AccountService(IAccountFactory accountFactory, IAccountRepository
  accountRepository)
    {
        this.accountFactory = accountFactory;
        this.accountRepository = accountRepository;
    }

    public void CreateAccount(AccountType accountType)
    {
        var newAccount = accountFactory.CreateAccount(accountType);
        accountRepository.NewAccount(newAccount);
    }

    private readonly IAccountRepository accountRepository;
    private readonly IAccountFactory accountFactory;
}
```

This service is starting to look as it should: an orchestration of more fine-grained interfaces designed to achieve a larger goal for the user interface layer. It is, for reasons of brevity and clarity, missing some guard clauses on the constructor, to prevent null dependencies, and some try/catch blocks on the `CreateAccount` method, to marshal domain exceptions to service exceptions.

A new account type

At this point, can you be confident enough that a request for a new account type results in minimal changes to existing code? Yes and no. In one case, you can trivially add an account, but in another, you will find that your current model makes some wrong assumptions that form *technical debt*.

A new reward account

Imagine that your client wants to add another kind of account—a Bronze account—that earns half of the reward points that the Silver account does. There are only two changes that need to be made to support this in the domain layer. First, you need to create a new subclass of the `AccountBase` class, as in Listing 4-37.

LISTING 4-37 The Bronze account is added as a new account type.

```
internal class BronzeAccount : AccountBase
{
    public override int CalculateRewardPoints(decimal amount)
    {
        return Math.Max((int)decimal.Floor(amount / BronzeTransactionCostPerPoint), 0);
    }

    private const int BronzeTransactionCostPerPoint = 20;
}
```

This is a simple change that involves new unit tests to provide your expectations, and a new class that provides the algorithm for calculating reward points for this class.

Whether you have a factory class or a factory method, you need to change it to support your new account type, along with the enumeration that defines possible account types to be created. Listing 4-38 shows how a factory class would change to support the new Bronze account.

```
public AccountBase CreateAccount(AccountType accountType)
{
    AccountBase account = null;
    switch (accountType)
    {
        case AccountType.Bronze:
            account = new BronzeAccount();
            break;
        case AccountType.Silver:
            account = new SilverAccount();
            break;
        case AccountType.Gold:
            account = new GoldAccount();
            break;
        case AccountType.Platinum:
            account = new PlatinumAccount();
            break;
    }
    return account;
}
```

Before moving on to the next new account for the client, is there any way you can refactor this method so that you do not have to amend it for every account? You cannot use the refactor detailed earlier in the "Replacing a conditional expression with polymorphism" section, because this is a result of such a refactor. Instead, is there a way to construct an AccountBase from an accountType name without directly referencing each value and subclass? Listing 4-39 provides the answer.

LISTING 4-39 If the accounts follow a certain naming convention, this factory will suffice for all account subclasses.

```
public AccountBase CreateAccount(string accountType)
{
    var objectHandle = Activator.CreateInstance(null, string.Format("{0}Account",
  accountType));
    return (AccountBase)objectHandle.Unwrap();
}
```

Note that the enumeration has been dropped in favor of a more flexible string value. This could be a problem, because any string value could be provided, rather than only those that match valid account types. Of course, this is the point of the exercise.

This sort of refactor is a little risky because it is in danger of creating a leaky abstraction of the factory—it might not work in all required scenarios. Several things have to be true before this sort of code is viable:

- Each account type must follow a naming convention of *[Type]Account*, where the *[Type]* prefix is the value of the enumeration.

- Each account type must be contained in the same assembly as this factory method.

- Each account type must have a public default constructor—the types cannot be parameterized with any values.

Due to these constraints, this usually means that you have refactored too much, and it causes problems later when one of these constraints needs to be circumvented. Proceed with caution.

Code smell: Refused bequest

Sometime after the launch of the new reward card scheme, the client's marketing department asks how many people are assigned to each account type. Your answer leads them to conclude that they have a 100-percent uptake in the reward card scheme: that every single customer has either a Bronze, Silver, Gold, or Platinum reward card. But this is not so. There was no provision made for creating an account that was *not* part of the reward card scheme, thus everyone was given a Bronze account by default. As a result of this conversation, another new account type is required: the Standard account.

This account serves a different purpose—it does not earn any reward points. There are two ways of modeling this. First, you can create a new `AccountBase` subclass, show in Listing 4-40, which does nothing in its `CalculateRewardPoints` override but return zero, effectively accumulating no points.

LISTING 4-40 A simple account without any reward point calculation.

```
internal class StandardAccount : AccountBase
{
    public override int CalculateRewardPoints(decimal amount)
    {
        return 0;
    }
}
```

The alternative solution is to acknowledge that not all accounts have reward points and, in fact, there are two different types in the domain model. In such a circumstance, rather than provide a "default implementation" for the `CalculateRewardPoints` method, the subclass effectively *refuses* what the superclass has *bequeathed* to it—hence the code smell "refused bequest." In the prior example, the StandardAccount has refused to implement the interface rather than to ignore it, whereas the next refactor will refuse the interface altogether.

Replacing inheritance with delegation

In practice, this means that you need to split the AccountBase class into two parts. Some of the interface will remain on the account, with some of it moving to a new class hierarchy to represent reward cards. In this way, the inheritance of accounts is replaced with delegation to reward cards.

The first change is to introduce a new IRewardCard interface to define the properties and behavior of each reward card, as shown in Listing 4-41.

LISTING 4-41 The reward points and their calculation have moved away from the Account class.

```
public interface IRewardCard
{
    int RewardPoints
    {
        get;
    }

    void CalculateRewardPoints(decimal transactionAmount, decimal accountBalance);
}
```

Previously, these two members were part of the AccountBase class, but they have been moved out because they are wholly dependent on the presence of reward cards. Note that the interface of CalculateRewardPoints has changed in two ways. First, there is no longer a return value on this method, because it is expected to mutate the RewardPoints property directly. Second, you must pass in the account balance as a parameter to this method because it is no longer available. This is an important side effect of splitting the two objects up in this manner: any context not directly encapsulated by the reward card object will need to be handed to it. This might cause the interface of this method to change in the future.

Listing 4-42 shows the implementations of this interface for the Bronze and Platinum cards after the refactor.

LISTING 4-42 Examples of the reward card implementations.

```
internal class BronzeRewardCard : IRewardCard
{
    public int RewardPoints
    {
        get;
        private set;
    }

    public void CalculateRewardPoints(decimal transactionAmount, decimal accountBalance)
    {
        RewardPoints += Math.Max((int)decimal.Floor(transactionAmount /
    BronzeTransactionCostPerPoint), 0);
    }
    private const int BronzeTransactionCostPerPoint = 20;
}
// . . .
internal class PlatinumRewardCard : IRewardCard
{
    public int RewardPoints
    {
        get;
        private set;
    }

    public void CalculateRewardPoints(decimal transactionAmount, decimal accountBalance)
    {
        RewardPoints += Math.Max((int)decimal.Ceiling((accountBalance /
PlatinumBalanceCostPerPoint) + (transactionAmount / PlatinumTransactionCostPerPoint)), 0);
    }

    private const int PlatinumTransactionCostPerPoint = 2;
    private const int PlatinumBalanceCostPerPoint = 1000;
}
```

These classes are very similar to their previous incarnation, with an extra local RewardPoints property.

As shown in Listing 4-43, the Account class is no longer abstract and therefore no longer requires the Base suffix. For construction, it accepts an IRewardCard instance and delegates to this when adding a transaction. Overall, this account looks more like it used to before the initial requirement for capturing reward points.

LISTING 4-43 Each account contains a reward card.

```
public class Account
{
    public Account(IRewardCard rewardCard)
    {
        this.rewardCard = rewardCard;
    }

    public decimal Balance
    {
        get;
        private set;
    }

    public void AddTransaction(decimal amount)
    {
        rewardCard.CalculateRewardPoints(amount, Balance);
        Balance += amount;
    }

    private readonly IRewardCard rewardCard;
}
```

To model a Standard account—an account without a reward card—you can either pass in `null` for the reward card constructor dependency (and protect against a `NullReferenceException` by testing for `null` before delegating) or you can model a `NullRewardCard`. The latter would be an implementation of the Null Object pattern that would not accumulate any reward points when `CalculateRewardPoints` was called.

Conclusion

This chapter has been a hybrid of unit testing and refactoring because the two should be paired together and performed in tandem.

Each unit test you write should represent an expectation of the code that, ideally, should be communicable to a layperson. Although as code they are technical artifacts, unit tests enforce real-world behavior in objects, just as those objects encapsulate real-world concepts.

When you diligently follow a test-first approach, you write no new production code without first constructing a failing unit test. Then you write the simplest production code possible to transition the unit test from a red failure state to a green success state. Taken to its logical conclusion, the production code becomes a natural side effect of fulfilling the expectations of its unit tests.

When you unit test code, you give yourself a firm foundation to subsequently alter the production code to make it clearly more adaptive to future requirements. The refactoring of code is an incremental process of improving the code's design. There are many options for refactoring, only some of which were explored in this chapter. Each option available might represent a tradeoff in one area for a certain improvement in another, and—as with many aspects of programming—the process is quite subjective.

With this chapter complete, the Agile foundation part of this book is closed. Next you will look at SOLID code and how it will help to further increase the adaptability of your code.

PART II

Writing SOLID code

SOLID is the acronym for a set of practices that, when implemented together, make code adaptive to change. The SOLID practices were introduced by Bob Martin almost 15 years ago. Even so, these practices are not as widely known as they could be—and perhaps should be.

In this part, a chapter is devoted to each of the SOLID principles:

- **S**   The single responsibility principle
- **O**   The open/closed principle
- **L**   The Liskov substitution principle
- **I**   Interface segregation
- **D**   Dependency injection

Even taken in isolation, each of these principles is a worthy practice that any software developer would do well to learn. When used in collaboration, these patterns give code a completely different structure—one that lends itself to change.

However, take note that these patterns and practices, just like all others, are merely tools for you to use. Deciding when and where to apply any pattern or practice is part of the art of software development. Overuse leads to code that is adaptive, but on too fine-grained a level to be appreciated or useful. Overuse also affects another key facet of code quality: readability. It is far more common for software to be developed in teams than as an individual pursuit. Thus, judiciously selecting when and where to apply each pattern, practice, or SOLID principle is imperative to ensure that the code remains comprehensible in the future.

CHAPTER 5

The single responsibility principle

After completing this chapter, you will be able to

- Understand the importance of the single responsibility principle.

- Identify classes that have too many responsibilities.

- Write modules, classes, and methods that have a single responsibility.

- Refactor monolithic classes into smaller classes with single responsibilities.

- Use design patterns to separate responsibilities.

The single responsibility principle (SRP) instructs developers to write code that has one *and only one* reason to change. If a class has more than one reason to change, it has more than one responsibility. Classes with more than a single responsibility should be broken down into smaller classes, each of which should have only one responsibility and reason to change.

This chapter explains that process and shows you how to create classes that only have a single responsibility but are still useful. Through a process of delegation and abstraction, a class that contains too many reasons to change should delegate one or more responsibilities to other classes.

It is difficult to overstate the importance of delegating to abstractions. It is the lynchpin of adaptive code and, without it, developers would struggle to adapt to changing requirements in the way that Scrum and other Agile processes demand.

Problem statement

To better explain the problem with having classes that hold too many responsibilities, this section explores an example. Listing 5-1 shows a simple batch processor class that reads records from a file and updates a database. Despite its small size, you need to continually add features to this batch processor so that it meets the needs of your business.

LISTING 5-1 An example of a class with too many responsibilities.

```
public class TradeProcessor
{
    public void ProcessTrades(System.IO.Stream stream)
    {
        // read rows
        var lines = new List<string>();
        using(var reader = new System.IO.StreamReader(stream))
        {
            string line;
            while((line = reader.ReadLine()) != null)
            {
                lines.Add(line);
            }
        }

        var trades = new List<TradeRecord>();

        var lineCount = 1;
        foreach(var line in lines)
        {
            var fields = line.Split(new char[] { ',' });

            if(fields.Length != 3)
            {
                Console.WriteLine("WARN: Line {0} malformed. Only {1} field(s) found.",
lineCount, fields.Length);
                continue;
            }

            if(fields[0].Length != 6)
            {
                Console.WriteLine("WARN: Trade currencies on line {0} malformed: '{1}'",
lineCount, fields[0]);
                continue;
            }

            int tradeAmount;
            if(!int.TryParse(fields[1], out tradeAmount))
            {
                Console.WriteLine("WARN: Trade amount on line {0} not a valid integer:
'{1}'", lineCount, fields[1]);
            }

            decimal tradePrice;
            if (!decimal.TryParse(fields[2], out tradePrice))
            {
                Console.WriteLine("WARN: Trade price on line {0} not a valid decimal:
'{1}'", lineCount, fields[2]);
            }
```

```csharp
            var sourceCurrencyCode = fields[0].Substring(0, 3);
            var destinationCurrencyCode = fields[0].Substring(3, 3);

            // calculate values
            var trade = new TradeRecord
            {
                SourceCurrency = sourceCurrencyCode,
                DestinationCurrency = destinationCurrencyCode,
                Lots = tradeAmount / LotSize,
                Price = tradePrice
            };

            trades.Add(trade);

            lineCount++;
        }

        using (var connection = new System.Data.SqlClient.SqlConnection("Data
Source=(local);Initial Catalog=TradeDatabase;Integrated Security=True"))
        {
            connection.Open();
            using (var transaction = connection.BeginTransaction())
            {
                foreach(var trade in trades)
                {
                    var command = connection.CreateCommand();
                    command.Transaction = transaction;
                    command.CommandType = System.Data.CommandType.StoredProcedure;
                    command.CommandText = "dbo.insert_trade";
                    command.Parameters.AddWithValue("@sourceCurrency", trade.
SourceCurrency);
                    command.Parameters.AddWithValue("@destinationCurrency", trade.
DestinationCurrency);
                    command.Parameters.AddWithValue("@lots", trade.Lots);
                    command.Parameters.AddWithValue("@price", trade.Price);

                    command.ExecuteNonQuery();
                }

                transaction.Commit();
            }
            connection.Close();
        }

        Console.WriteLine("INFO: {0} trades processed", trades.Count);
    }

    private static float LotSize = 100000f;
}
```

This is more than an example of a class that has too many responsibilities; it is also an example of a single *method* that has too many responsibilities. By reading the code carefully, you can discern what this class is trying to achieve:

1. It reads every line from a `Stream` parameter, storing each line in a list of strings.

2. It parses out individual fields from each line and stores them in a more structured list of `Trade-Record` instances.

3. The parsing includes some validation and some logging to the console.

4. Each `TradeRecord` is enumerated, and a stored procedure is called to insert the trades into a database.

The responsibilities of the `TradeProcessor` are reading streams, parsing strings, validating fields, logging, and database insertion. The single responsibility principle states that this class, like all others, should only have a single reason to change. However, the reality of the `TradeProcessor` is that it will change under the following circumstances:

- When you decide not to use a `Stream` for input but instead read the trades from a remote call to a web service.

- When the format of the input data changes, perhaps with the addition of an extra field indicating the broker for the transaction.

- When the validation rules of the input data change.

- When the way in which you log warnings, errors, and information changes. If you are using a hosted web service, writing to the console would not be a viable option.

- When the database changes in some way—perhaps the `insert_trade` stored procedure requires a new parameter for the broker, too, or you decide not to store the data in a relational database and opt for document storage, or the database is moved behind a web service that you must call.

For each of these changes, this class would have to be modified. Furthermore, unless you maintain a variety of versions, there is no possibility of adapting the `TradeProcessor` so that it is able to read from a different input source, for example. Imagine the maintenance headache when you are asked to add the ability to store the trades in a web service, but only if a certain command-line argument was supplied.

Refactoring for clarity

The first task on the road to refactoring the `TradeProcessor` so that it has one reason to change is to split the `ProcessTrades` method into smaller pieces so that each one focuses on a single responsibility. Each of the following listings shows a single method from the refactored `TradeProcessor` class, followed by an explanation of the changes.

First, Listing 5-2 shows the `ProcessTrades` method, which now does nothing more than delegate to other methods.

LISTING 5-2 The `ProcessTrades` method is very minimal because it delegates work to other methods.

```
public void ProcessTrades(System.IO.Stream stream)
{
    var lines = ReadTradeData(stream);
    var trades = ParseTrades(lines);
    StoreTrades(trades);
}
```

The original code was characterized by three distinct parts of a process—reading the trade data from a stream, converting the string data in the stream to `TradeRecord` instances, and writing the trades to persistent storage. Note that the output from one method feeds into the input to the next method. You cannot call `StoreTrades` until you have the trade records returned from the `Parse-Trades` method, and you cannot call `ParseTrades` until you have the lines returned from the `ReadTradeData` method.

Taking each of these methods in order, let's look at `ReadTradeData`, in Listing 5-3.

LISTING 5-3 `ReadTradeData` encapsulates the original code.

```
private IEnumerable<string> ReadTradeData(System.IO.Stream stream)
{
    var tradeData = new List<string>();
    using (var reader = new System.IO.StreamReader(stream))
    {
        string line;
        while ((line = reader.ReadLine()) != null)
        {
            tradeData.Add(line);
        }
    }
    return tradeData;
}
```

This code is preserved from the original implementation of the `ProcessTrades` method. It has simply been encapsulated in a method that returns the resultant string data as a string enumeration. Note that this makes the return value read-only, whereas the original implementation unnecessarily allowed subsequent parts of the process to add further lines.

The `ParseTrades` method, shown in Listing 5-4, is next. It has changed somewhat from the original implementation because it, too, delegates some tasks to other methods.

LISTING 5-4 ParseTrades delegates to other methods to limit its complexity.

```
private IEnumerable<TradeRecord> ParseTrades(IEnumerable<string> tradeData)
{
    var trades = new List<TradeRecord>();
    var lineCount = 1;
    foreach (var line in tradeData)
    {
        var fields = line.Split(new char[] { ',' });

        if(!ValidateTradeData(fields, lineCount))
        {
            continue;
        }

        var trade = MapTradeDataToTradeRecord(fields);

        trades.Add(trade);

        lineCount++;
    }
    return trades;
}
```

This method delegates validation and mapping responsibilities to other methods. Without this delegation, this section of the process would still be too complex and it would retain too many responsibilities. The ValidateTradeData method, shown in Listing 5-5, returns a Boolean value to indicate whether any of the fields for a trade line are invalid.

LISTING 5-5 All of the validation code is in a single method.

```
private bool ValidateTradeData(string[] fields, int currentLine)
{
    if (fields.Length != 3)
    {
        LogMessage("WARN: Line {0} malformed. Only {1} field(s) found.", currentLine,
    fields.Length);
        return false;
    }

    if (fields[0].Length != 6)
    {
        LogMessage("WARN: Trade currencies on line {0} malformed: '{1}'", currentLine,
    fields[0]);
        return false;
    }

    int tradeAmount;
    if (!int.TryParse(fields[1], out tradeAmount))
    {
        LogMessage("WARN: Trade amount on line {0} not a valid integer: '{1}'",
    currentLine, fields[1]);
```

```
        return false;
    }

    decimal tradePrice;
    if (!decimal.TryParse(fields[2], out tradePrice))
    {
        LogMessage("WARN: Trade price on line {0} not a valid decimal: '{1}'",
    currentLine, fields[2]);
        return false;
    }

    return true;
}
```

The only change made to the original validation code is that it now delegates to yet another method for logging messages. Rather than embedding calls to `Console.WriteLine` where needed, the LogMessage method is used, shown in Listing 5-6.

LISTING 5-6 The LogMessage method is currently just a synonym for `Console.WriteLine`.

```
private void LogMessage(string message, params object[] args)
{
    Console.WriteLine(message, args);
}
```

Returning up the stack to the `ParseTrades` method, Listing 5-7 shows the other method to which it delegates. This method maps an array of strings representing the individual fields from the stream to an instance of the `TradeRecord` class.

LISTING 5-7 Mapping from one type to another is a separate responsibility.

```
private TradeRecord MapTradeDataToTradeRecord(string[] fields)
{
    var sourceCurrencyCode = fields[0].Substring(0, 3);
    var destinationCurrencyCode = fields[0].Substring(3, 3);
    var tradeAmount = int.Parse(fields[1]);
    var tradePrice = decimal.Parse(fields[2]);

    var tradeRecord = new TradeRecord
    {
        SourceCurrency = sourceCurrencyCode,
        DestinationCurrency = destinationCurrencyCode,
        Lots = tradeAmount / LotSize,
        Price = tradePrice
    };

    return tradeRecord;
}
```

The sixth and final new method introduced by this refactor is `StoreTrades`, shown in Listing 5-8. This method wraps the code for interacting with the database. It also delegates the informational log message to the aforementioned `LogMessage` method.

LISTING 5-8 With the `StoreTrades` method in place, the responsibilities in this class are clearly demarcated.

```
private void StoreTrades(IEnumerable<TradeRecord> trades)
{
    using (var connection = new System.Data.SqlClient.SqlConnection("Data
  Source=(local);Initial Catalog=TradeDatabase;Integrated Security=True"))
    {
        connection.Open();
        using (var transaction = connection.BeginTransaction())
        {
            foreach (var trade in trades)
            {
                var command = connection.CreateCommand();
                command.Transaction = transaction;
                command.CommandType = System.Data.CommandType.StoredProcedure;
                command.CommandText = "dbo.insert_trade";
                command.Parameters.AddWithValue("@sourceCurrency", trade.SourceCurrency);
                command.Parameters.AddWithValue("@destinationCurrency",
trade.DestinationCurrency);
                command.Parameters.AddWithValue("@lots", trade.Lots);
                command.Parameters.AddWithValue("@price", trade.Price);

                command.ExecuteNonQuery();
            }

            transaction.Commit();
        }
        connection.Close();
    }

    LogMessage("INFO: {0} trades processed", trades.Count());
}
```

Looking back at this refactor, it is a clear improvement on the original implementation. However, what have you really achieved? Although the new `ProcessTrades` method is indisputably smaller than the monolithic original, and the code is definitely more readable, you have gained very little by way of adaptability. You can change the implementation of the `LogMessage` method so that it, for example, writes to a file instead of to the console, but that involves a change to the `TradeProcessor` class, which is precisely what you wanted to avoid.

This refactor has been an important stepping stone on the path to truly separating the responsibilities of this class. It has been a refactor for clarity, not for adaptability. The next task is to split each responsibility into different classes and place them behind interfaces. What you need is true abstraction to achieve useful adaptability.

Refactoring for abstraction

Building on the new `TradeProcessor` implementation, the next refactor introduces several abstractions that will allow you to handle almost any change request for this class. Although this running example might seem very small, perhaps even insignificant, it is a workable contrivance for the purposes of this tutorial. Also, it is *very* common for a small application such as this to grow into something much larger. When a few people start to use it, the feature requests begin to increase.

Often, the terms *prototype* and *proof of concept* are applied to such allegedly small applications, and the conversion from prototype to production application is relatively seamless. This is why the ability to refactor toward abstraction is such a touchstone of adaptive development. Without it, the myriad requests devolve into a "big ball of mud"—a class, or a group of classes in an assembly, with little delineation of responsibility and no discernible abstractions. The result is an application that has no unit tests and that is difficult to maintain and enhance, and yet that could be a critical piece of the line of business.

The first step in refactoring the `TradeProcessor` for abstraction is to design the interface or interfaces that it will use to perform the three high-level tasks of reading, processing, and storing the trade data. Figure 5-1 shows the first set of abstractions.

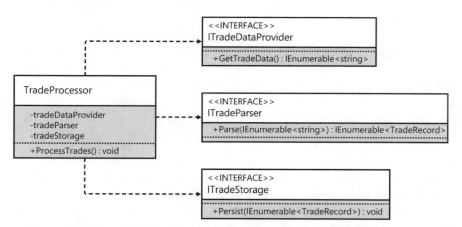

FIGURE 5-1 The `TradeProcessor` will now depend on three new interfaces.

Because you moved all of the code from `ProcessTrades` into separate methods in the first refactor, you should have a good idea of where the first abstractions should be applied. As prescribed by the single responsibility principle, the three main responsibilities will be handled by different classes. As you know from previous chapters, you should not have direct dependencies from one class to another but should instead work via interfaces. Therefore, the three responsibilities are factored out into three separate interfaces. Listing 5-9 shows how the `TradeProcessor` class looks after this change.

LISTING 5-9 The TradeProcessor is now the encapsulation of a process, and nothing more.

```
public class TradeProcessor
{
    public TradeProcessor(ITradeDataProvider tradeDataProvider, ITradeParser tradeParser,
    ITradeStorage tradeStorage)
    {
        this.tradeDataProvider = tradeDataProvider;
        this.tradeParser = tradeParser;
        this.tradeStorage = tradeStorage;
    }

    public void ProcessTrades()
    {
        var lines = tradeDataProvider.GetTradeData();
        var trades = tradeParser.Parse(lines);
        tradeStorage.Persist(trades);
    }

    private readonly ITradeDataProvider tradeDataProvider;
    private readonly ITradeParser tradeParser;
    private readonly ITradeStorage tradeStorage;
}
```

The class is now significantly different from its previous incarnation. It no longer contains the implementation details for the whole process but instead contains the *blueprint* for the process. The class models the process of transferring trade data from one format to another. This is its only responsibility, its only concern, and the only reason that this class should change. If the process itself changes, this class will change to reflect it. But if you decide you no longer want to retrieve data from a Stream, log on to the console, or store the trades in a database, this class remains as is.

As prescribed by the Stairway pattern (introduced in Chapter 2, "Dependencies and layering"), the interfaces that the TradeProcessor now depends on all live in a separate assembly. This ensures that neither the client nor the implementation assemblies reference each other. Separated into another assembly are the three classes that implement these interfaces, the StreamTradeDataProvider, SimpleTradeParser, and AdoNetTradeStorage classes. Note that there is a naming convention used for these classes. First, the prefix I was removed from the interface name and replaced with the implementation-specific context that is required of the class. So StreamTradeDataProvider allows you to infer that it is an implementation of the ITradeDataProvider interface that retrieves its data from a Stream object. The AdoNetTradeStorage class uses ADO.NET to persist the trade data. I have prefixed the ITradeParser implementation with the word Simple to indicate that it has no dependency context.

All three of these implementations are able to live in a single assembly due to their shared dependencies—core assemblies of the Microsoft .NET Framework. If you were to introduce an implementation that required a third-party dependency, a first-party dependency of your own, or a dependency from a non-core .NET Framework class, you should put these implementations into their own assemblies. For example, if you were to use the Dapper mapping library instead of ADO.NET, you would create an assembly called `Services.Dapper`, inside of which would be an `ITradeStorage` implementation called `DapperTradeStorage`.

The `ITradeDataProvider` interface does not depend on the `Stream` class. The previous version of the method for retrieving trade data required a `Stream` instance as a parameter, but this artificially tied the method to a dependency. When you are creating interfaces and refactoring toward abstractions, it is important that you do not retain dependencies where doing so would affect the adaptability of the code. The possibility of retrieving the trade data from sources other than a `Stream` has already been discussed, so the refactoring has ensured that this dependency is removed from the interface. Instead, the `StreamTradeDataProvider` requires a `Stream` as a constructor parameter, instead of a method parameter. By using the constructor, you can depend on almost anything without polluting the interface. Listing 5-10 shows the `StreamTradeDataProvider` implementation.

LISTING 5-10 Context can be passed into classes via constructor parameters, keeping the interface clean.

```
public class StreamTradeDataProvider : ITradeDataProvider
{
    public StreamTradeDataProvider(Stream stream)
    {
        this.stream = stream;
    }

    public IEnumerable<string> GetTradeData()
    {
        var tradeData = new List<string>();
        using (var reader = new StreamReader(stream))
        {
            string line;
            while ((line = reader.ReadLine()) != null)
            {
                tradeData.Add(line);
            }
        }
        return tradeData;
    }

    private Stream stream;
}
```

Remember that the `TradeProcessor` class, which is the client of this code, is aware of nothing other than the `GetTradeData` method's signature via the `ITradeDataProvider`. It has no knowledge whatsoever of how the real implementation retrieves the data—nor should it.

There are more abstractions that can be extracted from this example. Remember that the original `ParseTrades` method delegated responsibility for validation and for mapping. You can repeat the process of refactoring so that the `SimpleTradeParser` class does not have more than one responsibility. Figure 5-2 shows in Unified Markup Language (UML) how this can be achieved.

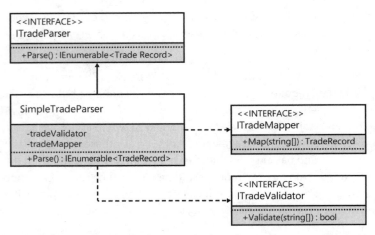

FIGURE 5-2 The `SimpleTradeParser` is also refactored to ensure that each class has a single responsibility.

This process of abstracting responsibilities into interfaces (and their accompanying implementations) is recursive. As you inspect each class, you must determine the responsibilities that it has and factor them out until the class has only one. Listing 5-11 shows the `SimpleTradeParser` class, which delegates to interfaces where appropriate. Its single reason for change is if the overall structure of the trade data changes—for instance, if the data no longer uses comma-separated values and changes to using tabs, or perhaps XML.

LISTING 5-11 The algorithm for parsing trade data is encapsulated in `ITradeParser` implementations.

```
public class SimpleTradeParser : ITradeParser
{
    public SimpleTradeParser(ITradeValidator tradeValidator, ITradeMapper tradeMapper)
    {
        this.tradeValidator = tradeValidator;
        this.tradeMapper = tradeMapper;
    }

    public IEnumerable<TradeRecord> Parse(IEnumerable<string> tradeData)
    {
        var trades = new List<TradeRecord>();
        var lineCount = 1;
        foreach (var line in tradeData)
        {
            var fields = line.Split(new char[] { ',' });

            if (!tradeValidator.Validate(fields))
            {
                continue;
            }

            var trade = tradeMapper.Map(fields);

            trades.Add(trade);
```

```
            lineCount++;
        }
        return trades;
    }


    private readonly ITradeValidator tradeValidator;
    private readonly ITradeMapper tradeMapper;
}
```

The final refactor aims to abstract logging from two classes. Both the `ITradeValidator` and `ITradeStorage` implementations are still logging directly to the console. This time, instead of implementing your own logging class, you will create an adapter for the popular logging library, Log4Net. The UML class diagram in Figure 5-3 shows how this all fits together.

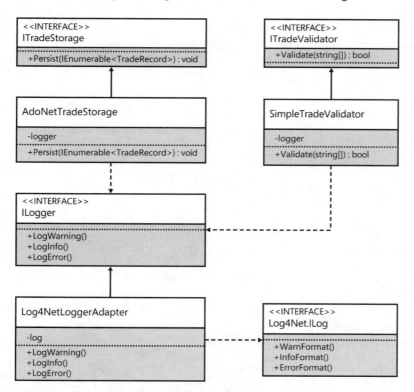

FIGURE 5-3 By implementing an adapter for Log4Net, you need not reference it in every assembly.

The net benefit of creating an adapter class such as `Log4NetLoggerAdapter` is that you can convert a third-party reference into a first-party reference. Notice that both `AdoNetTradeStorage` and `SimpleTradeValidator` both depend on the first-party `ILogger` interface. But, at run time, both will actually use Log4Net. The only references needed to Log4Net are in the entry point of the application (see Chapter 9, "Dependency injection," for more information) and the newly created

`Service.Log4Net` assembly. Any code that has a dependency on Log4Net, such as custom appenders, should live in the `Service.Log4Net` assembly. For now, only the adapter resides in this new assembly.

The refactored validator class is shown in Listing 5-12. It now has no reference whatsoever to the console. Because of Log4Net's flexibility, you can actually log to almost anywhere now. Total adaptability has been achieved as far as logging is concerned.

LISTING 5-12 The `SimpleTradeValidator` class after refactoring.

```
public class SimpleTradeValidator : ITradeValidator
{
    private readonly ILogger logger;    public SimpleTradeValidator(ILogger logger)
    {
        this.logger = logger;
    }

    public bool Validate(string[] tradeData)
    {
        if (tradeData.Length != 3)
        {
            logger.LogWarning("Line malformed. Only {1} field(s) found.",
tradeData.Length);
            return false;
        }

        if (tradeData[0].Length != 6)
        {
            logger.LogWarning("Trade currencies malformed: '{1}'", tradeData[0]);
            return false;
        }

        int tradeAmount;
        if (!int.TryParse(tradeData[1], out tradeAmount))
        {
            logger.LogWarning("Trade amount not a valid integer: '{1}'", tradeData[1]);
            return false;
        }

        decimal tradePrice;
        if (!decimal.TryParse(tradeData[2], out tradePrice))
        {
            logger.LogWarning("WARN: Trade price not a valid decimal: '{1}'",
tradeData[2]);
            return false;
        }

        return true;
    }
}
```

At this point, a quick recap is in order. Bear in mind that you have altered nothing as far as the functionality of the code is concerned. Functionally, this code does exactly what it used to do. However, if you wanted to enhance it in any way, you could do so with ease. The added ability to adapt this code to a new purpose more than justifies the effort expended to refactor it.

Referring back to the original list of potential enhancements to this code, this new version allows you to implement each one without touching the existing classes.

- *Request: You decide not to use a* `Stream` *for input but instead read the trades from a remote call to a web service.*

  - Solution: Create a new `ITradeDataProvider` implementation that supplies the data from the service.

- *Request: The format of the input data changes, perhaps with the addition of an extra field indicating the broker for the transaction.*

  - Solution: Alter the implementations for the `ITradeDataValidator`, `ITradeDataMapper`, and `ITradeStorage` interfaces, which handle the new broker field.

- *Request: The validation rules of the input data change.*

  - Solution: Edit the `ITradeDataValidator` implementation to reflect the rule changes.

- *Request: The way in which you log warnings, errors, and information changes. If you are using a hosted web service, writing to the console would not be a viable option.*

  - Solution: As discussed, Log4Net provides you with infinite options for logging, by virtue of the adapter.

- *Request: The database changes in some way—perhaps the* `insert_trade` *stored procedure requires a new parameter for the broker, too, or you decide not to store the data in a relational database and opt for document storage, or the database is moved behind a web service that you must call.*

  - Solution: If the stored procedure changes, you would need to edit the `AdoNetTradeStorage` class to include the broker field. For the other two options, you could create a `MongoTradeStorage` class that uses MongoDB to store the trades, and you could create a `ServiceTradeStorage` class to hide the implementation behind a web service.

I hope you are now fully convinced that a combination of abstracting via interfaces, decoupling assemblies to follow the Stairway pattern, aggressive refactoring, and adhering to the single responsibility principle are the foundation of adaptive code.

When you arrive at a scenario in which your code is neatly delegating to abstractions, the possibilities are endless. The rest of this chapter concentrates on other ways in which you can focus on a single responsibility per class.

SRP and the Decorator pattern

The Decorator pattern is excellent for ensuring that each class has a single responsibility. Classes can often do too many things without an obvious way of splitting the responsibilities into other classes. The responsibilities seem too closely linked.

The Decorator pattern's basic premise is that each decorator class fulfills the contract of a type and also accepts one or more of those types as constructor parameters. This is beneficial because functionality can be added to an existing class that implements a certain interface, and the decorator also acts—unbeknownst to clients—as an implementation of the required interface. Figure 5-4 shows a UML diagram of the Decorator design pattern.

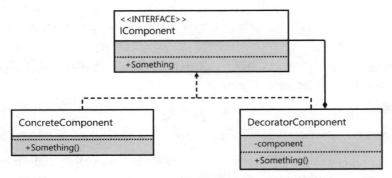

FIGURE 5-4 A UML diagram showing an implementation of the Decorator pattern.

A simple example of the pattern is shown in Listing 5-13, which does not pertain to a specific use of the pattern but provides a canonical example.

LISTING 5-13 A template example of the decorator pattern.

```
public interface IComponent
{
    void Something();
}
// . . .
public class ConcreteComponent : IComponent
{
    public void Something()
    {

    }
}
```

```
// . . .
public class DecoratorComponent : IComponent
{
    public DecoratorComponent(IComponent decoratedComponent)
    {
        this.decoratedComponent = decoratedComponent;
    }

    public void Something()
    {
        SomethingElse();
        decoratedComponent.Something();
    }

    private void SomethingElse()
    {

    }

    private readonly IComponent decoratedComponent;
}
// . . .
class Program
{
    static IComponent component;

    static void Main(string[] args)
    {
        component = new DecoratorComponent(new ConcreteComponent());
        component.Something();
    }
}
```

Because a client accepts the interface shown in the listing as a method parameter, you can provide either the original, undecorated type to that client or you can provide the decorated version. Note that the client will be oblivious: it will not have to change depending on which version it is being provided.

The Composite pattern

The Composite pattern is a specialization of the Decorator pattern and is one of the more common uses of that pattern. A UML diagram describing the Composite pattern's collaborators is shown in Figure 5-5.

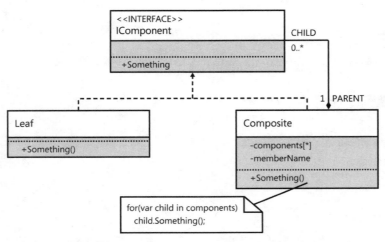

FIGURE 5-5 The Composite pattern closely resembles the Decorator pattern.

The Composite pattern's purpose is to allow you to treat many instances of an interface as if they were just one instance. Therefore, clients can accept just one instance of an interface, but they can be implicitly provided with many instances, without requiring the client to change. Listing 5-14 shows a composite decorator in practice.

LISTING 5-14 The composite implementation of an interface.

```
public interface IComponent
{
    void Something();
}
// . . .
public class Leaf : IComponent
{
    public void Something()
    {

    }
}
// . . .
public class CompositeComponent : IComponent
{
    public CompositeComponent()
    {
        children = new List<IComponent>();
    }

    public void AddComponent(IComponent component)
    {
        children.Add(component);
    }
```

```csharp
        public void RemoveComponent(IComponent component)
        {
            children.Remove(component);
        }

        public void Something()
        {
            foreach(var child in children)
            {
                child.Something();
            }
        }

        private ICollection<IComponent> children;
    }
    // . . .
    class Program
    {
        static void Main(string[] args)
        {
            var composite = new CompositeComponent();
            composite.AddComponent(new Leaf());
            composite.AddComponent(new Leaf());
            composite.AddComponent(new Leaf());

            component = composite;
            component.Something();
        }

        static IComponent component;
    }
```

In the CompositeComponent class, there are methods for adding and removing other instances of the IComponent. These methods do not form part of the interface and are for clients of the CompositeComponent class, directly. Whichever factory method or class is tasked with creating instances of the CompositeComponent class will also have to create the decorated instances and pass them into the Add method; otherwise, the clients of the IComponent would have to change in order to cope with compositions.

Whenever the Something method is called by the IComponent clients, the list of composed instances is enumerated, and their respective Something is called. This is how you reroute the call to a single instance of IComponent—of type CompositeComponent—to many other types.

Each instance that you supply to the CompositeComponent class must implement the IComponent interface—and this is enforced by the compiler due to C#'s strong typing—but the instances need not all be of the same concrete type. Because of the advantages of polymorphism, you can treat all implementations of an interface as instances of that interface. In the example shown in Listing 5-15, the CompositeComponent instances provided are of different types, further enhancing this pattern's utility.

LISTING 5-15 Instances provided to the composite can be of different types.

```csharp
public class SecondTypeOfLeaf : IComponent
{
    public void Something()
    {

    }
}
// . . .
public class AThirdLeafType : IComponent
{
    public void Something()
    {

    }
}
// . . .
public void AlternativeComposite()
{
    var composite = new CompositeComponent();
    composite.AddComponent(new Leaf());
    composite.AddComponent(new SecondTypeOfLeaf());
    composite.AddComponent(new AThirdLeafType());

    component = composite;
    composite.Something();
}
```

Taking this pattern to its logical conclusion, you can even pass in one or more instances of the CompositeComponent interface to the Add method, forming a chain of composite instances in a hierarchical tree structure.

Where should the composite live?

Chapter 2 introduced the Entourage anti-pattern, which states that implementations should not live in the same assemblies as their interfaces. However, there is an exception to that rule: implementations whose dependencies are a subset of their interface's dependencies.

Depending on how the composite is implemented, it is likely that no further dependencies will be introduced. If this is true, the assembly in which the interface resides could also include the composite implementation.

In Chapter 2, classes were shown to be modeled as object graphs. That theme continues here, to further demonstrate how the Composite pattern works. In Figure 5-6, the nodes of the graph represent object instances, and the edges represent method calls.

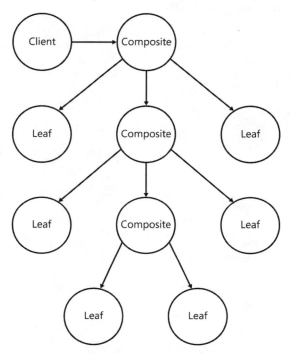

FIGURE 5-6 The object graph notation helps to visualize the runtime structure of the program.

Predicate decorators

The predicate decorator is a useful construct for hiding the conditional execution of code from clients. Listing 5-16 shows an example.

LISTING 5-16 This client will only execute the Something method on even days of the month.

```
public class DateTester
{
    public bool TodayIsAnEvenDayOfTheMonth
    {
        get
        {
            return DateTime.Now.Day % 2 == 0;
        }
    }
}
```

```
// . . .
class PredicatedDecoratorExample
{
    public PredicatedDecoratorExample(IComponent component)
    {
        this.component = component;
    }

    public void Run()
    {
        DateTester dateTester = new DateTester();
        if (dateTester.TodayIsAnEvenDayOfTheMonth)
        {
            component.Something();
        }
    }

    private readonly IComponent component;
}
```

The presence of the DateTester class in this example is a dependency that does not belong in this class. The initial temptation is to alter the code toward that of Listing 5-17. However, that is only a partial solution.

LISTING 5-17 An improvement is to require the dependency to be passed into the class.

```
class PredicatedDecoratorExample
{
    public PredicatedDecoratorExample(IComponent component)
    {
        this.component = component;
    }

    public void Run(DateTester dateTester)
    {
        if (dateTester.TodayIsAnEvenDayOfTheMonth)
        {
            component.Something();
        }
    }

    private readonly IComponent component;
}
```

You now require a parameter of the Run method, breaking the client's public interface and burdening its clients with providing an implementation of the DateTester class. By using the Decorator pattern, you are able to keep the client's interface the same, yet retain the conditional-execution functionality. Listing 5-18 proves that this is not too good to be true.

LISTING 5-18 The predicate decoration contains the dependency, and the client is much cleaner.

```
public class PredicatedComponent : IComponent
{
    public PredicatedComponent(IComponent decoratedComponent, DateTester dateTester)
    {
        this.decoratedComponent = decoratedComponent;
        this.dateTester = dateTester;
    }

    public void Something()
    {
        if(dateTester.TodayIsAnEvenDayOfTheMonth)
        {
            decoratedComponent.Something();
        }
    }

    private readonly IComponent decoratedComponent;
    private readonly DateTester dateTester;
}
// . . .
class PredicatedDecoratorExample
{
    public PredicatedDecoratorExample(IComponent component)
    {
        this.component = component;
    }

    public void Run()
    {
        component.Something();
    }

    private readonly IComponent component;
}
```

Note that this listing has added conditional branching to the code without modifying either the client code or the original implementing class. Also, this example has accepted the `DateTester` class as a dependency, but you could take this one step further by defining your own predicate interface for handling this scenario generically. After a few changes, the code looks like Listing 5-19.

LISTING 5-19 Defining a dedicated `IPredicate` interface makes the solution more general.

```
public interface IPredicate
{
    bool Test();
}
// . . .
public class PredicatedComponent : IComponent
{
    public PredicatedComponent(IComponent decoratedComponent, IPredicate predicate)
    {
        this.decoratedComponent = decoratedComponent;
        this.predicate = predicate;
    }

    public void Something()
    {
        if (predicate.Test())
        {
            decoratedComponent.Something();
        }
    }

    private readonly IComponent decoratedComponent;
    private readonly IPredicate predicate;
}
// . . .
public class TodayIsAnEvenDayOfTheMonthPredicate : IPredicate
{
    public TodayIsAnEvenDayOfTheMonthPredicate(DateTester dateTester)
    {
        this.dateTester = dateTester;
    }

    public bool Test()
    {
        return dateTester.TodayIsAnEvenDayOfTheMonth;
    }

    private readonly DateTester dateTester;
}
```

The `TodayIsAnEvenDayOfTheMonthPredicate` class converts the original dependent class, `DateTester`, to that of an `IPredicate`. This is an example of the Adapter pattern that was discussed earlier, in the "Refactoring for abstraction" section.

Note The .NET Framework, as of version 2.0, contains a Predicate<T> delegate, which models a predicate that accepts a single, generic parameter as context. I did not choose the Predicate<T> delegate for this example for two reasons: First, no context needs to be provided, because the original conditional test accepted no arguments. However, I could have used a Func<bool> delegate to model a context-free predicate, which brings me to the second reason: *delegates are not as versatile as interfaces*. By modeling an IPredicate, I will be able to decorate that interface just the same as any other in the future. In other words, I have defined another extension point that is infinitely decoratable.

Branching decorators

You can extend the predicate decorator further by accepting a decorated instance of the interface to execute something on the false branch of the conditional test, as shown in Listing 5-20.

LISTING 5-20 The branching decorator accepts two components and a predicate.

```
public class BranchedComponent : IComponent
{
    public BranchedComponent(IComponent trueComponent, IComponent falseComponent,
IPredicate predicate)
    {
        this.trueComponent = trueComponent;
        this.falseComponent = falseComponent;
        this.predicate = predicate;
    }

    public void Something()
    {
        if (predicate.Test())
        {
            trueComponent.Something();
        }
        else
        {
            falseComponent.Something();
        }
    }

    private readonly IComponent trueComponent;
    private readonly IComponent falseComponent;
    private readonly IPredicate predicate;
}
```

Whenever the predicate is tested, if it returns `true`, you call the equivalent interface method on the `trueComponent` instance. If it returns `false`, you instead call the interface method on the `falseComponent` instance.

Lazy decorators

The lazy decorator allows clients to be provided with a reference to an interface that will not be instantiated until its first use. Typically, and erroneously, clients are made aware of the presence of a lazy instance because a Lazy<T> is passed to them, as in Listing 5-21.

LISTING 5-21 This client has been given a Lazy<T>.

```
public class ComponentClient
{
    public ComponentClient(Lazy<IComponent> component)
    {
        this.component = component;
    }

    public void Run()
    {
        component.Value.Something();
    }

    private readonly Lazy<IComponent> component;
}
```

This client has no option but to accept that all instances of `IComponent` that it is provided with will be lazy. However, if you return to a more standard use of the interface, you can create a lazy decorator that prevents the client from knowing that it is dealing with a Lazy<T>, and allows some `ComponentClient` objects to accept `IComponent` instances that are not lazy. Listing 5-22 shows this decorator.

LISTING 5-22 LazyComponent implements a lazily instantiated `IComponent`, but `ComponentClient` is unaware of this.

```
public class LazyComponent : IComponent
{
    public LazyComponent(Lazy<IComponent> lazyComponent)
    {
        this.lazyComponent = lazyComponent;
    }

    public void Something()
    {
        lazyComponent.Value.Something();
    }
}
```

```
        private readonly Lazy<IComponent> lazyComponent;
}
// . . .
public class ComponentClient
{

    public ComponentClient(IComponent component)
    {
        this.component = component;
    }

    public void Run()
    {
        component.Something();
    }

    private readonly IComponent component;
}
```

Logging decorators

Listing 5-23 shows a common pattern that occurs whenever code contains extensive logging. The logging code becomes ubiquitous throughout the application, and the signal-to-noise ratio suffers.

LISTING 5-23 Logging code clouds the intent of methods.

```
public class ConcreteCalculator : ICalculator
{
    public int Add(int x, int y)
    {
        Console.WriteLine("Add(x={0}, y={1})", x, y);

        var addition = x + y;

        Console.WriteLine("result={0}", addition);

        return addition;
    }
}
```

Instead of proliferating the logging code throughout the application, you can limit it to one assembly that implements logging decorators, as shown in Listing 5-24.

```
public class LoggingCalculator : ICalculator
{
    public LoggingCalculator(ICalculator calculator)
    {
        this.calculator = calculator;
    }

    public int Add(int x, int y)
    {
        Console.WriteLine("Add(x={0}, y={1})", x, y);

        var result = calculator.Add(x, y);

        Console.WriteLine("result={0}", result);

        return result;
    }

    private readonly ICalculator calculator;
}
// . . .
public class ConcreteCalculator : ICalculator
{
    public int Add(int x, int y)
    {
        return x + y;
    }
}
```

Clients of the ICalculator interface will pass in various parameters, and some of the methods themselves will return values, too. Because the LoggingCalculator is in a position to intercept both of these artifacts, it can interrogate them directly. There are limitations to using logging decorators that should be considered. First, any private state contained in the decorated class remains unavailable to the logging decorator, which cannot access this state and write it to a log. Second, a logging decorator would need to be created for every interface in the application—a significant undertaking. For something so common, logging is better implemented as a logging aspect. Aspect-oriented programming (AOP) was covered in Chapter 2.

Profiling decorators

One of the major reasons to choose the .NET Framework as the target platform for developing an application is that it lends itself well to Rapid Application Development (RAD). A working application can be developed in a far shorter time frame than in a lower-level language like, for example, C++. This is for several reasons, including the .NET Framework's automatic memory management, the rich and varied list of libraries that can be used, and the .NET Framework itself. C# is often deemed fast at development time but slow at run time. C++, on the other hand, is considered to be slow at development time and fast at run time.

Although the .NET Framework can also be fast, bottlenecks do occur. How can you tell which part of the code is slow? By *profiling* the methods of the application, you gather statistics on which parts of the code are slower than others. See the code in Listing 5-25.

LISTING 5-25 This code is (intentionally and artificially) slow.

```
public class SlowComponent : IComponent
{
    public SlowComponent()
    {
        random = new Random((int)DateTime.Now.Ticks);
    }

    public void Something()
    {
        for(var i = 0; i<100; ++i)
        {
            Thread.Sleep(random.Next(i) * 10);
        }
    };

    private readonly Random random
}
```

The component's Something() method in this example is slow. *Slow* and *fast*, of course, mean different things to different people at different times. In this case, a slow method is defined as one that takes one second or more to execute. How can you tell that a method is slow? You can time the method to find out how long it took to execute from start to finish, much like in Listing 5-26.

LISTING 5-26 The System.Diagnostics.Stopwatch class can time how long a method takes to execute.

```
public class SlowComponent : IComponent
{
    public SlowComponent()
    {
        random = new Random((int)DateTime.Now.Ticks);
        stopwatch = new Stopwatch();
    }

    public void Something()
    {
        stopwatch.Start();
        for(var i = 0; i<100; ++i)
        {
            System.Threading.Thread.Sleep(random.Next(i) * 10);
        }
        stopwatch.Stop();
        Console.WriteLine("The method took {0} seconds to complete",
  stopwatch.ElapsedMilliseconds / 1000);
```

```
    }

    private readonly Random random;
    private readonly Stopwatch;
}
```

Here the Stopwatch class from the System.Diagnostics assembly is used to time each method from start to finish. Note that the Something method in the class starts the stopwatch on entry and then stops it on exit.

Of course, this can be factored out into a profiling decorator. The interface as a whole is decorated and, before delegating to the decorated instance, you start the stopwatch. When the delegated method returns, you stop the stopwatch before returning to the calling client. The stopwatch decorator code is shown in Listing 5-27.

LISTING 5-27 The profiling decorator code.

```
public class ProfilingComponent : IComponent
{
    public ProfilingComponent(IComponent decoratedComponent)
    {
        this.decoratedComponent = decoratedComponent;
        stopwatch = new Stopwatch();
    }

    public void Something()
    {
        stopwatch.Start();
        decoratedComponent.Something();
        stopwatch.Stop();
        Console.WriteLine("The method took {0} seconds to complete",
  stopwatch.ElapsedMilliseconds / 1000);
    }

    private readonly IComponent decoratedComponent;
    private readonly Stopwatch stopwatch;
}
```

There is one further change that you could make to the ProfilingComponent class: make it transparently log the profiling. First, you need to factor out the stopwatch code behind an interface, so that you can provide multiple implementations, including decorators. This is a common first step when refactoring toward a better separation of responsibilities. Listing 5-28 shows this intermediate step.

```
public class ProfilingComponent : IComponent
{
    public ProfilingComponent(IComponent decoratedComponent, IStopwatch stopwatch)
    {
        this.decoratedComponent = decoratedComponent;
        this.stopwatch = stopwatch;
    }

    public void Something()
    {
        stopwatch.Start();
        decoratedComponent.Something();
        var elapsedMilliseconds = stopwatch.Stop();
        Console.WriteLine("The method took {0} seconds to complete", elapsedMilliseconds /
    1000);
    }

    private readonly IComponent decoratedComponent;
    private readonly IStopwatch stopwatch;
}
```

Now that the `ProfilingComponent` class does not depend directly on the `System.Diagnostics.Stopwatch` class, you can vary the implementation of the `IStopwatch` class. A `LoggingStopwatch` decorator is created, as shown in Listing 5-29, to enhance any further `IStopwatch` implementations with logging facilities.

LISTING 5-29 The LoggingStopwatch decorator is an IStopwatch implementation that logs and delegates.

```
public class LoggingStopwatch : IStopwatch
{
    public LoggingStopwatch(IStopwatch decoratedStopwatch)
    {
        this.decoratedStopwatch = decoratedStopwatch;
    }

    public void Start()
    {
        decoratedStopwatch.Start();
        Console.WriteLine("Stopwatch started...");
    }

    public long Stop()
    {
        var elapsedMilliseconds = decoratedStopwatch.Stop();
```

```
        Console.WriteLine("Stopwatch stopped after {0} seconds",
    TimeSpan.FromMilliseconds(elapsedMilliseconds).TotalSeconds);
        return elapsedMilliseconds;
    }

    private readonly IStopwatch decoratedStopwatch;
}
```

Of course, you need a non-decorator implementation of the `IStopwatch` interface—one that acts as a real stopwatch. This is just a case of delegating to the .NET Framework's `System.Diagnostics.Stopwatch` class, as Listing 5-30 shows.

LISTING 5-30 The primary `IStopwatch` implementation uses the `Stopwatch` class.

```
public class StopwatchAdapter : IStopwatch
{
    public StopwatchAdapter(Stopwatch stopwatch)
    {
        this.stopwatch = stopwatch;
    }

    public void Start()
    {
        stopwatch.Start();
    }

    public long Stop()
    {
        stopwatch.Stop();
        var elapsedMilliseconds = stopwatch.ElapsedMilliseconds;
        stopwatch.Reset();
        return elapsedMilliseconds;
    }

    private readonly Stopwatch stopwatch;
}
```

Note that you could have chosen to implement `IStopwatch` as a subclass of the `System.Diagnostics.Stopwatch` class and used the existing `Start` and `Stop` methods. However, the `Start` method acts to resume functionality when a stopwatch is stopped, but what you need to do is to call `Reset` after you call `Stop`, and retrieve the `ElapsedMilliseconds` property value in between. This is another example of the Adapter pattern.

Asynchronous decorators

Asynchronous methods are those that run on a different thread than the client. This is useful when a method takes a long time to execute because, during synchronous execution, the client is blocked while waiting for a called method to return. In a desktop application using Windows Presentation

Foundation (WPF) and the Model-View-ViewModel (MVVM) pattern, for example, the ViewModels are bound to the View, and any commands that are executed are handled synchronously by those ViewModels *on the user interface thread*. In practice, this means that a long-running command will block the user interface from executing for as long as the command takes to finish its work. Listing 5-31 shows a snippet of this behavior.

LISTING 5-31 Commands handled on the UI thread will block it, making the UI unresponsive.

```
public class MainWindowViewModel : INotifyPropertyChanged
{
    public MainWindowViewModel(IComponent component)
    {
        this.component = component;
        calculateCommand = new RelayCommand(Calculate);
    }

    public string Result
    {
        get
        {
            return result;
        }
        private set
        {
            if (result != value)
            {
                result = value;
                PropertyChanged(this, new PropertyChangedEventArgs("Result"));
            }
        }
    }

    public ICommand CalculateCommand
    {
        get
        {
            return calculateCommand;
        }
    }

    public event PropertyChangedEventHandler PropertyChanged = delegate { };

    private void Calculate(object parameter)
    {
        Result = "Processing...";
        component.Process();
        Result = "Finished!";
    }

    private string result;
    private IComponent component;
    private RelayCommand calculateCommand;
}
```

By creating an asynchronous decorator, you can instruct the called method to execute on a separate thread. This can be accomplished by delegating the work to a Task class, which becomes a dependency of your decorator, as Listing 5-32 shows.

LISTING 5-32 An asynchronous decorator for WPF that uses the Dispatcher class.

```
public class AsyncComponent : IComponent
{
    public AsyncComponent(IComponent decoratedComponent)
    {
        this.decoratedComponent = decoratedComponent;
    }

    public void Process()
    {
        Task.Run((Action)decoratedComponent.Process);
    }

    private readonly IComponent decoratedComponent;
}
```

There is a problem with the AsyncComponent class: its dependency on the Task class is implicit, meaning that it is hard to test this class. Unit testing code with static dependencies is difficult, so you would be better off replacing this *skyhook* with a *crane*.

The limitations of asynchronous decorators

Not all conceivable methods can make use of the Decorator pattern to create asynchronous versions that clients do not know about. In fact, the only asynchronous methods to which this approach is applicable are *fire-and-forget* methods.

A fire-and-forget method has no return value, and clients do not need to know when such a method returns. When it is implemented as an asynchronous decorator, clients *cannot* know when a method call truly was completed because the call returns immediately—while the real work being performed is probably still in progress.

Request-response methods are common data-retrieval methods that are often very usefully implemented asynchronously, because they tend to take a while and block the UI thread. Clients need to know that the method is asynchronous, so that they can be coded explicitly to accept a callback when the asynchronous method is complete. Therefore, request-response methods cannot be implemented by using asynchronous decorators.

Decorating properties and events

So far, you have learned how to decorate the methods of an interface, but what about properties and events? Both of those syntactic elements can also be decorated, as long as you do not use auto-properties or auto-events: you need to explicitly define both in order to decorate them properly.

Listing 5-33 shows the manual creation of a property, but rather than having a backing field, for both the getter and the setter this code delegates to the decorated instance of the interface.

LISTING 5-33 Properties can also use the Decorator pattern, just like methods.

```
public class ComponentDecorator : IComponent
{
    public ComponentDecorator(IComponent decoratedComponent)
    {
        this.decoratedComponent = decoratedComponent;
    }

    public string Property
    {
        get
        {
            // We can do some mutation here after retrieving the value
            return decoratedComponent.Property;
        }
        set
        {
            // And/or here, before we set the value
            decoratedComponent.Property = value;
        }
    }

    private readonly IComponent decoratedComponent;
}
```

Listing 5-34 shows the manual creation of an event, but rather than having a backing field, for both the adder and remover this code delegates to the decorated instance of the interface.

LISTING 5-34 Events can also use the Decorator pattern, just like methods.

```
public class ComponentDecorator : IComponent
{
    public ComponentDecorator(IComponent decoratedComponent)
    {
        this.decoratedComponent = decoratedComponent;
    }
```

```
public event EventHandler Event
{
    add
    {
        // We can do something here, when the event handler is registered
        decoratedComponent.Event += value;
    }
    remove
    {
        // And/or here, when the event handler is deregistered
        decoratedComponent.Event -= value;
    }
}

private readonly IComponent decoratedComponent;
}
```

Using the Strategy pattern instead of `switch`

To understand when the Strategy pattern is best applied, you can look at instances of conditional branching. Whenever you use `switch` statements, you can use the Strategy pattern to simplify the client so that it delegates complexity to dependent interfaces. Listing 5-35 shows an example of a `switch` statement that could be replaced with the Strategy pattern.

LISTING 5-35 This method uses a `switch` statement, but the Strategy pattern would be more adaptive.

```
public class OnlineCart
{
    public void CheckOut(PaymentType paymentType)
    {
        switch(paymentType)
        {
            case PaymentType.CreditCard:
                ProcessCreditCardPayment();
                break;
            case PaymentType.Paypal:
                ProcessPaypalPayment();
                break;
            case PaymentType.GoogleCheckout:
                ProcessGooglePayment();
                break;
            case PaymentType.AmazonPayments:
                ProcessAmazonPayment();
                break;
        }
    }
}
```

```
    private void ProcessCreditCardPayment()
    {
        Console.WriteLine("Credit card payment chosen");
    }

    private void ProcessPaypalPayment()
    {
        Console.WriteLine("Paypal payment chosen");
    }

    private void ProcessGooglePayment()
    {
        Console.WriteLine("Google payment chosen");
    }

    private void ProcessAmazonPayment()
    {
        Console.WriteLine("Amazon payment chosen");
    }
}
```

In the example, for each case of the switch statement, the behavior of the class changes. This presents a code maintenance problem because the addition of a new case option requires a change to this class. If, instead, you replace each case statement with a new implementation of an interface, further implementations can be created to encapsulate new functionality—and the client would not need to change. This is shown in Listing 5-36.

LISTING 5-36 After the switch statement is replaced, the client looks far more adaptive to change.

```
public class OnlineCart
{
    public OnlineCart()
    {
        paymentStrategies = new Dictionary<PaymentType, IPaymentStrategy>();
        paymentStrategies.Add(PaymentType.CreditCard, new PaypalPaymentStrategy());
        paymentStrategies.Add(PaymentType.GoogleCheckout, new
GoogleCheckoutPaymentStrategy());
        paymentStrategies.Add(PaymentType.AmazonPayments, new
AmazonPaymentsPaymentStrategy());
        paymentStrategies.Add(PaymentType.Paypal, new PaypalPaymentStrategy());
    }

    public void CheckOut(PaymentType paymentType)
    {
        paymentStrategies[paymentType].ProcessPayment();
    }

    private IDictionary<PaymentType, IPaymentStrategy> paymentStrategies;
}
```

In the tradition of object-oriented programming, this code has objectified the different payment types into various classes, each of which implements the IPaymentStrategy interface. In this example, the OnlineCart class has a private dictionary that maps each value of the PaymentType enumeration onto an instance of the strategy interface. This simplifies the CheckOut method significantly. The switch statement has been removed and, along with it, the knowledge of how to process each different type of payment. The OnlineCart class did not need to know how to process the payments, which could vary greatly and introduce many unnecessary dependencies on this class. Now its job is to select the right payment strategy and delegate the processing to it.

There is still a maintenance burden here for adding new payment strategy implementations. If you want to add support for WePay, for example, the constructor will need to be updated to map the new WePayPaymentStrategy class to the associated WePay enumeration value.

Conclusion

The single responsibility principle has a hugely positive impact on the adaptability of code. Compared to equivalent code that does not adhere to the principle, SRP-compliant code leads to a greater number of classes that are smaller and more directed in scope. Where there would otherwise have been a single class or suite of classes with interdependencies and a confusion of responsibility, the SRP introduces order and clarity.

The SRP is primarily achieved through abstracting code behind interfaces and delegating responsibility for unrelated functionality to whichever implementation happens to be behind the interface at run time. Some design patterns are excellent at supporting efforts to strictly regiment the SRP—in particular, the Adapter pattern and the Decorator pattern. The former enables much of your code to maintain first-party references to interfaces under your direct control, although in reality utilizing a third-party library. The latter can be applied whenever some of a class's functionality needs to be removed but it is too tightly coupled with the intent of the class to stand alone.

What this chapter did not cover is how all of these classes are orchestrated at run time. Passing interfaces into constructors was taken for granted in this chapter, but Chapter 9 describes a variety of ways in which this can be accomplished.

CHAPTER 6

The open/closed principle

After completing this chapter, you will be able to

- Understand different interpretations of the open/closed principle.

- Treat SOLID code as append-only.

- Compare and contrast different class extension-point mechanisms.

- Use protected variation as a guideline for extension points.

The oxymoronic nature of the open/closed principle causes some confusion. Its pithy name suggests code that is permissive but at the same time restrictive. The several variations of the definition serve only to cloud matters further.

Picking one definition over another and using it alone would be remiss of me. Rather, this chapter compares each definition and its consequences to try to distill the principle down to its essence. The goal is a very useful guideline that will enable you to create code that is more adaptive to future changes.

Introduction to the open/closed principle

There are two definitions of the open/closed principle that must be examined, the original coining from the 1980s and a more contemporary definition. The latter seeks to elaborate on the former by giving it more context and clarifying the principle's scope.

The Meyer definition

Bertrand Mayer, in his 1988 book, *Object-Oriented Software Construction* (Prentice Hall), defined the open/closed principle (OCP) as follows:

> *Software entities should be open for extension, but closed for modification.*
>
> *—Bertrand Meyer*

The Meyer definition is the most commonly cited definition of the principle, but there is a second: the Martin definition.

The Martin definition

Robert C. Martin has defined the OCP in many different writings over the years. A more verbose version has been chosen here to contrast with the brief original:

> *"Open for extension." This means that the behavior of the module can be extended. As the requirements of the application change, we are able to extend the module with new behaviors that satisfy those changes. In other words, we are able to change what the module does.*
>
> *"Closed for modification." Extending the behavior of a module does not result in changes to the source or binary code of the module. The binary executable version of the module, whether in a linkable library, a DLL, or a Java .jar, remains untouched.*
>
> —Robert C. Martin, *Agile Software Development: Principles, Patterns, and Practices*
> *(Prentice Hall, 2003)*

For both sides of the open/closed principle, Martin explains in further detail what is meant by the key terms from the Meyer definition. To be open for extension, Martin explains, developers must be able to respond to changing requirements and support new features. This must be achieved despite modules being closed to modification. Developers must support new functionality without editing the source code—or compiled assembly—of the existing modules.

Before this chapter begins to describe how this is possible, there are exceptions to the restrictive "closed for modification" clause of the OCP that are sometimes cited: changes for fixing bugs or defects and changes that can be made without any client awareness.

Bug fixes

Bugs are a common problem in software, and they are impossible to prevent entirely. When they do occur, though, you need to respond by fixing the problem code. Of course, this involves a modification to an existing class—that is, unless you are willing to duplicate the class and implement the bug fix on the new version. This sounds needlessly convoluted and runs counter to the guiding principle of erring on the side of pragmatism rather than purity.

The two-step process for fixing a bug is outlined as follows:

1. Write a failing unit test and/or integration test that specifically targets the bug. This requires reliable and repeatable reproduction steps to create the conditions under which the code fails. Referring back to the AAA syntax of a unit test, you need to be able to *Arrange* the system under test so that it is in a state that might exhibit the defect, perform the specific *Act* in which the defect resides, and finally *Assert* the *expected* behavior. When you write such a test, the test will initially fail. This demonstrates the fact that all bugs are the result of missing tests. If a test is present that captures the defect, the test fails and, by extension, so does the build on the build server, when continuous integration is used.

2. The source code is *modified* so that the unit test passes. The bug fix exception to the OCP becomes necessary at this juncture because, without it, you would not be able to modify any existing code. Editing the system under test allows you to transition the failing test from red to green—from failure to success. When you ensure that no other tests are failing as a side effect, the bug is fixed.

Client awareness

A more permissive exception to the "closed for modification" rule is that any change is allowed to existing code as long as it does not also require a change to any client of that code. This places an emphasis on how coupled the software modules are, at all levels of granularity: between classes and classes, assemblies and assemblies, and subsystems and subsystems.

If a change in one class forces a change in another, the two are said to be *tightly* coupled. Conversely, if a class can change in isolation without forcing other classes to change, the participating classes are *loosely* coupled. At all times and at all levels, loose coupling is preferable. Maintaining loose coupling limits the impact that the OCP has if you allow modifications to existing code that does not force further changes to clients.

Extension points

Now that the "closed for modification" rule of the OCP is clarified, the "open for extension" rule can be considered. Classes that honor the OCP should be open to extension by containing defined extension points where future functionality can hook into the existing code and provide new behaviors.

Some options for different kinds of extension points are detailed in this section, with their pros and cons explored. These examples continue the `TradeProcessor` example of the previous chapter, this time focusing on the client's interaction with the class.

Code without extension points

First, what does code look like when it has no extension points? Figure 6-1 shows what happens when a class that has no extension points needs new functionality.

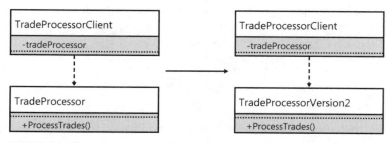

FIGURE 6-1 When there are no extension points, clients are forced to change.

The `TradeProcessorClient` depends directly on the `TradeProcessor` class. A new requirement is handed to you, resulting in necessary changes to the `TradeProcessor` class. Without modifying the original class, you create a new version (`TradeProcessorVersion2`) that contains the new functionality as specified in your new requirement. Because the client directly depends on the `TradeProcessor` class, and because of the lack of extension points in the `TradeProcessor` class, you need to place the new functionality inside a new class. The side effect of this change is that the `TradeProcessorClient` must be edited so that it depends on the new version of the class.

If you allow changes to existing code as long as they have no client impact, you might not have to create an entirely new version of the `TradeProcessor`. If the `ProcessTrades` method were to change, this would not simply be an implementation change for the class, it would also be an interface change. All interface changes force client changes because clients are always tightly coupled to the interfaces of their services.

Virtual methods

An alternative implementation for the `TradeProcessor` class contains an extension point: the `ProcessTrades` method is *virtual*. Figure 6-2 shows how the three classes are now arranged.

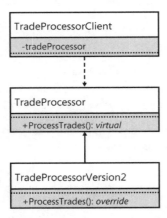

FIGURE 6-2 The client depends on the `TradeProcessor` class, which can be extended via inheritance.

Any class that marks one of its members as virtual is open to extension. This type of extension is via implementation inheritance. When your requirement for a new feature in the `TradeProcessor` class arrives, you can subclass the existing `TradeProcessor` and—without modifying its source code—alter the `ProcessTrades` method.

The `TradeProcessorClient` does not need to change in this case, because you can use polymorphism to supply the client with the new version of the `TradeProcessor` and have it call the subclass's implementation of the `ProcessTrades` method.

You are somewhat limited in the scope of your reimplementation, however. You have access to the base class—so you can call `TradeProcessor.ProcessTrades()`—but you cannot alter individual lines of the original method. You either call the original method in its entirety, perhaps implementing the new feature before or after the call, or you reimplement it completely. There is no middle ground with a virtual method. Remember, subclasses can only access members from their base class that are marked as protected. If the `TradeProcessor` was created with many private members, you would not have access to them, and altering the original class is, of course, prohibited by the OCP.

Abstract methods

A more flexible extension point that uses implementation inheritance is an *abstract* method. In this case, the `TradeProcessor` is an abstract class that defines a public `ProcessTrades` method, which delegates the work of the processing algorithm to three protected abstract methods. The client has no knowledge of these protected methods and, because they are abstract, no implementation is provided. Figure 6-3 shows the relationships between the classes involved.

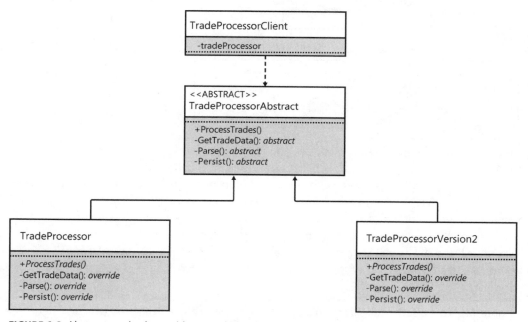

FIGURE 6-3 Abstract methods provide extension points for future subclasses.

Two versions of the trade processor are provided. Both inherit the `ProcessTrades` method directly from the abstract base class, and both provide their own implementations for the abstract methods. The client depends on the abstract base class, so either concrete subclass—or a new subclass for new requirements—could be provided and the OCP would be preserved.

This is an example of the *Template Method pattern*, in which an algorithm is modeled but its general steps are customizable because of delegation to abstract methods. In effect, the base class delegates the individual steps of the process to subclasses.

Interface inheritance

The final type of extension point discussed in this chapter is the alternative to implementation inheritance: interface inheritance. Here, the client's dependency on a *class* is replaced with the now-familiar delegation to an *interface*. Figure 6-4 shows the client's dependency on the interface and the two implementations of the interface.

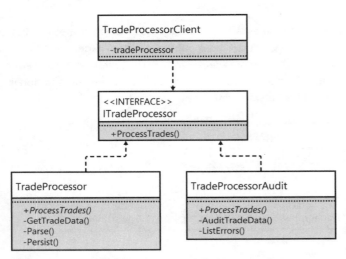

FIGURE 6-4 The client depends on an interface rather than a class.

Interface inheritance is preferable to implementation inheritance. With implementation inheritance, all subclasses—present and future—are *clients*. This prevents modification because, with implementation inheritance, subclasses depend on the *implementation*, too. All implementation changes are thus potentially client-aware changes. This echoes the advice to prefer composition over inheritance and to keep inheritance hierarchies shallow, with few layers of subclassing. If a change is made to add a member at the top of the inheritance graph, that change affects all members of the hierarchy.

Interfaces are also better extension points because they can be decorated with rich object graphs of functionality that calls upon many different contexts. They are more flexible than classes. I don't mean that the virtual and abstract methods that form the extension points of class inheritance are not useful, but that they do not provide quite the same level of adaptability that interfaces do.

"Design for inheritance or prohibit it"

In his book *Effective Java* (Addison-Wesley, 2008), Joshua Bloch has this to say about inheritance:

> *Design and document for inheritance or else prohibit it.*
>
> —*Joshua Bloch*

If you choose to use implementation inheritance as an extension point, you must design and document the class properly so as to protect and inform future programmers who extend the class. Inheritance of classes can be tricky—new subclasses can break existing code in unpredictable ways.

It is very important to note that any class that is not marked with the sealed keyword claims to support inheritance. A class does not need to be abstract or to contain virtual methods in order to be subclassed. The new keyword can be used to hide inherited members, but this blocks polymorphism, possibly defying expectations.

Prohibiting inheritance by sealing a class communicates a clear message to other programmers who might use the class: inheritance is not just unsupported in this class, it is prevented. This removes the temptation to try to extend the class, so programmers will redirect their efforts to finding an alternative.

Protected variation

You are now armed with several tools with which to implement the OCP. You know under which circumstances you can edit existing classes, and you know that you need to implement extension points in your code in order to support future changes in requirements. You also know that you can use interfaces as extension points to make your code truly adaptable and, perhaps, future-proof.

The missing ingredient is the knowledge of *when* and *where* to apply this principle. Taken to its logical extreme, should you add extension points everywhere, all the time? Would this make your code infinitely flexible, or is there a law of diminishing returns that applies?

This is where another principle related to the OCP is of vital importance: *protected variation*. Alistair Cockburn coined the term:

> *Identify points of predicted variation and create a stable interface around them.*
> —Alistair Cockburn, Pattern Languages of Program Design, vol. 2 (Addison-Wesley, 1996)

Somewhat confusingly, the definition references *predicted variation*, yet the principle itself is called *protected variation*. However, "predicted variation" is, to my mind, a more accurate term. The two major facets of this definition bear a closer examination.

Predicted variation

The requirements of an individual class should be linked directly to a business client's requirement. If this link is ignored, there is a risk that the class will not serve any purpose that the business client requested. Over the course of a sprint, user stories are taken from the sprint backlog, and developers and the product owner converse. At this point, questions should be asked as to the potential for future, related requirements. This informs the *predicted variation* that can be translated into extension points.

A stable interface

Even if you delegate only to interfaces, clients are still dependent on those interfaces. If the interface changes, the client must also change. A key advantage of depending on interfaces is that they are much less likely to change than implementations. If you place the interface in a separate assembly from its implementation, as the Stairway pattern suggests, the two can vary without affecting each other, and the implementation can change without affecting clients.

Clearly, it is very important that all interfaces chosen to represent an extension point should be stable. The likelihood and frequency of interface changes should be low, otherwise you will need to amend all clients to use the new version.

Just enough adaptability

There is a "Goldilocks Zone" where code contains just the right amount of extension points—in the right places—to enable change in areas where it is needed without increasing complexity or over-engineering the solution. For any individual problem, there can be too little, too much, or *just enough* adaptability.

Programmers who are beginning their careers tend to write code that is quite procedural, even in object-oriented languages such as C#. They tend to use classes as storage mechanisms for methods, regardless of whether those methods truly belong together. There is no discernible architecture to the code, and there are few extension points (and those that exist are misplaced). Any changes to re-quirements necessitate direct changes to the existing class or classes. This is how the original Trade-Processor was organized in Chapter 5, "The single responsibility principle." It was a "god object" that had perfect knowledge of everything to do with the program.

However, sometimes, this is the correct solution. If you assess the predicted variation for a small tool such as the TradeProcessor and conclude that it is very unlikely to change in any way, the orig-inal version of the code would suffice. Or perhaps the version that was refactored for clarity would be sufficient. The extra time spent refactoring for abstraction is wasted effort if you never make use of the extension points provided. Not only that, but the code is less readable, spread over different files and assemblies, with implementations hidden behind interfaces.

At the opposite end of the spectrum is the programmer who has started abstracting code behind interfaces. This programmer has discovered a new hammer, and now everything looks like a nail. The code produced by this programmer is a mass of extension points, most of which will never be used. A significant effort is required to piece together the code, which constantly delegates responsibilities to interfaces, and a significant effort is required to write this code in the first place.

If these two archetypal programmers—and their code—were combined, the result might be a har-monious middle ground where there are sufficient extension points, but where code can be adapted only in areas where requirements are unclear, changeable, or difficult to implement. This comes with experience, however, and it is difficult to arrive at this Zen-like state of protected variation without first being a naïve beginner and then transitioning to a know-it-all super-abstractor.

Conclusion

The open/closed principle is a guideline for the overall design of classes and interfaces and how developers can build code that allows change over time. With each passing sprint, new requirements are inevitable and should be embraced. Acknowledging that change is a good thing is only part of the answer, however. If the code you have produced up until this point is not built to enable change, change will be difficult, time consuming, error prone, and costly.

By ensuring that your code is open to extension but closed to modification, you effectively disallow future changes to existing classes and assemblies, which forces programmers to create new classes that can plug into the extension points. There are two main types of extension point available: implementation inheritance and interface inheritance. Virtual and abstract methods allow you to create subclasses that customize methods in a base class. If classes delegate to interfaces, this provides you with more flexibility in your extension points by virtue of a variety of patterns.

Knowing that you can integrate extension points into code is not sufficient, however. You also need to know when this is applicable. The concept of protected variation suggests that you identify parts of the requirements that are likely to change or that are particularly troublesome to implement, and factor these out behind extension points. Code can be quite rigidly defined, with little scope for extension or elaboration, or it can be very fluid, with myriad extension points ready to handle new requirements. Either of these options can be correct, depending on the specific scenario and context.

CHAPTER 7

The Liskov substitution principle

After completing this chapter, you will be able to

- Understand the importance of the Liskov substitution principle.

- Avoid breaking the rules of the Liskov substitution principle.

- Further solidify your single responsibility principle and open/closed principle habits.

- Create derived classes that honor the contracts of their base classes.

- Use code contracts to implement preconditions, postconditions, and data invariants.

- Write correct exception-throwing code.

- Understand covariance, contravariance, and invariance and where each applies.

Introduction to the Liskov substitution principle

The Liskov substitution principle (LSP) is a collection of guidelines for creating inheritance hierarchies in which a client can reliably use any class or subclass without compromising the expected behavior.

If the rules of the LSP are not followed, an extension to a class hierarchy—that is, a new subclass—might necessitate changes to any client of the base class or interface. If the LSP is followed, clients can remain unaware of changes to the class hierarchy. As long as there are no changes to the interface, there should be no reason to change any existing code. The LSP, therefore, helps to enforce both the open/closed principle and the single responsibility principle.

Formal definition

The definition of the LSP by prominent computer scientist Barbara Liskov is a bit dry, so it requires further explanation. Here is the official definition:

> *If S is a subtype of T, then objects of type T may be replaced with objects of type S, without breaking the program.*
>
> —*Barbara Liskov*

There are three code ingredients relating to the LSP:

- **Base type** The type (T) that clients have reference to. Clients call various methods, any of which can be overridden—or partially specialized—by the subtype.

- **Subtype** Any one of a possible family of classes (S) that inherit from the base type (T). Clients should not know which specific subtype they are calling, nor should they need to. The client should behave the same regardless of the subtype instance that it is given.

- **Context** The way in which the client interacts with the subtype. If the client doesn't interact with a subtype, the LSP can neither be honored nor contravened.

LSP rules

There are several "rules" that must be followed for LSP compliance. These rules can be split into two categories: contract rules (relating to the expectations of classes) and variance rules (relating to the types that can be substituted in code).

Contract rules

These rules relate to the contract of the supertype and the restrictions placed on the contracts that can be added to the subtype.

- Preconditions cannot be strengthened in a subtype.

- Postconditions cannot be weakened in a subtype.

- Invariants—conditions that must remain true—of the supertype must be preserved in a subtype.

To understand the contract rules, you should first understand the concept of contracts and then explore what you can do to ensure that you follow these rules when creating subtypes. The "Contracts" section later in this chapter covers both in depth.

Variance rules

These rules relate to the variance of arguments and return types.

- There must be contravariance of the method arguments in the subtype.

- There must be covariance of the return types in the subtype.

- No new exceptions can be thrown by the subtype unless they are part of the existing exception hierarchy.

The concept of type variance in the languages of the Common Language Runtime (CLR) of the Microsoft .NET Framework is limited to generic types and delegates. However, variance in these scenarios is well worth exploring and will equip you with the requisite knowledge to write code that is LSP compliant for variance. This will be explored in depth in the "Covariance and contravariance" section later in this chapter.

Contracts

It is often said that developers should *program to interfaces*, and a related idiom is to *program to a contract*. However, beyond the apparent method signatures, interfaces convey a very loose notion of a contract. A method signature reveals little about the actual requirements and guarantees of the method's implementation, as Figure 7-1 shows. In a strongly typed language like C#, there is at least a notion of passing the correct type for an argument, but this is largely where the interface ends and the concept of the contract must begin.

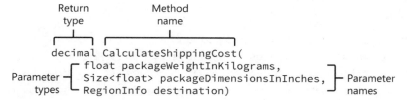

FIGURE 7-1 Method signatures reveal little about the expectations of the implementation.

All methods have at least an optional return type, a name, and an optional list of formal parameters. Each parameter consists of a type specifier and a name. When calling the method shown in Figure 7-1, you know—from only looking at the signature—that you need to pass in three parameters, one of type `float`, one of type `Size<float>`, and another of type `RegionInfo`. You also know that you can save the return value, of type `decimal`, in a variable or otherwise operate on this value after the call has been made.

> **Note** It is not advisable to use the `decimal` type to represent currency values, as is done in Figure 7-1. Instead, a Money[1] value type should be used. Although effort has been taken to ensure that the examples in this book are, as much as possible, relevant to a real-world context and are not just contrivances, some concessions have been made in the interest of brevity.

As a method writer, you can control the names given to parameters and methods. Take extra care to ensure that the method name truly represents the method's purpose and that the parameter names are as descriptive as possible. The `CalculateShippingCost` function's name uses a verb-noun form. Here the verb—the action performed by the method—is `Calculate`, and the noun—the object of the verb—is `ShippingCost`. This noun is, in a sense, the name of the return value. Descriptive names have also been chosen for the parameters: `packageDimensionsInInches` and `packageWeightIn-Kilograms` are self-explanatory parameter names, especially in the context of the method. They form a starting point for documenting the method.

---

[1] http://moneytype.codeplex.com/

Tip For further information on good variable and method naming and other best practices, Steve McConnell's *Code Complete*2 is essential reading.

What is missing, though, is the *contract* of the method. For example, the `packageWeightIn-Kilograms` parameter is of type `float`. What clients of this method might infer is that *any* `float` value is valid, including a negative value. Because the parameter represents a weight, a negative value should not be valid. The contract of this method should enforce a weight of greater than zero. For this, the method must implement a *precondition*.

Tip Although contracts as outlined in this chapter add run-time protection against many invalid calls to methods, the importance of good method and parameter naming is hard to exaggerate. If the formal parameters of the `CalculateShippingCost` method did not specify that they are in inches or kilograms, clients could, for example, call the method with values representing centimeters and pounds, respectively.

Preconditions

Preconditions are defined as all of the conditions necessary for a method to run reliably and without fault. Every method requires some preconditions to be true before it should be called. By default, interfaces force no guarantees on any of the implementers of their methods. Listing 7-1 shows how you can implement a precondition by using a guard clause at the start of a method.

LISTING 7-1 Throwing an exception is an effective way of enforcing precondition contracts.

```
public decimal CalculateShippingCost(
    float packageWeightInKilograms,
    Size<float> packageDimensionsInInches,
    RegionInfo destination)
{
    if (packageWeightInKilograms <= 0f) throw new Exception();

    return decimal.MinusOne;
}
```

The `if` statement at the very start of the method is one way to enforce a precondition, such as the requirement for a positive weight. If the condition `packageWeightInKilograms <= 0f` is met, an exception is thrown and the method stops executing immediately. This certainly prevents a method

---

2 http://www.stevemcconnell.com/cc.htm

from being executed unless all parameters have valid values. By using a more descriptive exception, you can provide more context to the caller, as shown in Listing 7-2.

LISTING 7-2 It is important to provide as much context as possible about why the precondition caused a failure.

```
public decimal CalculateShippingCost(
    float packageWeightInKilograms,
    Size<float> packageDimensionsInInches,
    RegionInfo destination)
{
    if (packageWeightInKilograms <= 0f)
        throw new ArgumentOutOfRangeException("packageWeightInKilograms", "Package weight
    must be positive and non-zero");

    return decimal.MinusOne;
}
```

This is an improvement on the first exception that was thrown. In addition to using an exception specifically for the purpose of out-of-range arguments, the client is also informed which parameter is errant and a description of the problem is provided.

By chaining more guard clauses like this together, you can add more conditions that must be fulfilled in order to call the method without generating an exception. The changes shown in Listing 7-3 include exceptions that are thrown when the package dimensions are out of range, too.

LISTING 7-3 As many preconditions as necessary can be added to prevent the method from being called with invalid parameters.

```
public decimal CalculateShippingCost(
    float packageWeightInKilograms,
    Size<float> packageDimensionsInInches,
    RegionInfo destination)
{
    if (packageWeightInKilograms <= 0f)
        throw new ArgumentOutOfRangeException("packageWeightInKilograms", "Package weight
    must be positive and non-zero");

    if (packageDimensionsInInches.X <= 0f || packageDimensionsInInches.Y <= 0f)
        throw new ArgumentOutOfRangeException("packageDimensionsInInches", "Package
    dimensions must be positive and non-zero");

    return decimal.MinusOne;
}
```

With these preconditions in place, clients must ensure that the parameters that they provide are within valid ranges before calling. One corollary from this is that all of the state that is checked in a precondition *must* be publically accessible by clients. If the client is unable to verify that the method they are about to call will throw an error due to an invalid precondition, the client won't be able to ensure that the call will succeed. Therefore, private state should not be the target of a precondition; only method parameters and the class's public properties should have preconditions.

Postconditions

Postconditions check whether an object is being left in a valid state as a method is exited. Whenever state is mutated in a method, it is possible for the state to be invalid due to logic errors.

Postconditions are implemented in the same manner as preconditions, through guard clauses. However, rather than placing the clauses at the start of the method, postcondition guard clauses must be placed at the end of the method after all edits to state have been made, as Listing 7-4 shows.

LISTING 7-4 The guard clause at the end of the method is a postcondition that ensures that the return value is in range.

```
public virtual decimal CalculateShippingCost(float packageWeightInKilograms, Size<float>
    packageDimensionsInInches, RegionInfo destination)
{
    if (packageWeightInKilograms <= 0f)
        throw new ArgumentOutOfRangeException("packageWeightInKilograms", "Package weight
must be positive and non-zero");

    if (packageDimensionsInInches.X <= 0f || packageDimensionsInInches.Y <= 0f)
        throw new ArgumentOutOfRangeException("packageDimensionsInInches", "Package
dimensions must be positive and non-zero");

    // shipping cost calculation

    var shippingCost = decimal.One;

    if(shippingCost <= decimal.Zero)
        throw new ArgumentOutOfRangeException("return", "The return value is out of
range");

    return shippingCost;
}
```

By testing state against a predetermined valid range—and throwing an exception if the value falls outside of that range—you can enforce a postcondition on the method. The postcondition here relates not to the state of the object but to the return value. Much like method argument values are tested against preconditions for validity, so are method return values tested against postconditions for validity. If, at any point during the method, the return value is set to zero or a negative value, the postcondition will detect this and halt execution at the end of the method. This way, clients of this method will never inadvertently receive an invalid value and they can continue to assume that it will always be valid. Note that the interface of the method does not communicate that the return value will always be non-zero and positive—that is a feature of the interface's contract with clients.

Data invariants

A third type of contract is the data invariant. A *data invariant* is a predicate that remains true for the lifetime of an object; it is true after construction and must remain true until the object is out of scope. Data invariants relate to the expected internal state of the object. An example of a data invariant for the `ShippingStrategy` call is that the flat rate provided is positive and non-zero. If, as shown in Listing 7-5, the flat rate is set on construction, a simple guard clause in the constructor will prevent an invalid value from being set.

LISTING 7-5 Adding a precondition to a constructor can help protect a data invariant.

```
public class ShippingStrategy
{
    public ShippingStrategy(decimal flatRate)
    {
        if (flatRate <= decimal.Zero)
            throw new ArgumentOutOfRangeException("flatRate", "Flat rate must be positive
and non-zero");

        this.flatRate = flatRate;
    }

    protected decimal flatRate;
}
```

Because the `flatRate` value is a protected member variable, the only opportunity that clients have for setting the value is through the constructor. If `flatRate` is set to a valid value at this point, it is guaranteed to be valid for the rest of the lifetime of the object because clients have no way of changing this value.

However, if the `flatRate` variable is instead a publically settable property, the guard clause would have to be moved to the setter block in order to protect the data invariant. Listing 7-6 shows the flat rate refactored as a public property, with an accompanying guard clause.

LISTING 7-6 When a data invariant is a public property, the guard clause moves to the setter.

```
public class ShippingStrategy
{
    public ShippingStrategy(decimal flatRate)
    {
        FlatRate = flatRate;
    }

    public decimal FlatRate
    {
        get
        {
            return flatRate;
        }
        set
        {
            if (value <= decimal.Zero)
                throw new ArgumentOutOfRangeException("value", "Flat rate must be positive
and non-zero");

            flatRate = value;
        }
    }
}
```

Now clients might be able to change the value of the FlatRate property but, because of the if statement and exception, the invariant cannot be broken.

Encapsulation vs. contracts

The contracts implemented in this example make sense, but they are caused by a poor choice of types for each value. The precondition contract for ensuring that the package weight argument is non-zero and positive is intrinsically linked with the type of the variable: weight should never be zero or negative. This makes weight a candidate for encapsulation into its own type. If, as is likely, another class or method requires a weight, you would need to carry this precondition across to the new code. This is inefficient, hard to maintain, and error-prone. It makes more sense to create a new type and define the precondition with it so that all uses of the Weight type must have a non-zero and positive value. It is, in fact, an invariant of the type rather than a precondition of the CalculateShippingCost method.

Similarly, the flat rate is modeled poorly by the decimal type. Instead, this should be promoted to its own value type, and the invariant requiring it to also be non-zero and positive should be applied to this type.

Liskov contract rules

All of this method contract discussion is merely preamble to some of the tenets of the Liskov substitution principle. The LSP sets rules by which types must inherit contracts. A reminder of the definition of the LSP is shown here:

> *If S is a subtype of T, then objects of type T may be replaced with objects of type S, without breaking the program.*

Where contracts are concerned, this leads to the guidelines that were stated earlier:

- Preconditions cannot be strengthened in a subtype.

- Postconditions cannot be weakened in a subtype.

- Invariants of the supertype must be preserved in a subtype.

If you follow all of these rules when creating subclasses of existing classes, substitutability will be retained when you are dealing with contracts.

Whenever a subclass is created, it brings with it all of the methods, properties, and fields that make up the parent class. This also includes the contracts inside the methods and property setters. Preconditions, postconditions, and data invariants are all expected to be maintained in the same way that they were in the parent class. Subclasses are, where applicable, allowed to override method implementations, which includes the possibility for changing the contracts. Liskov substitution stipulates that some changes are not allowed, because they could break existing clients that must be able to use the new subclass as if it were an instance of the superclass.

Preconditions cannot be strengthened

Whenever a subclass overrides an existing method that contains preconditions, it must never *strengthen* the existing preconditions. Doing so would potentially break any client code that already assumes that the subclass defines the strongest possible precondition contracts for any method.

Listing 7-7 shows the addition of a new `WorldWideShippingStrategy`. Due to the large number of similarities in how the classes behave, this new class is implemented as a subclass of the `ShippingStrategy` class. The `CalculateShippingCost` method is overridden to provide a new value that takes into account the destination of the package being sent via the `RegionInfo` parameter. Although the `ShippingStrategy` class did not make any guarantees that the destination of the package would be provided, `WorldWideShippingStrategy` now requires this parameter to be provided, otherwise it cannot correctly calculate how much it would cost to send the package to that location.

LISTING 7-7 This subclass adds a new guard clause, thus strengthening the preconditions.

```
public class WorldWideShippingStrategy : ShippingStrategy
{
    public override decimal CalculateShippingCost(
        float packageWeightInKilograms,
        Size<float> packageDimensionsInInches,
        RegionInfo destination)
    {
        if (packageWeightInKilograms <= 0f)
            throw new ArgumentOutOfRangeException("packageWeightInKilograms", "Package
weight must be positive and non-zero");

        if (packageDimensionsInInches.X <= 0f || packageDimensionsInInches.Y <= 0f)
            throw new ArgumentOutOfRangeException("packageDimensionsInInches", "Package
dimensions must be positive and non-zero");

        if (destination == null)
            throw new ArgumentNullException("destination", "Destination must be
provided");

        return decimal.One;
    }
}
```

The temptation is to strengthen the preconditions so that you can guarantee that the destination parameter is provided. This creates a conflict that calling code is unable to solve. If a class calls the CalculateShippingCost method of the ShippingStrategy class, it is free to pass in a null value for the destination parameter without experiencing a side effect. But if it is calling the Calculate-ShippingCost method of the WorldWideShippingStrategy class, it must not pass in a null value for the destination parameter. Doing so would violate a precondition and cause an exception to be thrown. As earlier chapters have demonstrated, client code must never make assumptions about what type it is acting on. Doing so only leads to strong coupling between classes and an inability to adapt to changes in requirements.

To demonstrate the problem, examine the unit test shown in Listing 7-8.

LISTING 7-8 When the precondition is strengthened, clients cannot reliably use a WorldWideShippingStrategy where a ShippingStrategy is required.

```
[Test]
public void ShippingRegionMustBeProvided()
{
    strategy.Invoking(s => s.CalculateShippingCost(1f, ValidDimensions, null))
        .ShouldThrow<ArgumentNullException>("Destination must be provided")
        .And.ParamName.Should().Be("destination");
}
```

If the strategy used by this test is of type `WorldWideShippingStrategy`, the test will pass; no destination is provided but one is required, thus an exception meeting the specification is thrown. If a `ShippingStrategy` is used instead, this test will fail because no precondition exists to prevent the null value for the destination and no exception will be thrown.

Listing 7-9 shows a refactored set of unit tests that do not attempt to test the same preconditions on both strategy types. A test asserting that the shipping region must be provided is only valid for the `WorldWideShippingStrategy`. However, regardless of shipping strategy, the precondition that the shipping weight must be positive is always valid, so this is included in a base class of tests that will be run for each shipping strategy class.

LISTING 7-9 These refactored unit tests separately target the two shipping strategy classes.

```
[TestFixture]
public class WorldWideShippingStrategyTests : ShippingStrategyTestsBase
{
    [Test]
    public void ShippingRegionMustBeProvided()
    {
        strategy.Invoking(s => s.CalculateShippingCost(1f, ValidSize, null))
            .ShouldThrow<ArgumentNullException>("Destination must be provided")
            .And.ParamName.Should().Be("destination");
    }

    protected override ShippingStrategy CreateShippingStrategy()
    {
        return new WorldWideShippingStrategy(decimal.One);
    }
}
// . . .
public abstract class ShippingStrategyTestsBase
{
    [Test]
    public void ShippingWeightMustBePositive()
    {
        strategy.Invoking(s => s.CalculateShippingCost(-1f, ValidSize, null))
            .ShouldThrow<ArgumentOutOfRangeException>("Package weight must be positive and
    non-zero")
            .And.ParamName.Should().Be("packageWeightInKilograms");
    }
}
```

Postconditions cannot be weakened

When applying postconditions to subclasses, the opposite rule applies. Instead of not being able to strengthen postconditions, you cannot weaken them. As for all of the Liskov substitution rules relating to contracts, the reason that you cannot weaken postconditions is because existing clients might break when presented with the new subclass. Theoretically, if you comply with the LSP, any subclass you create should be usable by all existing clients without causing them to fail in unexpected ways.

One such example of causing an unexpected failure in an existing client is explored in Listing 7-10. The unit test and implementation relate to the `WorldWideShippingStrategy`, the `ShippingStrategy` subclass for international packages.

LISTING 7-10 The new implementation requires a weakening of the postcondition.

```
[Test]
public void ShippingDomesticallyIsFree()
{
    strategy.CalculateShippingCost(1f, ValidDimensions, RegionInfo.CurrentRegion)
        .Should().Be(decimal.Zero);
}
// . . .
public override decimal CalculateShippingCost(float packageWeightInKilograms, Size<float>
  packageDimensionsInInches, RegionInfo destination)
{
    if (destination == null)
        throw new ArgumentNullException("destination", "Destination must be provided");

    if (packageWeightInKilograms <= 0f)
        throw new ArgumentOutOfRangeException("packageWeightInKilograms", "Package weight
 must be positive and non-zero");

    if (packageDimensionsInInches.X <= 0f || packageDimensionsInInches.Y <= 0f)
        throw new ArgumentOutOfRangeException("packageDimensionsInInches", "Package
 dimensions must be positive and non-zero");

    var shippingCost = decimal.One;

    if(destination == RegionInfo.CurrentRegion)
    {
        shippingCost = decimal.Zero;
    }

    return shippingCost;
}
```

The unit test asserts that, when the current region is used for the destination—that is, the shipping is domestic—the `WorldWideShippingStrategy` does not charge for shipping at all. This is reflected in the accompanying implementation. This assertion is, again, in conflict with an existing unit test for the base class that asserts the original postcondition: that the result is always positive and non-zero, as shown in Listing 7-11.

LISTING 7-11 This unit test shows the original unit test, which fails when the strategy is a `WorldWideShipping-Strategy`.

```
[Test]
public void ShippingCostMustBePositiveAndNonZero()
{
    strategy.CalculateShippingCost(1f, ValidDimensions, RegionInfo.CurrentRegion)
        .Should().BeGreaterThan(0m);
}
```

A client could easily be broken by this change in behavior due to its assumption of the value of the shipping cost. For example, the client assumes that the shipping cost is always positive and non-zero, as indicated by the postcondition contract of the `ShippingStrategy`. This client then uses the shipping cost as the denominator in a subsequent calculation. When a switch is made to use the new `WorldWideShippingStrategy`, the client unexpectedly starts throwing `DivideByZeroException` errors for all domestic orders.

Had the LSP been honored and the postcondition never weakened, this defect would never have been introduced.

Invariants must be maintained

Whenever a new subclass is created, it must continue to honor all of the data invariants that were part of the base class. This is an easy problem to introduce because subclasses have a lot of freedom to introduce new ways of changing previously private data.

Listing 7-12 returns to the previous data invariant example from earlier in the chapter. However, in this instance, the `ShippingStrategy` accepts the flat rate value as a constructor parameter and maintains this value as a read-only data invariant. The new `WorldWideShippingStrategy` is introduced, and the means to change the flat rate value is made public through a property.

LISTING 7-12 The subclass breaks the data invariant of the superclass, violating the LSP.

```
[Test]
public void ShippingFlatRateCanBeChanged()
{
    strategy.FlatRate = decimal.MinusOne;

    strategy.FlatRate.Should().Be(decimal.MinusOne);
}
// . . .
public class WorldWideShippingStrategy : ShippingStrategy
{
    public WorldWideShippingStrategy(decimal flatRate)
        : base(flatRate)
    {

    }
```

```
    public decimal FlatRate
    {
        get
        {
            return flatRate;
        }
        set
        {
            flatRate = value;
        }
    }
}
```

Although the subclass reuses the base class's constructor and guard clause, it does not maintain the data invariant and therefore breaks the Liskov substitution principle. The unit test proves that clients are able to set the value to a negative number, which should be disallowed by the class if it is to correctly protect its data invariants.

Listing 7-13 shows that when the base class is reworked to disallow direct write access to the flat rate field, the invariant is properly honored by the subclass. This is a very common pattern whereby fields are private but have protected or public properties that contain guard clauses to protect the invariants.

LISTING 7-13 The base class allows the subclass write access to the field only through the guarded property setter.

```
public class WorldWideShippingStrategy : ShippingStrategy
{
    public WorldWideShippingStrategy(decimal flatRate)
        : base(flatRate)
    {

    }

    public new decimal FlatRate
    {
        get
        {
            return base.FlatRate;
        }
        set
        {
            base.FlatRate = value;
        }
    }
}
// . . .
public class ShippingStrategy
{
```

```
    public ShippingStrategy(decimal flatRate)
    {
        if (flatRate <= decimal.Zero)
            throw new ArgumentOutOfRangeException("flatRate", "Flat rate must be positive
and non-zero");

        this.flatRate = flatRate;
    }

    protected decimal FlatRate
    {
        get
        {
            return flatRate;
        }
        set
        {
            if (value <= decimal.Zero)
                throw new ArgumentOutOfRangeException("value", "Flat rate must be positive
and non-zero");

            flatRate = value;
        }
    }
}
```

Tightening the visibility of the field and instead providing access only through the property setter protects the invariant with a guard clause. Doing this at subclass level is also preferable because it means that all future subclasses are absolved of this responsibility and simply cannot directly write to the field at all.

A new unit test can be created that asserts this new behavior, as shown in Listing 7-14.

LISTING 7-14 With the invariant maintained, this unit test passes.

```
[Test]
public void ShippingFlatRateCannotBeSetToNegativeNumber()
{
    strategy.Invoking(s => s.FlatRate = decimal.MinusOne)
        .ShouldThrow<ArgumentOutOfRangeException>("Flat rate must be positive and non-
zero")
        .And.ParamName.Should().Be("value");
}
```

If a client tries to set the FlatRate property to a negative value, or even to zero, the guard clause prevents the assignment and an ArgumentOutOfRangeException is thrown.

Code contracts

Throughout the previous section, the guard clauses that formed the basis of the contracts were all written in long form, using `if` statements and exceptions. It is worth exploring an alternative to these manual guard clauses: code contracts.

Previously a separate library, code contracts were integrated into the .NET Framework 4.0 main libraries. In addition to being easier to read, write, and comprehend than manual guard clauses, code contracts bring with them the possibility of using static verification and automatic generation of reference documentation.

With static contract verification, code contracts are able to check for contract violations without executing the application. This helps expose implicit contracts such as null dereferences and problems with array bounds, in addition to the explicitly coded contracts shown throughout this section.

Generating reference documentation relating to the contract of a method or class is important because client code has no other way of knowing the exp   ectations. When more detail is included in the XML comments that form the documentation to methods and classes, clients can view the expectations via IntelliSense. This makes working with classes that use contracts a bit easier.

Preconditions

Preconditions can be written succinctly by using code contracts. You will need to include the `System.Diagnostics.Contracts` namespace, which is part of the `mscorlib.dll` and so should not need an additional assembly reference. The static `Contract` class provides the majority of the functionality that is required to implement contracts.

> **Note** If you make the decision to use code contracts, the static `Contract` class will permeate throughout almost all of your code base. This is less of a problem than it is with most static references because code contracts are ubiquitous infrastructure that, it is assumed, will not be removed or replaced. Thus, it is a significant undertaking to undo the decision to use code contracts, and it is best to use them from the outset of a project, or not at all.

Listing 7-15 shows the declarative nature of a code contract precondition.

```csharp
using System.Diagnostics.Contracts;

public class ShippingStrategy
{
    public decimal CalculateShippingCost(float packageWeightInKilograms, Size<float>
  packageDimensionsInInches, RegionInfo destination)
    {
        Contract.Requires(packageWeightInKilograms > 0f);
        Contract.Requires(packageDimensionsInInches.X > 0f && packageDimensionsInInches.Y
  > 0f);

        return decimal.MinusOne;
    }
}
```

The `Contract.Requires` method accepts a Boolean predicate value. This represents the state that the method requires in order to proceed. Note that this is the exact opposite of the predicate used in an `if` statement in manual guard clauses. In that case, the clauses were checking for state that was invalid before throwing an exception. With code contracts, the predicate is closer to an assertion: that the Boolean value must return `true`, otherwise the contract fails. This example requires that the `packageWeightInKilograms` parameter is non-zero and positive and that the `packageDimensionsInInches` parameter is non-zero and positive for both its X and Y properties.

This version of the `Contract.Requires` method throws an exception when the contract predicate is not met, but the type of exception is a `ContractException`, which does not match the expected exception in the existing unit tests. Therefore, they fail.

```
Expected System.ArgumentOutOfRangeException because Package dimension must be positive and non-
    zero, but found System.Diagnostics.Contracts.__ContractsRuntime+ContractException with message
    "Precondition failed: packageDimensionsInInches.X > 0f && packageDimensionsInInches.Y > 0f"
```

Furthermore, if you run this example while passing in an invalid value for one of the parameters, you will get the message shown in Figure 7-2. This informs you that you have not properly configured code contracts for use.

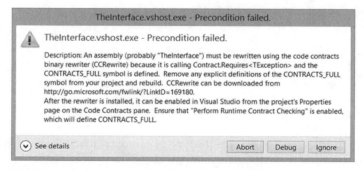

FIGURE 7-2 Code contracts must be configured before use.

The property pages of each project include a Code Contracts tab on which you can configure code contracts. A minimal working setup is shown in Figure 7-3.

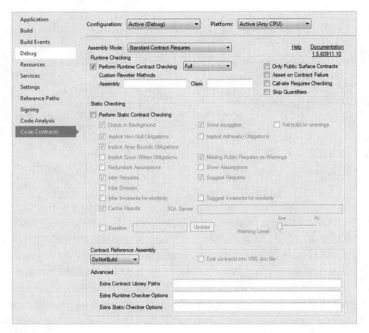

FIGURE 7-3 The property pages for code contracts contain a lot of settings.

When they are configured correctly, the contract preconditions can be rewritten to use an alternative version of the `Contract.Requires` method. Listing 7-16 shows this version.

LISTING 7-16 This version of the `Requires` method accepts the type of the exception to be thrown.

```
public class ShippingStrategy
{
    public decimal CalculateShippingCost(float packageWeightInKilograms, Size<float>
packageDimensionsInInches, RegionInfo destination)
    {
        Contract.Requires<ArgumentOutOfRangeException>(packageWeightInKilograms > 0f,
"Package weight must be positive and non-zero");
        Contract.Requires<ArgumentOutOfRangeException>(packageDimensionsInInches.X > 0f &&
packageDimensionsInInches.Y > 0f, "Package dimensions must be positive and non-zero");

        return decimal.MinusOne;
    }
}
```

This generic version of the `Requires` method accepts the type of exception that you would like the contract to throw when the predicate fails. This, along with the exception message included in a subsequent method parameter, will cause the existing unit tests to pass.

Postconditions

Code contracts can similarly provide a shortcut to defining postconditions. The `Contract` static class contains an `Ensures` method that is the postcondition complement to the precondition's `Requires` method. This method also accepts a Boolean predicate that must be true in order to progress through to the return statement. It is worth noting that the return statement must be the only line that follows a call to `Contract.Ensures`. This makes intuitive sense because, otherwise, it would be possible to further modify state in a way that might break the postcondition.

Listing 7-17 reiterates the `ShippingCostMustBePositive` unit test and includes a rewritten `CalculateShippingCost` implementation that uses the `Contract.Ensures` method as a postcondition.

LISTING 7-17 The `Ensures` method creates a postcondition that should be true on exiting the method.

```
[Test]
public void ShippingCostMustBePositive()
{
    strategy.CalculateShippingCost(1, ValidSize, null)
        .Should().BeGreaterThan(decimal.MinusOne);
}
// . . .
public class ShippingStrategy
{
    public decimal CalculateShippingCost(float packageWeightInKilograms, Size<float>
    packageDimensionsInInches, RegionInfo destination)
    {
        Contract.Requires<ArgumentOutOfRangeException>(packageWeightInKilograms > 0f,
    "Package weight must be positive and non-zero");
        Contract.Requires<ArgumentOutOfRangeException>(packageDimensionsInInches.X > 0f &&
    packageDimensionsInInches.Y > 0f, "Package dimensions must be positive and non-zero");

        Contract.Ensures(Contract.Result<decimal>() > 0m);

        return decimal.MinusOne;
    }
}
```

The predicate in this example is a bit different from the ones in prior examples and demonstrates a common use of the postcondition: testing that a return value is valid. Checking that the shipping cost is positive (and, in fact, non-negative) requires knowledge of the return value. The return value is often, but not always, a local variable that is declared and defined within the method. You could trivially assert that the value you are returning is greater than zero, but this is not really foolproof. To access the value that is actually returned from the method, you can use the `Contract.Result` method to retrieve it. This generic method accepts the return type of the method and returns whichever result is eventually returned by the method. This is how you can ensure that no subsequent lines can replace a valid value with an invalid value without the postcondition failing and an exception being thrown.

Data invariants

It is common for each method in a class to contain its own preconditions and postconditions, but data invariants relate to the class as a whole. Code contracts allow you to create a private method on the class that contains declarative definitions of the class's invariants.

Each invariant is defined by another method of the Contract static class, as Listing 7-18 shows.

LISTING 7-18 Data invariants can be protected by a method dedicated to the purpose.

```
public class ShippingStrategy
{
    public ShippingStrategy(decimal flatRate)
    {
        this.flatRate = flatRate;
    }

    [ContractInvariantMethod]
    private void ClassInvariant()
    {
        Contract.Invariant(this.flatRate > 0m, "Flat rate must be positive and non-zero");
    }

    protected decimal flatRate;
}
```

The Contract.Invariant method follows the same pattern as the Requires and Ensures methods in that it accepts a Boolean predicate that must be true in order to satisfy the contract. In this example, there is also a second string parameter provided that describes the fault if this contract fails to be met and the invariant is unprotected. The client is allowed to make as many calls to the Invariant method as necessary, so it is best to break the invariants down to their most granular, rather than logically AND them all together with the && operator. This gives you the maximum benefit of knowing exactly which data invariant has been broken.

If this were a normal private method, you would be obliged to call the method at the start and end of every method, to ensure that the invariants were correctly protected. Luckily, you can have code contracts do this on your behalf by marking the method with the ContractInvariantMethod-Attribute. Remember that attributes do not require the Attribute suffix, so this has been shortened in the example to ContractInvariantMethod. This flags the method as one that code contracts must call when entering and leaving a method, to confirm that the class's data invariants are not being violated. The prerequisites for marking a method as a ContractInvariantMethod are that it must return void and accept no arguments. However, it can be public or private, and you can choose any name to describe the method. Classes can have more than one ContractInvariantMethod, so logically grouping them is also possible. The body of the method must only make calls to the Contract.Invariant method.

Interface contracts

The final feature of code contracts to be covered here is that of interface contracts. So far, you have embedded all of your calls to `Contract.Requires`, `Contract.Ensures`, and `Contract.Invariant` in the class implementation itself. As has been mentioned, the static nature of the `Contract` class makes this code ubiquitous and difficult to remove or change in favor of an alternative library in the future. This is somewhat contrary to the adaptive codebase that is the ideal, but some infrastructural concessions are justifiable for pragmatic reasons.

A more immediate concern is the drop in readability that occurs when code contracts are liberally applied to classes. In fact, this is not really a fault of code contracts but a result of diligently applying contracts in general. Preconditions, postconditions, and data invariants are naturally implemented in code, but this code tends to increase the noise-to-signal ratio.

An interface contract, such as that shown in Listing 7-19 for the ongoing `ShippingStrategy` example, can alleviate this problem in addition to providing another helpful feature.

LISTING 7-19 A dedicated class can define preconditions, postconditions, and invariants for every implementation of an interface.

```
[ContractClass(typeof(ShippingStrategyContract))]
interface IShippingStrategy
{
    decimal CalculateShippingCost(
        float packageWeightInKilograms,
        Size<float> packageDimensionsInInches,
        RegionInfo destination);
}
//. . .
[ContractClassFor(typeof(IShippingStrategy))]
public abstract class ShippingStrategyContract : IShippingStrategy
{
    public decimal CalculateShippingCost(float packageWeightInKilograms, Size<float>
    packageDimensionsInInches, RegionInfo destination)
    {
        Contract.Requires<ArgumentOutOfRangeException>(packageWeightInKilograms > 0f,
    "Package weight must be positive and non-zero");
        Contract.Requires<ArgumentOutOfRangeException>(packageDimensionsInInches.X > 0f &&
    packageDimensionsInInches.Y > 0f, "Package dimensions must be positive and non-zero");

        Contract.Ensures(Contract.Result<decimal>() > 0m);

        return decimal.One;
    }

    [ContractInvariantMethod]
    private void ClassInvariant()
    {
        Contract.Invariant(flatRate > 0m, "Flat rate must be positive and non-zero");
    }
}
```

For interface contracts, you of course need an interface to work with. In this example, the `CalculateShippingCost` method has been extracted into its own `IShippingStrategy` interface. It is this interface, rather than a single implementation, that is going to have the contracts applied. This is an important departure from the previous examples because it means that all implementations of this interface will acquire the applied contracts. This is how you can enhance a simple interface that provides few instructions for implementation and use, to give it more powerful requirements and assurances.

When writing an interface contract, you also need a class that is going to implement the methods of the interface but only fill them with uses of the `Contract.Requires` and `Contract.Ensures` methods. The abstract `ShippingStrategyContract` provides this functionality and looks like the prior examples, but what the prior examples lacked was the real functionality of the method. Even in production code, this is the limit of the code contained in a contract class. There is also a `Contract-InvariantMethod` to house any calls to `Contract.Invariant`, just as if this class were the real implementation.

To link the interface to the contract class implementation, you unfortunately need a two-way reference via an attribute. This is somewhat unfortunate because it adds noise to the interface, which it would be nice to avoid. Nevertheless, by marking the interface with the `ContractClass` attribute and the contract class with the `ContractClassFor` attribute, you can write your preconditions, postconditions, and data invariant protection code once and have it apply to all subsequent implementations of the interface. Both the `ContractClass` and `ContractClassFor` attributes accept a Type argument. The `ContractClass` is applied to the interface and has the contract class type passed in, whereas the `ContractClassFor` is applied to the contract class and has the interface type passed in.

This concludes the introduction to code contracts and the foray into the Liskov substitution principle's rules relating to contracts. One final important point needs to be emphasized. Whether they are implemented manually or by using code contracts, if a precondition, postcondition, or invariant fails, *clients should not catch the exception*. Catching an exception is an action that indicates that the client can recover from this situation, which is seldom likely or perhaps even possible when a contract is broken. The ideal is that all contract violations will happen during functional testing and that the offending code will be fixed before shipping. This is why it is so important to unit test contracts. If a contract violation is not fixed before shipping and an end user is unfortunate enough to trigger an exception, it is most likely the best course of action to force the application to close. It is advisable to allow the application to fail because it is now in a potentially invalid state. For a web application, this will mean that the global error page is displayed. For a desktop application, the user can be shown a friendly message and be given a chance to report the problem. In any and all cases, a log should be made of the exception, with full stack trace and as much context as possible.

The next section covers the rest of the LSP's rules—those that apply to covariance and contra-variance.

Covariance and contravariance

The remaining rules of the Liskov substitution principle all relate to covariance and contravariance. Generally, *variance* is a term applied to the expected behavior of subtypes in a class hierarchy containing complex types.

Definitions

As previously demonstrated, it is important to cover the basics of this topic before diving in to the specifics of the LSP's requirements for variance.

Covariance

Figure 7-4 shows a very small class hierarchy of just two types: the generically named Supertype and Subtype, which are conveniently named after their respective roles in the inheritance structure. Supertype defines some fields and methods that are inherited by Subtype. Subtype enhances the Supertype by defining its own fields and methods.

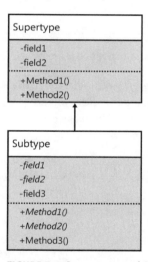

FIGURE 7-4 Supertype and Subtype have a parent/child relationship in this class hierarchy.

Polymorphism is the ability of a subtype to be treated as if it were an instance of the supertype. Thanks to this feature of object-oriented programming, which C# supports, any method that accepts an instance of Supertype will also be able to accept an instance of Subtype without any casting required by either the client or service code, and also without any type sniffing by the service. To the service, it has been handed an instance of Supertype, and this is the only fact it is concerned with. It doesn't care what specific subtype has been handed to it.

Variance enters the discussion when you introduce another type that might use Supertype and/or Subtype through a generic parameter.

Figure 7-5 is a visual explanation of the concept of *covariance*. First, you define a new interface called `ICovariant`. This interface is a generic of type T and contains a single method that returns this type, T. Because the `out` keyword is used before the generic type argument T, this interface is well named because it exhibits covariant behavior.

The second half of the class diagram details a new inheritance hierarchy that has been created thanks to the covariance of the `ICovariant` interface. By plugging in the values for the `Supertype` and `Subtype` classes that were defined previously, `ICovariant<Supertype>` becomes a supertype for the `ICovariant<Subtype>` interface.

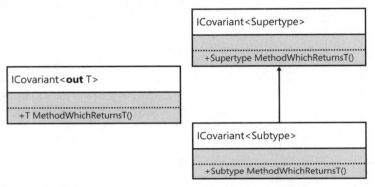

FIGURE 7-5 Due to covariance of the generic parameter, the base-class/subclass relationship is preserved.

Polymorphism applies here, just as it did previously, and this is where it gets interesting. Thanks to covariance, whenever a method requires an instance of `ICovariant<Supertype>`, you are perfectly at liberty to provide it with an instance of `ICovariant<Subtype>`, instead. This will work seamlessly thanks to the simultaneous interoperating of both covariance and polymorphism.

So far, this is of limited general use. To firm up this explanation, I'll move away from class diagrams and instructive type names to a more real-world scenario. Listing 7-20 shows a class hierarchy between a general `Entity` base class and a specific `User` subclass. All `Entity` types inherit a GUID unique identifier and a string name, and each `User` has an `EmailAddress` and a `DateOfBirth`.

LISTING 7-20 In this small domain, a User is a specialization of the Entity type.

```
public class Entity
{
    public Guid ID { get; private set; }

    public string Name { get; private set; }
}
// . . .
public class User : Entity
{
    public string EmailAddress { get; private set; }

    public DateTime DateOfBirth { get; private set; }
}
```

This is directly analogous to the Supertype/Subtype example, but with a more directed purpose. This small domain is going to have the Repository pattern applied to it. The Repository pattern provides you with an interface for retrieving objects as if they were in memory but that could realistically be loaded from a very different storage medium. Listing 7-21 shows an `EntityRepository` class and its `UserRepository` subclass.

LISTING 7-21 Without involving generics, all inheritance in C# is invariant.

```
public class EntityRepository
{
    public virtual Entity GetByID(Guid id)
    {
        return new Entity();
    }
}
// . . .
public class UserRepository : EntityRepository
{
    public override User GetByID(Guid id)
    {
        return new User();
    }
}
```

This example is not the same as that previously described because of one key difference: in the absence of generic types, C# is not covariant for method return types. In fact, a compilation error is generated due to an attempt to change the return type of the `GetByID` method in the subclass to match the `User` class.

```
error CS0508: 'SubtypeCovariance.UserRepository.GetByID(System.Guid)': return type must be
  'SubtypeCovariance.Entity' to match overridden member
  'SubtypeCovariance.EntityRepository.GetByID(System.Guid)'
```

Perhaps experience tells you that this will not work, but the reason is a lack of covariance in this scenario. If C# supported covariance for general classes, you would be able to enforce the change of return type in the `UserRepository`. Because it does not, you have only two options. You can amend the `UserRepository.GetByID` method's return type to be `Entity` and use polymorphism to allow you to return a `User` in its place. This is dissatisfying because clients of the `UserRepository` would have to downcast the return type from an `Entity` type to a `User` type, or they would have to sniff for the `User` type and execute specific code if the expected type was returned.

Instead, you should redefine `EntityRepository` as a generic class that requires the `Entity` type it intends to operate on via a generic type argument. This generic parameter can be marked `out`, thus covariant, and the `UserRepository` subclass can specialize its parent base class for the `User` type. Listing 7-22 exemplifies this.

LISTING 7-22 Make base classes generic to take advantage of covariance and allow subclasses to override the return type.

```
public interface IEntityRepository<TEntity>
    where TEntity : Entity
{
    TEntity GetByID(Guid id);
}
// . . .
public class UserRepository : IEntityRepository<User>
{
    public User GetByID(Guid id)
    {
        return new User();
    }
}
```

Rather than maintaining `EntityRepository` as a concrete class that can be instantiated, this code has converted it into an interface that removes the default implementation of `GetByID`. This is not entirely necessary, but the benefits of clients depending on interfaces rather than implementations have been demonstrated consistently, so it is a sensible reinforcement of that policy.

Note also that there is a `where` clause applied to the generic type parameter of the `Entity-Repository` class. This clause prevents subclasses from supplying a type that is not part of the `Entity` class hierarchy, which would have made this new version more permissive than the original implementation.

This version prevents the need for `UserRepository` clients to mess around with downcasting because they are guaranteed to receive a `User` object, rather than an `Entity` object, and yet the inheritance of `EntityRepository` and `UserRepository` is preserved.

Contravariance

Contravariance is a similar concept to covariance. Whereas covariance relates to the treatment of types that are used as return values, *contravariance* relates to the treatment of types that are used as method parameters.

Using the same `Supertype` and `Subtype` class hierarchy as previously discussed, Figure 7-6 explores the relationship between types that are marked as contravariant via generic type parameters.

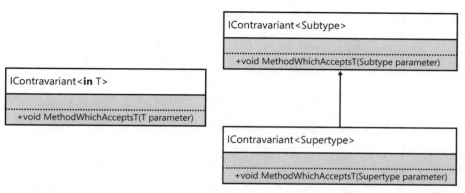

FIGURE 7-6 Due to contravariance of the generic parameter, the base-class/subclass relationship is inverted.

The `IContravariant` interface defines a method that accepts a single parameter of the type dictated by the generic parameter. Here, the generic parameter is marked with the `in` keyword, meaning that it is contravariant.

The subsequent class hierarchy can be inferred, indicating that the inheritance hierarchy has been inverted: `IContravariant<Subtype>` becomes the superclass, and `IContravariant<Supertype>` becomes the subclass. This seems strange and counterintuitive, but it will soon become apparent why contravariance exhibits this behavior—and why it is useful.

In Listing 7-23, the .NET Framework `IEqualityComparer` interface is provided for reference and an application-specific implementation is created. The `EntityEqualityComparer` accepts the previous `Entity` class as a parameter to the `Equals` method. The details of the comparison are not relevant, but a simple identity comparison is used.

LISTING 7-23 The `IEqualityComparer` interface allows the definition of function objects like `EntityEqualityComparer`.

```
public interface IEqualityComparer<in TEntity>
    where TEntity : Entity
{
    bool Equals(TEntity left, TEntity right);
}
// . . .
public class EntityEqualityComparer : IEqualityComparer<Entity>
{
    public bool Equals(Entity left, Entity right)
    {
        return left.ID == right.ID;
    }
}
```

The unit test in Listing 7-24 explores the affect that contravariance has on the `EntityEquality-Comparer`.

LISTING 7-24 Contravariance inverts class hierarchies, allowing a more general comparer to be used wherever a more specific comparer is requested.

```
[Test]
public void UserCanBeComparedWithEntityComparer()
{
    SubtypeCovariance.IEqualityComparer<User> entityComparer = new
  EntityEqualityComparer();
    var user1 = new User();
    var user2 = new User();
    entityComparer.Equals(user1, user2)
        .Should().BeFalse();
}
```

Without contravariance—the innocent-looking `in` keyword applied to generic type parameters—the following error would be shown at compile time.

```
error CS0266: Cannot implicitly convert type 'SubtypeCovariance.EntityEqualityComparer' to
  'SubtypeCovariance.IEqualityComparer<SubtypeCovariance.User>'. An explicit conversion exists
  (are you missing a cast?)
```

There would be no type conversion from `EntityEqualityComparer` to `IEqualityComparer<User>`, which is intuitive because `Entity` is the supertype and `User` is the subtype. However, because the `IEqualityComparer` supports contravariance, the existing inheritance hierarchy is inverted and you are able to assign what was originally a less specific type to a more specific type via the `IEqualityComparer` interface.

Invariance

Beyond covariant or contravariant behavior, types are said to be invariant. This is not to be confused with the term *data invariant* used earlier in this chapter as it relates to code contracts. Instead, invariant in this context is used to mean "not variant." If a type is not variant at all, no arrangement of types will yield a class hierarchy. Listing 7-25 uses the `IDictionary` generic type to demonstrate this fact.

LISTING 7-25 Some generic types are neither covariant or contravariant. This makes them *invariant*.

```
[TestFixture]
public class DictionaryTests
{
    [Test]
    public void DictionaryIsInvariant()
    {
        // Attempt covariance...
        IDictionary<Supertype, Supertype> supertypeDictionary = new Dictionary<Subtype,
Subtype>();

        // Attempt contravariance...
        IDictionary<Subtype, Subtype> subtypeDictionary = new Dictionary<Supertype,
Supertype>();
    }
}
```

The first line of the `DictionaryIsInvariant` test method attempts to assign a dictionary whose key and value parameters are of type Subtype to a dictionary whose key and value parameters are of type Supertype. This will not work because the `IDictionary` type is not covariant, which would preserve the class hierarchy of Subtype and Supertype.

The second line is also invalid, because it attempts the inverse: to assign a dictionary of Supertype to a dictionary of Subtype. This fails because the `IDictionary` type is not contravariant, which would invert the class hierarchy of Subtype and Supertype.

The fact that the `IDictionary` type is neither covariant nor contravariant leads to the conclusion that it must be invariant. Indeed, Listing 7-26 shows how the `IDictionary` type is declared, and you can tell that there is no reference to the out or in keywords that would specify covariance and contravariance, respectively.

LISTING 7-26 None of the generic parameters of the `IDictionary` interface are marked with in or out.

```
public interface IDictionary<TKey, TValue> : ICollection<KeyValuePair<TKey, TValue>>,
    IEnumerable<KeyValuePair<TKey, TValue>>, IEnumerable
```

As previously proven for the general case—that is, without generic types—C# is invariant for both method parameter types and return types. Only when generics are involved is variance customizable on a per-type basis.

Liskov type system rules

Now that you have a grounding in variance, this section can circle back and relate all of this to the Liskov substitution principle. The LSP defines the following rules, two of which relate directly to variance:

- There must be contravariance of the method arguments in the subtype.

- There must be covariance of the return types in the subtype.

- No new exceptions are allowed.

Without contravariance of method arguments and covariance of return types, you cannot write code that is LSP-compliant.

The third rule stands alone as not relating to variance and bears its own discussion.

No new exceptions are allowed

This rule is more intuitive than the other LSP rules that relate to the type system of a language. First, you should consider: what is the purpose of exceptions?

Exceptions aim to separate the reporting of an error from the handling of an error. It is common for the reporter and the handler to be very different classes with different purposes and context. The exception object represents the error that occurred through its type and the data that it carries with it. Any code can construct and throw an exception, just as any code can catch and respond to an exception. However, it is recommended that an exception only be caught if something meaningful can be done at that point in the code. This could be as simple as rolling back a database transaction or as complex as showing users a fancy user interface for them to view the error details and to report the error to the developers.

It is also often inadvisable to catch an exception and silently do nothing, or catch the general `Exception` base type. Both of these two scenarios together are even more discouraged. With the latter scenario, you end up attempting to catch and respond to *everything*, including exceptions that you realistically have no meaningful way of recovering from, like `OutOfMemoryException`, `StackOverflowException`, or `ThreadAbortException`. You could improve this situation by ensuring that you always inherit your exceptions from `ApplicationException`, because many unrecoverable exceptions inherit from `SystemException`. However, this is not a common practice and relies on third-party libraries to also follow this practice.

Listing 7-27 shows two exceptions that have a sibling relationship in the class hierarchy. It is important to note that this precludes the ability to create a catch block specifically targeting one of the exception types and to intercept both types of exception.

LISTING 7-27 Both of these exceptions are of type `Exception`, but neither inherits from the other.

```
public class EntityNotFoundException : Exception
{
    public EntityNotFoundException()
        : base()
    {

    }

    public EntityNotFoundException(string message)
        : base(message)
    {

    }
}
//. . .
public class UserNotFoundException : Exception
{
    public UserNotFoundException()
        : base()
    {

    }

    public UserNotFoundException(string message)
        : base(message)
    {

    }
}
```

Instead, in order to catch both an `EntityNotFoundException` and a `UserNotFoundException` with a single catch block, you would have to resort to catching the general `Exception`, which is not recommended.

This problem is exacerbated in the potential code taken from the `EntityRepository` and `UserRepository` classes, as shown in Listing 7-28.

LISTING 7-28 Two different implementations of an interface might throw different types of exception.

```
public Entity GetByID(Guid id)
{
    Contract.Requires<EntityNotFoundException>(id != Guid.Empty);

    return new Entity();
}
//. . .
public User GetByID(Guid id)
{
    Contract.Requires<UserNotFoundException>(id != Guid.Empty);

    return new User();
}
```

Both of these classes use code contracts to assert a precondition: that the provided `id` parameter must not be equal to `Guid.Empty`. Each uses its own exception type if the contract is violated. Think for a second about the impact that this would have on a client using the repository. The client would need to catch both kinds of exception and could not use a single catch block to target both exceptions without resorting to catching the `Exception` type. Listing 7-29 shows a unit test that is a client to these two repositories.

LISTING 7-29 This unit test will fail because a `UserNotFoundException` is not assignable to an `EntityNotFoundException`.

```
[TestFixture(typeof(EntityRepository), typeof(Entity))]
[TestFixture(typeof(UserRepository), typeof(User))]
public class ExceptionRuleTests<TRepository, TEntity>
    where TRepository : IEntityRepository<TEntity>, new()
{
    [Test]
    public void GetByIDThrowsEntityNotFoundException()
    {
        var repo = new TRepository();
        Action getByID = () => repo.GetByID(Guid.Empty);

        getByID.ShouldThrow<EntityNotFoundException>();
    }
}
```

This unit test fails because the `UserRepository` does not, as required, throw an `EntityNotFoundException`. If the `UserNotFoundException` was a subclass of the type `EntityNotFoundException`, this test would pass and a single catch block could guarantee catching both kinds of exception.

This becomes a problem of client maintenance. If the client is using an interface as a dependency and calling methods on that interface, it should not know anything about the classes behind that interface. This is a return to the argument concerning the Entourage anti-pattern versus the Stairway pattern. If new exceptions that are not part of an expected exception class hierarchy are introduced, clients must start referencing these exceptions directly. And—even worse—clients will have to be updated whenever a new exception type is introduced.

Instead, it is important that every interface have a unifying base class exception that conveys the necessary information about an error from the exception reporter to the exception handler.

Conclusion

On the surface, the Liskov substitution principle is one of the more complex facets of the SOLID principles. It requires a foundational knowledge of both contracts and variance to build rules that guide you toward more adaptive code.

By default, interfaces do not convey rules for preconditions or postconditions to clients. Creating guard clauses that halt the application at run time serves to further narrow the allowed range of valid values for parameters. The LSP provides guidelines such that each subclass in a class hierarchy cannot strengthen preconditions or weaken postconditions.

Similarly, the LSP suggests rules for variance in subtypes. There should be contravariance of method arguments in subtypes and covariance of return values in subtypes. Additionally, any new exception that is introduced, perhaps with the creation of a new interface implementation, should inherit from an existing base exception. To do otherwise would be to potentially cause an existing client to miss the catch—effectively to fumble the exception and allow it to cause an application crash.

If the LSP is violated with respect to these rules, it becomes harder for clients to treat all types in a class hierarchy the same. Ideally, clients would be able to hold a reference to a base type or interface and not alter its own behavior depending on the concrete subclass that it is actually using at run time. Such mixed concerns create dependencies between sections of the code that are better kept separate. Any violation of the LSP should be considered technical debt and, as demonstrated in prior chapters, this debt should be paid off sooner rather than later.

CHAPTER 8

Interface segregation

After completing this chapter, you will be able to

- Understand the importance of interface segregation.

- Write interfaces with the client code's requirements as a primary concern.

- Create smaller interfaces with more directed purposes.

- Identify scenarios where interface segregation can be used.

- Split interfaces by their implementations' dependencies.

The interface, as earlier chapters have established, is a key tool in the modern object-oriented programmer's toolkit. Interfaces represent the boundaries between what client code requires and how that requirement is implemented. The interface segregation principle states that interfaces should be *small*.

Each member of an interface needs to be implemented in its entirety: properties, events, and methods. Unless every client of an interface requires every member, it does not make sense to require every implementation to fulfill such a large contract. Bearing in mind the single responsibility principle and how developers can make liberal use of the Decorator pattern, for every member present in an interface, there needs to be a valid analogy for the decoration being implemented.

At their simplest, interfaces contain single methods that serve a single purpose. At this level of granularity, they are akin to delegates, but with many added benefits.

A segregation example

This chapter works through a complete example that progresses from a single monolithic interface to multiple smaller interfaces. Along the way, a variety of decorators will be created to elaborate on one of the key benefits of liberally applying interface segregation.

A simple CRUD interface

The interface itself is quite simple, with only five methods. It is used to allow clients to interact with persistent storage for an entity through the traditional CRUD operations. *CRUD* stands for *create*, *read*, *update*, and *delete*. These are the common operations that clients need to maintain persistent storage for an entity. Figure 8-1 shows a UML class diagram explaining the operations available to the `ICreateReadUpdateDelete` interface.

```
<<INTERFACE>>
ICreateReadUpdateDelete

+Create()
+ReadOne()
+ReadAll()
+Update()
+Delete()
```

FIGURE 8-1 The initial interface before segregation.

The read operations are split into two methods, one for retrieving a single record from storage and another for reading all of the records. In code, this interface is as shown in Listing 8-1.

LISTING 8-1 A simple interface for CRUD operations on an entity.

```
public interface ICreateReadUpdateDelete<TEntity>
{
    void Create(TEntity entity);

    TEntity ReadOne(Guid identity);

    IEnumerable<TEntity> ReadAll();

    void Update(TEntity entity);

    void Delete(TEntity entity);
}
```

The `ICreateReadUpdateDelete` interface is generic, allowing reuse across different entity types. However, by making the interface generic, rather than making each individual method generic, you force clients to declare up front which `TEntity` you are dealing with, which clarifies its dependencies. If a client wants to perform CRUD operations on more than one entity, it will have to request multiple `ICreateReadUpdateDelete<TEntity>` instances, one for each entity type.

> **Note** Though clients will require an *instance* of `ICreateReadUpdateDelete<TEntity>` per entity, there could still only be one *implementation* of `ICreateReadUpdateDelete <TEntity>` that would suffice for all concrete `TEntity` types. This implementation would also be generic.

Every operation of CRUD is performed by each implementation of the `ICreateReadUpdate-Delete` interface—including any decorator. This would be acceptable for decorators such as logging or transaction handling, as Listing 8-2 shows.

LISTING 8-2 Some decorators apply to all methods.

```
public class CrudLogging<TEntity> : ICreateReadUpdateDelete<TEntity>
{
    private readonly ICreateReadUpdateDelete<TEntity> decoratedCrud;
    private readonly ILog log;
    public CrudLogging(ICreateReadUpdateDelete<TEntity> decoratedCrud, ILog log)
    {
        this.decoratedCrud = decoratedCrud;
        this.log = log;
    }

    public void Create(TEntity entity)
    {
        log.InfoFormat("Creating entity of type {0}", typeof(TEntity).Name);
        decoratedCrud.Create(entity);
    }

    public TEntity ReadOne(Guid identity)
    {
        log.InfoFormat("Reading entity of type {0} with identity {1}",
 typeof(TEntity).Name, identity);
        return decoratedCrud.ReadOne(identity);
    }

    public IEnumerable<TEntity> ReadAll()
    {
        log.InfoFormat("Reading all entities of type {0}", typeof(TEntity).Name);
        return decoratedCrud.ReadAll();
    }

    public void Update(TEntity entity)
    {
        log.InfoFormat("Updating entity of type {0}", typeof(TEntity).Name);
        decoratedCrud.Update(entity);
    }

    public void Delete(TEntity entity)
    {
        log.InfoFormat("Deleting entity of type {0}", typeof(TEntity).Name);
        decoratedCrud.Delete(entity);
    }

}
// . . .
public class CrudTransactional<TEntity> : ICreateReadUpdateDelete<TEntity>
{
    private readonly ICreateReadUpdateDelete<TEntity> decoratedCrud;
    public CrudTransactional(ICreateReadUpdateDelete<TEntity> decoratedCrud)
    {
        this.decoratedCrud = decoratedCrud;
    }
```

```csharp
    public void Create(TEntity entity)
    {
        using (var transaction = new TransactionScope())
        {
            decoratedCrud.Create(entity);

            transaction.Complete();
        }
    }

    public TEntity ReadOne(Guid identity)
    {
        TEntity entity;
        using (var transaction = new TransactionScope())
        {
            entity = decoratedCrud.ReadOne(identity);

            transaction.Complete();
        }
        return entity;
    }

    public IEnumerable<TEntity> ReadAll()
    {
        IEnumerable<TEntity> allEntities;
        using (var transaction = new TransactionScope())
        {
            allEntities = decoratedCrud.ReadAll();

            transaction.Complete();
        }
        return allEntities;
    }

    public void Update(TEntity entity)
    {
        using (var transaction = new TransactionScope())
        {
            decoratedCrud.Update(entity);

            transaction.Complete();
        }
    }

    public void Delete(TEntity entity)
    {
        using (var transaction = new TransactionScope())
        {
            decoratedCrud.Delete(entity);

            transaction.Complete();
        }
    }
}
```

The decorators for logging and transaction management are *cross-cutting concerns*. Irrespective of the method on the interface and, in many cases, irrespective of the interface itself, logging and transaction management could be applied. Thus, to avoid repetitive implementations for multiple interfaces, you can decorate all implementations by using aspect-oriented programming.

Some other decorators apply only to a subset of the methods of a single interface, rather than to all of them. For example, you might want to prompt the user before you permanently delete an entity from persistent storage—a common requirement. Remember that you do not want to edit an existing class, which would violate the open/closed principle. Instead, you should create a new implementation of an existing interface that clients are already using to perform the delete action. This is the `Delete` method of the `ICreateReadUpdateDelete<TEntity>` interface. Such an implementation would look like Listing 8-3.

LISTING 8-3 If a decorator targets part of an interface, segregation is an option.

```
public class DeleteConfirmation<TEntity> : ICrud<TEntity>
{
    private readonly ICreateReadUpdateDelete<TEntity> decoratedCrud;
    public DeleteConfirmation(ICreateReadUpdateDelete<TEntity> decoratedCrud)
    {
        this.decoratedCrud = decoratedCrud;
    }

    public void Create(TEntity entity)
    {
        decoratedCrud.Create(entity);
    }

    public TEntity ReadOne(Guid identity)
    {
        return decoratedCrud.ReadOne(identity);
    }

    public IEnumerable<TEntity> ReadAll()
    {
        return decoratedCrud.ReadAll();
    }

    public void Update(TEntity entity)
    {
        decoratedCrud.Update(entity);
    }

    public void Delete(TEntity entity)
    {
        Console.WriteLine("Are you sure you want to delete the entity? [y/N]");
        var keyInfo = Console.ReadKey();
        if (keyInfo.Key == ConsoleKey.Y)
        {
            decoratedCrud.Delete(entity);
        }
    }
}
```

The DeleteConfirmation<TEntity> class decorates only the Delete method, as its name suggests. The other methods are implemented with pass-through delegation to the wrapped interface. *Pass-through* means that there is no decoration for that method: the call is merely *passed through* the decorator to the underlying implementation, almost as if it had been called directly. Despite the fact that these pass-through methods apparently do nothing special, in order to maintain unit test coverage and ensure that they are delegating properly, test methods should still be written to verify that their behavior is correct. This is laborious when compared to the alternative: interface segregation.

By separating the Delete method from the rest of the ICreateReadUpdateDelete<TEntity> interface, you have two interfaces, as shown in Listing 8-4.

LISTING 8-4 The ICreateReadUpdateDelete interface is split in two.

```
public interface ICreateReadUpdate<TEntity>
{
    void Create(TEntity entity);

    TEntity ReadOne(Guid identity);

    IEnumerable<TEntity> ReadAll();

    void Update(TEntity entity);
}
// . . .
public interface IDelete<TEntity>
{
    void Delete(TEntity entity);
}
```

This allows the confirmation decorator to be replaced with an implementation only for the IDelete<TEntity> interface, as shown in Listing 8-5.

LISTING 8-5 The confirmation decorator is applied only to the interface to which it pertains.

```
public class DeleteConfirmation<TEntity> : IDelete<TEntity>
{
    private readonly IDelete<TEntity> decoratedDelete;

    public DeleteConfirmation(IDelete<TEntity> decoratedDelete)
    {
        this.decoratedDelete = decoratedDelete;
    }

    public void Delete(TEntity entity)
    {
        Console.WriteLine("Are you sure you want to delete the entity? [y/N]");
        var keyInfo = Console.ReadKey();
        if (keyInfo.Key == ConsoleKey.Y)
```

```
        {
            decoratedDelete.Delete(entity);
        }
    }
}
```

This is an improvement, because there is less code overall, without the pass-through decoration methods, so the intent is much clearer. Also, less code means less testing.

Before moving on to the next decorator, consider the following refactor that is available for the DeleteConfirmation decorator. You should encapsulate the user interrogation into a simple interface. This way, you could write multiple different implementations of this new interface—one for each user interface type (for example, console, Windows Forms, and Windows Presentation Foundation)—and the decorator would not need to change. You should do this because the DeleteConfirmation class does not currently adhere to the single responsibility principle. As it is now, it contains two reasons to change: the interface that it delegates to has changed, *and* you want to elicit confirmation from the user in a different manner. Asking users whether they want to delete an entity requires a very simple predicate-like interface, as shown in Listing 8-6.

LISTING 8-6 A very simple interface for asking the user to confirm something.

```
public interface IUserInteraction
{
    bool Confirm(string message);
}
```

Caching

The next decorator that you could implement is for the read methods: ReadOne and ReadAll. For both of these methods, you want to cache the returned value from the decorated implementation and return the contents of the cache in all subsequent requests. Again, with no equivalent analogy for caching the Create or Update methods, the first decorator contains needless methods, as in Listing 8-7.

LISTING 8-7 The caching decorator includes redundant, pass-through methods.

```
public class CrudCaching<TEntity> : ICreateReadUpdate<TEntity>
{
    private TEntity cachedEntity;
    private IEnumerable<TEntity> allCachedEntities;
    private readonly ICreateReadUpdate<TEntity> decorated;
```

```
    public CrudCaching(ICreateReadUpdate<TEntity> decorated)
    {
        this.decorated = decorated;
    }

    public void Create(TEntity entity)
    {
        decorated.Create(entity);
    }

    public TEntity ReadOne(Guid identity)
    {
        if(cachedEntity == null)
        {
            cachedEntity = decorated.ReadOne(identity);
        }
        return cachedEntity;
    }

    public IEnumerable<TEntity> ReadAll()
    {
        if (allCachedEntities == null)
        {
            allCachedEntities = decorated.ReadAll();
        }
        return allCachedEntities;
    }

    public void Update(TEntity entity)
    {
        decorated.Update(entity);
    }

}
```

By applying interface segregation a second time, you can factor out the two methods used for reading data into their own interface, and they can now be decorated separately. The new IRead interface, and its accompanying caching decorator, is shown in Listing 8-8.

LISTING 8-8 The IRead interface is targeted specifically by the ReadCaching decorator.

```
public interface IRead<TEntity>
{
    TEntity ReadOne(Guid identity);

    IEnumerable<TEntity> ReadAll();
}
// . . .
public class ReadCaching<TEntity> : IRead<TEntity>
{
```

```
    private TEntity cachedEntity;
    private IEnumerable<TEntity> allCachedEntities;

    private readonly IRead<TEntity> decorated;
    public ReadCaching(IRead<TEntity> decorated)
    {
        this.decorated = decorated;
    }

    public TEntity ReadOne(Guid identity)
    {
        if(cachedEntity == null)
        {
            cachedEntity = decorated.ReadOne(identity);
        }
        return cachedEntity;
    }

    public IEnumerable<TEntity> ReadAll()
    {
        if (allCachedEntities == null)
        {
            allCachedEntities = decorated.ReadAll();
        }
        return allCachedEntities;
    }

}
```

Before you implement the final decorator, the remaining interface contains only two methods, as Listing 8-9 shows.

LISTING 8-9 The remaining methods can probably be unified.

```
public interface ICreateUpdate<TEntity>
{
    void Create(TEntity entity);

    void Update(TEntity entity);
}
```

The Create and Update methods have identical signatures. Not only that, they serve very similar purposes: the former saves a new entity, and the latter saves an existing entity. You could unify these methods into one Save method, which acknowledges that the distinction between creating and updating is an implementation detail that clients don't need to know about. After all, a client is likely to want to both save and update an entity, so requiring two interfaces that are so similar seems needless when there is a viable alternative. All that clients of the interface want to do is persist an entity. The refactored interface looks like the one in Listing 8-10.

LISTING 8-10 ISave implementations will either create or update an entity, as appropriate.

```
public interface ISave<TEntity>
{
    void Save(TEntity entity);
}
```

After this refactor, you can add a new decorator that is specific to this interface—audit tracking. Every time a user saves an entity, you want to add some metadata to persistent storage. Specifically, you want to know which user enacted the save and at what time. Listing 8-11 shows the SaveAuditing decorator.

LISTING 8-11 Two ISave interfaces are used by the audit decorator.

```
public class SaveAuditing<TEntity> : ISave<TEntity>
{
    private readonly ISave<TEntity> decorated;
    private readonly ISave<AuditInfo> auditSave;
    public SaveAuditing(ISave<TEntity> decorated, ISave<AuditInfo> auditSave)
    {
        this.decorated = decorated;
        this.auditSave = auditSave;
    }

    public void Save(TEntity entity)
    {
        decorated.Save(entity);
        var auditInfo = new AuditInfo
        {
            UserName = Thread.CurrentPrincipal.Identity.Name,
            TimeStamp = DateTime.Now
        };
        auditSave.Save(auditInfo);
    }

}
```

The SaveAuditing decorator implements the ISave interface, but it also needs to be constructed with two further ISave implementations. The first must match the TEntity generic type parameter of the decorator and is used to do the real work of saving (or, of course, to provide further decoration on the way to doing the real work of saving). The second is an ISave implementation that is specifically for saving AuditInfo types. This class is not shown, but it can be inferred to contain string UserName and DateTime TimeStamp properties. When clients call the Save method, a new AuditInfo instance is created and its properties are set. The real implementation responsible for saving this instance will then persist this new record to storage.

Again, it is worth reiterating that client code has no idea that this is happening; it is entirely unaware that auditing is occurring and does not need to change as a result of its implementation. Similarly, the leaf implementation of the ISave<TEntity> interface—that is, the nondecorator version that is responsible for the actual work of saving—is also unaware of the decorator and does not need to change to accommodate any specific decoration.

You now have three different interfaces where before you had one, and each has a decorator that provides some different, meaningful, real-world function. Figure 8-2 shows a UML class diagram of the new interfaces and their decorators after segregation.

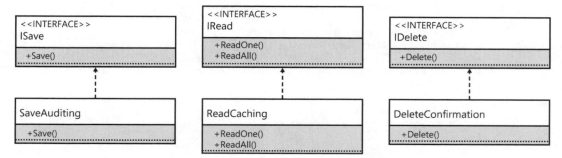

FIGURE 8-2 Interface segregation allows you to target methods for decoration without redundancy.

Multiple interface decoration

Each decorator so far has maintained a one-to-one relationship with the interface that it enhances. This is true because each decorator implements the interface that it is decorating. But you can use the Adapter pattern in conjunction with the Decorator pattern to produce multiple decorators while minimizing the code you must write.

The next decorator you will create is intended to publish an event whenever a record is saved or deleted. This notification will allow disparate subscribers to act upon any change to persistent storage. Note that there is no analogous event for reading any records, so the IRead interface will not be targeted in this instance.

For this, you first need a mechanism for publishing and subscribing events. Continuing the theme of interface segregation, this is split into the two interfaces shown in Listing 8-12.

LISTING 8-12 Two interfaces for publishing and subscribing to events.

```
public interface IEventPublisher
{
    void Publish<TEvent>(TEvent @event)
        where TEvent : IEvent;
}
// . . .
public interface IEventSubscriber
{
    void Subscribe<TEvent>(TEvent @event)
        where TEvent : IEvent;
}
```

The IEvent interface is extremely simple, containing just a `string Name` property. By using these two interfaces, a decorator can be created, as in Listing 8-13, that publishes a specific event when an entity is deleted.

LISTING 8-13 This decorator publishes an event when an entity is deleted.

```
public class DeleteEventPublishing<TEntity> : IDelete<TEntity>
{
    private readonly IDelete<TEntity> decorated;
    private readonly IEventPublisher eventPublisher;

    public DeleteEventPublishing(IDelete<TEntity> decorated, IEventPublisher
  eventPublisher)
    {
        this.decorated = decorated;
        this.eventPublisher = eventPublisher;
    }

    public void Delete(TEntity entity)
    {
        decorated.Delete(entity);
        var entityDeleted = new EntityDeletedEvent<TEntity>(entity);
        eventPublisher.Publish(entityDeleted);
    }

}
```

From here, you have two choices: implementing the equivalent ISave decorator for publishing events on the same class or implementing the ISave decorator in a new class. Listing 8-14 shows the former option, which involves renaming the existing class and adding a new Save method.

LISTING 8-14 Two decorators can be implemented in one class.

```
public class ModificationEventPublishing<TEntity> : IDelete<TEntity>, ISave<TEntity>
{
    private readonly IDelete<TEntity> decoratedDelete;
    private readonly ISave<TEntity> decoratedSave;
    private readonly IEventPublisher eventPublisher;

    public ModificationEventPublishing(IDelete<TEntity> decoratedDelete, ISave<TEntity>
  decoratedSave, IEventPublisher eventPublisher)
    {
        this.decoratedDelete = decoratedDelete;
        this.decoratedSave = decoratedSave;
        this.eventPublisher = eventPublisher;
    }
```

```
    public void Delete(TEntity entity)
    {
        decoratedDelete.Delete(entity);
        var entityDeleted = new EntityDeletedEvent<TEntity>(entity);
        eventPublisher.Publish(entityDeleted);
    }

    public void Save(TEntity entity)
    {
        decoratedSave.Save(entity);
        var entitySaved = new EntitySavedEvent<TEntity>(entity);
        eventPublisher.Publish(entitySaved);
    }

}
```

A single class can be the implementation for multiple decorators—but only when the context of the decorator is shared, as in this example. The `ModificationEventPublishing` decorator is implementing the same functionality—event publication—for both of the interfaces that it implements. It would be unwise, however, to combine decorators for event publishing with those for auditing, for example. This is due to the relative dependencies involved. One decorator depends on the `IEventPublisher` interface, whereas the other depends on the `AuditInfo` class. It would be better instead to separate those implementations into their own assemblies with their own dependency chains.

Client construction

The design of interfaces—segregated or otherwise—affects the classes that implement the interfaces and also the clients that use the interfaces. If clients are to use interfaces, they must in some way be supplied them. This chapter will continue, for the most part, to manually construct the implementations and provide them to clients via constructor parameters. For an alternative option, see the next chapter, which covers dependency injection.

The manner in which you supply the implementations to clients is partly dictated by the number of implementations of the segregated interfaces. If each interface is given its own implementation, each of those implementations needs to be constructed and supplied to the client. Alternatively, if all of the interfaces are implemented in a single class, a single instance is sufficient for all of the related dependencies on the client.

Multiple implementations, multiple instances

Continuing the CRUD example, assume that the `IRead`, `ISave`, and `IDelete` interfaces have all been implemented by different, distinct classes. A client needing to use these interfaces will, because of segregation, require three interfaces whereas it previously only required one. Such a client is shown in Listing 8-15.

LISTING 8-15 The order-specific controller requires each facet of CRUD as a separate dependency.

```
public class OrderController
{
    private readonly IRead<Order> reader;
    private readonly ISave<Order> saver;
    private readonly IDelete<Order> deleter;

    public OrderController(IRead<Order> orderReader, ISave<Order> orderSaver,
    IDelete<Order> orderDeleter)
    {
        reader = orderReader;
        saver = orderSaver;
        deleter = orderDeleter;
    }

    public void CreateOrder(Order order)
    {
        saver.Save(order);
    }

    public Order GetSingleOrder(Guid identity)
    {
        return reader.ReadOne(identity);
    }

    public void UpdateOrder(Order order)
    {
        saver.Save(order);
    }

    public void DeleteOrder(Order order)
    {
        deleter.Delete(order);
    }
}
```

This controller works specifically with order entities. This means that each of the interfaces supplied contains the Order class as the generic parameter. If you were to alter any of those declarations to use a different type, the operations provided by that interface would then require that type. For example, if you decided to change the delete interface parameter to IDelete<Customer>, the DeleteOrder method of the OrderController would complain that you were trying to delete an Order with a method that only accepts Customers. This is simply strong typing and generics in action.

Each method of this controller class requires a different interface to perform its function. For clarity, each method maps one to one with the operations on the respective interfaces. It is quite likely that this will not always be the case, of course.

As its name suggests, the OrderController deals only with Order classes. You can make use of the fact that the service interfaces are each generic by implementing a controller that is similarly generic. This is shown in Listing 8-16.

```
public class GenericController<TEntity>
{
    private readonly IRead<TEntity> reader;
    private readonly ISave<TEntity> saver;
    private readonly IDelete<TEntity> deleter;

    public GenericController(IRead<TEntity> entityReader, ISave<TEntity> entitySaver,
    IDelete<TEntity> entityDeleter)
    {
        reader = entityReader;
        saver = entitySaver;
        deleter = entityDeleter;
    }

    public void CreateEntity(TEntity entity)
    {
        saver.Save(entity);
    }

    public TEntity GetSingleEntity(Guid identity)
    {
        return reader.ReadOne(identity);
    }

    public void UpdateEntity(TEntity entity)
    {
        saver.Save(entity);
    }

    public void DeleteEntity(TEntity entity)
    {
        deleter.Delete(entity);
    }
}
```

There is little difference between this version of the controller and the prior one, but the impact on the amount of code that you might have to write could be significant. This controller can be instantiated to operate on any entity, and the service interfaces that are required are all forced to agree on the same operation. No longer can you supply different types for each one—such as ISave<Customer>, IRead<Order>, IDelete<LineItem>.

Either version of the controller can be created in much the same way. Listing 8-17 shows how you must instantiate an instance of each class that implements the required interfaces before passing them in to the controller's constructor.

LISTING 8-17 Creating the `OrderController` with separate instances of the dependencies.

```
static OrderController CreateSeparateServices()
{
    var reader = new Reader<Order>();
    var saver = new Saver<Order>();
    var deleter = new Deleter<Order>();

    return new OrderController(reader, saver, deleter);
}
```

By creating classes for each individual segregated interface, the segregation has, in effect, permeated the implementations. The key point to note is that the three parameters to the `OrderController` class—reader, saver, and delete—are not just distinct instances, they are also distinct *types*.

Single implementation, single instance

A second approach to implementing segregated interfaces is to inherit all of them into one single class. This might at first appear somewhat counterintuitive (after all, what is the point of segregating interfaces just to unify them all again in the implementation?), but be patient. Listing 8-18 shows all three interfaces on a single class.

LISTING 8-18 All interfaces can be implemented in a single class.

```
public class CreateReadUpdateDelete<TEntity> :
    IRead<TEntity>, ISave<TEntity>, IDelete<TEntity>
{
    public TEntity ReadOne(Guid identity)
    {
        return default(TEntity);
    }

    public IEnumerable<TEntity> ReadAll()
    {
        return new List<TEntity>();
    }

    public void Save(TEntity entity)
    {

    }

    public void Delete(TEntity entity)
    {

    }
}
```

Remember, clients are not aware of the existence of this class. At compile time, they are only aware of the individual interfaces, which it requires one by one. To the client, each interface will still only have the members declared on that interface, regardless of the fact that the underlying implementation has other operations available. This is how interfaces are used for encapsulation and information hiding—they are analogous to a small window onto the implementing class, masking out what it does not allow the client to see.

Even with this change, the controller from the multiple implementation example is still sufficient: it correctly asks for each interface as a separate constructor parameter. What needs to change is how you construct the controller and supply it with those parameters. This is shown in Listing 8-19.

LISTING 8-19 Although it might look unusual, this is an expected side effect of interface segregation.

```
public OrderController CreateSingleService()
{
    var crud = new CreateReadUpdateDelete<Order>();

    return new OrderController(crud, crud, crud);
}
```

First, you only need a single instance of the CreateReadUpdateDelete class. It implements all three interfaces, so it suffices for *all three constructor parameters*.

As unusual as that might look—passing in the same instance three times—it makes sense because each parameter requires a different facet of the class. This is a common side effect of the interface segregation principle.

Of the two variations explored, this single implementation for a suite of related—but segregated—interfaces is not as versatile as having multiple implementations. It is most commonly used for the leaf implementation of the interfaces—that is, the implementation that is neither decorator nor adapter. It is the one that does the actual work. The reason for this is that the context is the same across all implementations. Whether you are using NHibernate, ADO.NET, Entity Framework, or some other persistence framework, the leaf implementation is the one that directly uses these libraries. In each case —reading, saving, or deleting—that library will be used to do the main work.

Some decorators and adapters also apply to the full suite of segregated interfaces, but it is more common for these to be implemented individually only on the appropriate interface.

The Interface Soup anti-pattern

A common mistake is to take the segregated interfaces and reunify them in an aggregate for some reason, as Listing 8-20 demonstrates. This is usually done to avoid the odd-looking multiple injection that you saw previously.

LISTING 8-20 Interface segregation is wrongly circumvented when all interfaces are thrown together to form a soup.

```
interface IInterfaceSoupAntiPattern<TEntity> : IRead<TEntity>, ISave<TEntity>,
  IDelete<TEntity>
{
}
```

This creates an "interface soup" that is made from constituent interfaces but undermines the benefits of interface segregation. Implementers will again be required to provide implementations of all operations and so there is no scope for targeted decoration.

Splitting interfaces

The ability—or requirement—to decorate interfaces is only one reason that you might want to split a large interface into smaller constituents. However, I view this as a good enough reason for the practice.

Two more utilitarian reasons for interface segregation are based on client need and architectural design.

Client need

Different developers work on different parts of code. Therefore, it is likely that two or more developers will converge at some point, with one using the interface of another. Having detailed, step-by-step instructions for an interface is not only unlikely, but also impractical. Writing any code—especially code that is sufficiently unit tested—takes time. Writing extensive documentation, even for the end user, is tedious and time consuming. Instead, it is better to program as defensively as is possible, to prevent other developers—or even yourself in the future—from inadvertently doing something they shouldn't with your interface.

It helps to remember that clients need only what they need. Monolithic interfaces tend to hand too much control to clients. Interfaces with a large number of members allow clients to do more than they perhaps should, clouding the intent and misdirecting the focus. All classes should *always* have a single responsibility.

Listing 8-21 shows an interface that allows clients to interact with a user's settings—specifically, the user interface theme that the clients have set for the application. This example is surprising—it is an interface with a single property that, in this particular scenario, is *still* exposing too much to its client. How can you possibly segregate this further?

LISTING 8-21 The user settings interface allows access to the application's current theme.

```
public interface IUserSettings
{
    string Theme
    {
        get;
        set;
    }
}
```

First, see the implementation in Listing 8-22, which uses the ConfigurationManager class to read and write to the AppSettings section of the configuration files.

LISTING 8-22 An implementation that loads settings from the configuration file.

```
public class UserSettingsConfig : IUserSettings
{
    private const string ThemeSetting = "Theme";

    private readonly Configuration config;

    public UserSettingsConfig()
    {
        config = ConfigurationManager.OpenExeConfiguration(ConfigurationUserLevel.None);
    }

    public string Theme
    {
        get
        {
            return config.AppSettings.Settings[ThemeSetting].Value;
        }
        set
        {
            config.AppSettings.Settings[ThemeSetting].Value = value;
            config.Save();
            ConfigurationManager.RefreshSection("appSettings");
        }
    }
}
```

So far, so what? Well, there are two clients to this interface. One is focused only on *reading* the data and the other is focused on *writing* the data. Herein lies the problem, as shown in Listing 8-23.

LISTING 8-23 The clients of the interface use the property for different purposes.

```
public class ReadingController
{
    private readonly IUserSettings settings;

    public ReadingController(IUserSettings settings)
    {
        this.settings = settings;
    }

    public string GetTheme()
    {
        return settings.Theme;
    }
}
// . . .
public class WritingController
{
    private readonly IUserSettings settings;

    public WritingController(IUserSettings settings)
    {
        this.settings = settings;
    }

    public void SetTheme(string theme)
    {
        settings.Theme = theme;
    }
}
```

As is to be expected, the ReadingController only uses the getter of the Theme property, whereas the WritingController only uses the setter of the Theme property. However, due to a lack of segregation, there is nothing to stop the writer from retrieving the theme nor, which is more problematic, the reader from modifying the theme.

In order to be truly defensive and eliminate the possibility of interface misuse, you can segregate the read and write portions of the interface, as shown in Listing 8-24.

LISTING 8-24 The interface is split into two parts: one for reading the theme, and one for writing it.

```
public interface IUserSettingsReader
{
    string Theme
    {
        get;
    }
}
```

```
// . . .
public interface IUserSettingsWriter
{
    string Theme
    {
        set;
    }
}
```

Although this might look a little odd, it is absolutely valid C#. It is perhaps not unusual that an interface can dictate that implementers only supply a getter for a property, but it is slightly more unusual that it require only a setter.

Each controller is now able to depend only on the interface that it truly requires. As Listing 8-25 shows, the `ReadingController` is paired with the `IUserSettingsReader`, and the `Writing-Controller` is paired with the `IUserSettingsWriter`.

LISTING 8-25 Each of the two controllers now depends only on the interface that it requires.

```
public class ReadingController
{
    private readonly IUserSettingsReader settings;

    public ReadingController(IUserSettingsReader settings)
    {
        this.settings = settings;
    }

    public string GetTheme()
    {
        return settings.Theme;
    }
}
// . . .
public class WritingController
{
    private readonly IUserSettingsWriter settings;

    public WritingController(IUserSettingsWriter settings)
    {
        this.settings = settings;
    }

    public void SetTheme(string theme)
    {
        settings.Theme = theme;
    }
}
```

Via interface segregation, you have prevented the reader from being able to write the user settings, and you have prevented the writer from being able to read the user settings. Developers are thus not able to accidently dilute the purpose of the controller by mistakenly performing an operation that they should not.

The implementing class, which uses the `ConfigurationManager`, changes only very subtly, as shown in Listing 8-26.

LISTING 8-26 The `UsersSettingsConfig` class now implements both interfaces, but clients are unaware.

```
public class UserSettingsConfig : IUserSettingsReader, IUserSettingsWriter
{
    private const string ThemeSetting = "Theme";

    private readonly Configuration config;

    public UserSettingsConfig()
    {
        config = ConfigurationManager.OpenExeConfiguration(ConfigurationUserLevel.None);
    }

    public string Theme
    {
        get
        {
            return config.AppSettings.Settings[ThemeSetting].Value;
        }
        set
        {
            config.AppSettings.Settings[ThemeSetting].Value = value;
            config.Save();
            ConfigurationManager.RefreshSection("appSettings");
        }
    }
}
```

Other than in the fact that it inherits from both reader and writer interfaces, this class is identical to the previous version. Remember that this same implementation can easily be passed to both the `ReadingController` and the `WritingController`, yet the window provided by the interface means that the set and get operations, respectively, will not be available.

The requirement that some clients should be able to read without writing is particularly likely. The other scenario, where writers are not allowed to read, is less likely. In this case, instead of total segregation, you can segregate and inherit the interfaces, as shown in Listing 8-27.

LISTING 8-27 Now using methods, the writer inherits from the reader.

```
public interface IUserSettingsReader
{
    string GetTheme();
}
// . . .
public interface IUserSettingsWriter : IUserSettingsReader
{
    void SetTheme(string theme);
}
```

In order to do this, the Theme property had to be converted to GetTheme and SetTheme methods. This is because the language doesn't quite support property inheritance cleanly. The Theme property is present on both interfaces. Although classes are able to cleanly implement the get and set parts of an interface from two different interfaces, this is unfortunately not the case with interface inheritance. When property names clash through interface inheritance, the compiler warns that the base class property is *hidden* by the subclass property. This would not achieve the result that you want, and the compiler's suggestion that you replace the base class property with the new keyword is not a solution, either—the getter would still not be inherited.

Instead, you can change from properties to methods with the same semantic function. The GetTheme method is the same as Theme.get, and the SetTheme method is the same as Theme.set. Now the inheritance works as expected—implementers and clients of the reader interface will only have access to the GetTheme method, and implementers and clients of the writer interface will have access to both the GetTheme and SetTheme methods. Additionally, any implementation of the IUserSettings-Writer interface is *automatically* an implementation of the IUserSettingsReader interface.

Listing 8-28 shows a change to the writing controller: it first checks whether the theme has been changed before it tries to set a new theme. This is now acceptable because the user settings writer service is also the user settings reader service. In this case, the two interfaces do not need to be supplied separately in order to be used.

LISTING 8-28 The writing controller has access to both the getter and setter through one interface.

```
public class WritingController
{
    private readonly IUserSettingsWriter settings;

    public WritingController(IUserSettingsWriter settings)
    {
        this.settings = settings;
    }
```

```
    public void SetTheme(string theme)
    {
        if (settings.GetTheme() != theme)
        {
            settings.SetTheme(theme);
        }
    }
}
```

Authorization

Another example of segregation by client need is when a certain set of operations is only available when the application is in a specific state. For example, the operations that a user can perform are typically different depending on whether that user is logged in or not.

The unauthorized interface shown in Listing 8-29 contains operations that can be done by an anonymous, unauthenticated user.

LISTING 8-29 This interface only contains operations that anonymous users can perform.

```
public interface IUnauthorized
{
    IAuthorized Login(string username, string password);

    void RequestPasswordReminder(string emailAddress);
}
```

Note that the Login method returns an interface. It is only returned when the credentials are correct, and it allows clients to perform authorized actions, as shown in Listing 8-30.

LISTING 8-30 After logging in, the user will have access to privileged operations.

```
public interface IAuthorized
{
    void ChangePassword(string oldPassword, string newPassword);

    void AddToBasket(Guid itemID);

    void Checkout();

    void Logout();
}
```

The operations on this interface are only available to a user who has entered his credentials and is logged in as authenticated.

Segregating interfaces by client need prevents *programmers* from doing something they should not. In this case, it prevents them from executing a privileged action with an anonymous user. Of course, there are ways around this, but it is hoped that developers will realize that they are making a very fundamental change to the application in order to do something that they should not.

Architectural need

A second driver of the interface segregation principle is architectural design. High-level decisions can have a large impact on the low-level organization of the code.

In this example, the decision has been made to have an asymmetric architecture. Similar to the read/write split shown earlier, the `IPersistence` interface shown in Listing 8-31 contains a combination of queries and commands.

LISTING 8-31 This persistence-layer interface contains both commands and queries.

```
public interface IPersistence
{
    IEnumerable<Item> GetAll();

    Item GetByID(Guid identity);

    IEnumerable<Item> FindByCriteria(string criteria);

    void Save(Item item);

    void Delete(Item item);
}
```

The asymmetric architecture that this interface is part of is specifically CQRS: Command/Query Responsibility Segregation. The recurrence of the word *segregation* is no accident here, because this architectural pattern is about to cause you to perform some interface segregation.

A first implementation of the `IPersistence` interface is shown in Listing 8-32.

LISTING 8-32 When commands and queries are handled asymmetrically, the implementation is muddled.

```
public class Persistence : IPersistence
{
    private readonly ISession session;
    private readonly MongoDatabase mongo;

    public Persistence(ISession session, MongoDatabase mongo)
    {
        this.session = session;
        this.mongo = mongo;
    }
```

```
public IEnumerable<Item> GetAll()
{
    return mongo.GetCollection<Item>("items").FindAll();
}

public Item GetByID(Guid identity)
{
    return mongo.GetCollection<Item>("items").FindOneById(identity.ToBson());
}

public IEnumerable<Item> FindByCriteria(string criteria)
{
    var query = BsonSerializer.Deserialize<QueryDocument>(criteria);
    return mongo.GetCollection<Item>("Items").Find(query);
}

public void Save(Item item)
{
    using(var transaction = session.BeginTransaction())
    {
        session.Save(item);

        transaction.Commit();
    }
}

public void Delete(Item item)
{
    using(var transaction = session.BeginTransaction())
    {
        session.Delete(item);

        transaction.Commit();
    }
}
}
```

There are two very different dependencies here: NHibernate is used for commands, and MongoDB is used for queries. The former is an Object/Relational Mapper for use with a domain model. The latter is a document storage library for fast querying. This class has two disparate dependencies and therefore two reasons to change. With such differing dependencies, it is very likely that their respective decorators will similarly be different. Rather than split the entire interface into very small operations, as was done with the previous CRUD interface, this interface will only be split into two parts: commands and queries. Figure 8-3 shows a UML class diagram of how this will be orchestrated.

With the commands and queries split between two interfaces, the implementations can then depend on totally different packages. The commands implementation will depend only on NHibernate, and the queries implementation will depend only on MongoDB.

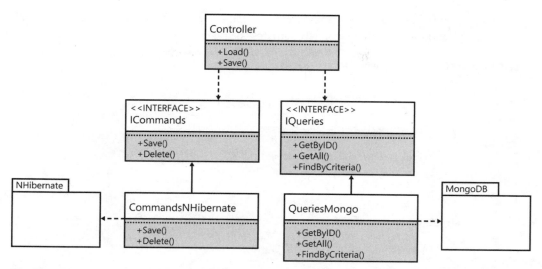

FIGURE 8-3 Splitting interfaces by architectural need allows implementations to have very different dependencies.

Ideally, these two implementations will not only be different classes, but those classes will reside in different packages—assemblies—too. If not, the problem is only partially alleviated because it will be impossible to reuse one implementation without depending on the other, plus the chain of dependencies that comes with it.

Listing 8-33 shows the interfaces after they have been split. The two can now be implemented separately.

LISTING 8-33 The interface has been split into query and command methods.

```
public interface IPersistenceQueries
{
    IEnumerable<Item> GetAll();

    Item GetByID(Guid identity);

    IEnumerable<Item> FindByCriteria(string criteria);
}
// . . .
public interface IPersistenceCommands
{
    void Save(Item item);

    void Delete(Item item);
}
```

As shown in Listing 8-34, the queries class is the same implementation as before, except for the commands—and the dependency on NHibernate—being completely excised.

LISTING 8-34 The query implementation depends only on MongoDB.

```
public class PersistenceQueries : IPersistenceQueries
{
    private readonly MongoDatabase mongo;

    public Persistence(MongoDatabase mongo)
    {
        this.mongo = mongo;
    }

    public IEnumerable<Item> GetAll()
    {
        return mongo.GetCollection<Item>("items").FindAll();
    }

    public Item GetByID(Guid identity)
    {
        return mongo.GetCollection<Item>("items").FindOneById(identity.ToBson());
    }

    public IEnumerable<Item> FindByCriteria(string criteria)
    {
        var query = BsonSerializer.Deserialize<QueryDocument>(criteria);
        return mongo.GetCollection<Item>("Items").Find(query);
    }
}
```

In exactly the same manner, the commands class contains no queries, nor any reference to MongoDB, as shown in Listing 8-35.

LISTING 8-35 The command implementation depends only on NHibernate.

```
public class PersistenceCommands : IPersistenceCommands
{
    private readonly ISession session;
    public PersistenceCommands(ISession session)
    {
        this.session = session;
    }

    public void Save(Item item)
    {
        using(var transaction = session.BeginTransaction())
        {
```

```
            session.Save(item);

            transaction.Commit();
        }
    }

    public void Delete(Item item)
    {
        using(var transaction = session.BeginTransaction())
        {
            session.Delete(item);

            transaction.Commit();
        }
    }
}
```

Single-method interfaces

Interface segregation taken to its logical conclusion results in very small interfaces. The smaller the interface, the more versatile it becomes. Such interfaces have analogies in the framework: `Action`, `Func`, and `Predicate`. However, delegates are not as versatile as interfaces. Though delegates certainly have their uses, the fact that interfaces can be decorated, adapted, and composed in all kinds of different ways sets them apart. Because interfaces must be implemented, there can also be extra context provided through other interfaces implemented on the same class, or via constructor parameters.

The simplest interface available has a single method. The simplest method available accepts no parameters and returns no value, as shown in Listing 8-36.

LISTING 8-36 ITask is the simplest interface possible.

```
public interface ITask
{
    void Do();
}
```

This interface is extremely decoratable. Because it returns no value, it can even have an asynchronous fire-and-forget decorator. It can be used whenever a client needs to send a message but does not have any context to provide it, nor does it require any response to be returned.

A step up from this is the action interface, which is analogous to the `Action` delegate in the framework. It takes a generic parameter that dictates the type of its context. The `IAction` interface is shown in Listing 8-37.

LISTING 8-37 The IAction interface adds a context parameter.

```
public interface IAction<TContext>
{
    void Do(TContext context);
}
```

This is only slightly more complex than the task. If you introduce a return value, instead of a parameter, you create a function, as shown in Listing 8-38.

LISTING 8-38 IFunction interfaces have return values.

```
public interface IFunction<TReturn>
{
    TReturn Do();
}
```

A further specialization of this interface is to require that the function return a Boolean value. This creates a predicate, as shown in Listing 8-39.

LISTING 8-39 IPredicate is a function that returns a Boolean value.

```
public interface IPredicate
{
    bool Test();
}
```

The predicate can be used to encapsulate a branching test, such as an if statement or the clause of a loop.

Although these interfaces look unassuming, a lot can be achieved by decorating, adapting, and composing a number of different instances of these interfaces.

Conclusion

This chapter has been dedicated to the art of good interface design. Too often, interfaces are large facades behind which huge subsystems are hidden. At a certain critical mass, interfaces lose the adaptability that makes them so fundamental to developing solid code.

There are plenty of reasons why interfaces should be segregated—to aid decoration, to correctly hide functionality from clients, as self-documentation for other developers, or as a side effect of architectural design. Whatever the reason, it is a technique that should be kept at the forefront of your mind whenever you are creating an interface. As with most programming tools, it is easier to start out on the right path than to go back and heavily refactor.

CHAPTER 9

Dependency injection

After completing this chapter, you will be able to

- Understand the importance of dependency injection.

- Use dependency injection as the glue that holds SOLID code together.

- Choose between Poor Man's Dependency Injection, an Inversion of Control container, or convention over configuration.

- Avoid dependency injection anti-patterns.

- Organize your solutions around composition roots and resolution roots.

- Know how the Factory pattern collaborates with dependency injection to manage object lifetimes correctly.

Dependency injection (DI) is a very simple concept with a similarly simple implementation. However, this simplicity belies the importance of the pattern. DI is the glue without which the techniques of the previous SOLID chapters—and much of the Agile foundation chapters—would not be possible.

When something is so simple, yet so important, people tend to overcomplicate it. DI is no exception, but there are a number of pitfalls that you should be aware of. These include anti-patterns and general bad practices that subvert the intent of this pattern.

Implemented correctly, dependency injection is invisible to the majority of a project's code. It is limited to a very small amount of the code, often in a single assembly. The trick is to plan for dependency injection from the outset, because integrating it into an established project is difficult and time consuming.

Humble beginnings

The following example highlights the underlying problem that dependency injection solves. Imagine that you are developing a task management application that allows the user to manage a to-do list. In this hypothetical scenario, you are still in the early stages of development, using Windows Presentation Foundation (WPF) for the user interface. So far, you have a main window for the application that does little other than show the current state of your to-do list, which is read from persistent storage. Figure 9-1 shows this window.

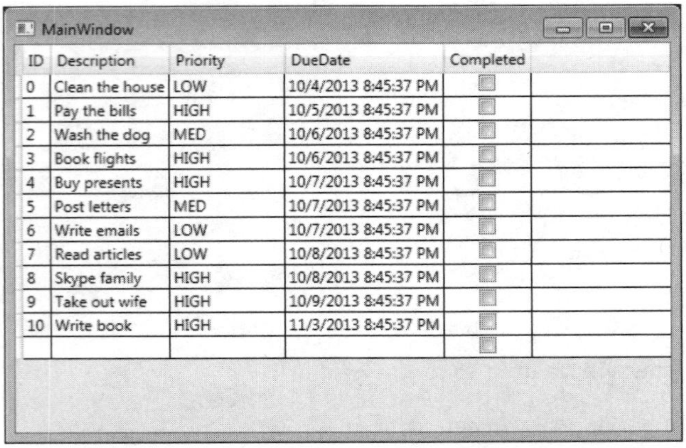
MainWindow

ID	Description	Priority	DueDate	Completed
0	Clean the house	LOW	10/4/2013 8:45:37 PM	
1	Pay the bills	HIGH	10/5/2013 8:45:37 PM	
2	Wash the dog	MED	10/6/2013 8:45:37 PM	
3	Book flights	HIGH	10/6/2013 8:45:37 PM	
4	Buy presents	HIGH	10/7/2013 8:45:37 PM	
5	Post letters	MED	10/7/2013 8:45:37 PM	
6	Write emails	LOW	10/7/2013 8:45:37 PM	
7	Read articles	LOW	10/8/2013 8:45:37 PM	
8	Skype family	HIGH	10/8/2013 8:45:37 PM	
9	Take out wife	HIGH	10/9/2013 8:45:37 PM	
10	Write book	HIGH	11/3/2013 8:45:37 PM	

FIGURE 9-1 The task list has some state beyond the task description: priority, due date, and the task's completion state.

Because this is a WPF application, you are using the Model-View-ViewModel (MVVM) pattern to ensure a separation of concerns between the layers. The application strives to use best practices—although dependency injection is still to come. One of the view models is the backing controller for the main window. `TaskListController` delegates to a `TaskService` to retrieve all of the tasks. An example of how this is currently accomplished without dependency injection is shown in Listing 9-1.

LISTING 9-1 This controller does not use dependency injection.

```
{
    public event PropertyChangedEventHandler PropertyChanged = delegate { };

    private readonly ITaskService taskService;
    private readonly IObjectMapper mapper;
    private ObservableCollection<TaskViewModel> allTasks;

    public TaskListController()
    {
        this.taskService = new TaskServiceAdo();
        this.mapper = new MapperAutoMapper();

        var taskDtos = taskService.GetAllTasks();
        AllTasks = new
  ObservableCollection<TaskViewModel>(mapper.Map<IEnumerable<TaskViewModel>>(taskDtos));
    }

    public ObservableCollection<TaskViewModel> AllTasks
    {
        get
        {
            return allTasks;
        }
        set
        {
```

```
            allTasks = value;
            PropertyChanged(this, new PropertyChangedEventArgs("AllTasks"));
        }
    }
}
```

The problems with this approach include:

- Difficulty in unit testing the controller due to a dependency on an implementation.

- Lack of clarity as to what this view model requires—depends on—unless its source is checked.

- Implied dependency from this class to the dependencies of the service.

- Lack of flexibility in providing alternative service implementations.

The rest of this section investigates these problems in greater depth by comparing the original class with a refactored version that uses dependency injection, as shown in Listing 9-2. (The changes have been highlighted in bold.)

LISTING 9-2 After refactoring, this controller uses dependency injection.

```
public class TaskListController : INotifyPropertyChanged
{
    public event PropertyChangedEventHandler PropertyChanged = delegate { };

    private readonly ITaskService taskService;
    private readonly IObjectMapper mapper;
    private ObservableCollection<TaskViewModel> allTasks;

    public TaskListController(ITaskService taskService, IObjectMapper mapper)
    {
        this.taskService = taskService;
        this.mapper = mapper;
    }

    public void OnLoad()
    {
        var taskDtos = taskService.GetAllTasks();
        AllTasks = new
 ObservableCollection<TaskViewModel>(mapper.Map<IEnumerable<TaskViewModel>>(taskDtos));
    }

    public ObservableCollection<TaskViewModel> AllTasks
    {
        get
        {
            return allTasks;
        }
        set
        {
```

```
            allTasks = value;
            PropertyChanged(this, new PropertyChangedEventArgs("AllTasks"));
        }
    }

}
```

To unit test the first class in isolation, as you should, the TaskService would need to be mocked. However, it is unlikely that the TaskService can be mocked by conventional means. It is not likely to be a proxiable class, nor should you be forced to make it so. The second class accepts an ITaskService, which is an interface, rather than a class. This is more testable because interfaces are always proxiable.

> **Note** A class is said to be *proxiable* if an alternative implementation—known as a *proxy*—can be provided to the client. Classes are only proxiable if they declare all of their methods as virtual. Interfaces, on the other hand, are always proxiable.

If a class arbitrarily constructs classes inside its methods, you cannot know externally what it requires in order to function correctly. The first example, without DI, is a black box of dependencies. You can only discover what it needs by opening the class file and reading through it studiously. It declares none of its dependencies as part of its interface or method signatures. The second example, with DI, clearly states that it needs an implementation of the task service in order to function. This is discoverable from client code by using IntelliSense, which is included with Microsoft Visual Studio.

When a dependency exists between class A and class B, if class B has a dependency on class C, it follows that class A is implicitly dependent on class C. This is how the Entourage anti-pattern manifests and leads to an interconnected web of dependencies that are very difficult to rectify. If you ensure that your interfaces generalize—that is, that they correctly abstract their behavior—a class that depends on an interface does not depend on anything further. This holds true even though implementations of the interface might depend on something heavy and external, such as a database. This is the Stairway pattern correctly applied.

When objects are instantiated directly, you also lose a possible extension point that an interface would otherwise provide. You cannot inherit from the TaskService and enhance its methods—assuming that they are declared virtual—because you would have to amend the controller to directly construct a new instance of this subclass. Interfaces lend themselves to all sorts of interesting patterns that can be used to provide alternative implementations or enhance the existing implementation. Additionally, as you have learned, this can be done after the initial version of the class has been written, before new requirements have been discovered. *This is the key to code adaptability.*

The Task List application

Figure 9-2 shows the package-level and class-level organization that you are aiming for with the Task List application.

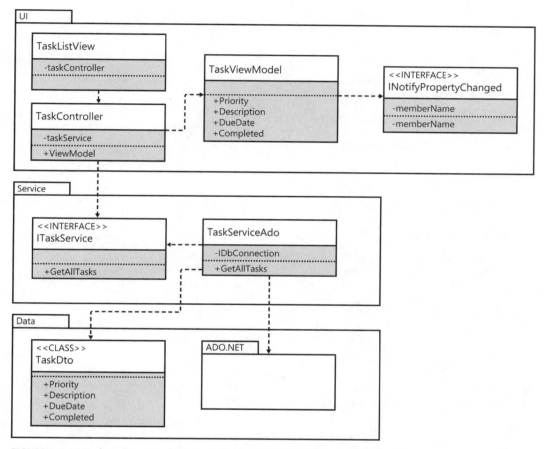

FIGURE 9-2 UML class diagram of the three-layered Task List application, with packages.

The user interface consists of WPF and controller/view model–specific code. The service layer is abstracted from the controllers via an interface, which has an implementation that uses a simple ADO.NET call to retrieve the tasks from persistent storage.

The TaskDto class is returned by the service as an in-memory representation of a task row from storage. This is a Plain Old CLR Object (POCO) and, as such, it is not as feature rich as a WPF view model really should be. Thus, when TaskController retrieves the TaskDto objects from the ITaskService, it asks an IObjectMapper to convert them to TaskViewModel objects, which implement INotify-PropertyChanged and can be embellished with other view-specific features.

The ADO.NET implementation of the `ITaskService` interface is shown in Listing 9-3. The constructor is your main concern, but later this chapter will discuss a lingering code smell in this class.

LISTING 9-3 The `TaskService` is responsible for retrieving the task list data.

```
public class TaskServiceAdo : ITaskService
{
    public TaskServiceAdo(ISettings settings)
    {
        this.settings = settings;
    }

    public IEnumerable<TaskDto> GetAllTasks()
    {
        var allTasks = new List<TaskDto>();


    private readonly ISettings settings;

    private const int IDIndex = 0;
    private const int DescriptionIndex = 1;
    private const int PriorityIndex = 2;
    private const int DueDateIndex = 3;
    private const int CompletedIndex = 4;
        using(var connection = new
SqlConnection(settings.GetSetting("TaskDatabaseConnectionString")))
        {
            connection.Open();

            using(var transaction = connection.BeginTransaction())
            {
                var command = connection.CreateCommand();
                command.Transaction = transaction;
                command.CommandType = CommandType.StoredProcedure;
                command.CommandText = "[dbo].[get_all_tasks]";

                using(var reader = command.ExecuteReader(CommandBehavior.CloseConnection))
                {
                    if (reader.HasRows)
                    {
                        while (reader.Read())
                        {
                            allTasks.Add(
                                new TaskDto
```

```
                                {
                                    ID = reader.GetInt32(IDIndex),
                                    Description = reader.GetString(DescriptionIndex),
                                    Priority = reader.GetString(PriorityIndex),
                                    DueDate = reader.GetDateTime(DueDateIndex),
                                    Completed = reader.GetBoolean(CompletedIndex)
                                }
                            );
                        }
                    }
                }
            }
        }

        return allTasks;
    }
}
```

The `ISettings` interface abstracts away from this class the details of retrieving the connection string. An implementation that is an adapter for the Microsoft .NET Framework's `Configuration-Manager` class is provided. It is not hard to imagine that the settings could end up being stored elsewhere at some point, which justifies the use of an interface. Another problem is that the `ConfigurationManager` class is static and, thus, hard to mock. Using it directly would not only limit your options for retrieving application settings such as connection strings, it would also make the `TaskServiceAdo` class less testable.

Constructing the object graph

Often in this book, it has been an accepted fact that interfaces are injected into constructors. Eventually, of course, interfaces prove to be insufficient, and you must commit to an implementation. There are two main options for accomplishing this: Poor Man's Dependency Injection and using an Inversion of Control container. In order to exemplify how dependency injection works, this section will first look at Poor Man's DI.

Poor Man's Dependency Injection

This pattern is so named because it does not require any external dependencies in order to function. It involves constructing the necessary object graph for the controller ahead of time. Listing 9-4 shows how to construct the refactored `TaskListController` and provide it to the `TaskListView`, which is the application's main window.

LISTING 9-4 Poor Man's DI is verbose but flexible.

```
public partial class App : Application
{
    private void OnApplicationStartup(object sender, StartupEventArgs e)
    {
        CreateMappings();

        var settings = new ApplicationSettings();
        var taskService = new TaskServiceAdo(settings);
        var objectMapper = new MapperAutoMapper();
        controller = new TaskListController(taskService, objectMapper);
        MainWindow = new TaskListView(controller);
        MainWindow.Show();

        controller.OnLoad();
    }

    private void CreateMappings()
    {
        AutoMapper.Mapper.CreateMap<TaskDto, TaskViewModel>();
    }

    private TaskListController controller;
}
```

This code is the entry point to your application. The OnApplicationStartup method is an event handler that is called by internal WPF code to inform you that you can initialize things. In different types of applications, the entry point varies in style but is always a good place to put your dependency injection code.

The process of bootstrapping the application is very simple. The target is to construct a Task-ListView, because that is the view class that acts as the resolution root of the application. Resolution roots are covered later in this chapter. In order to construct that class, you need a TaskList-Controller instance. But that class requires both an ITaskService and an IObjectMapper, so you instantiate classes for both—this is where you are committing to the implementations. The TaskServiceAdo, in turn, requires an ISettings implementation, so you commit to the ApplicationSettings, which is an adapter for the ConfigurationManager .NET Framework class. Figure 9-3 clarifies this with a class diagram.

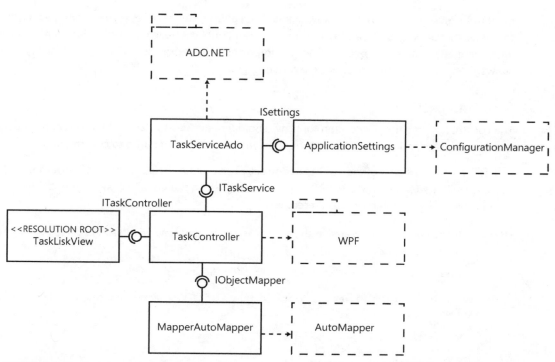

FIGURE 9-3 The interfaces, their implementations, and their dependencies, all of which make up the Task List application.

Each class requires one or more dependencies as sockets that are implemented by other classes that might also require dependencies. It is common for an implementation to be an adapter, such as the MapperAutoMapper and the ApplicationSettings classes. These simply fulfil the interface required of the dependency but delegate the actual work to another class. Even if the class is not an adapter, it is likely to have some dependencies of its own to which it delegates some of the work, like the TaskServiceAdo, which uses ADO .NET for the real retrieval of data. Other implementations of the ITaskService could get the task list from anywhere—a TaskServiceNHibernate class would be an alternative implementation that delegated much of the work to NHibernate. A Task-ServiceOutlook class could depend on the Microsoft Outlook Add-In framework and read the tasks directly from the built-in task list of Outlook. It is imperative to note that, because the interface does not tie itself to any of these technologies, *anything* could be the source of tasks, assuming that it can fulfil the interface.

Poor Man's DI is verbose. When this application is extended to support adding new tasks, editing tasks, or perhaps notifying of an imminent due date, it is clear that these few lines of construction code will grow significantly, to the point where they are no longer easily understood. However, Poor Man's DI is flexible. Whatever complex object graph you want to construct, the way to construct it is obvious because there is only one way: manually creating instances of everything and passing them to classes that aggregate their functionality, repeating until you reach the resolution root. You can implement any number of decorators for the interfaces that each class depends on; Poor Man's DI allows you to meticulously construct the resulting graph.

Method injection

The constructor isn't the only option for providing dependencies to classes. Methods and properties can also be used, and they both have different use cases when compared to constructors.

Listing 9-5 shows part of the `TaskListController` that has been rewritten to furnish the `ITask-Service` with its `ISettings` dependency as a parameter on the `GetAllTasks` method. This requires the interface for the method to be altered.

LISTING 9-5 The task service now accepts the settings as a method parameter instead of a constructor parameter.

```
public class TaskListController : INotifyPropertyChanged
{
    public TaskListController(ITaskService taskService, IObjectMapper mapper, ISettings settings)
    {
        this.taskService = taskService;
        this.mapper = mapper;
        this.settings = settings;
    }

    public void OnLoad()
    {
        var taskDtos = taskService.GetAllTasks(settings);
        AllTasks = new
    ObservableCollection<TaskViewModel>(mapper.Map<IEnumerable<TaskViewModel>>(taskDtos));
    }
}
```

This is useful when the method being called is the only one that requires the dependency. Constructor dependencies indicate that sufficient behavior in the class requires delegation to the dependency, but if only a small percentage of methods truly use the dependency, it might make more sense to pass it in to those methods specifically. The downside of method injection is that it requires the clients who call the method to "acquire" an instance of the dependency. They can do so either through a constructor parameter or through a method parameter that causes clients to pass the parameter down the call stack until it is used by the target class.

Property injection

Similar to method injection, property injection can be used to inject dependencies. Listing 9-6 refactors the prior example to show how the ITaskService could have its ISettings dependencies set by a property. Bear in mind that, again, the interface needs to be changed to support the property, not just the implementation.

LISTING 9-6 Dependency injection can also be accomplished via property injection.

```
public class TaskListController : INotifyPropertyChanged
{
    public TaskListController(ITaskService taskService, IObjectMapper mapper, ISettings
    settings)
    {
        this.taskService = taskService;
        this.mapper = mapper;
        this.settings = settings;
    }

    public void OnLoad()
    {
        taskService.Settings = settings;
        var taskDtos = taskService.GetAllTasks();
        AllTasks = new
    ObservableCollection<TaskViewModel>(mapper.Map<IEnumerable<TaskViewModel>>(taskDtos));
    }
}
```

The benefit to this approach is that the instance property can be changed at run time. Whereas a constructor dependency is injected and that instance is used for the lifetime of the class, a property value can be replaced midway through the class's lifetime.

Inversion of Control

Throughout this book, the examples have focused on developing classes that delegate to abstractions. These abstractions are then implemented by other classes, which delegate some work to more abstractions. Eventually, a class is so small and directed that it need not delegate any further, and the chain of dependency is ended. In order to construct the dependent classes, first their dependencies are constructed and then injected in as dependencies. You have learned how this dependency injection can be implemented by manually constructing classes and passing instances into the constructors. Though this elevates you from a situation in which dependent implementations cannot be swapped or decorated to one in which they can, the object graph is still constructed statically: which part goes where is known at compile time. Inversion of Control (IoC) allows you to defer this construction to run time.

IoC is most well known in the context of IoC *containers*. These systems allows you to link the interfaces of your application to their implementations and retrieve an instance of a class by *resolving* all of the dependencies.

The code in Listing 9-7 shows the application entry point rewritten to use the Unity IoC container. The first step is to instantiate a new `UnityContainer` instance. Note that when you are bootstrapping the IoC container like this, there is no alternative but to directly create instances of infrastructural components.

LISTING 9-7 With an IoC container, instead of manually constructing implementations, types are mapped to interfaces.

```
public partial class App : Application
{
    private IUnityContainer container;
    private void OnApplicationStartup(object sender, StartupEventArgs e)
    {
        CreateMappings();

        container = new UnityContainer();
        container.RegisterType<ISettings, ApplicationSettings>();
        container.RegisterType<IObjectMapper, MapperAutoMapper>();
        container.RegisterType<ITaskService, TaskServiceAdo>();
        container.RegisterType<TaskListController>();
        container.RegisterType<TaskListView>();

        MainWindow = container.Resolve<TaskListView>();
        MainWindow.Show();

        ((TaskListController)MainWindow.DataContext).OnLoad();
    }

    private void CreateMappings()
    {
        AutoMapper.Mapper.CreateMap<TaskDto, TaskViewModel>();
    }
}
```

After the Unity container is created, you need to make it aware of each interface that will need to be resolved at some point during the application's lifetime and map a concrete implementation to each interface. Whenever Unity encounters an interface, it will know which implementation it needs to resolve. If you fail to indicate which class to use for an interface, Unity will loudly remind you that it cannot instantiate interfaces.

After all registration is complete, you need to get an instance of your resolution root: the `TaskList-View`. The `Resolve` method of the container will examine the constructor of this class and try to instantiate any dependencies by examining their constructors and trying to instantiate their dependencies, and so on down the chain. Eventually, when there are no more classes to instantiate, the `Resolve` method is able to call the constructors that it found by passing in the instances it has created so far. This is exactly the same process that you follow when using Poor Man's DI, but with that approach you examine the constructors manually and instantiate the classes directly.

The Register, Resolve, Release pattern

All Inversion of Control containers reduce to a simple interface with only three methods, as shown in Listing 9-8. Unity is no exception to this and follows a similar pattern.

LISTING 9-8 Although each implementation will embellish it, this is the general interface for all IoC containers.

```
public interface IContainer : IDisposable
{
    void Register<TInterface, TImplementation>()
        where TImplementation : TInterface;

    TImplementation Resolve<TInterface>();

    void Release();
}
```

The purpose of each of the three methods is explained in the following list:

- **Register**   This method is called first, at application initialization. It will be called many times to register many different interfaces to their implementations. The where clause enforces the constraint that the TImplementation type must implement—that is, inherit the interface of— the TInterface type. Other permutations of this method allow you to register an already-constructed instance of a class and a type without a specific interface. (Such a type will be registered against all the interfaces it implements.)

- **Resolve**   This method is called during the running of the application. It is common for a particular family of classes to be resolved as the top-level object of the graph. For example, this would be the controllers in an ASP.NET Model-View-Controller (MVC) application, the view-models in a ViewModel-first WPF application, and the views in a Windows Forms Model-View-Presenter (MVP) application. The call to this method should be an infrastructural concern. That is, you should not call Resolve inside your application's classes for controllers, views, presenters, services, domain, business logic, or data access.

- **Release**   At some point, the classes will no longer be needed and their resources can be released. This might happen at the end of the application, but it also could happen at a more opportune moment during the application's lifetime. In a web scenario, for example, it is common for resources to live only *per-request*. Thus, Release could be called at the end of each request. This sort of object lifetime concern is discussed in more detail later.

- **Dispose**   Most IoC containers will implement the IDisposable interface, so it has been included in this reference interface, too. The Dispose method will be called once when the application is shut down. It is distinct from Release in that the Dispose call will clear out the internal dictionaries of the container so that it has no registrations and is unable to resolve anything.

The first IoC example (shown in Listing 9-7) can be rewritten so that all interaction with the container is encapsulated in a class. This moves the verbose registration code away from the code-behind in the WPF application. This is shown in Listing 9-9.

LISTING 9-9 The startup event handler delegates much of its work to a configuration class.

```
public partial class App : Application
{
    private IocConfiguration ioc;

    private void OnApplicationStartup(object sender, StartupEventArgs e)
    {
        CreateMappings();

        ioc = new IocConfiguration();
        ioc.Register();

        MainWindow = ioc.Resolve();
        MainWindow.Show();

        ((TaskListController)MainWindow.DataContext).OnLoad();
    }

    private void OnApplicationExit(object sender, ExitEventArgs e)
    {
        ioc.Release();
    }

    private void CreateMappings()
    {
        AutoMapper.Mapper.CreateMap<TaskDto, TaskViewModel>();
    }
}
```

The entry point is now simpler than it was before, and the IoC registration has been moved to a dedicated class. Listing 9-10 shows this class for the Task List application. When the application exits, it calls the Release method, which you can hook into by registering a handler to the appropriate Application event.

LISTING 9-10 The configuration class has methods for all three phases of the Register, Resolve, Release pattern.

```
public class IocConfiguration
{

    private readonly IUnityContainer container;
    public IocConfiguration()
    {
        container = new UnityContainer();
    }

    public void Register()
    {
        container.RegisterType<ISettings, ApplicationSettings>();
        container.RegisterType<IObjectMapper, MapperAutoMapper>();
        container.RegisterType<ITaskService, TaskServiceAdo>();
        container.RegisterType<TaskListController>();
        container.RegisterType<TaskListView>();
    }

    public Window Resolve()
    {
        return container.Resolve<TaskListView>();
    }

    public void Release()
    {
        container.Dispose();
    }
}
```

The `Register` method contains exactly the same code as before. As this method grows, however, it can be refactored into multiple methods and generally kept neater than it otherwise might be if it was contained in the application entry point.

The `Resolve` method returns a generic `Window`, which is a common resolution root for a WPF application. Specifically, the `TaskListView` is returned because it is the main window for your application. In other application types, such as ASP.NET MVC, there are often multiple resolution roots—one for each controller. The organization of the composition root for MVC and other applications is discussed later in this chapter.

Imperative vs. declarative registration

The registration code to this point has been written imperatively with procedural calls to methods on a container object. This gives you some advantages: it is easy to read, it is relatively succinct, and it provides a minimum of compile-time checking, such as protection against typographical errors. One disadvantage is that you are tying yourself to an implementation at compile time. If you want to swap out one of your implementations for an alternative, this requires a recompile of the code.

If, instead, you use declarative registration via XML, you can obviate the need for a recompile by moving the decision to configuration time. Listing 9-11 shows Unity's support for XML registration.

LISTING 9-11 A section in the application configuration file can describe how interfaces should map to implementations.

```xml
<configuration>
  <configSections>
    <section name="unity"
            type="Microsoft.Practices.Unity.Configuration.UnityConfigurationSection,
  Microsoft.Practices.Unity.Configuration" />
  </configSections>
  <appSettings>
    <add key="TaskDatabaseConnectionString" value="Data Source=(local);Initial
  Catalog=TaskDatabase;Integrated Security=True;Application Name=Task List Editor" />
  </appSettings>
  <unity xmlns="http://schemas.microsoft.com/practices/2010/unity">
    <typeAliases>
      <typeAlias alias="ISettings" type="ServiceInterfaces.ISettings, ServiceInterfaces"
  />
      <typeAlias alias="ApplicationSettings" type="UI.ApplicationSettings, UI" />
      <typeAlias alias="IObjectMapper" type="ServiceInterfaces.IObjectMapper,
  ServiceInterfaces" />
      <typeAlias alias="MapperAutoMapper" type="UI.MapperAutoMapper, UI" />
      <typeAlias alias="ITaskService" type="ServiceInterfaces.ITaskService,
  ServiceInterfaces" />
      <typeAlias alias="TaskServiceAdo" type="ServiceImplementations.TaskServiceAdo,
  ServiceImplementations" />
      <typeAlias alias="TaskListController" type="Controllers.TaskListController,
  Controllers" />
      <typeAlias alias="TaskListView" type="UI.TaskListView, UI" />
    </typeAliases>
    <container>
      <register type="ISettings" mapTo="ApplicationSettings" />
      <register type="IObjectMapper" mapTo="MapperAutoMapper" />
      <register type="ITaskService" mapTo="TaskServiceAdo" />
    </container>
  </unity>
  <startup>
    <supportedRuntime version="v4.0" sku=".NETFramework,Version=v4.5" />
  </startup>
</configuration>
```

This XML is the content of the application configuration file for the WPF Task List. Adding a configuration section for Unity enables the `typeAlias` and `container` elements. The former is used to alias shorter names for longer types, which need to be specified by their assembly-qualified names so that Unity can find them at run time. After the types have been aliased, the latter section performs the same job as the `Register` method: mapping an interface to an implementation.

Some changes need to be made to the application entry point for Unity to read this XML configuration. Listing 9-12 shows that these changes are minimal.

LISTING 9-12 Now the registration phase involves passing the configuration section to the container.

```
public partial class App : Application
{
    private IUnityContainer container;

    private void OnApplicationStartup(object sender, StartupEventArgs e)
    {
        CreateMappings();

        var section = (UnityConfigurationSection)ConfigurationManager.GetSection("unity");
        container = new UnityContainer().LoadConfiguration(section);

        MainWindow = container.Resolve<TaskListView>();
        MainWindow.Show();

        ((TaskListController)MainWindow.DataContext).OnLoad();
    }

    private void CreateMappings()
    {
        AutoMapper.Mapper.CreateMap<TaskDto, TaskViewModel>();
    }
}
```

Just two lines are required. First, you load the `unity` section from the configuration file by using the `ConfigurationManager` class. This is cast to the `UnityConfigurationSection` type so that it can be passed to the `LoadConfiguration` method of a newly instantiated `UnityContainer`. After this, the container can be used, as before, to resolve the main window of the application.

Although declarative registration brings the benefit of configuration-time type mapping, it has significant drawbacks that make it impractical in many situations. The biggest problem is its verbosity. This small example is already a lot more typing than before, but this example is small. In some cases, the registration code could be a few times larger than this, or more. As XML, it would be even larger still. If a typographical error was made in any of the alias or registration sections, it would not be caught until run time, whereas such errors are caught by the compiler in procedural code.

The most compelling reason that declarative registration is suboptimal is that most IoC containers allow for a lot of variation in registration. This can include lambda factories, whereby a lambda method is provided to the registration method, to be called whenever the interface is resolved. Such procedural code is not possible in declarative XML.

Object lifetime

It is important to acknowledge that not every object in the application has an equal lifetime. That is, some objects might need to live longer than others. Of course, in the managed languages of .NET, there is no deterministic way to destroy an object, but you can ask it to relinquish its resources by calling the IDispose.Dispose() method, if it implements that interface.

For example, the TaskService from Listing 9-3 had a remaining code smell of manually creating a SqlConnection instance. This was left there because the lifetime of that connection could not be matched to that of the TaskService, which is created on application startup and exists for the duration of the application. If the SqlConnection was injected into the TaskService, as shown in Listing 9-13, it would live for the lifetime of the application. This does not mean, however, that the connection would be open for the duration, because opening the connection is a separate operation from its construction.

LISTING 9-13 Some resources have a lifetime that must be carefully managed.

```
private void OnApplicationStartup(object sender, StartupEventArgs e)
{
    CreateMappings();

    container = new UnityContainer();
    container.RegisterType<ISettings, ApplicationSettings>();
    container.RegisterType<IObjectMapper, MapperAutoMapper>();
    container.RegisterType<ITaskService, TaskServiceAdo>(new InjectionFactory(c => new
TaskServiceAdo(new
SqlConnection(c.Resolve<ISettings>().GetSetting("TaskDatabaseConnectionString")))));
    container.RegisterType<TaskListController>();
    container.RegisterType<TaskListView>();

    MainWindow = container.Resolve<TaskListView>();
    MainWindow.Show();

    ((TaskListController)MainWindow.DataContext).OnLoad();
}
// . . .
public class TaskServiceAdo : ITaskService
{

    private readonly IDbConnection connection;
    public TaskServiceAdo(IDbConnection connection)
    {
        this.connection = connection;
    }

    public IEnumerable<TaskDto> GetAllTasks()
    {
        var allTasks = new List<TaskDto>();

        using (connection)
        {
```

```
        connection.Open();

        using (var transaction = connection.BeginTransaction())
        {
            var command = connection.CreateCommand();
            command.Transaction = transaction;
            command.CommandType = CommandType.StoredProcedure;
            command.CommandText = "[dbo].[get_all_tasks]";

            using (var reader =
command.ExecuteReader(CommandBehavior.CloseConnection))
            {
                while (reader.Read())
                {
                    allTasks.Add(
                        new TaskDto
                        {
                            ID = reader.GetInt32(IDIndex),
                            Description = reader.GetString(DescriptionIndex),
                            Priority = reader.GetString(PriorityIndex),
                            DueDate = reader.GetDateTime(DueDateIndex),
                            Completed = reader.GetBoolean(CompletedIndex)
                        }
                    );
                }
            }
        }

    return allTasks;
    }

}
```

The first change is made to the entry point, where an injection factory is used for constructing the service. This is a lambda expression that has access to the container for resolving parameters and returns a new instance of the service. The call to the ISettings service's GetSettings method has been moved to this injection factory to retrieve the connection string. This is passed to the SqlConnection constructor which, in turn, is passed to the service.

In the GetAllTasks() method, the presence of the using(connection) is problematic. This ensures that SqlConnection.Dispose() is called at the end of the using scope. After this call, the connection can no longer be used, yet you could feasibly call this method again.

Instead, what if the TaskServiceAdo implemented IDisposable and delegated its Dispose method to that of the connection? This is explored in Listing 9-14.

LISTING 9-14 The service implements IDisposable so that it can dispose of the connection.

```
public class TaskServiceAdo : ITaskService, IDisposable
{
    public TaskServiceAdo(IDbConnection connection)
    {
        this.connection = connection;
    }

    public IEnumerable<TaskDto> GetAllTasks()
    {
        var allTasks = new List<TaskDto>();

        connection.Open();

        try
        {
            using (var transaction = connection.BeginTransaction())
            {
                var command = connection.CreateCommand();
                command.Transaction = transaction;
                command.CommandType = CommandType.StoredProcedure;
                command.CommandText = "[dbo].[get_all_tasks]";

                using (var reader =
    command.ExecuteReader(CommandBehavior.CloseConnection))
                {
                    while (reader.Read())
                    {
                        allTasks.Add(
                            new TaskDto
                            {
                                ID = reader.GetInt32(IDIndex),
                                Description = reader.GetString(DescriptionIndex),
                                Priority = reader.GetString(PriorityIndex),
                                DueDate = reader.GetDateTime(DueDateIndex),
                                Completed = reader.GetBoolean(CompletedIndex)
                            }
                        );
                    }
                }
            }
        }
        finally
        {
            connection.Close();
        }

        return allTasks;
    }

    public void Dispose()
    {
        connection.Dispose();
    }
}
```

Instead of disposing the connection in the method, the connection is disposed of only when the service is disposed. This raises the important question of when the task service should be disposed. Should all of the task's clients, which will receive `ITaskService` as a constructor parameter, also implement `IDisposable`? Who will dispose of these objects? Eventually, you would need to call `Dispose()` on something.

It is important to note that if a class is handed a dependency via its constructor, *it should not manually dispose of the dependency itself.* The class cannot guarantee that it has been given the one and only instance of the dependency; it might share it with others and therefore cannot dispose of it without potentially having a negative impact on other classes.

The answer to the question of how to manage the lifetime of objects when using dependency injection is much closer to how the service was originally implemented.

The connection factory   Recall that the Factory pattern is a way of replacing manual object instantiation with delegation to a class whose purpose is to create objects.

A connection factory could look something like the interface shown in Listing 9-15. This interface has been made slightly more general by returning the `IDbConnection` interface, rather than committing all of its clients to the `SqlConnection` class.

LISTING 9-15 The connection factory interface is very simple.

```
public interface IConnectionFactory
{
    IDbConnection CreateConnection();
}
```

This interface will be injected into the task service so that you have a way of retrieving a connection without manually constructing it, keeping the service testable through mocking. Listing 9-16 shows the refactored service.

LISTING 9-16 Dependency injection can work in tandem with the Factory pattern.

```
public class TaskServiceAdo : ITaskService
{
    private readonly IConnectionFactory connectionFactory;

    public TaskServiceAdo(IConnectionFactory connectionFactory)
    {
        this.connectionFactory = connectionFactory;
    }

    public IEnumerable<TaskDto> GetAllTasks()
    {
        var allTasks = new List<TaskDto>();
```

```
            using(var connection = connectionFactory.CreateConnection())
            {
                connection.Open();

                using (var transaction = connection.BeginTransaction())
                {
                    var command = connection.CreateCommand();
                    command.Transaction = transaction;
                    command.CommandType = CommandType.StoredProcedure;
                    command.CommandText = "[dbo].[get_all_tasks]";

                    using (var reader =
        command.ExecuteReader(CommandBehavior.CloseConnection))
                    {
                        while (reader.Read())
                        {
                            allTasks.Add(
                                new TaskDto
                                {
                                    ID = reader.GetInt32(IDIndex),
                                    Description = reader.GetString(DescriptionIndex),
                                    Priority = reader.GetString(PriorityIndex),
                                    DueDate = reader.GetDateTime(DueDateIndex),
                                    Completed = reader.GetBoolean(CompletedIndex)
                                }
                            );
                        }
                    }
                }
            }

            return allTasks;
        }
    }
```

Note that the return value from the CreateConnection method is being disposed by the using block. This is viable in this instance, because the product from the factory implements IDisposable. Through interface inheritance, it is possible to enforce multiple interfaces on implementors.

However, the question must be asked whether every implementation will definitely need every interface. Sometimes they do, but given the wide variety of implementations that an interface can have—long after it was originally written—it is a big assumption to make. When it comes to IDisposable, I'm not sure it always applies.

The Responsible Owner pattern   Instead of artificially forcing the IDisposable interface onto every implementation, you can use it only on those that truly need it. This does cause a problem, though. If the product of the factory—your interface—does not implement IDisposable, you can no longer use a using block to neatly dispose of the product after it falls out of scope. In this case, you must use the Responsible Owner pattern.

Listing 9-17 shows that the using block can be replaced with a try/finally block, and that you can check at run time to find out whether the product implements the IDisposable interface.

LISTING 9-17 The Responsible Owner pattern ensures that resources are disposed of appropriately.

```
public IEnumerable<TaskDto> GetAllTasks()
{
    var allTasks = new List<TaskDto>();

    var connection = connectionFactory.CreateConnection();
    try
    {
        connection.Open();

        using (var transaction = connection.BeginTransaction())
        {
            var command = connection.CreateCommand();
            command.Transaction = transaction;
            command.CommandType = CommandType.StoredProcedure;
            command.CommandText = "[dbo].[get_all_tasks]";

            using (var reader = command.ExecuteReader(CommandBehavior.CloseConnection))
            {
                while (reader.Read())
                {
                    allTasks.Add(
                        new TaskDto
                        {
                            ID = reader.GetInt32(IDIndex),
                            Description = reader.GetString(DescriptionIndex),
                            Priority = reader.GetString(PriorityIndex),
                            DueDate = reader.GetDateTime(DueDateIndex),
                            Completed = reader.GetBoolean(CompletedIndex)
                        }
                    );
                }
            }
        }
    }
    finally
    {
        if(connection is IDisposable)
        {
            var disposableConnection = connection as IDisposable;
            disposableConnection.Dispose();
        }
    }

    return allTasks;
}
```

Only if the connection is of type `IDisposable` do you then attempt to call the `Dispose` method on it. This will work regardless of whether the product returned by the factory implements `IDisposable` or not, but if it does, it will correctly dispose of it, correctly cleaning up its resources.

The Responsible Owner pattern deterministically disposes of objects if they implement `IDisposable`. The pattern effectively ignores the objects if they do not implement `IDisposable`. However, SOLID code often results in multiple decorators that wrap around each other to add extra functionality. In this case, only if the top-layer object implements `IDisposable` will the Responsible Owner pattern function correctly. When the outer decorator does not implement `IDisposable`, but subsequent layers do, the Responsible Owner pattern will not correctly dispose of these instances. Instead, you must use the Factory Isolation pattern.

The Factory Isolation pattern   This pattern is able to deterministically dispose of the complex object graphs that often form as a result of SOLID code. It is named after the glove box isolators that are commonly found in laboratories. These are glass or metal boxes with integrated gloves to allow safe, protected access to the contents. In a similar fashion, the Factory Isolation pattern allows safe, protected access to an instance of an object that will be correctly disposed of after use.

The Factory Isolation pattern is only required when the target interface does not implement `IDisposable`. Extending the `IDisposable` interface burdens all implementations with the requirement that they implement a `Dispose` method, even in circumstances where this is unnecessary. Instead, `IDisposable` should be treated as an implementation detail and assigned to classes on an individual basis. This then leads naturally to the application of the Responsible Owner pattern and the Factory Isolation pattern.

The examples so far have all targeted the lifetime of the `IDbConnection` interface. Unfortunately, this interface extends the `IDisposable` interface. If, instead, the assumption is made that the target interface does not extend `IDisposable`, the client-side view of the Factory Isolation pattern would look like the code in Listing 9-18.

LISTING 9-18 An example of a client using the Factory Isolation pattern.

```
public IEnumerable<TaskDto> GetAllTasks()
{
    var allTasks = new List<TaskDto>();
    connectionFactory.With(connection =>
    {
        connection.Open();
        using (var transaction = connection.BeginTransaction())
        {
            var command = connection.CreateCommand();
            command.Transaction = transaction;
            command.CommandType = CommandType.StoredProcedure;
            command.CommandText = "[dbo].[get_all_tasks]";
            using (var reader = command.ExecuteReader(CommandBehavior.CloseConnection))
            {
                while (reader.Read())
                {
```

```
                    allTasks.Add(
                        new TaskDto
                        {
                            ID = reader.GetInt32(IDIndex),
                            Description = reader.GetString(DescriptionIndex),
                            Priority = reader.GetString(PriorityIndex),
                            DueDate = reader.GetDateTime(DueDateIndex),
                            Completed = reader.GetBoolean(CompletedIndex)
                        }
                    );
                }
            }
        }
    });

    return allTasks;
}
```

The Factory Isolation pattern replaces the common `Create` method, which returns an instance of a factory product, instead providing a `With` method, which accepts a lambda method that has the factory product as a parameter.

The advantage here is that the lifetime of the factory product is explicitly linked to the lambda method's scope. This succinctly communicates to the client that it is not in control of the product's lifetime. The factory implementation itself is very simple, as shown in Listing 9-19.

LISTING 9-19 Creating an isolating factory is simple.

```
public class IsolationConnectionFactory : IConnectionIsolationFactory
{
    public void With(Action<IDbConnection> do)
    {
        using(var connection = CreateConnection())
        {
            do(connection);
        }
    }
}
```

The `With` method is able to construct a florid object graph of decorators, adapters, and composites—just as SOLID suggests—and manage their lifetimes without the calling client concerning itself with anything but using the final product.

Note that it is possible to circumvent the Factory Isolation pattern by assigning the lambda-scoped product instance to a variable that has wider scope, so client code is discouraged from doing this.

Beyond simple injection

Dependency injection can be implemented in many different ways, by using a variety of different frameworks. Some patterns out there are benevolent, supporting and enhancing DI while reinforcing what it aims to accomplish. Other patterns do the opposite: they detract from the underlying purpose of DI, actively undermining it and detracting from the whole point.

Two such patterns are particularly insidious. The Service Locator anti-pattern is, unfortunately, all too common. It is used in many frameworks and libraries—sometimes, it is the only way to create a hook to use dependency injection. Worse than the Service Locator is an anti-pattern with an unfortunate moniker that I shall eschew in favor of something a bit more sanitized: *Illegitimate Injection*. This is a middle ground where dependency injection is used "sometimes," allowing the construction of services, controllers, and similar entities without properly providing their dependencies.

When you are using DI, each type of application requires a different kind of setup. With each, you need to identify the composition root in order to correctly integrate your registration code. The location of the composition root in a WPF application differs from that of a Windows Forms application. Both will differ from that of an ASP.NET MVC application.

In advanced scenarios, the manual composition of classes through Poor Man's DI and the individual registration of classes through an Inversion of Control container are both too laborious and verbose. By deferring registration to one or more conventions, you can eliminate a lot of boilerplate code but also provide some manual registration, to handle the edge cases when conventions do not suffice.

The Service Locator anti-pattern

Service locators look very similar to Inversion of Control containers, which is precisely why they are not always thought of as detrimental to the code. Listing 9-20 shows an example of the service locator provided by the Patterns and Practices team at Microsoft.

LISTING 9-20 The `IServiceLocator` interface appears to be just another IoC container.

```
public interface IServiceLocator : IServiceProvider
{
    object GetInstance(Type serviceType);

    object GetInstance(Type serviceType, string key);

    IEnumerable<object> GetAllInstances(Type serviceType);

    TService GetInstance<TService>();

    TService GetInstance<TService>(string key);

    IEnumerable<TService> GetAllInstances<TService>();
}
```

Note that methods such as `TService GetInstance<TService>()` could have been taken directly from the `IUnityContainer` interface—just by swapping the name for `Resolve`. The problem arises from how a service locator is *used*, thanks to the static `ServiceLocator` class, as shown in Listing 9-21.

LISTING 9-21 This static class is the cause of the anti-pattern.

```
/// <summary>
/// This class provides the ambient container for this application. If your
/// framework defines such an ambient container, use ServiceLocator.Current
/// to get it.
/// </summary>
public static class ServiceLocator
{
    private static ServiceLocatorProvider currentProvider;

    public static IServiceLocator Current
    {
        get { return currentProvider(); }
    }

    public static void SetLocatorProvider(ServiceLocatorProvider newProvider)
    {
        currentProvider = newProvider;
    }
}
```

The class summary comment, which I have left in, hints toward the problem. The concept of an *ambient container* implies a leak of knowledge that a container exists. Although there is a laudable decoupling of the specific implementation of the service locator behind an interface, the problem is the acknowledgement—inside any class other than the composition root—of the service locator or container. Listing 9-22 shows how the `TaskListController` would look if it was rewritten to use the `ServiceLocator`.

LISTING 9-22 A service locator allows classes to retrieve anything at all, whether appropriate or not.

```
public class TaskListController : INotifyPropertyChanged
{
    public void OnLoad()
    {
        var taskService = ServiceLocator.Current.GetInstance<ITaskService>();
        var taskDtos = taskService.GetAllTasks();
        var mapper = ServiceLocator.Current.GetInstance<IObjectMapper>();
        AllTasks = new
    ObservableCollection<TaskViewModel>(mapper.Map<IEnumerable<TaskViewModel>>(taskDtos));
    }
```

```
    public ObservableCollection<TaskViewModel> AllTasks
    {
        get
        {
            return allTasks;
        }
        set
        {
            allTasks = value;
            PropertyChanged(this, new PropertyChangedEventArgs("AllTasks"));
        }
    }

    public event PropertyChangedEventHandler PropertyChanged = delegate { };

    private ObservableCollection<TaskViewModel> allTasks;
}
```

Now there is no constructor, nor is there constructor injection. Instead, when required, the class makes a call to the static `ServiceLocator` class and returns the service requested. Recall that static classes like this are *skyhooks*—a code smell.

Worse still, the class is able to retrieve anything and everything from the service locator. You are no longer following the "Hollywood Principle" of dependency injection: *Don't call us, we'll call you.* Instead, you are directly asking for the things you need, rather than having them handed to you. How can you tell what dependencies this class needs? With the service locator, you have to examine the code, searching for capricious calls that retrieve a required service. Constructor injection allowed you to view dependencies—all of them—with a glance at the constructor, or at a distance, via IntelliSense.

The problem is not necessarily one of unit testing. The service locator allows you to set an `IServiceLocator` implementation before use, which means that it can be mocked and the classes can be unit tested. At least it does not prevent that. It just seems absurd to register classes and map them to their interfaces—a not-insignificant task—only to pollute controllers, services, and other classes with infrastructural code such as this. It is doubly absurd when there is no problem to be solved—constructor injection did not need to be circumvented in this way.

An adapter for the service locator is provided for Unity. Listing 9-23 shows how this is registered after the mappings have been set up.

```
private void OnApplicationStartup(object sender, StartupEventArgs e)
{
    CreateMappings();

    container = new UnityContainer();
    container.RegisterType<ISettings, ApplicationSettings>();
    container.RegisterType<IObjectMapper, MapperAutoMapper>();
    container.RegisterType<ITaskService, TaskServiceAdo>();
    container.RegisterType<TaskListController>();
    container.RegisterType<TaskListView>();

    ServiceLocator.SetLocatorProvider(() => new UnityServiceLocator(container));

    MainWindow = container.Resolve<TaskListView>();
    MainWindow.Show();

    ((TaskListController)MainWindow.DataContext).OnLoad();
}
```

This looks remarkably similar to the prior versions except for setting the locator provider. The call to `Resolve`, though, does not truly "resolve" the object graph; there are no longer any dependencies to inject into the `TaskListView`. They are all fetched individually as and when needed within the methods of the class.

The Service Locator anti-pattern is a good example of literal irony applied to a programming context, in that what is claimed is contrary to the reality. It is claimed that classes do not have dependencies, due to their default constructor, but that is simply not the case: they *do* have dependencies, otherwise you wouldn't be trying to fetch them from a service locator!

Unfortunately, the service locator is sometimes an unavoidable anti-pattern. In some application types—particularly Windows Workflow Foundation—the infrastructure does not lend itself to constructor injection. In these cases, the only alternative is to use a service locator. This is better than not injecting dependencies at all. For all my vitriol against the (anti-)pattern, it is infinitely better than manually constructing dependencies. After all, it still enables those all-important extension points provided by interfaces that allow decorators, adapters, and similar benefits.

Injecting the container

Closely related to the service locator is the concept of injecting the container directly into a class. This, similarly, hands the class the keys to the safe, in that it is then free to retrieve anything that it wants from the container. Imagine such a class that, scattered throughout its many methods, retrieves a dozen services. Now compare it with a class that has a constructor that requires those dozen services and enforces their presence with up-front preconditions that throw exceptions if null references are passed in. Both of these classes are clearly doing too much—as indicated by the dependencies they require—and should be refactored into smaller classes or their dependencies grouped into meaningful decorators. However, only the latter makes it explicitly obvious at a glance that this smell exists.

Added to this, the class that requires the container as a constructor parameter must also reference the container's assembly. This will proliferate infrastructural code throughout the entire codebase, because each class accepts the container in order to access the services it *truly* needs.

Illegitimate Injection

Illegitimate Injection looks much like normal, correctly implemented, dependency injection. There is a constructor that accepts dependencies, and these are provided either by Poor Man's DI or an Inversion of Control container.

However, the pattern is polluted—indeed, fatally poisoned—by the presence of a second, default constructor. As Listing 9-24 shows, this second constructor proceeds to construct some implementations for the dependencies directly, circumventing DI.

LISTING 9-24 Having a constructor that directly references implementation negates some of the benefits of dependency injection.

```
public class TaskListController : INotifyPropertyChanged
{
    public event PropertyChangedEventHandler PropertyChanged = delegate { };

    private readonly ITaskService taskService;
    private readonly IObjectMapper mapper;
    private ObservableCollection<TaskViewModel> allTasks;

    public TaskListController(ITaskService taskService, IObjectMapper mapper)
    {
        this.taskService = taskService;
        this.mapper = mapper;
    }

    public TaskListController()
    {
        this.taskService = new TaskServiceAdo(new ApplicationSettings());
        this.mapper = new MapperAutoMapper();
    }

    public void OnLoad()
    {
        var taskDtos = taskService.GetAllTasks();
        AllTasks = new
    ObservableCollection<TaskViewModel>(mapper.Map<IEnumerable<TaskViewModel>>(taskDtos));
    }
```

```
public ObservableCollection<TaskViewModel> AllTasks
{
    get
    {
        return allTasks;
    }
    set
    {
        allTasks = value;
        PropertyChanged(this, new PropertyChangedEventArgs("AllTasks"));
    }
}

}
```

This means that this class must reference whichever assemblies the implementations are in and, concomitantly, all subsequent dependencies. This is the Entourage anti-pattern all over again. Although the first constructor, which accepts only interfaces, sets the scene for the Stairway pattern and well-mannered DI, the second, default constructor undermines this.

What happens when this "default" implementation is not what you want anymore? This class will be edited to construct the preferred class instead. What about when one default constructor is not enough and, in some scenarios, you want implementation A whereas in others, you want implementation B? That's enough to make a person nauseous.

Sometimes this anti-pattern is used to support unit testing, with the defaults being mock implementations that do not have dependencies and that might reside local to this class. Classes should never contain anything that exists only to support unit testing. A common example of this sort of practice is converting `private` methods to `internal` and using the `InternalsVisibleToAttribute` to allow test assemblies to access these methods—rather than testing classes solely through their `public` interface. True, this might appear to be an arbitrarily fine line—after all, DI is much vaunted for its enabling of unit testing. But that is precisely the point: you have already enabled unit testing through the use of interfaces and their injection via the constructor. Mocks can, and should, be provided through that constructor.

It is worth noting that the classification of Illegitimate Injection as an anti-pattern does not hinge on the visibility of the constructor. Whether the constructor is public, protected, private, or internal, the outcome is the same: you are referencing implementations where you should not be.

The composition root

Only one location in an application should have any knowledge of dependency injection: the composition root. This is where classes are constructed when you are using Poor Man's DI, or where interfaces and class mappings are registered when you are using an Inversion of Control container.

The ideal is for the composition root to be as close to the entry point of the application as possible. This allows you to bootstrap DI as soon as possible, gives you a recognized location to find the DI configuration, and helps you avoid leaking dependencies on the container throughout the application. It also means that for each application type there is a different composition root.

The resolution root

Closely related to the composition root is the resolution root. This is the object type that forms the root of the object graph to be resolved. As in the prior WPF examples, it could be that the resolution root is even a single *instance*, but it is more commonly a family of types unified by a common base.

In some cases, you will manually resolve the resolution root yourself, but some application types that facilitate dependency injection—like MVC—require you to register the mappings while the application resolves the roots itself.

ASP.NET MVC

MVC projects lend themselves very well to dependency injection via an IoC container. They have clearly defined resolution roots and composition roots, and they are extensible enough to support any library that you might need to integrate into the framework for IoC.

The resolution root of an MVC application is the controller. All requests from the browser are made to routes that map directly to methods—called *actions*—on a controller. As the request comes in, the MVC framework maps the URL to a controller name, finds the type to which this name corresponds, instantiates it, and then invokes the action on the instance. Figure 9-4 depicts this interaction in a UML sequence diagram.

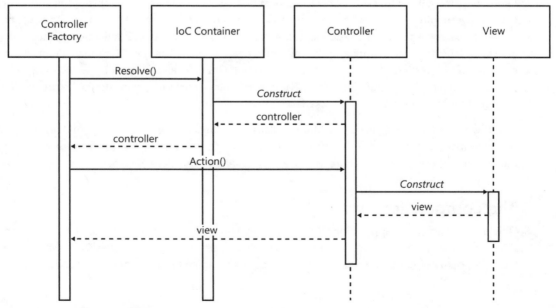

FIGURE 9-4 A UML sequence diagram showing how MVC constructs controllers via a factory.

When you are using IoC for dependency injection, the instantiation of the controller is, more accurately, the *resolution* of the controller. This means that you can easily follow the Register, Resolve, Release pattern, keeping the `Resolve` call down to the ideal minimum, which is in one place.

Listing 9-25 shows the composition root of an ASP.NET MVC user interface for the Task List application.

LISTING 9-25 The `Application_Start` method of the `HttpApplication` is a common composition root in web applications.

```
public class MvcApplication : HttpApplication
{
    public static UnityContainer Container;

    protected void Application_Start()
    {
        AreaRegistration.RegisterAllAreas();

        FilterConfig.RegisterGlobalFilters(GlobalFilters.Filters);
        RouteConfig.RegisterRoutes(RouteTable.Routes);
        BundleConfig.RegisterBundles(BundleTable.Bundles);

        AutoMapper.Mapper.CreateMap<TaskDto, TaskViewModel>();

        Container = new UnityContainer();
        Container.RegisterType<ISettings, ApplicationSettings>();
        Container.RegisterType<IObjectMapper, MapperAutoMapper>();
        Container.RegisterType<ITaskService, TaskServiceAdo>();
        Container.RegisterType<TaskViewModel>();
        Container.RegisterType<TaskController>();

        ControllerBuilder.Current.SetControllerFactory(new
  UnityControllerFactory(Container));
    }
}
```

Some of this code is boilerplate that is created by default when a new MVC application is created. This includes all of the MVC-specific initialization code, such as that for registering areas, filtering, routes, and bundles. This is all performed at the first opportunity—in the `Application_Start` method. This method is called when the first request is made after the application has been started in IIS. It is located in the code-behind file of the `Global.asax` and contains the application-specific subclass of the `HttpApplication` class.

Other than for the MVC-specific `TaskController` class, the rest of the service interfaces and implementations have been reused. The previous `TaskController` was centered around WPF, so it could not be reused outside of that context. Instead, the new `TaskController` does much the same job—retrieving tasks and converting them to a more view-friendly format via the `IObjectMapper`—but inherits from an MVC base class for controllers. This cements it as a resolution root for the application, because it inherits from the `System.Web.Mvc.Controller` class. Listing 9-26 shows this new controller.

LISTING 9-26 This TaskController is a resolution root and has a constructor requiring dependencies.

```
public class TaskController : Controller
{
    private readonly ITaskService taskService;
    private readonly IObjectMapper mapper;

    public TaskController(ITaskService taskService, IObjectMapper mapper)
    {
        this.taskService = taskService;
        this.mapper = mapper;
    }

    public ActionResult List()
    {
        var taskDtos = taskService.GetAllTasks();
        var taskViewModels = mapper.Map<IEnumerable<TaskViewModel>>(taskDtos);
        return View(taskViewModels);
    }
}
```

The List method is the action method that is called by the same view that renders all of the tasks. Just as in the WPF application, the controller first delegates to the ITaskService to retrieve the tasks, and then delegates to the IObjectMapper to convert the returned data transfer objects into viewmodels for use by the view.

> **Note** The same ViewModel that was used for WPF is used here, too. This is okay because the INotifyPropertyChanged interfaces is not strictly WPF-centric (it is located in the System.ComponentModel namespace). However, MVC does not care about that interface and will not respond to any events that are fired on the ViewModel. Furthermore, MVC allows you to decorate ViewModels with validation hints and other such attributes that are part of the MVC assemblies, so it is best to create MVC-specific ViewModels.

By default, MVC controllers are required to have public default constructors so that the framework can construct instances of them before calling an action method. But when you are using dependency injection, you need to have constructors that accept the interfaces of your required services. Luckily, MVC uses the Factory pattern for creating the controller and provides an extension point for you to provide your own implementation, as Listing 9-27 shows.

```
public class UnityControllerFactory : DefaultControllerFactory
{
    private readonly IUnityContainer container;

    public UnityControllerFactory(IUnityContainer container)
    {
        this.container = container;
    }

    protected override IController GetControllerInstance(RequestContext requestContext,
    Type controllerType)
    {
        if (controllerType != null)
        {
            var controller = container.Resolve(controllerType) as IController;
            if (controller == null)
            {
                controller = base.GetControllerInstance(requestContext, controllerType);
            }
            if (controller != null)
                return controller;
        }
        requestContext.HttpContext.Response.StatusCode = 404;
        return null;
    }
}
```

When you constructed the `UnityControllerFactory` in the `Application_Start` method, you passed in the container as a parameter. Here, as emphasized in bold, you can tell that the `Get-ControllerInstance` override uses the container's `Resolve` method to create an instance of the requested controller by type. This is where the controller—the resolution root—is resolved, along with the rest of the object graph that might be required.

It is necessary to bear in mind the different lifetimes involved in this example. The IoC container is created, and mappings are registered, at application startup. The controllers, however, are resolved *per request*. As the request comes in, the controller is resolved, and as the request ends, the controller falls out of scope and is no longer used.

Windows Forms

In a Windows Forms application, bootstrapping dependency injection is more like that of a WPF application than an ASP.NET MVC application. The resolution root of both is the view, with the presenter or controller being passed in as a constructor parameter and the object graph proceeding from there.

Listing 9-28 shows the composition root of the Windows Forms front end for the Task List application. It is located in the `Program` class—in the `Main` method—which is the entry point of the application. As usual, it is important to try to keep the registration code as close to the entry point as possible.

LISTING 9-28 The `Program` class's `Main` method is the entry point to the application and makes a good composition root.

```
static class Program
{
    public static UnityContainer Container;

    [STAThread]
    static void Main()
    {
        AutoMapper.Mapper.CreateMap<TaskDto, TaskViewModel>();

        Application.EnableVisualStyles();
        Application.SetCompatibleTextRenderingDefault(false);

        Container = new UnityContainer();
        Container.RegisterType<ISettings, ApplicationSettings>();
        Container.RegisterType<IObjectMapper, MapperAutoMapper>();
        Container.RegisterType<ITaskService, TaskServiceAdo>();
        Container.RegisterType<TaskListController>();
        Container.RegisterType<TaskListView>();

        var mainForm = Container.Resolve<TaskListView>();
        Application.Run(mainForm);
    }
}
```

Note that, in this case, you are able to reuse not only the service implementations, but also the `TaskListViewController` because it doesn't (yet) depend on anything wholly specific to WPF. Of course, in the future, it probably will, so it might be necessary to create a controller or presenter specifically to support the Windows Forms application.

The view in this application is very simple, in that the code-behind merely accepts the controller as a constructor parameter and initializes the data binding, as shown in Listing 9-29. When you are using the Model-View-Presenter pattern, the view implements an interface to which the presenter can manually delegate calls for setting data.

LISTING 9-29 This view uses data binding to set the retrieved task list to a data grid control.

```
public partial class TaskListView : Form
{
    public TaskListView(TaskListController controller)
    {
        InitializeComponent();

        controller.OnLoad();
        this.taskListControllerBindingSource.DataSource = controller;
    }
}
```

Without a framework to resolve your view for you, you must do it yourself before passing the form into the `Application.Run` method, which starts the Windows Forms application. This is only applicable if there is only one main view for the application, which is often the case in desktop applications. Dialog boxes and other child windows would be created via service calls from the controllers or presenters that are implemented by the view.

Convention over configuration

Registering by configuration involves painstakingly mapping interfaces to implementations. Aside from being time consuming, it is also verbose. Instead, you can use conventions to cut down on the amount of code written.

Conventions are instructions to the container that tell it how to automatically map interfaces to implementations. These instructions form the inputs to the container, in place of the registrations. Ideally, the container takes this input and processes it, with the output being exactly the same registrations that you would otherwise have done manually.

 Note The "over" here can be read as "instead of." Thus, this topic is about convention *instead of* configuration.

Listing 9-30 shows how the continuing example could use convention over configuration for registering.

LISTING 9-30 The registration phase can be greatly simplified by using conventions.

```
private void OnApplicationStartup(object sender, StartupEventArgs e)
{
    CreateMappings();

    container = new UnityContainer();
    container.RegisterTypes(
        AllClasses.FromAssembliesInBasePath(),
        WithMappings.FromMatchingInterface,
        WithName.Default
    );

    MainWindow = container.Resolve<TaskListView>();
    MainWindow.Show();

    ((TaskListController)MainWindow.DataContext).OnLoad();
}
```

The registrations have been replaced by a call to `RegisterTypes`, which is the method used to provide the container with instructions on how to find classes and map them to interfaces. The instructions provided in this example tell the container to:

- Register all classes from the assemblies in the `bin` folder (which is the base path).

- Map those classes to the interface that matches the name of the class. The *convention* here is that the `Service` implementation class would be registered against the `IService` interface.

- Use the default to name the mapping when registering each mapping. This default is `null`, meaning that the mapping is unnamed.

As a result, the container will iterate through each public class in each assembly that is in the `bin` folder, find its implemented interfaces, and map it to the one that matches the class's name (prefixed with an `I`, for `Interface`), without providing a name for the mapping. It is not hard to imagine that the resulting registration will be quite greedy, potentially registering more classes to interfaces than you usually would if you were registering manually. However, a more important concern is whether it correctly registers the classes you want to the correct interfaces. This is the new problem introduced by conventions.

The registration is undeniably simpler than its previous incarnation, but only insofar as it is *shorter*: less code. With registration by configuration, it was easy to comprehend which implementation was being used for each interface—and that they were definitely registered correctly.

The first parameter to `RegisterTypes` is a collection of the types to register. The `AllClasses` static class provides some helper methods for retrieving such a collection by using various common strategies. The second parameter requires a function that accepts a Type passed in from the collection in the first parameter—the implementation type—and returns a collection of Type instances to which it will be mapped—the interface types. The `WithMappings` static helper provides some methods that match this signature and use various strategies for finding appropriate interfaces to map to each type.

The third parameter is another function, this time requiring that you return a name for the mapping for each type. The WithName static helper class provides two alternatives: Default, which always returns null (thus the mapping is unnamed), and TypeName, whereby the type's name is used for the mapping name. This allows you to call Resolve<IService>("MyServiceImplementation") to retrieve the mapped type by its name.

Of course, with the parameters of this method being so general, you are at liberty to provide whatever methods match the signature so that you can tailor the convention to your needs. As Listing 9-31 shows, the crux of registering by convention is in the conventions that are used to find types, map them, and name them.

LISTING 9-31 Conventions can be tailored to your specifications.

```
public partial class App : Application
{
    private void OnApplicationStartup(object sender, StartupEventArgs e)
    {
        CreateMappings();

        container = new UnityContainer();
        container.RegisterTypes(
            AllClasses.FromAssembliesInBasePath().Where(type =>
    type.Assembly.FullName.StartsWith(MatchingAssemblyPrefix)),
            UserDefinedInterfaces,
            WithName.Default
        );

        MainWindow = container.Resolve<TaskListView>();
        MainWindow.Show();

        ((TaskListController)MainWindow.DataContext).OnLoad();
    }

    private IEnumerable<Type> UserDefinedInterfaces(Type implementingType)
    {
        return WithMappings.FromAllInterfaces(implementingType)
            .Where(iface => iface.Assembly.FullName.StartsWith(MatchingAssemblyPrefix));
    }
}
```

You start by retrieving all of the types from the assemblies in the bin folder again. But this time, you limit the acceptable assemblies by returning only those whose full name starts with a specific prefix string. It is common practice to use a dot notation for naming assemblies so that they match the top-level namespace that they contain. So Microsoft.Practices.Unity is the name of the DLL in which that namespace resides. If that assembly exists in your bin folder—and it is certain to if you are using Unity—you might want to omit it from the scan for types to map. A simple way to do this is to retrieve only those types that match the prefix of your own application. Instead of Microsoft, you would use something like MyBusiness or OurProject.

The second parameter has been replaced with a reference to your own local method, which matches the required signature. Given a Type, which is the implementation type, you need to return a collection of other types that represent the interfaces to map to. Rather than write anything particularly complex, you specialize `WithMappings.FromAllInterfaces`, which returns all of the interfaces that the type implements. This list could feasibly include interfaces that you really do not want to map to—`INotifyPropertyChanged` or `IDataErrorInfo`, for example. So again, you only return the interfaces that reside in assemblies that match your assembly prefix. This ensures that you map only your own types to your own interfaces.

Pros and cons

Much like Poor Man's Dependency Injection and vanilla registration with an Inversion of Control container, using conventions involves a tradeoff. You have less code to write, but that code is more algorithmic than the declarative alternatives.

Conventions are initially harder to set up. If you are writing truly SOLID code, not everything will lend itself to a perfect one-to-one mapping of class to interface. In fact, if an interface only has one implementation, that is itself a code smell—and mocks for unit tests do not count toward that total. Whether they are adapters, decorators, or different strategies, it should be common to have more than one implementation per interface, making registration by convention that much more difficult. As it becomes more commonplace to have florid object graphs injected into classes, it becomes harder to devise a general rule by which classes and interfaces can be mapped to each other. Under such circumstances, the conventions cover only a small portion of the required registration code, rather than being the general case.

Mark Seemann, author of the excellent *Dependency Injection in .NET* (Manning Publications, 2011), has explored the three options available for DI and has arrived at the conclusion summarized by Figure 9-5. In brief, the tradeoffs are between two criteria: value and complexity. Value is a utilitarian measure of the worth of the option, ranging from pointless to valuable. Complexity measures the relative difficulty of the options, ranging from simple to sophisticated. As shown in the figure, all three options exist at different points of the bell curve. Poor Man's DI is simple and valuable, whereas convention over configuration is sophisticated and valuable. The main difference between them, then, is that using conventions is more complex than manually constructing the classes and forming an object graph from those classes.

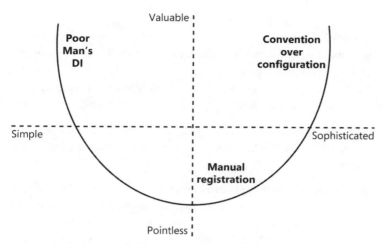

FIGURE 9-5 The tradeoffs between the three options for dependency injection mapped on two axes.

Interestingly, Seemann considers manual registration to sit somewhere between simple and sophisticated on the complexity scale but claims that it is pointless on the utilitarian scale. Why is this? The main reason is because registering types manually with a container is *weakly typed*. If you try to construct a class and pass in an instance for one of its parameters that does not match the type required, the compiler will complain when you try to build. However, no such compile-time error is generated by an IoC container. Instead, you defer the error to run time, which causes you to enter an inefficient loop of write > compile > run > test. Not only that, but you have spent time and energy learning how to register mappings with the container, for little gain and some extra pain.

The choice seems simple: either Poor Man's DI or conventions. If the project is simple and a limited amount of mappings will be required, Poor Man's DI is as simple as can be: just construct the objects manually. If the project is likely to be more complex, requiring many interfaces and classes to be mapped together, target the majority of the registrations with conventions, with the rest of the more specialized mappings being manually registered.

I also highly recommend Mark Seemann's blog, where he explores many topics and is always methodical in his approach[1].

---

[1] *blog.ploeh.dk*

Conclusion

Dependency injection is the glue that holds together every other facet of this book. Without DI, it would not be possible to focus so keenly on factoring dependencies out of classes and hiding their implementation behind general interfaces. Such extension points are key to the development of adaptive code and key to the steady progress of an application as it gains in size and complexity.

There are different options for the implementation of DI, each of which has its own place. Whether you use Poor Man's DI or conventions (with some minimal manual mapping), having DI at all is more important than how it is accomplished.

Some common uses of DI are actually *abuses* that fit better into the category of code smell or anti-pattern. Service Locator and Illegitimate Injection are two abuses that negate some of the positive effects of properly implemented DI.

Each application type has a composition root and a resolution root, the identification of which help you understand how the classes should be organized to facilitate DI. The composition root is always very close to the entry point of the application, assuming that registration is an initialization concern. The resolution root is the only type of object that should be resolved. In some applications, there is only one instance of the resolution root, whereas in others, a family of different subclasses will be resolved.

For all its far-reaching effects, dependency injection is actually a deceptively simple pattern that is nonetheless powerful and misunderstood.

Adaptive sample

This part of the book takes you through the initial phases of developing a software product. Using a fictitious team and project, the following chapters describe the conversations the team members have and the decisions they must make along the way.

The code examples reflect a selection of some of the patterns and practices that were covered in Parts I and II. Not everything is covered, but some of the more common implementation questions are answered.

As in the rest of this book, working code samples are available on GitHub. See Appendix A, "Adaptive tools," for a brief introduction to using Git for source control, and Appendix B, "GitHub code samples," which you can download from this book's catalog page in the Microsoft Press Store, for a reference of code listings for each chapter to branch names in the Adaptive Code repository on GitHub.

CHAPTER 10

Adaptive sample: Introduction

In this chapter, you will

- Learn about the team that will develop the adaptive sample application.

- Understand the features of the product for the adaptive sample application.

- Create an initial product backlog for the application in sprint zero.

The chapters in this part of the book incrementally build a working application by using Scrum and by adhering to the adaptive design principles detailed in this book. It is the culmination of all of the content thus far, presented to form a coherent whole picture. As with the rest of the chapters, I recommend that you study the accompanying code1 while reading these chapters. Without the content of these chapters, the code alone lacks context. Similarly, without the full Microsoft Visual Studio solution, the listings provided in the following chapters will only give you a small window onto the full picture.

The format of this chapter is intended to mirror a real-world scenario, but there are some concessions made for brevity and clarity. The rest of this chapter is an introduction to a fictitious Scrum team and an outline of the product that is to be developed.

Trey Research

The sample application will be developed by an imaginary company, Trey Research. The company prides itself on writing adaptive code that is resilient to change.

The team

The sample application will be developed by using the Scrum process, so the team needs members who will fulfill the roles of Scrum. For a refresher of these roles and the Scrum process, refer to Chapter 1, "Introduction to Scrum."

The team includes all of the roles that are required to advance the application from its inception to its delivery. The product owner has knowledge of how she wants the application to function, which features are of the highest priority, and which features will generate the greatest amount of revenue

---

1 See Appendix A, "Adaptive tools," for instructions on how to access the code for the sample application and the rest of the code in this book.

for the business. The Scrum master is focused on the process that is being used by the team. His concern is that the process works for the team, that the team has no impediments to its work, and that the product owner is informed of any issues that arise during the development of user stories. Trey Research's development team consists of developers who will implement stories and a test analyst who will design test cases and verify that stories meet a certain standard of delivery.

Product owner

The product owner is Petra. She is a veteran business analyst who has recently joined the company. Her specialization is in finding exactly what the customer wants—an invaluable skill for a product owner. She readily admits that Agile processes are alien to her, but she is eager to learn more about her new role.

Throughout the development process, Petra liaises with the client company to find out exactly what it is that they want and why they want it. Also, she will calculate the value of various features to the client so that she can better prioritize work for the development team.

Scrum master

Steve holds two roles in the company. He is simultaneously a Scrum master and the technical team lead. This is a common scenario that the company is keen to remedy in the near future, freeing Steve up to concentrate on his preferred role as Scrum master. To facilitate this, the company is looking to hire an experienced developer into a dedicated technical team lead role.

In his capacity as Scrum master, Steve ensures that the team follows the Scrum process and that the team members are happy with the current incarnation of the process. He prides himself on working honestly and transparently with any assigned product owner or customer—never altering metrics or over-promising on delivery.

Although Steve rarely has time to write code, he still attends design meetings and tries to steer the development team in the right direction whenever he can.

Developers

David and Dianne are the company's two dedicated developers. David is considered a junior developer because he was brought into the company after graduating from college, whereas Dianne is at more of an intermediate level.

One of the reasons that Steve hired David is his continued self-education on programming practices and techniques. David tries to stay current on the latest trends and is always hungry to learn. However, he does tend to view each new technique or technology as a cure-all and liberally applies it whenever he can. This is excellent practice for David, but often his code is a morass of needless indirection.

Dianne is more advanced than David, but she has a tendency to sound jaded by the tidal wave of new technologies that have emerged over the last few years. She has been burnt by the same issues that David is currently working through. Dianne is vying for the technical team lead role and is determined to prove her credentials to be promoted from within. To this end, she is keen to work closely with David to help him to improve.

The Hype Cycle

The Hype Cycle was developed by Gartner, an IT research and advisory firm. It is a useful tool for assessing the progress of new techniques and technologies. It is shown in Figure 10-1.

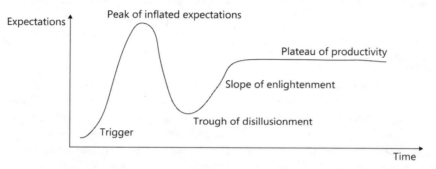

FIGURE 10-1 The Hype Cycle can help explain attitudes toward new techniques and technologies.

The x-axis of the graph represents advancing time, and the y-axis represents expectations. Initially there is a trigger, which could be a new technological discovery or a helpful new technique or procedure. Soon thereafter, expectations rise rapidly until they hit the "peak of inflated expectations." At this point, the technology or technique begins to be viewed as less all-powerful than was initially believed. This causes expectations to plummet rapidly to the "trough of disillusionment." All is not lost, however, because the "slope of enlightenment" gradually leads to a "plateau of productivity." At this point, the technology or technique is established and has more realistic expectations attached to it.

The expectations of developers are often located somewhere on this graph with respect to one or more programming technologies or techniques. For example, at Trey Research, David is nearing the peak of inflated expectations with respect to design patterns, the SOLID principles, unit testing, and refactoring. Dianne is just crawling out of the trough of disillusionment. In the sprint meetings detailed throughout this chapter, pay close attention to their questions and responses and consider how they are shaped by their relative positions on the Hype Cycle.

For completeness, it is worth noting that Steve's experience has moved him along the graph sufficient for him to be on the plateau of productivity. Not only that, but Steve is no longer as susceptible to the Hype Cycle as he once was. He is cautious when approaching new techniques and technologies that are purported to increase productivity, quality, efficiency—or any other metric. As a result, his expectations do not oscillate as wildly when he is presented with a new technique or technology.

Test analyst

Tom is the team's test analyst. His focus is on test automation. He has always had an ability to find a software product's weaknesses and improve the overall user experience through an increased robustness. He likes to treat features as black boxes and is less concerned with how something is implemented than in whether it works to specification—and beyond.

Tom feels like he is overworked in the team because he is constantly rejecting work that has been implemented. This means that he has to test and retest a story at least twice before it works to his exacting standards. It is a point of pride for Tom that defects are rarely deployed to a client's machine and are instead caught early by his automated tests.

The product

Trey Research has been hired by a client to develop a new online chat application called Proseware. This is a web-based application that will allow people to chat from around the world. During first discussions with the client, Petra was able to determine that the client has a lot of ideas for the project but would like to put something small together so that they are better able to decide the direction of the application. Trey Research is well suited to this product because of its incremental development style and its ability to balance this against potentially rapid changes in requirements.

Petra spoke to the client before the project started so that she could prepare the team with some information about what they will develop. The client wants Proseware to be hosted by Trey Research, thus the team is free to choose whichever platforms and tools the team members think are best for the project. Petra was sure to ask the client what their requirements were with regard to Proseware's capacity for users. She agreed with the client that the application needs to only support 20 concurrent users at a time, and this has become a key nonfunctional requirement of Proseware.

Before the team sets to work on writing any code, Petra calls a team meeting so that the team members can discuss the project and try to create an initial backlog of user stories. With these stories in place, the team can set to work on creating something demonstrable within a single sprint.

Initial backlog

The client provided Petra and the team with a list of features for Proseware. This was provided as a prose description, and the team's goal for the meeting is to turn this into one or more user stories.

We view Proseware as the primary site for people to chat. However, we realize that Rome was not built in a day, so we have limited our mission statement somewhat so that something can be delivered in the fastest possible timeframe.

Although we do want to allow users to be able to send each other images or files, the key functionality will be centered around textual communication. Anyone who is in a room should receive all the messages that are sent from anyone else.

Because the textual side of chat is so important, we need the members of a room to be able to send each other formatted text—something like HTML. Of course, they shouldn't be able to spam the chat with lots of meaningless images or videos!

Some of the conversations in Proseware should be not be editable by some users, and some users should only be allowed to read, but not contribute.

Petra brings this short description to the meeting, and the team sets to work trying to find the user stories.

Finding stories in prose

Sometimes clients write prose descriptions of their expectations, as in the previous section. From this, the team must extract and negotiate the user stories to be implemented. The Trey Research team arranges a meeting to find the user stories in the description of Proseware that was supplied by the client.

PETRA: Okay, has everyone read the description? [Everyone nods, displaying a range of enthusiasm.]

STEVE: There's a lot here!

DAVID: Not really—we could probably get through this in a single sprint. [Steve smiles broadly.]

PETRA: Can someone please show me how this is going to give us a list of user stories?

DIANNE: First thing we can do is pick out the verbs and nouns: *send, receive, format, spam...room, conversation, users, members, chat...*

STEVE: True, that's a lot right there.

PETRA: As a user, I want to... So that...

DIANNE: Are they just *users*?

STEVE: Sounds like there's more than one role here.

DAVID: They call them *users*, and then they call them *members*.

TOM: Aren't you a *participant* in a conversation, though?

STEVE: Perhaps, but we should use their ubiquitous language. There are some roles around conversations being read-only or not, surely?

DIANNE: Yeah, that sounds like it's hinting toward some kind of permissions system.

PETRA: Can someone pick out a story, please?

DAVID: As a member, I want to send formatted text so that others can... view... *stuff*?

STEVE: Shall we focus on the roles and the behavior for now? Petra, you can add the business value bit, can't you?

PETRA: Sure.

DIANNE: Yeah, but even that seems a little bit too big. It feels like an epic, not a user story.

PETRA: Sorry, what's an *epic* again?

DAVID: It's just a big story, really. Dianne thinks this story is too big to fit into a single sprint, but I don't know how it could be smaller.

DIANNE: Well, what's simpler than formatted text? Ignore the HTML part—that's just the client imposing implementation! Think about *any* formatted text: what's simpler?

DAVID: Err... *Un*formatted text?

STEVE: Also known as *plain* text. [David smiles sheepishly.]

DIANNE: As a room member, I want to send plain text messages to other room members. [Petra looks for dissenters but finds tacit consensus.]

TOM: Excellent! Ladies and gentlemen, we have our first user story! [Everyone but Petra bursts into a spontaneous round of applause.]

PETRA: But they asked for formatted text?

STEVE: Don't worry, that's another story—it just comes later, after plain text has been delivered.

PETRA: Okay. As a room member, I want to send formatted text messages to other room members.

STEVE: That's two. Any more?

DAVID: I want to create rooms?

DIANNE: Yes. I think this will surely make that person a room owner, won't it? As a room owner, I want to create rooms for categorizing conversations?

STEVE: Good.

TOM: They said they wanted to send images and files, too.

PETRA: Yes, that's another story.

STEVE: One more: I want to create read-only conversations.

DIANNE: That's the last sentence covered. I think we're done.

Story point estimation

By now, the team members agree that they have found the user stories from the client's requirements. They create user story cards from each of the following bullet points:

- I want to send plain text messages to other room members.

- I want to create rooms for categorizing conversations.

- I want to send formatted text to other room members.

- I want to send images and/or files.

- I want to create read-only conversations.

The team arranges the cards on the table ready for assigning story points. There are only five stories, so the team decides to use planning poker to estimate the effort required.

PETRA: Sending plain text messages can't be too difficult, surely?

DAVID: It would only take me an hour! [Steve and Dianne raise their eyebrows. Tom rolls his eyes.]

STEVE: Well, you can't really do this one first. Without rooms, you have no participants.

DIANNE: True, there's a dependency there, but it doesn't alter the size. [Steve nods in agreement.]

PETRA: Is everyone ready?

After some final card shuffling, the team members show their cards:

PETRA	TOM	STEVE	DIANNE	DAVID
3	3	5	5	1

PETRA: Hmm, that's a bit of a mix. David, why one?

DAVID: There's almost nothing to do here: it's just taking some input and writing it to the screen.

DIANNE: Not exactly, David. There's more to it than that. We need to save the text somewhere and be able to read it back. Other room members need to read it, too.

STEVE: Indeed, Dianne's right. We need to think about the architecture here.

DAVID: Oh, yeah. I thought it was just about writing it out to the browser window. But, of course, that's only going to be viewed by the person who wrote it—not shared. Wow, that's much harder!

PETRA: Okay, shall we re-estimate?

The team members count down from three and show their cards again:

PETRA	TOM	STEVE	DIANNE	DAVID
5	5	5	5	5

STEVE: Can we split this story up into "reading" and "writing"?

DIANNE: Sorry—I'm not sure what you mean.

TOM: I think he means that we could have a story for viewing the messages that have been sent to a room and another story for sending messages to that room. Right, Steve?

STEVE: Yes. I just think it would help for us to start really small. I know an estimate of five is not all that large, but it is significant at such an early stage of development.

DIANNE: Okay, I'm happy with that. Shall we re-estimate sending messages?

PETRA	TOM	STEVE	DIANNE	DAVID
3	3	3	3	3

DIANNE: And now let's estimate just viewing the messages already sent to a room.

PETRA	TOM	STEVE	DIANNE	DAVID
2	3	2	2	1

STEVE: Tom, David—will you accept a two?

TOM: Yes, two is fine.

DAVID: I agree. Two makes sense.

STEVE: Excellent. Two it is. [Steve marks a two on the user story and reads out the next.] I want to create rooms for categorizing conversations.

DIANNE: How do we demonstrate this?

TOM: Petra and I spoke about this, and one of the acceptance criteria is that we should be able to view the list of the rooms that have been created.

DIANNE: Another candidate for splitting into "read" and "write" stories?

STEVE: I think so, yes.

DIANNE: Let's estimate the read part first: I want to view a list of rooms that represent conversations.

The team members show their cards:

PETRA	TOM	STEVE	DIANNE	DAVID
2	2	2	2	2

DIANNE: Wow! Unanimous. And now the story for creating new rooms?

The team members show their cards:

PETRA	TOM	STEVE	DIANNE	DAVID
2	2	2	2	1

STEVE: David, are you okay to take a two?

DAVID: Yeah, that's fine.

STEVE: Next: I want to send formatted text to other room members.

PETRA: So this is just adding in formatted text?

STEVE: Yes—assume that the plain text story has been completed and is a prerequisite to this story.

TOM: What sort of formatting do they want? Embedded images or something?

DAVID: Images is a separate story. I think of this more as bold, italic, underline—things like that.

PETRA: Yes, that's what the client said that they wanted. HTML was the only format they could think of, but I don't think we'd want to go there. Just simple text formatting, nothing too strenuous.

STEVE: Okay, ready?

The team members show their cards:

PETRA	TOM	STEVE	DIANNE	DAVID
1	1	1	1	1

STEVE: Hurray! We're all agreed on that, then. Next: I want to send images and/or files.

DIANNE: I don't like the "and/or" bit in this story. Can we be less ambiguous?

TOM: Well, what's the difference between sending an image and sending a file?

PETRA: From my conversation with the client, they wanted images to be shown in the browser, whereas files would be downloaded to other users' machines.

DAVID: Then this is surely two different stories, isn't it? One for downloading files and one for showing images.

DIANNE: Exactly, this is too big at the moment. We should tackle them separately. It feels like files would be the simpler of the two, so we could put that first, with images using it as a prerequisite.

STEVE: I agree. So let's change this to two stories. I want to send files to other room members. I want to show images to the room. Let's estimate them separately.

The team members show their cards for the first story:

PETRA	TOM	STEVE	DIANNE	DAVID
5	5	3	3	3

STEVE: Hmm, why fives?

TOM: Testing this is going to be difficult. There are a lot of unusual test cases that we will need to consider. For instance, what if the file is very large? What if the file is malicious? Will we keep hold of the file on our servers? For how long?

STEVE: I take your point. I was considering only the development effort here, sorry. I can tell now that you will be spending a lot of time trying to break this.

DAVID: Shall we re-estimate, or just take five?

STEVE: I'm happy with five.

DIANNE: Me too.

STEVE: And what about images?

PETRA: This is just about showing the image to the users on the page?

STEVE: Yes, the upload part should have been completed by now, so this is just about showing the image on the page.

The team members show their cards:

PETRA	TOM	STEVE	DIANNE	DAVID
3	3	3	3	5

STEVE: David, a five?

DAVID: Yes—I think this is a bit harder than it looks. What if the image is inappropriate? What if there are a lot of users and the image takes a long time to download? That will put a load on our servers.

DIANNE: I agree, those are all concerns, but I think they are out of scope for now. Petra, make a note to ask the client what they think of a content filter—not just for images, but for text, too. But, at the moment, we only need to support 20 users. That should not represent a significant load.

PETRA: Good idea about the content filter, David.

STEVE: Happy to take a three, David?

DAVID: Actually, now I think it's a two! But, yes—a three is fine.

STEVE: Good stuff. Final story: I want to create read-only conversations.

The team members show their cards:

PETRA	TOM	STEVE	DIANNE	DAVID
8	1	5	8	3

STEVE: Oh dear. That's all a bit random! Tom, one?

TOM: Sorry, forgot about analysis and development effort. This just seems really, really easy to test in comparison to the other stories.

STEVE: Okay. Petra, Dianne, eight?

DIANNE: At this point, we won't have roles or permissions, which we'll need. I think there's a lot of work here.

DAVID: Oh, I didn't think we needed roles or permissions at this point. I thought we'd just flag a conversation as read-only.

STEVE: It needs to be read-only on a per-user basis. Still, I don't think we need any heavy in-frastructure for permissions or roles as yet. I think it should be implemented with a very simple solution first, and we can elaborate on it later.

DIANNE: That sounds fine to me.

PETRA: Yeah, I trust you guys.

STEVE: The average here was exactly five. Shall we take that? [Everybody agrees.]

STEVE: David, still think this is a single sprint of work?

DAVID: Hmm... No!

The meeting ends.

Summary

Over the course of the meeting, the team has taken a short description from the client and broken it down into user stories. The team then estimated the stories and created a prioritized backlog. They can now begin development.

Notice how the conversation allowed all sides of the development process to give input: analysis, implementation, and testing. For each story, the team reached a consensus for the effort required to complete the story.

CHAPTER 11

Adaptive sample: Sprint 1

In this chapter, you will

- Observe the team's first sprint planning session.

- Follow the implementation and evolution of the first user stories.

- Observe the team's sprint demo and retrospective.

In this chapter, the Trey Research team implements its first four user stories. These are the only stories that the team has assigned to Sprint 1 of the project. The team has set the following sprint goal:

> *To demonstrate a dynamic list of rooms, to be able to create a new room, to view the messages written in a room, and for at least two users to be able to share messages in the room*

By defining a sprint goal, the team set something challenging but achievable to be completed within the sprint. All work should be aligned to the sprint goal so that the team knows that it is on track and working on only what the client has asked for.

Planning

The team arranges a planning meeting for the sprint and takes to it the stories that relate to the sprint goal. For this sprint, the stories that the team will implement are:

- I want to create rooms for categorizing conversations.

- I want to view a list of rooms that represent conversations.

- I want to view the messages that have been sent to a room.

- I want to send plain text messages to other room members.

The team begins its discussion.

PETRA: Okay, four stories to talk about, but these are the first to be implemented, so I expect there are some key decisions to be made here.

STEVE: Perhaps, yes. Certainly we need to consider a few technologies before we begin. Does anyone have any suggestions?

DIANNE: This is a web application, so we should probably go with something that we are all comfortable and familiar with. ASP.NET MVC seems the obvious choice. Does everyone agree?

STEVE: I'm happy with that.

DAVID: Hmm. I think this is a perfect Node.js application, to be honest.

TOM: I have no experience with Node, unfortunately. Does anyone else?

STEVE: Not really, no. I think Dianne is right to say that we should stick to what we know.

DIANNE: With MVC, we already have much of the code structure set out for us. Look at this sequence diagram.

Dianne shows the team the UML sequence diagram in Figure 11-1.

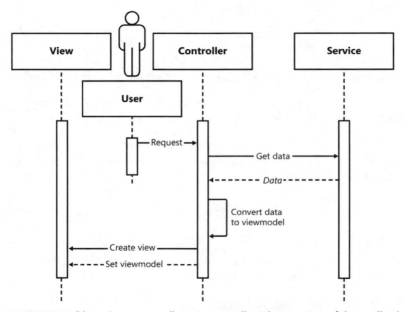

FIGURE 11-1 Dianne's sequence diagram generalizes the structure of the application.

STEVE: Okay, I understand what you've done here. That looks okay to me, for now.

DAVID: It doesn't look like there's anything to do with rooms or messages.

DIANNE: Yes, I'll explain. It's quite generic. Rather than create a sequence diagram for every user story, I decided to generalize the solution so that we can tell what classes we will need—in the short term, at least.

DAVID: Oh, I see. So *Get data* is a placeholder for *Get room* and *Get messages*, right?

DIANNE: Yes, you've got it.

STEVE: So, what's the service part? Will it be event-driven messaging or some kind of database that we poll?

DIANE: HTTP is a disconnected, stateless protocol. We will have to poll the server for messages.

DAVID: But only the messages since the last check. We don't want to return all messages all the time.

STEVE: Yes, that wouldn't scale well.

DIANNE: Speaking of which, is this really a scalable solution?

PETRA: Good point. Although the client wants to support only 20 users in the short term, you can tell that this is going to expand quite quickly. There's no way to know what the upper limit might be. We shouldn't limit the application's scalability.

STEVE: Perhaps not, no. But, as long as we build adaptability into the code from the outset, we should be able to discover the most appropriate architecture as we progress.

TOM: What about the user interface? If we're going to demonstrate this next week, it should at least look respectable.

PETRA: Tom's right—a lot of confidence from clients is lost by functionally great but aesthetically poor demonstrations.

DAVID: Well, MVC uses bootstrap, so we could implement a couple of bootstrap templates. We'll need a page for the room list and a page for the room's messages. At least then it will look a bit modern, if a little minimalist.

PETRA: Don't worry about minimalism. I think they will probably want this application to be themed by the user, anyway. Any effort we spend on perfecting the user interface would probably be wasted at such an early stage.

STEVE: Tom, what about testing? Is there anything here you're worried about?

TOM: No, I made sure that the sprint goal was limited to just two users so that I can defer the automated load testing until later. At this point we can just focus on manually testing things until I get some automation set up. I'll probably want you three to unit test, though, so let me know if you need help with any of that.

STEVE: Brilliant—I think we're done for now. We can discuss things in further detail as and when we need to.

The meeting ends, and the team is ready to implement its first story.

"I want to create rooms for categorizing conversations."

A couple of days later, David indicates that he is ready for a code review of the room creation story. Dianne comes over to David's desk, and the two discuss the code. The goal of this discussion is to identify both positive and negative aspects of the chosen implementation. Peer reviews such as this offer developers a chance to identify whether something is not up to the required standard or lacks adaptability, so that final changes can be made before the code is committed to source control.

The controller

When David starts implementing the controller, he calls Dianne over to ask for her input.

DAVID: So, I've used the MVC pattern as you suggested. The controller itself doesn't do much yet—it is merely delegating down to an `IRoomRepository` interface to interact with whatever persistent storage we put in place.

DIANNE: Let's look at the controller code now.

David shows Dianne the controller code in Listing 11-1.

LISTING 11-1 The `RoomController` is the entry point of the `Create` requests.

```
public class RoomController : Controller
{
    private readonly IRoomRepository roomRepository;
    public RoomController(IRoomRepository roomRepository)
    {
        Contract.Requires<ArgumentNullException>(roomRepository != null);

        this.roomRepository = roomRepository;
    }

    [HttpGet]
    public ActionResult List()
    {
        return View();
    }

    [HttpGet]
    public ActionResult Create()
    {
        return View(new CreateRoomViewModel());
    }

    [HttpPost]
    public ActionResult Create(CreateRoomViewModel model)
    {
        ActionResult result;
```

```
        if(ModelState.IsValid)
        {
            roomRepository.CreateRoom(model.NewRoomName);

            result = RedirectToAction("List");
        }
        else
        {
            result = View("Create", model);
        }

        return result;
    }
}
```

DIANNE: Okay, this looks good. We've got dependency injection for the IRoomRepository, so that gives us some flexibility. And it is enforced with code contracts, which is great.

DAVID: Yes—I also ensure that the preconditions are in place with unit tests. I'll show them to you if you want.

DIANNE: That would be great, but could you just explain the Create method for the POST request handler, please? Specifically, why does it redirect after delegating to the CreateRoom method on the repository?

DAVID: That's the Post-Redirect-Get pattern. Basically, if we just return to the List view directly at this point, any attempts to refresh the page by the user will result in a second POST request. This would mean that we try to create another room with the same name, and it just doesn't feel right from a user experience perspective.

DIANNE: Excellent! This looks really good for now.

DAVID: One thing I'm not so sure of is directly instantiating a new CreateRoomViewModel. Shouldn't I use a factory for this?

DIANNE: Good question. I would say no—not in this case. The reason is that there is unlikely to be any variation in the returned type. Viewmodels like this are tailored to a specific use, and it would be needless indirection to delegate to a factory here.

Controller unit tests

David opens the file containing the unit tests, as shown in Listing 11-2, and asks Dianne to peer review his work.

DAVID: Here are the unit tests for the RoomController constructor.

LISTING 11-2 Validating the RoomController constructor through unit tests.

```
[Test]
public void ConstructingWithoutRepositoryThrowsArgumentNullException()
{
    Assert.Throws<ArgumentNullException>(() => new RoomController(null));
}

[Test]
public void ConstructingWithValidParametersDoesNotThrowException()
{
    Assert.DoesNotThrow(() => CreateController());
}
```

DAVID: The first one ensures that we always have a valid reference for the IRoomRepository field in the RoomController.

DIANNE: Yes, it is part of the implied contract of the RoomController that it always has a valid, not-null repository field.

DAVID: These next two tests are asserting the behavior of the Create method used to service GET requests.

David scrolls down through the tests file and finds the code shown in Listing 11-3.

LISTING 11-3 Unit tests for the GET request of the Create action.

```
[Test]
public void GetCreateRendersView()
{
    var controller = CreateController();

    var result = controller.Create();

    Assert.That(result, Is.InstanceOf<ViewResult>());
}

[Test]
public void GetCreateSetsViewModel()
{
    var controller = CreateController();

    var viewResult = controller.Create() as ViewResult;

    Assert.That(viewResult.Model, Is.InstanceOf<CreateRoomViewModel>());
}
```

DAVID: We need to know two things: that the request gives a `ViewResult` instance, and that the `Model` property is of the expected type, `CreateRoomViewModel`.

DIANNE: Could you unify these into one unit test with two assertions?

DAVID: I suppose I could, but then it wouldn't be immediately clear from the name of the unit test which assertion had failed. I prefer to write quite fine-grained tests with as few assertions as make sense. When a unit test fails, it is then easy to identify the errant behavior.

DIANNE: That's fine. What about the POST request side of the `Create` action, the one that delegates to the service?

DAVID: Here it is.

David scrolls down further and shows Dianne the unit tests of Listing 11-4.

LISTING 11-4 Unit tests for the POST request of the `Create` action.

```
[Test]
[TestCase(null)]
[TestCase("")]
[TestCase("     ")]
public void PostCreateNewRoomWithInvalidRoomNameCausesValidationError(string roomName)
{
    var controller = CreateController();

    var viewModel = new CreateRoomViewModel { NewRoomName = roomName };

    var context = new ValidationContext(viewModel, serviceProvider: null, items: null);
    var results = new List<ValidationResult>();

    var isValid = Validator.TryValidateObject(viewModel, context, results);

    Assert.That(isValid, Is.False);
}

[Test]
[TestCase(null)]
[TestCase("")]
[TestCase("     ")]
public void PostCreateNewRoomWithInvalidRoomNameShowsCreateView(string roomName)
{
    var controller = CreateController();

    var viewModel = new CreateRoomViewModel { NewRoomName = roomName };
    controller.ViewData.ModelState.AddModelError("Room Name", "Room name is required");
    var result = controller.Create(viewModel);

    Assert.That(result, Is.InstanceOf<ViewResult>());
```

```
    var viewResult = result as ViewResult;
    Assert.That(viewResult.View, Is.Null);
    Assert.That(viewResult.Model, Is.EqualTo(viewModel));
}

[Test]
public void PostCreateNewRoomRedirectsToViewResult()
{
    var controller = CreateController();

    var viewModel = new CreateRoomViewModel { NewRoomName = "Test Room" };
    var result = controller.Create(viewModel);

    Assert.That(result, Is.InstanceOf<RedirectToRouteResult>());

    var redirectResult = result as RedirectToRouteResult;
    Assert.That(redirectResult.RouteValues["Action"], Is.EqualTo("List"));
}

[Test]
public void PostCreateNewRoomDelegatesToRoomRepository()
{
    var controller = CreateController();

    var viewModel = new CreateRoomViewModel { NewRoomName = "Test Room" };
    controller.Create(viewModel);

    mockRoomRepository.Verify(repository => repository.CreateRoom("Test Room"));
}
```

DAVID: The first two tests assert that the room name is a required field—it cannot be omitted—
          and that a validation error drops the user back at the room creation form.

DIANNE: I like your use of the TestCase attribute to provide the unit test with some erroneous
          room names.

DAVID: Thanks. I thought it would allow me to write fewer tests.

DIANNE: So far, so good. What's next?

The room repository

David is unsure of his implementation for the room repository. He opens the file shown in Listing 11-5
so that Dianne can offer her opinion.

DAVID: I've created an implementation of the IRoomRepository interface for ADO.NET. Here it is.

```
public class AdoNetRoomRepository : IRoomRepository
{
    public AdoNetRoomRepository(IConnectionIsolationFactory factory)
    {
        this.factory = factory;
    }

    public void CreateRoom(string name)
    {
        factory.With(connection =>
        {
            using(var transaction = connection.BeginTransaction())
            {
                var command = connection.CreateCommand();
                command.CommandText = "dbo.create_room";
                command.CommandType = CommandType.StoredProcedure;
                command.Transaction = transaction;
                var parameter = command.CreateParameter();
                parameter.DbType = DbType.String;
                parameter.ParameterName = "name";
                parameter.Value = name;
                command.Parameters.Add(parameter);

                command.ExecuteNonQuery();
            }
        });
    }

    private readonly IConnectionIsolationFactory factory;
}
```

DAVID: I've used the Factory Isolation pattern here, and I'm delegating down to a factory inter-
          face to control the lifetime of the database connection object. The body of the Create-
          Room method is pretty standard ADO.NET code aside from there.

DIANNE: Hmm, I'm not so sure that the Factory Isolation pattern is warranted here. Let me just ask
          Steve.

Factory Isolation pattern misapplied

Dianne beckons Steve over to get a second opinion on David's use of the Factory Isolation pattern.

STEVE: How can I help?

DIANNE: Well, look at this class. David's used the Factory Isolation pattern here, but I'm just not
          sure it's appropriate.

STEVE: Hmm, indeed. I think I understand the problem here. You're using ADO.NET here, right?
          Let's have a look at the implementation of the factory.

David opens the file and shows Dianne and Steve the code in Listing 11-6.

LISTING 11-6 The isolation factory aims to manage the lifetime of a database connection.

```
public class AdoNetConnectionIsolationFactory : IConnectionIsolationFactory
{
    private readonly IApplicationSettings applicationSettings;
    private readonly DbProviderFactory dbProviderFactory;
    public AdoNetConnectionIsolationFactory(IApplicationSettings applicationSettings)
    {
        this.applicationSettings = applicationSettings;
        this.dbProviderFactory = DbProviderFactories
                .GetFactory(applicationSettings.GetValue("DatabaseProviderName"));
    }

    public void With(Action<IDbConnection> action)
    {
        using(var connection = dbProviderFactory.CreateConnection())
        {
            connection.ConnectionString = applicationSettings
                    .GetValue("ProsewareConnectionString");
            connection.Open();

            action(connection);
        }
    }
}
```

STEVE: The DbProviderFactory.CreateConnection method returns an IDbConnection.

DAVID: Yes, that's right.

DIANNE: I understand the problem now. The Factory Isolation pattern is only applicable when the product of the factory may or may not implement IDisposable. The IDbConnection interface inherits from IDisposable, so it effectively forces all implementations to provide a public Dispose method.

STEVE: Exactly. So you don't need to use factory isolation because...

DAVID: Because I can just add in a using block, instead.

DIANNE: That's right.

DAVID: Okay, so should this just be a normal factory, instead?

DIANNE: I would say no. If you look at what's happening in this class, it's effectively hiding the DbProviderFactory from clients. I think the factory is needless indirection in this case.

STEVE: I agree.

DAVID: But that means I'll have to call DbProviderFactory directly from the room repository implementation. Isn't that inflexible, especially because DbProviderFactory is a static class?

STEVE: That's true—it would be nice if DbProviderFactory wasn't a static class. But the room repository implementation depends on ADO.NET, so it isn't really pollution. The introduction of the factory has made public something that is a concern only internally to the repository's implementation.

DAVID: Okay, that makes sense. And we can ignore this static class call because it is generic enough as it is, right?

DIANNE: Yes. Consider what meaningful decoration or adaptation you might make to a DbProviderFactory if it was an interface. Any alternative behavior is more likely to be injected at a higher level—around the IRoomRepository interface.

DAVID: I've got it. Let me make these changes, and I'll get back to you.

Refactoring

David sets to work on refactoring the room repository, resulting in the code shown in Listing 11-7. He calls Dianne and Steve over to assess the changes.

LISTING 11-7 The refactored room repository uses the DbProviderFactory directly.

```
public class AdoNetRoomRepository : IRoomRepository
{
    private readonly IApplicationSettings applicationSettings;
    private readonly DbProviderFactory databaseFactory;
    public AdoNetRoomRepository(IApplicationSettings applicationSettings,
  DbProviderFactory databaseFactory)
    {
        Contract.Requires<ArgumentNullException>(applicationSettings != null);
        Contract.Requires<ArgumentNullException>(databaseFactory != null);

        this.applicationSettings = applicationSettings;
        this.databaseFactory = databaseFactory;
    }

    public void CreateRoom(string name)
    {
        using(var connection = databaseFactory.CreateConnection())
        {
            connection.ConnectionString =
  applicationSettings.GetValue("ProsewareConnectionString");
            connection.Open();

            using(var transaction = connection.BeginTransaction())
            {
```

```
                        var command = connection.CreateCommand();
                        command.CommandText = "dbo.create_room";
                        command.CommandType = CommandType.StoredProcedure;
                        command.Transaction = transaction;
                        var parameter = command.CreateParameter();
                        parameter.DbType = DbType.String;
                        parameter.ParameterName = "name";
                        parameter.Value = name;
                        command.Parameters.Add(parameter);

                        command.ExecuteNonQuery();
                }
            }
        }

    }
```

DAVID: I made a few changes. I've integrated the code from the connection factory into the repository class. I wasn't happy with the arbitrary use of the DbProviderFactories static class. The DbProviderFactory class is at least an abstract class, which gives us some extension points that we can work with. This way, we're using normal dependency injection, but instead of an interface, the injection is an abstract class.

DIANNE: That's great. I think you've made good changes there.

STEVE: Could you show me the Inversion of Control container's registration configuration for the DbProviderFactory? I'm interested in how you're registering this.

David shows Steve and Dianne the Unity registration code shown in Listing 11-8.

LISTING 11-8 The Unity Inversion of Control (IoC) registration for the DbProviderFactory.

```
container.RegisterType<DbProviderFactory>(new InjectionFactory(c =>
  DbProviderFactories.GetFactory(
  c.Resolve<IApplicationSettings>().GetValue("DatabaseProviderName"))));
```

STEVE: That's fine. I expected it would be a little unusual and contrived due to the static nature of the class involved, but I think you've done well to abstract it away from the repository implementation.

DIANNE: I think this is good to be integrated now, don't you, Steve?

STEVE: Yes, I think that's our first story completed.

David commits the code, and the team moves on to the next story.

"I want to view a list of rooms that represent conversations."

The next day, David completes the second story—viewing the list of all created rooms. Before committing the code to source control, he asks Dianne to review his work.

DAVID: I've made some changes to the RoomController so that it supports reading the rooms and displaying them on a page.

DIANNE: Okay, let's start there. Open up the RoomController and show me what's new.

David shows Dianne the code in Listing 11-9. To keep this snippet small and focused, the room creation actions have been omitted.

LISTING 11-9 The RoomController has a new action for listing the rooms.

```csharp
public class RoomController : Controller
{
    private readonly IRoomRepository roomRepository;
    private readonly IRoomViewModelMapper viewModelMapper;
    public RoomController(IRoomRepository roomRepository, IRoomViewModelMapper mapper)
    {
        Contract.Requires<ArgumentNullException>(roomRepository != null);
        Contract.Requires<ArgumentNullException>(mapper != null);

        this.roomRepository = roomRepository;
        this.viewModelMapper = mapper;
    }

    [HttpGet]
    public ActionResult List()
    {
        var roomListViewModel = new RoomListViewModel();

        var allRoomRecords = roomRepository.GetAllRooms();

        foreach(var roomRecord in allRoomRecords)
        {
            roomListViewModel.Rooms
                    .Add(viewModelMapper.MapRoomRecordToRoomViewModel(roomRecord));
        }

        return View(roomListViewModel);
    }

}
```

DAVID: There's a new constructor argument here—a mapper—the presence of which is enforced with code contracts. I added a new unit test for that, too.

DIANNE: Okay, that's good. There's one change I would make here, though. Talk me through the List method, and I'll let you know what I think we can do to simplify this class.

DAVID: It has two parts, really. First, the room repository is queried to retrieve all room records. However, those room records are models, not viewmodels, so I've introduced some mapping from one data type to another. This is delegated down to the mapper interface. After the data is converted to RoomViewModel objects, we can pass that to the view so that it can render the list of rooms.

DIANNE: I think there's a leak in one of the abstractions here. The RoomRecord class, which is what the IRoomRepository returns, belongs down at the data persistence layer. I'm not sure whether it should have propagated all the way up to this controller. This is the underlying reason that the mapper is necessary.

DAVID: But what other option do I have? I can only retrieve RoomRecord instances, but I also need to return RoomViewModel objects.

DIANNE: Absolutely. But there is no need for this controller to know about RoomRecords and the fact that they need to be mapped. Instead, how about making the controller depend on neither the IRoomRepository nor the IRoomViewModelMapper but on a new interface instead? We could call it an IRoomViewModelService. This would allow the controller to be ignorant of the RoomRecord. One implementation of this new service would use the room repository and the mapper that you have here to return RoomViewModel instances, which is the only data that the controller needs to know about here.

DAVID: I understand. However, what about the existing CreateRoom call that exists on the IRoomRepository interface? Without a repository, this controller will not be able to call that method.

DIANNE: Good point. I would suggest that you use interface segregation here. Instead of the IRoomViewModelService, you could have an IRoomViewModelReader and an IRoomViewModelWriter. That gives us the option in the future of varying the implementation of the read and write sides of the requests.

DAVID: Okay, I think my unit tests are going to change quite a lot due to this. Instead of showing them to you now, I will perform these refactors and get back to you.

DIANNE: How will this affect our delivery of the sprint goals? Will this compromise our meeting the deadline?

DAVID: No, the refactors are quite small. I should be able to complete this in an hour or two.

DIANNE: Sounds good.

David sets to work fixing the issues that Dianne had pointed out.

Refactoring

David spends a few hours refactoring his code to make Dianne's suggested changes. He then calls Dianne over to inspect the results.

DAVID: This is the controller after the refactors. What do you think?

Listing 11-10 shows the new controller after refactoring.

LISTING 11-10 The controller has been refactored to depend on reader and writer interfaces.

```
public class RoomController : Controller
{
    private readonly IRoomViewModelReader reader;
    private readonly IRoomViewModelWriter writer;
    public RoomController(IRoomViewModelReader reader, IRoomViewModelWriter writer)
    {
        Contract.Requires<ArgumentNullException>(reader != null);
        Contract.Requires<ArgumentNullException>(writer != null);

        this.reader = reader;
        this.writer = writer;
    }

    [HttpGet]
    public ActionResult List()
    {
        var roomListViewModel = new RoomListViewModel(reader.GetAllRooms());

        return View(roomListViewModel);
    }

    [HttpGet]
    public ActionResult Create()
    {
        return View(new RoomViewModel());
    }

    [HttpPost]
    public ActionResult Create(RoomViewModel model)
    {
        ActionResult result;

        if(ModelState.IsValid)
        {
            writer.CreateRoom(model.Name);

            result = RedirectToAction("List");
        }
        else
        {
            result = View("Create", model);
        }

        return result;
    }
}
```

DIANNE: This has removed the dependency on the mapper quite nicely. The injection of a reader and a writer means that we have the option of varying the implementation in the future, in case we move toward a CQRS architecture.

DAVID: Could you remind me what CQRS is, please?

DIANNE: Command/Query Responsibility Segregation. It's where the commands and the queries of your application do not align: they are asymmetrical. In our case, we might write to transactional storage, but we might read from nontransactional document storage. I think Steve has been tinkering with a possible architecture if this does not scale well, as we suspect.

DAVID: I remember now—that sounds interesting. Shall we take a look at the IRoomViewModelReader and IRoomViewModelWriter implementation?

Dianne nods, and David opens the file containing that class, as shown in Listing 11-11.

LISTING 11-11 A service that more closely resembles the original controller code.

```
public class RepositoryRoomViewModelService : IRoomViewModelReader, IRoomViewModelWriter
{
    private readonly IRoomRepository repository;
    private readonly IRoomViewModelMapper mapper;
    public RepositoryRoomViewModelService(IRoomRepository repository,
IRoomViewModelMapper mapper)
    {
        Contract.Requires<ArgumentNullException>(repository != null);
        Contract.Requires<ArgumentNullException>(mapper != null);

        this.repository = repository;
        this.mapper = mapper;
    }

    public IEnumerable<RoomViewModel> GetAllRooms()
    {
        var allRooms = new List<RoomViewModel>();
        var allRoomRecords = repository.GetAllRooms();
        foreach(var roomRecord in allRoomRecords)
        {
            allRooms.Add(mapper.MapRoomRecordToRoomViewModel(roomRecord));
        }
        return allRooms;
    }

    public void CreateRoom(string roomName)
    {
        repository.CreateRoom(roomName);
    }

}
```

DAVID: I decided to implement both interfaces in one class, because they both shared a dependency on the `IRoomRepository`. However, I think this resembles the original controller class—what have we gained with this refactor?

DIANNE: The main benefit is that the controller is now more focused on its main responsibilities. Instead of being responsible for orchestrating the mapping from records to viewmodels, it can now focus on responding to validation. The fact that the controller no longer has knowledge of the `RoomRecord` class is compelling enough.

DAVID: Yes, I suppose it was starting to do too much, wasn't it?

DIANNE: It didn't really obey the single responsibility principle. If we weren't using a repository, we wouldn't need a mapper. This would be a change lower down in the architectural layers. Controllers should not be concerned with such changes.

David and Dianne agree that this story is now ready to be committed.

"I want to view the messages that have been sent to a room."

Dianne works on the next story in tandem with David, by using pair programming. While Dianne writes the code, David looks on and offers suggestions.

> **Note** *Pair programming* is a common practice in Agile software development that originated with the Extreme Programming (XP) methodology: two programmers work together on a particular functionality. While one of the pair types, the other is able to consider the best way of implementing a method, class, or unit test.

DIANNE: Shall we start with the controller?

DAVID: Yes, that seems like a good place to begin.

DIANNE: We're going to need a new `HttpGet` handler for viewing room messages. What shall we call this?

DAVID: Something like `GetMessages`?

DIANNE: That would be good, but ASP.NET MVC uses the controller name and method name to form the URL for the request.

DAVID: Of course, I forgot. How about just calling it `Messages`? It is part of the `RoomController`, so the URL will be `/Room/Messages`.

DIANNE: Okay, that makes sense. We'll also need a parameter for identifying which room's messages we want to see.

DAVID: We've got the room ID, which uniquely identifies a room. Could we use that?

DIANNE: Is it an `integer` or a `long`?

DAVID: I thought an `integer` would suffice.

DIANNE: We'll also need a new viewmodel for this view. Following the naming convention you've used so far, this should be `MessageListViewModel`, right?

DAVID: Yes. We can just pass an instance of it to the `View` method on the controller and return the resulting `ViewResult`.

DIANNE: The `IRoomViewModelReader` will need a new method for querying the messages in a room.

DAVID: I suppose that should be called `GetRoomMessages`, and it should also accept the room ID as a parameter.

DIANNE: I'll define it on the interface and create a stub on any implementing classes so that we can determine how the controller changes might work.

Dianne creates the method shown in Listing 11-12.

LISTING 11-12 The `Messages` method retrieves all messages associated with a room, by ID.

```
[HttpGet]
public ActionResult Messages(int roomID)
{
    var messageListViewModel = new MessageListViewModel(reader.GetRoomMessages(roomID));

    return View(messageListViewModel);
}
```

DIANNE: This looks good. Let's fill in the implementation of the `IRoomViewModelReader.Get-RoomMessages` method.

DAVID: Okay, the only implementation so far makes use of an `IRoomRepository` interface. I think we'll need a new `IMessageRepository` interface so that we can retrieve messages.

DIANNE: Agreed. We should inject it in just like the other dependencies.

DAVID: When we have that repository available in the class, we need to request from it the messages for a given room ID and pass them to the mapper.

DIANNE: So the mapper is responsible for converting records from the repository to viewmodels that the controller can use, right? It looks like there's only an `IRoomViewModelMapper` available. It feels a little too much to create a new `IMessageViewModelMapper`. Can we rename this interface to something more generic?

DAVID: How about IViewModelMapper? That way it becomes useful for mapping all records to viewmodels.

DIANNE: How does this look?

Dianne shows David the code in Listing 11-13.

LISTING 11-13 The class that maps records to viewmodels now contains a method for retrieving room messages.

```
public class RepositoryRoomViewModelService : IRoomViewModelReader, IRoomViewModelWriter
{
    private readonly IRoomRepository roomRepository;
    private readonly IMessageRepository messageRepository;
    private readonly IViewModelMapper mapper;
    public RepositoryRoomViewModelService(IRoomRepository roomRepository,
   IMessageRepository messageRepository, IViewModelMapper mapper)
    {
        Contract.Requires<ArgumentNullException>(roomRepository != null);
        Contract.Requires<ArgumentNullException>(messageRepository != null);
        Contract.Requires<ArgumentNullException>(mapper != null);

        this.roomRepository = roomRepository;
        this.messageRepository = messageRepository;
        this.mapper = mapper;
    }


    public IEnumerable<MessageViewModel> GetRoomMessages(int roomID)
    {
        var roomMessages = new List<MessageViewModel>();
        var roomMessageRecords = messageRepository.GetMessagesForRoomID(roomID);
        foreach(var messageRecord in roomMessageRecords)
        {
            roomMessages.Add(mapper.MapMessageRecordToMessageViewModel(messageRecord));
        }
        return roomMessages;
    }

}
```

DAVID: That looks good to me.

David and Dianne continue to implement the repository method IMessageRepository.Get-MessageForRoomID(), which loads the message from the Microsoft SQL Server database. After this method is implemented, they move on to the next user story.

"I want to send plain text messages to other room members."

David swaps places with Dianne to implement the final story of the sprint.

DAVID: This should be really easy now that we have a pattern in place for reading and writing data.

DIANNE: Sort of, yes. But remember, one of the requirements of this story is that the request will be made asynchronously.

DAVID: Oh. So it won't be a full-page postback?

DIANNE: No, the user interface will send the data via an AJAX request.

 Note Some definitions: AJAX stands for Asynchronous JavaScript and XML. XML stands for Extensible Markup Language. AJAJ stands for Asynchronous JavaScript and JSON. JSON stands for JavaScript Object Notation.

DAVID: Hold on. You mean AJAJ, don't you?

DIANNE: I suppose I do!

DAVID: What makes this controller action different, then?

DIANNE: Two things, really. When the `ModelState.IsValid` property is true, we should use the `IRoomViewModelWriter` to save the message. But we should then return the viewmodel as a `JsonResult`.

DAVID: And what do we do when the model state is not valid?

DIANNE: In that case, return an `HttpStatusCodeResult` with an HTTP 400 error.

DAVID: That's a client error response code, isn't it?

DIANNE: Yes. Specifically, it's a Bad Request response.

David shows Dianne the code in Listing 11-14.

LISTING 11-14 The AddMessage method on the RoomController class.

```
[HttpPost]
public ActionResult AddMessage(MessageViewModel messageViewModel)
{
    ActionResult result;

    if(ModelState.IsValid)
    {
        writer.AddMessage(messageViewModel);

        result = Json(messageViewModel);
    }
```

```
    else
    {
        result = new HttpStatusCodeResult(400);
    }

    return result;
}
```

DAVID: What about the `AddMessage` method on the `IRoomViewModelWriter`?

DIANNE: I think we can use the same pattern as before. This part of the code does not care
          whether it is called synchronously or asynchronously, so it will not change the pattern
          that we've established so far.

David proceeds to follow the same pattern that the `IRoomViewModelWriter.CreateRoom`
method uses, which results in the `AddMessage` method shown in Listing 11-15.

LISTING 11-15 The AddMessage method on the RoomViewModelWriter class.

```
public void AddMessage(MessageViewModel messageViewModel)
{
    var messageRecord = mapper.MapMessageViewModelToMessageRecord(messageViewModel);
    messageRepository.AddMessageToRoom(messageRecord.RoomID, messageRecord.AuthorName,
    messageRecord.Text);
}
```

With this change, and the creation of a further repository method to retain the message record in
Microsoft SQL Server via ADO.NET, the story is complete.

David and Dianne have now finished the stories that were assigned to the sprint, just in time for
the sprint demo.

Sprint demo

At the end of the week, the team arranges to meet the client and demonstrate its progress thus far.
The stories to be completed are assembled, and the functionality of each one is shown. The client is
invited to provide feedback and alter the direction in which to take the product from here.

The sprint demo has many benefits. First, it allows the team to ensure that it is always aligned with
the client's current wants and needs. The demonstration also motivates the team members to always
produce their best work because they must be confident that they can show the current state of
the product to the client. Clients also benefit because they are able to view tangible progress on the
product at an early stage and regularly throughout development. If a client wants to change anything
about how the software works, the product demonstration is a great time to do so. The backlog of

user stories can be altered and reprioritized as a result, and the software will immediately change direction to meet the needs of the client.

First demonstration of Proseware

On demonstration day, the team assembles in a meeting room with a representative from the client company. The team briefly discusses how the sprint has progressed and prepares to show the current state of the software.

Unfortunately at such a key time, it is discovered that the projector in the meeting room is not working correctly. This delays the presentation for a few minutes while a technician who can correct the problem is found. After the projector is up and running, the team discovers that the resolution of the screen is far lower than that of the development machines. This degrades the appearance of the user interface, making it harder for the client to understand which parts are where on the page.

The team apologizes and the client seems understanding, though a little disheartened that the application doesn't look as his company had hoped. After some tweaking of display settings, the application starts to look a little better, though it still does not appear exactly as it did in the development environment.

The team runs through the four stories that have been implemented during the sprint and then asks whether the client has any questions or comments. The response is generally favorable: although the application does not yet do much, it is clear that some core functionality is in place at a very early stage.

Petra suggests that their next tasks will include formatting the messages sent to a room. She also mentions David's idea of a content filter. The client appears very receptive to this idea and requests that the team make this a high priority for the coming sprint.

At the end of the meeting, the client leaves and the team stays back to hold their sprint retrospective.

Sprint retrospective

At the end of the sprint, the team convenes to discuss progress over the week. All team members are present and answer the following questions:

- What went well?
- What went badly?
- Are there any parts of the process that we need to change?
- Were any new things done in the sprint that we need to keep?
- Were there any surprises discovered over the course of the sprint?

The aim is to generate a list of actionable items to prioritize and take forward. As usual, the outcome of this meeting is not to generate a lot of discussion without tangible action.

What went well?

The team members are assembled in a suitable meeting space and work through the list of questions, one at a time. They start with what went well during the sprint.

STEVE: So, what did everyone think went well in this first sprint?

PETRA: The demo was good, I think. It might not have been exactly what the customer was expecting, but I think it was positive.

TOM: Absolutely, I agree. I think that they were realistic enough to know that this isn't a finished product, or even a first release, but that there was tangible value in what we had produced in just a short space of time.

DIANNE: They turned up, provided constructive feedback and—even at such an early stage—changed our direction.

PETRA: Yes, I think that's worthy of a separate entry here. David, your idea for a content filter was very well received, and they have increased its priority so that we will be working on that in the next sprint.

DAVID: I'm glad that they were so clearly enthused by what we were doing. We just need to manage their expectations a little: I wouldn't want them to oversell our work so far.

STEVE: What else went well?

DIANNE: I think that the code is in good shape. Even though there is only a small amount of code, what is there will certainly provide a good foundation for future work.

DAVID: Thanks—I think collaboration between Dianne, Steve, and myself really helped with that. If not for their guidance throughout the process, the code would already contain some significant technical debt.

STEVE: Okay, I'll mark both of those down. Anything else?

The room falls silent, so Steve marks the following points on the whiteboard and moves on to the next question.

- Demonstration was good, even if there was little to show at this stage.

- Client was present at demo and gave good-quality feedback.

- Code seems to be in good shape.

What went badly?

The next question for the team to answer is what went badly during the sprint.

STEVE: Be honest but realistic here: what went badly during the sprint?

TOM: I think I was underutilized this sprint. I realize there's not a huge amount that I could be doing to contribute at this early stage, but there was very little to test, and what there was came in waves.

PETRA: Okay—that's very valuable. What's the root cause here?

STEVE: I think it's because David was the only developer actively working on stories, while Dianne and I prepared some architectural designs for another project.

PETRA: Will this be an ongoing problem, or can we remedy this?

DIANNE: This is to be noted more in the "things to change" section, but Steve and I are going to become less like chickens and more like pigs from here on with the Proseware project.

TOM: Remind me what that means again, please.

STEVE: Basically, we've been contributing to Proseware but not fully committed resources as yet. We were needed elsewhere as another project reached maintenance mode.

DIANNE: Indeed. We'll be able to write stories in subsequent sprints, which will give you a steady stream of new functionality to test, rather than the one or two flurries of activity.

TOM: Sounds good to me.

STEVE: Anything else go badly?

PETRA: Obviously, the problem with the projector at the start of the demonstration was not good.

DAVID: Yes, I'm really not sure what happened there! It was embarrassing, but I think we recovered well.

DIANNE: Absolutely, we recovered well. But we need to be able to prevent this from happening again.

STEVE: I think the problem was simply a lack of ample preparation time. Just as in all other environments, we need to integrate early and often! In the future, we should take half an hour before the demonstration to run through what we will be presenting in the meeting room, using the projector. The client will forgive that sort of error once, but any repeat will look amateurish.

Steve marks down the following items on the whiteboard:

- QA was underutilized throughout the sprint.

- Demonstration was almost disastrous because of environmental issues.

STEVE: Anything else?

All team members shake their heads to indicate no, and Steve proceeds.

Things to change?

Agile processes are very malleable, and teams should take the opportunity to reflect on whether the process is working for them—or against them. Making actionable items out of the things to change about the process, work environment, or other practices is an excellent way to improve the way a team works.

STEVE: Right, we've already driven out some changes with things that went badly. First, Dianne and myself will have to be more available to the project in this sprint. Second, we need to take an extra half-hour to prepare for the demo in the meeting room. Anything else?

The room is quiet.

STEVE: Okay—is the daily stand-up meeting working?

TOM: Actually, it isn't—I wasn't there twice during this sprint because I hit traffic on the way in and couldn't make it, remember?

DIANNE: Of course—I completely forgot about that.

STEVE: Would it be better at 9:30 A.M.?

TOM: I think so. It's just too difficult for me to guarantee that I can be here at 9:00 A.M..

PETRA: I'll inform management that we should look into flexible working hours, Tom.

TOM: Thanks—that would be great.

DAVID: I think we need to do the demo less often. The client expressed surprise that they had to be here every week and also that we were showing them a small amount of functionality. Why not tackle both issues at the same time by demonstrating once every fortnight, instead?

STEVE: That's a good idea—definitely worth looking in to. However, I think the demo is a great motivator for delivery. I would like to retain the weekly demonstration, but what do you think about limiting the demos for the client to every other week, with internal demos in between? We don't need to involve management, just this team.

PETRA: I think that would work. It would allow us to perfect the demo process and show off more functionality to the client at the same time.

David looks happy, and Steve marks the following on the whiteboard:

- Dianne and Steve to commit to the Proseware project and focus on story delivery.

- Demonstrate once a fortnight to the client.

- Demonstrate in between just to the team.

- Take an extra half-hour before the demo to run through the agenda and check that everything is working.

Things to keep?

Sometimes, the best course of action is inaction—in other words, making a note of something positive that a team does but that is not yet habitual. This is the topic of the "things to keep" question.

STEVE: What about things to keep? Is there anything that we took initiative on that we should keep doing?

Everyone remains quiet.

STEVE: Okay, if anyone thinks of anything after this meeting, let me know and we'll create an action item.

Surprises?

Almost every sprint will have revealed some surprises. The team could have discovered an antiquated process that needs updating, a requirement that wasn't properly captured, or a piece of software that suddenly stopped working. The "surprises" section of the sprint retrospective aims to capture all of these items so that they cannot be classed as surprises in the future.

STEVE: How about surprises?

DAVID: I was quite surprised that they liked my content filter idea!

DIANNE: I think it makes great sense, to be honest. They're targeting Proseware at a certain demographic, and it is likely to represent a lot of value to them.

PETRA: I agree, it was a great idea. Perhaps that's something that we should keep doing: keep thinking of ideas.

Steve writes it down in the appropriate column on the whiteboard.

TOM: It surprised me that Steve and Dianne weren't working on this project full time.

PETRA: Okay, anyone else?

DIANNE: It surprised me, too. I was under the impression that I was to be a full-time part of Proseware, but Steve and I needed to put out a fire on another project.

STEVE: We should get some kind of agreement from management that someone else will pick that up next sprint, rather than us.

DIANNE: Good plan.

Steve notes this down on the whiteboard.

STEVE: Okay, thanks guys. A good sprint overall and great start to this project. Let's keep it up.

PETRA: I agree. Let's make the changes agreed in this retrospective and ensure that we continue on this same path next week.

The meeting ends and the team departs.

Summary

The first sprint has been a qualified success for the team. Although not everything has gone according to plan, the team has gathered some valuable feedback in a short amount of time. This is a key part of any Agile process: the constructive criticism required to take corrective action is always nearby.

In the next chapter, the team continues working on sprint two and carries forward the stories that have not yet been implemented.

CHAPTER 12

Adaptive sample: Sprint 2

In this chapter, you will

- Observe the team's second sprint planning session.

- Follow the implementation and evolution of the next user stories.

- Observe the team's second sprint demo and retrospective.

In this chapter, the Trey Research team continues to implement user stories for the Proseware project. The direction has changed slightly due to the feedback received from the client at the sprint demonstration during sprint 1. The team has set the following sprint goal:

> *To add optional markdown-formatted text to conversations, to filter message content so that it is appropriate, and to ensure that 300 users can be served concurrently*

This sprint goal incorporates all of the stories that the team has committed to completing during the sprint. As usual, the team will conclude the sprint with a demonstration to the client—to elicit feedback and to inform the client of progress—and a sprint retrospective in which the team will address any problems that the sprint presented and to acknowledge the good work that the team did during the sprint.

First, though, the team begins the sprint with a planning session.

Planning

The second planning meeting for the project allows the members of the team to discuss the user stories that they have committed to in their sprint goal. The second sprint includes the following user stories:

- I want to send markdown that will be correctly formatted.

- I want to filter message content so that it is appropriate.

- I want to serve hundreds of users concurrently.

With the whole team assembled in a meeting room, the discussion begins:

PETRA: We've got a new story on the backlog as a result of the feedback from the sprint demo in the last sprint.

STEVE: Instead of implementing read-only conversations, the client wants us to prioritize the content filter.

DIANNE: So we should estimate this story now.

STEVE: Yes, if we get an estimate for this story we can understand how much capacity we have for this sprint.

DIANNE: Okay, so on the count of three, let's show our estimates.

Everyone shuffles their cards before showing them.

PETRA	TOM	STEVE	DIANNE	DAVID
3	3	8	5	8

STEVE: Wow, we have a bit of variety here. Tom, could you explain your three?

TOM: I chose three mainly because I can automate the testing for this fairly easily. Providing a text message with a disallowed word in it and asserting that you could not post the message is simple enough. If there's more technical complexity to the implementation, I'd be happy to increase the estimate.

STEVE: David, would you like to explain your eight? Then I'll explain mine.

DAVID: Yes, I think this is difficult because we need to add another table to data storage for the disallowed words. This is going to take some time to implement.

STEVE: Yes, I thought that, too. I also considered that we don't want to limit disallowed words to the messages users write in conversations—we should also include the names of the rooms. In fact, any time we take input from the user we should submit it to the content filter.

DIANNE: How about instead of implementing a data-driven content filter right away, we just simplify it and hardcode the blocked list of words?

STEVE: Okay, I think that's a good idea. Later we can add stories to target administration of the content filter.

PETRA: Great—shall we re-estimate or take the five?

TOM: I'm happy with a five.

STEVE: Yes, a five seems fair.

DAVID: I agree, five it is.

PETRA: Excellent, thanks everyone. Let's make sure we hit all our goals this sprint so we can show the client a great demo this week.

Everyone files out of the meeting room ready to get to work.

"I want to send markdown that will be correctly formatted."

Before he starts this story, David asks Steve about parsing markdown.

DAVID: I assume I should be using a third-party library for parsing markdown and transforming it into HTML, but I'm not sure which library to use.

STEVE: Okay, hold on. I think Dianne has some experience in this area—we'll ask her.

Steve beckons Dianne over to quiz her about markdown libraries.

STEVE: Dianne, you've used some markdown libraries before, right? Which one did you prefer?

DIANNE: I evaluated a few previously. Try MarkdownDeep—it seemed simple enough to use. There's a NuGet package for it, too.

STEVE: Thanks, Dianne. David, try MarkdownDeep. Also, make sure you create a new class library project for any classes that depend on this library.

DAVID: Okay—thanks.

David sets to work on implementing the markdown transform for the application. After a few hours, he is ready to show Steve and Dianne his work. He asks them to peer review what he has done.

DAVID: I wondered where the best place to put the implementation of the markdown transform was. I knew I wanted to intercept the room message text by implementing a decorator for an existing interface. I thought that if I implemented it on the `AddMessageToRoom` method on the `IMessageRepository` interface we could save on processing reads. If we just transform the markdown to HTML as the message is saved, we don't need to worry about it again.

DIANNE: That would save us from transforming markdown to HTML on every read, but it wouldn't really work.

DAVID: Yes, I realized that we wouldn't be able to edit messages if we did that. I know that we don't have that feature yet, but I thought we might in the future and didn't want to artificially prevent users from editing.

STEVE: Good—we will almost certainly want that feature in the future, so it's probably correct to perform the transform when reading, not writing.

DAVID: The other question I had was about client-side or server-side transforms. I've kept it server-side at the moment, but I wondered whether we might prefer doing it client-side in the browser.

DIANNE: Perhaps we could use that in the future for a side-by-side preview of the markdown and HTML as the user is typing a message.

STEVE: Great idea, Dianne—I'll make a note of that for the demo and find out what the client thinks.

DAVID: In the end, I implemented the transform as a decorator on the `IRoomViewModelReader` interface. This is because markdown and HTML are user interface concerns and the `IRoomViewModelReader` is a UI contract. The other option was decorating the `IRoom-Repository` and `IMessageRepository`—but these are data contracts. Still, despite this, I'm not entirely happy with it at the moment, but here it is.

David shows Steve and Dianne the code for this markdown decorator, as shown in Listing 12-1.

LISTING 12-1 The markdown decorator transforms user-entered markdown to HTML.

```
public class RoomViewModelReaderMarkdownDecorator : IRoomViewModelReader
{
    public RoomViewModelReaderMarkdownDecorator(
        IRoomViewModelReader @delegate,
        Markdown markdown)
    {
        this.@delegate = @delegate;
        this.markdown = markdown;
    }

    public IEnumerable<RoomViewModel> GetAllRooms()
    {
        return @delegate.GetAllRooms();
    }

    public IEnumerable<MessageViewModel> GetRoomMessages(int roomID)
    {
        var roomMessages = @delegate.GetRoomMessages(roomID);

        foreach(var viewModel in roomMessages)
        {
            viewModel.Text = markdown.Transform(viewModel.Text);
        }

        return roomMessages;
    }

    private readonly IRoomViewModelReader @delegate;
    private readonly Markdown markdown;
}
```

STEVE: I like it—it looks good to me. What weren't you sure about?

DAVID: Two things, really. The first is that we're dependent directly on the `Markdown` class from MarkdownDeep. Should this not be placed behind its own interface?

DIANNE: I think injecting that class as a dependency of this decorator is sufficient. The class is small enough to be replaced if we need to use a different library.

DAVID: Okay, that's good. It also allowed me to write a simple unit test with a test case for each expected transform. Here's what I have so far.

David opens the file containing his markdown unit tests, as shown in Listing 12-2.

LISTING 12-2 The unit tests for the markdown transform decorator.

```
[TestFixture]
public class MarkdownTests
{
    [Test]
    [TestCase(
        "This message has only paragraph markdown...",
        "<p>This message has only paragraph markdown...</p>\n")]
    [TestCase(
        "This message has *some emphasized* markdown...",
        "<p>This message has <em>some emphasized</em> markdown...</p>\n")]
    [TestCase(
        "This message has **some strongly emphasized** markdown...",
        "<p>This message has <strong>some strongly emphasized</strong>
markdown...</p>\n")]
    public void MessageTextIsAsExpectedAfterMarkdownTransform(string markdownText,
string expectedText)
    {
        message1.Text = markdownText;
        var markdownDecorator = new
RoomViewModelReaderMarkdownDecorator(mockRoomViewModelReader.Object, markdown);

        var roomMessages = markdownDecorator.GetRoomMessages(12345);

        var actualMessage = roomMessages.FirstOrDefault();

        Assert.That(actualMessage, Is.Not.Null);

        Assert.That(actualMessage.Text, Is.EqualTo(expectedText));
    }

    [SetUp]
    public void SetUp()
    {
        markdown = new Markdown();
        message1 = new MessageViewModel
        {
            AuthorName = "Dianne",
            ID = 1,
            RoomID = 12345,
            Text = "Test!"
        };
        mockRoomViewModelReader = new Mock<IRoomViewModelReader>();
        var roomMessages = new MessageViewModel[]
        {
            message1
        };
        mockRoomViewModelReader.Setup(reader =>
                reader.GetRoomMessages(It.IsAny<int>())).Returns(roomMessages);
    }

    private MessageViewModel message1;
    private Mock<IRoomViewModelReader> mockRoomViewModelReader;
    private Markdown markdown;
}
```

STEVE: Again, that's great. Didn't you say you had a second query?

DAVID: Yeah—notice that the markdown class decorates the `IRoomViewModelReader`, but that class also has a `GetAllRooms` method. Is this a good candidate for interface segregation? At the moment, the `GetAllRooms` method isn't transformed, so I just delegate straight down to the wrapped instance.

DIANNE: Should we allow the user to use markdown in the room names, too? That way, the `GetAllRooms` method would be decorated, too.

STEVE: I think we should leave it as it is for now. Let's not split the interface or allow markdown in the room names. Depending on the client's feedback during the demo, we can make a decision either way.

"I want to filter message content so that it is appropriate."

Dianne and David have both been assigned to the message content filtering story. Together they will implement the functionality required by using pair programming.

DIANNE: As mentioned in the planning session, we don't have time to implement a fully data-driven message content filter during this sprint. Instead, we need to make some progress toward that goal.

DAVID: So will we just implement the data access part for this sprint and come back to it next week?

DIANNE: No, we can't do that. We need to deliver a vertical slice of functionality: something that is demonstrable to the client, but not necessarily complete. Just implementing the data access would not add any value.

DAVID: I don't understand how we can deliver some value yet not implement the whole content filter.

DIANNE: What we will do is compromise somewhere so that we can be finished in a short amount of time yet provide some value to the client. For this story, the compromise is simple: we should hardcode the list of values that are considered inappropriate, instead of retrieving them from persistent storage like a database.

DAVID: I guess that makes sense. But I've always been told that hardcoding things is bad. Isn't this poor design?

DIANNE: Sort of, yes. It's technical debt. We are making a prudent decision to compromise on some desirable functionality in order to deliver something sooner rather than later. Perhaps the client knows exactly the list of words that they want to limit and they will never change. If so, we could complete this story just by hardcoding that list.

DAVID: I suppose it's quite clever, really. Rather than take a lot of time to implement something, we aim for a simpler solution as an objective on the way to the goal.

DIANNE: Exactly! And, as each objective is met, it is possible that the next objective could be totally different—or that the goal itself changes dramatically.

DAVID: Another thing I'm unsure of: how are we going to implement this story? Should we create a decorator for the message writer that throws an exception when an inappropriate word is included in the message?

DIANNE: The trouble with that solution is that it uses exceptions for control flow. Exceptions are better reserved for situations that are truly "exceptional." This is more of a validation scenario.

DAVID: Oh, I see! So we could hook into the MVC validation and just fail validation if the message contains something from the blocked words list?

DIANNE: I think that's a better idea. How about this...?

Dianne starts typing and, a few minutes later, arrives at the class in Listing 12-3.

LISTING 12-3 A custom validation attribute is perfect for the content filter.

```
public class ContentFilteredAttribute : ValidationAttribute
{
    private readonly string[] blockedWords = new string[]
    {
        "heffalump",
        "woozle",
        "jabberwocky",
        "frabjous",
        "bandersnatch"
    };

    protected override ValidationResult IsValid(object value,
ValidationContext validationContext)
    {
        var validationResult = ValidationResult.Success;

        if (value != null && value is string)
        {
            var valueString = (string)value;
            if(blockedWords.Any(inappropriateWord =>
                    valueString.ToLowerInvariant()
                    .Contains(inappropriateWord.ToLowerInvariant())))
            {
                var errorMessage = FormatErrorMessage(validationContext.DisplayName);
                validationResult = new ValidationResult(errorMessage);
            }
        }

        return validationResult;
    }
}
```

DIANNE: I've obviously used words that wouldn't be included in a proper content filter blocked words list, but I wouldn't want the demonstration to the client to include anything truly inappropriate!

DAVID: No, of course! I think this will demonstrate the functionality they want well enough. How about some tests?

DIANNE: Oh, of course. Here they are.

The two unit tests from the `RoomControllerTests` class are shown in Listing 12-4.

LISTING 12-4 Unit tests are added to enforce the validation rule on the room name and message text.

```
[Test]
[TestCase("Callooh! Callay! O frabjous day!")]
[TestCase("The frumious Bandersnatch!")]
[TestCase("A heffalump or woozle is very confusel...")]
public void PostCreateNewRoomWithBlockedWordsCausesValidationError(string roomName)
{
    var controller = CreateController();

    var viewModel = new RoomViewModel { Name = roomName };
    var context = new ValidationContext(viewModel, serviceProvider: null, items: null);
    var results = new List<ValidationResult>();

    var isValid = Validator.TryValidateObject(viewModel, context, results, true);

    Assert.That(isValid, Is.False);
}
// . . .
[Test]
[TestCase("Callooh! Callay! O frabjous day!")]
[TestCase("The frumious Bandersnatch!")]
[TestCase("A heffalump or woozle is very confusel...")]
public void PostAddMessageWithBlockedWordsCausesValidationError(string text)
{
    var controller = CreateController();

    var viewModel = new MessageViewModel { AuthorName = "David", Text = text};
    var context = new ValidationContext(viewModel, serviceProvider: null, items: null);
    var results = new List<ValidationResult>();

    var isValid = Validator.TryValidateObject(viewModel, context, results, true);

    Assert.That(isValid, Is.False);
}
```

DAVID: With the two properties on the view models marked with the `ContentFiltered` attribute, these tests will pass quite nicely.

DIANNE: Absolutely. Still, there are a few things that I'm not happy about with this design at the moment.

DAVID: What?

DIANNE: Obviously, the hardcoding of the blocked word list. I would consider this to be prudent technical debt, but I would still like to request the blocked word list from a provider interface. This way, I could create an implementing class that returns a static, hardcoded list and provide a more data-driven implementation in future.

DAVID: Yes, that would nicely split the data for the blocked word list from the algorithm of validating the property. Could you use dependency injection?

DIANNE: Unfortunately not. These custom attributes are not very flexible and will not be constructed through the controller or any other extension point exposed by MVC.

DAVID: That's a shame. How about the service locator pattern?

DIANNE: I usually refer to service locator as an anti-pattern, but in this case it might be the best choice available to us.

DAVID: Shall we leave this as is for now and accept that there is some more technical debt associated with this attribute? That way, we get to make progress and revisit this code if necessary.

DIANNE: I agree. I think that this is likely to change quite drastically in the future, so there is no point in guessing which direction it will take at this point.

"I want to serve hundreds of users concurrently."

The final story of the sprint involves Dianne and Steve increasing the scalability of the application. The client has requested that the application support scaling horizontally, rather than vertically. Horizontal scaling means that the application should be able to support more concurrent users through the addition of extra machines. In comparison, vertical scaling is the ability to support more concurrent users through the addition of extra resources to a single machine.

Dianne and Steve understand that the limiting factor to horizontal scaling is the presence in the architecture of a relational database management system (RDBMS), such as Microsoft SQL Server. In comparison to solutions with purpose-built distributed storage that is intended to scale horizontally, it is difficult to add a new instance of SQL Server to a cluster of machines.

Because of this, Dianne investigates the team's options for replacing the SQL Server database with document storage. She presents MongoDB to the team as a solid and popular alternative that will allow the team to scale the application by adding new machines to a cluster. The only problem standing in the way is current reliance of the application on SQL Server to store and retrieve room and message data.

Luckily, the team has already prepared for this eventuality by programming to interfaces.

DIANNE: All we need to do is create new implementations for the repository interfaces: `IRoomRepository` and `IMessageRepository`.

STEVE: We certainly could do that, but I think we could cut out the mapping from record data to view model data and, instead, just serialize and deserialize our view models directly.

DIANNE: That sounds interesting! That way we would just need to create new implementations of the `IRoomViewModelReader` and `IRoomViewModelWriter` interfaces that delegate down to MongoDB.

STEVE: Exactly.

The pair sets to work implementing the `MongoRoomViewModelStorage` class, as shown in Listing 12-5.

LISTING 12-5 The implementation of the data persistence layer for MongoDB.

```
public class MongoRoomViewModelStorage : IRoomViewModelReader, IRoomViewModelWriter
{
    public MongoRoomViewModelStorage(IApplicationSettings applicationSettings)
    {
        this.applicationSettings = applicationSettings;
    }

    public IEnumerable<RoomViewModel> GetAllRooms()
    {
        var roomsCollection = GetRoomsCollection();
        return roomsCollection.FindAll();
    }

    public void CreateRoom(RoomViewModel roomViewModel)
    {
        var roomsCollection = GetRoomsCollection();
        roomsCollection.Save(roomViewModel);
    }

    public IEnumerable<MessageViewModel> GetRoomMessages(int roomID)
    {
        var messageQuery = Query<MessageViewModel>
                .EQ(viewModel => viewModel.RoomID, roomID);
        var messagesCollection = GetMessagesCollection();
        return messagesCollection.Find(messageQuery);
    }

    public void AddMessage(MessageViewModel messageViewModel)
    {
        var messagesCollection = GetMessagesCollection();
        messagesCollection.Save(messageViewModel);
    }

    private MongoCollection<MessageViewModel> GetMessagesCollection()
    {
        var database = GetDatabase();
        var messagesCollection = database.
                GetCollection<MessageViewModel>(MessagesCollection);
        return messagesCollection;
```

```
        }

        private MongoCollection<RoomViewModel> GetRoomsCollection()
        {
            var database = GetDatabase();
            var roomsCollection = database.GetCollection<RoomViewModel>(RoomsCollection);
            return roomsCollection;
        }

        private MongoDatabase GetDatabase()
        {
            var connectionString = applicationSettings.GetValue(MongoConnectionString);
            var client = new MongoClient(connectionString);
            var server = client.GetServer();
            return server.GetDatabase(ProsewareDatabase);
        }

        private readonly IApplicationSettings applicationSettings;
        private static string MongoConnectionString = "MongoConnectionString";
        private static string ProsewareDatabase = "Proseware";
        private static string MessagesCollection = "messages";
        private static string RoomsCollection = "rooms";
    }
```

With this implementation in place, the team is able to unleash the potential of horizontal scalability for the Proseware application and the client.

Sprint demo

At the end of the second sprint, the team prepares to give another demonstration to the client. All of the stories completed in this sprint are collated and their functionality is shown. One of the key actions taken from the sprint retrospective meeting for sprint 1 was to improve the preparation of the demonstration. The team follows up on this diligently, meeting ahead of schedule to run through each story's functionality without the client present. This helps to mitigate any problems due to differences in the development and demonstration environments. The rehearsal proceeds without a problem, so the team is ready to demonstrate its progress to the client.

During the demonstration of the markdown story, the team asks the client representative whether the client would like the room names to be subject to the same formatting as the messages in a room. The client seems receptive to the idea and asks that the team schedule this into the backlog, but indicates that it should only receive a low priority because there are more important features that the client would like to have sooner. The client is also pleased that the team has used markdown, rather than the requested HTML formatting, because the client understands that it is becoming a more popular and informal style of text formatting.

The next story is the message content filtering. The client is happy that the team has already applied the content filter to the room name and message text inputs and concurs that every future input received from users should similarly be subject to the same filtering. However, the client requests that this feature have the ability to be turned on or off via configuration in the future.

The final story of the sprint involves Tom simulating 300 users at a time, with the data storage spanning two separate machines. The client again requests that the data source to be used be controlled by configuration settings.

After all of the stories have been demonstrated, the client representative impresses upon the team how pleased he is with the incremental but tangible progress that the team has made in just two short sprints.

Sprint retrospective

At the end of the second sprint, just as at the end of the first sprint, the team convenes to discuss progress over the week. All team members are present and answer the following questions:

- What went well?

- What went badly?

- Are there any parts of the process that we need to change?

- Were any new things done in the sprint that we need to keep?

- Were there any surprises discovered over the course of the sprint?

The aim is to generate a list of actionable items to prioritize and take forward. As usual, the outcome of this meeting is not to generate a lot of discussion without tangible action.

Assembled in a suitable meeting space, the team works through the list, one question at a time.

What went well?

The team starts with what went well during the sprint.

STEVE: What does everyone think went well in this sprint?

PETRA: Personally, I think this sprint was a great success: we met our sprint goal in a timely fashion, we prepared excellently for the demonstration, and we ensured, through preparation, that nothing went wrong. The client was very impressed, and we can be satisfied with our efforts.

DIANNE: I agree. It was a template for how future sprints should progress. Let's not lose focus, though: we must aim to sustain this same level over time.

STEVE: Absolutely—there should be no room for complacency.

What went badly?

The next question for the team to answer is what went badly during the sprint.

STEVE: How about what went badly? Surely something didn't go according to plan.

DAVID: I think there were a few questions that went unanswered during the sprint. These questions would have had a minor impact on implementation overall, but I think it would have been good to get these questions answered as soon as possible, rather than at the end of the sprint.

PETRA: What sort of questions, David? Do you have an example?

DAVID: In the markdown story, Dianne asked whether we should be transforming the room names in addition to the messages. We elected not to but, really, we didn't know the definitive answer.

Things to change?

The team members move on to discussing anything that they feel needs to change about their process or working practices.

DIANNE: Yes, I agree. I think it's something that we need to change: if we have a question about implementation, we should ask Petra. If she doesn't know the answer, she can schedule a call with the client and ask them directly.

PETRA: Absolutely, I'm here to ensure that you have all of the knowledge you need about the client's requirements. If you don't ask me something and I haven't been specific enough with the acceptance criteria in the story, something crucial might be missed.

STEVE: In this case, waiting to ask the question during the demonstration didn't hurt us much, but with other more important questions it will be imperative that we seek the correct answer as soon as possible.

PETRA: Anything else that needs to change? No? Let's move on, then.

Things to keep?

The team members start talking about the positive actions that they need to form into habits.

STEVE: I'll pitch in with something to keep. We changed the preparation for the sprint and it worked well. We should make a note to keep that going until it becomes habitual.

PETRA: Great point. This next sprint will determine whether the quality of this sprint's work is sustainable or is an anomaly, so noting how we achieved such a good sprint and bearing it in mind in the future is a good idea.

STEVE: What else should we keep?

DIANNE: I can't think of anything else out of the ordinary that we especially need to keep doing.

Surprises?

The "surprises" section of the sprint retrospective aims to capture anything that has surprised the team during the sprint so that these things cannot be classed as surprises in the future.

STEVE: Final question, everyone: were there any surprises in this sprint that we need to investigate or prevent in the future?

DAVID: I'm a bit surprised at how well this sprint went!

The team concludes the meeting and the members file out of the room, buoyant with their recent success.

Summary

The second sprint has been a success and is an improvement for the team. By developing adaptability into the chosen solution's code, the team has shown that it is able to gracefully handle the sort of change that is expected in Agile software development projects. Had the team not introduced any extension points in the code, it would have been very difficult for the team members to enhance the software by adding functionality without significantly rewriting, refactoring, or contorting the code to the breaking point.

Adaptive tools

This appendix gives you an introduction to source control with Git, which is required to use the code samples for this book. If you have used Git before, you're already aware of its deserved reputation as the foremost source control software. If you have not encountered Git before, this appendix will bring you up to a level at which you can interact with local and remote repositories of code. These skills will translate to working with any codebase that is stored in Git; the content herein is not limited to the code samples for this book. Many popular open-source projects use Git, and it is being adopted by companies to manage their proprietary code, too.

In all contexts, the concept of continuous integration (CI) is an important part of keeping code synchronized between various contributors, so a section of this appendix briefly discusses the concept of CI and a common workflow for its implementation.

Source control with Git

Source control evolved slowly for a long time before being revolutionized with the advent of distributed source control systems such as Mercurial and Git. I would argue that *any* source control is better than no source control, but my preference is certainly for Git.

The purpose of source control in general is to track changes in code over time, making it easy to travel forward and backward in time through the code. It also provides a ready-made backup of the source.

With Git, every developer has his own repository that contains the full source code (see Figure A-1). To make edits to the source, developers should create local branches to which they can commit successive changes. Each branch should have a clearly delineated purpose—to fix a defect, implement a new feature, or make some experimental changes. Whatever their purpose, these changes remain local to the developer's repository until the developer elects to push the branch elsewhere.

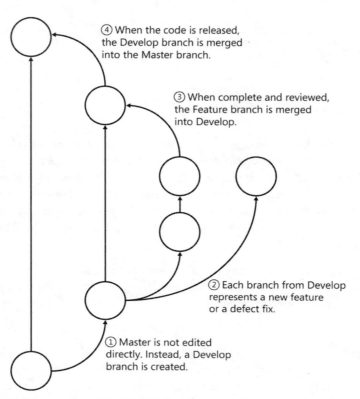

Master **Develop** **Feature 1** **Feature 2**

④ When the code is released, the Develop branch is merged into the Master branch.

③ When complete and reviewed, the Feature branch is merged into Develop.

② Each branch from Develop represents a new feature or a defect fix.

① Master is not edited directly. Instead, a Develop branch is created.

FIGURE A-1 A possible branching strategy for using Git.

Although it is not necessary to have a central repository, it is common to consider one of the repositories the authoritative location for the source. Take a look at Figure A-2. By pushing branches to this repository, developers can subsequently request that their changes be pulled into the main branch of the code. This is called a *pull request* and is often the catalyst for a code review by a developer's peers, which helps to maintain the quality of the code. Each peer who reviews the code can approve or reject the pull request, as appropriate. Each peer can also functionally test the code by pulling the branch to her local repository, compiling it, and testing it locally. If the code is rejected, the original developer can continue to make edits and push the changes back to the central repository until it is accepted. The accepted pull request is then merged into a main development branch, and the other developers will receive those changes when they next update their local repositories with the main branches. They will also need to merge any changes with those of their own in-progress branches.

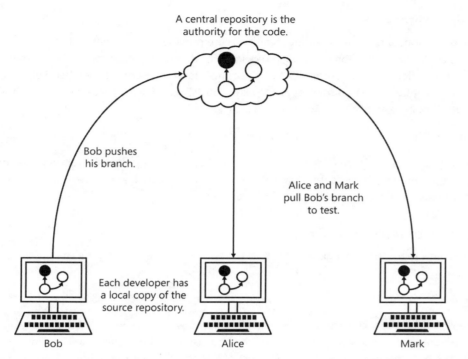

FIGURE A-2 Distributed source control is a peer-to-peer system, but it often uses a central repository.

Git lessons

Git for Windows can be downloaded from *http://git-scm.com/download/win*.

All of the code listings in this book are available on GitHub, which is a community centered on Git repositories. Appendix B, "GitHub code samples" (available online), provides a reference for each chapter's code listings and the Git branch to which they belong.

For those who are new to Git, the following subsections provide a short orientation for navigating code stored in a Git repository. This is far from an extensive introduction to Git, but it should provide you with enough knowledge to follow the code examples and compile them. For more information, the Git Reference[1] is an excellent introduction.

If you don't like working with the command line, there are several good GUIs available for Git. They are available from *http://git-scm.com/downloads/guis*. Atlassian's SourceTree is the best-in-class at the time of this writing.

---

[1] *http://gitref.org/*

Cloning a repository

The first step is to clone a repository. All Git commands are provided as parameters to the `git` command-line application. The `clone` command requires the address of a repository to clone. The following command clones the repository for this book into a local repository. Remember that Git is distributed source control, so many repositories can exist. You will have full read access to the remote repository but will only be able to write to your own local clone.

```
git clone https://github.com/garymcleanhall/AdaptiveCode.git
```

This command creates a new directory called AdaptiveCode under the current working directory. By default, the `master` branch is selected. Each of the samples in this book are, however, located on different branches, so you need to be able to switch branches.

Switching to a different branch

After cloning a new repository, change the directory to your local clone by using the change directory command.

```
cd AdaptiveCode
```

The currently selected branch is the default, which for this repository is `master`. There is not much on the `master` branch for this repository. Instead, the code is located on other branches. Initially, only the `master` branch is replicated locally. The rest of the branches are still remote. To view which branches are available locally, supply `git` with the `branch` command.

```
git branch
```

This lists only the `master` branch. To list all of the branches that are available remotely, add the `remote` switch to the `branch` command.

```
git branch --remote
```

This lists all of the branches that are available in this repository. Note that all of the branches start with the prefix `origin/`, which specifies the remote location on which these branches reside. Each repository can have multiple remotes, with `origin` being the name designated for the remote from which this local repository was cloned.

As a personal preference, I have prefixed every branch with a chX- short code (although branch names can be pretty much anything). This indicates the chapter number to which the branch relates. The rest of the branch name is a more free-form description of its content. Appendix B provides a reference of code listings as they correspond to branch names. Now, by using the `checkout` command, you can create a local version of the remote branch and move onto it.

```
git checkout ch9-problem-statement
```

This creates a local version of the remote branch `origin/ch9-problem-statement` and alters the current working directory so that the changes present on that branch are brought in. If you list the contents of the current directory, as shown in the following listing, there is now a new directory called `DependencyInjectionMvc`, which, in turn, contains a Microsoft Visual Studio solution file and some more directories for its constituent projects.

```
C:\dev\AdaptiveCode [ch9-problem-statement]> ls


    Directory: C:\dev\AdaptiveCode


Mode                LastWriteTime     Length Name
----                -------------     ------ ----
d----         3/16/2014  12:47 PM            DependencyInjectionMvc
-a---         3/16/2014  12:47 PM       1522 .gitignore
-a---         3/16/2014  12:30 PM         84 README.md
```

If you move back to the `master` branch, this folder will no longer be relevant and will be deleted.

Updating local branches

If the remote version of the branch changes at some point, you will want to retrieve the latest changes. The `fetch` command downloads any changes to remote branches.

```
git fetch
```

If you don't supply a branch name, the command downloads changes to all branches, including newly created branches. You can also specify the name of the branch you want to fetch.

```
git fetch origin master
```

Note that the name of the remote is also specified, because the `master` branch might exist on more than one remote.

After you have downloaded the changes by using the `fetch` command, you can switch to the target branch by using the `checkout` command.

```
git checkout ch9-problem-statement
```

From here, the local branch is out of sync with the remote branch because the changes have not been replicated locally. The `merge` command is able to apply any changes made to a remote branch onto the local branch.

```
git merge origin/ch9-problem-statement
```

When the `merge` command is finished, the local branch is identical to the remote and all updates have been applied.

Continuous integration

Whenever a developer's code is pushed to a central repository, it is common for that code to be compiled on the server. This continuous integration of developers' changes provides invaluable feedback about the state of the code base. If the source fails to compile, it has failed to meet the first prerequisite to the pull request being accepted: without a working build, the request will be summarily denied.

However, compiling the code is often insufficient to confirm that the developer has not broken anything as he was fixing a defect or implementing a new feature. Thus, after compiling the code, the CI server runs all unit tests, and then checks that enough of the code is covered by unit tests. After that, it might even attempt to generate deployment packages from the output of the build.

All of these steps are carried out serially, with the success of each step being a requirement for continuing with the build process. There is no value in running unit tests if the code won't compile; similarly, it makes no sense to check unit test coverage if the unit tests failed, or to generate deployment packages if the unit test coverage was insufficient. A CI server set up to build each pushed branch in this way relieves developers of a great burden. Instead of taking the significant additional time that such checks add to their tasks, they can just compile the code and run the unit tests that they have written, leaving the rest up to the CI. Figure A-3 shows a flowchart for such a continuous integration build process.

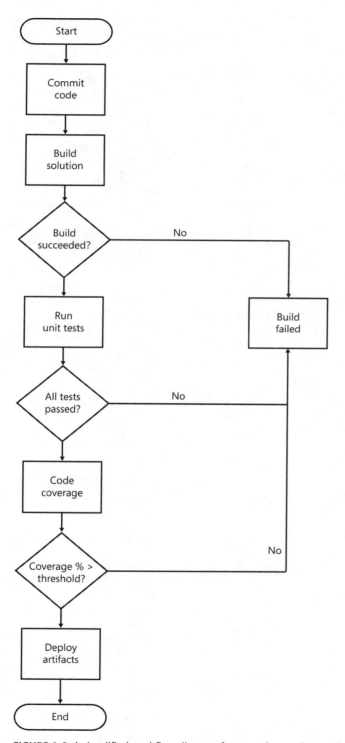

FIGURE A-3 A simplified workflow diagram for a continuous integration service.

Index

A

Entourage anti-pattern
    dependency injection and, 284
    described, 63–65
    Illegitimate Injection and, 311
    solving with Stairway pattern, 85
epics vs. features, 13
estimating
    features, 29
    stories, 30, 31, 35
    story points, 330–335
events
    decorating, 203
    publishing and subscribing to, 261–263
exceptions
    catching, 238, 246–249
    enforcing preconditions with, 220, 221
    purpose of, 246, 371
    wrapping, 146, 149
expected behavior
    asserting in unit tests, 128
    Liskov substitution principle, 217
    naming test methods and, 132
    refactoring code and, 152
    test-driven development and, 130
    variance and, 239
ExpectedExceptionAttribute, 144, 145, 147
explicit interface implementation, 97–101
extension
    methods, 118–120
    open/closed principle and, 208
    points, 209–214
    points, adaptive code and, 322
external dependencies. *See* third-party software
    dependencies
external mocking frameworks, 140, 141
Extreme Programming (XP), user stories and, 13

F

factories
    connection, 301, 302
    injection, 299
    isolating, 304
factory classes, replacing constructors with, 159
Factory Isolation pattern, 304, 305

factory methods, replacing with constructors, 157–159
Factory pattern, 301, 302, 314, 345–347
failing unit tests
    bug fixes and, 208
    described, 130, 139
    writing for bug fixes, 148
fakes, testing with, 137–140
fast-track items, 18
features
    burnup charts, 25–27
    estimating, 29
    prioritizing, 29
    Scrum board cards and, 12, 13
fire-and-forget methods, 202
first-party software dependencies, 43, 44–48
fluent interfaces, 123, 124
foreach loops, CLR duck-typing support and, 116–118
framework dependencies, 48, 49, 66
Fusion log, 68–70

G

GAC (global assembly cache), 67, 68
generalizing specialists, 8
generic
    controllers, 265
    interfaces, 252, 265
    type parameters, 242–245
Git, 379–383
GitHub, 381
Given, When, Then pattern, 126
global assembly cache (GAC), 67, 68
goals, defining for sprints, 337
Goldilocks Zone, extension points and, 214
graphs
    modeling dependencies in, 51–55
    object, 287–291, 312, 320
green icon, as indicator of successful unit test, 130
greenfield projects, 27
guard clauses
    vs. code contracts, 232
    data invariants and, 223, 230, 231
    postconditions and, 222
    preconditions and, 220, 221, 226

Agile processes and, 1
Arrange, Act, Assert (AAA), 126–130
Class Adapter, 109, 110
Command/Query Responsibility Segregation (CQRS), 90
Composite, 185–189
Decorator, 184, 185, 251
described, 56
Factory, 301, 302, 314, 345–347
Factory isolation, 304, 305
history of, 102
layering, 82–84
Model-View-ViewModel (MVVM), 282
Null Object, 103–105, 108
Object Adapter, 110, 111
overuse vs. underuse, 102
Poor Man's Dependency Injection, 287
Register, Resolve, Release, 293–295
Repository, 241
Responsible Owner, 302–304
Stairway, 65, 66, 284
Strategy, 111–113, 204–206
Template Method, 211
peak of inflated expectations, 327
peer reviews, 340–357, 380
performing unit tests. *See* unit tests
persistent storage, CRUD operations and, 251, 252
pigs and chickens, 9
Plain Old CLR Object (POCO), 285
planning poker, story point estimation and, 331–335
plateau of productivity, 327
PO (product owner) role, 7, 325, 326
POCO (Plain Old CLR Object), 285
poker, planning, story point estimation and, 331–335
polymorphism
covariance and, 239, 240
described, 101, 102
replacing conditional expressions with, 154–157
Poor Man's Dependency Injection (Poor Man's DI)
composition root and, 311
described, 287–290
post mortems. *See* sprint retrospectives
postconditions
code contracts and, 235
described, 222, 223
Liskov Substitution Principle and, 227–229
PostSharp, 88

preconditions
arranging for unit tests, 126, 127
code contracts and, 232–234
of constructors, 143
contracts and, 224
described, 220–222
enforcing with exceptions, 221
enforcing with preconditions, 220
Liskov Substitution Principle and, 225–227
predicate decorators, 189–193
predicted variation, 213
prioritizing features, 29
Prism (Windows Presentation Foundation/Model-View-ViewModel library), 122
private methods, 236
product backlogs
described, 27
responsibility for setting priorities, 7, 27
Scrum process and, 4
product owner (PO) role, 7, 325, 326
production code
defined, 125
test-driven development and, 130
profiling decorators, 196–200
proof of concept, refactoring toward abstraction and, 177
properties
decorating, 203
signatures, 99
property injection, 291
property setters, 230, 231
protected variation, 213, 214
prototypes, refactoring toward abstraction and, 177
proxiable classes, 284
proxies
classes, 70
discovery, 71
services, 70, 71
prudent technical debt, 20
publishing events, 261–263
pull requests, 380

Q

Quality Assurance (QA), swimlanes for, 18
queries, separating from commands, 89–91

About the author

GARY MCLEAN HALL lives in Manchester, England, with his wife, daughter, and dog. He is an experienced Microsoft .NET Framework developer specializing in patterns and practices. In his many years of contracting, he has worked on numerous Agile teams that have maintained a strict focus on creating code that is adaptive to change. He has worked for companies such as Eidos, Xerox, Nephila Capital Ltd., and The LateRooms Group. He has also run a software consultancy company for several years and lived and worked in Bermuda for three years. In each role, he excelled at balancing the delivery of a software product and the quality of its source code.